Commentary
on the
Second Epistle
to the
Corinthians

CHARLES HODGE

WILLIAM B. EERDMANS PUBLISHING COMPANY
GRAND RAPIDS, MICHIGAN

Published by Wm. B. Eerdmans Publishing Co.
255 Jefferson Ave. S.E., Grand Rapids, Michigan 49503

First printing 1950
Paperback edition published 1994

ISBN 0-8028-8032-0

II. CORINTHIANS

———•••———

CHAPTER I.

Paul's gratitude for the deliverance and consolation which he had experienced. Vs. 1–11.

After the apostle had written his former letter to the Corinthians, and had sent Titus, either as the bearer of the letter or immediately after its having been sent by other hands, to ascertain the effect which it produced, he seems to have been in a state of unusual depression and anxiety. The persecutions to which he had been exposed in Asia placed him in continued danger of death, 1, 8; and his solicitude about the church in Corinth allowed him no inward peace, 7, 5. After leaving Ephesus he went to Troas; but although the most promising prospects of usefulness there presented themselves, he could not rest, but passed over into Macedonia in hopes of meeting Titus and obtaining from him intelligence from Corinth, 2, 12. 23. This letter is the outpouring of his heart occasioned by the information which he received. More than any other of Paul's epistles, it bears the impress of the strong feelings under the influence of which it was written. That the Corinthians had received his former letter with a proper spirit, that it brought them to repentance, led them to excommunicate the incestuous person, and called forth, on the

part of the larger portion of the congregation, the manifestation of the warmest affection for the apostle, relieved his
mind from a load of anxiety, and filled his heart with gratitude to God. On the other hand, the increased boldness and
influence of the false teachers, the perverting errors which
they inculcated, and the frivolous and calumnious charges
which they brought against himself, filled him with indignation. This accounts for the abrupt transitions from one subject to another, the sudden changes of tone and manner which
characterize this epistle. When writing to the Corinthians as
a church obedient, affectionate, and penitent, there is no limit
to his tenderness and love. His great desire seems to be to
heal the temporary breach which had occurred between them,
and to assure his readers that all was forgiven and forgotten,
and that his heart was entirely theirs. But when he turns to
the wicked, designing corrupters of the truth among them,
there is a tone of severity to be found in no other of his writings, not even in his epistle to the Galatians. Erasmus compares this epistle to a river which sometimes flows in a gentle
stream, sometimes rushes down as a torrent bearing all before
it ; sometimes spreading out like a placid lake ; sometimes
losing itself, as it were, in the sand, and breaking out in
its fulness in some unexpected place. Though perhaps the
least methodical of Paul's writings, it is among the most in-
teresting of his letters as bringing out the man before the
reader and revealing his intimate relations to the people for
whom he laboured. The remark must be borne in mind
(often made before), that the full play allowed to the peculiarities of mind and feeling of the sacred writers, is in no way
inconsistent with their plenary inspiration. The grace of
God in conversion does not change the natural character of
its subjects, but accommodates itself to all their peculiarities
of disposition and temperament. And the same is true with
regard to the influence of the Spirit in inspiration.

The salutation in this epistle is nearly in the same words
as in the former letter, vs. 1. 2. Here also as there, the introduction is a thanksgiving. As these expressions of gratitude
are not mere forms, but genuine effusions of the heart, they
vary according to the circumstances under which each epistle
was written. Here the thanksgiving was for consolation.
Paul blesses God as the God of all mercy for the consolation
which he had experienced. He associates, or rather identifies
himself with the Corinthians ; representing his afflictions as

theirs and his consolation also as belonging to them, vs. 3–7. He refers to the afflictions which came upon him in Asia, so that he despaired of life, but through their prayers God who had delivered, still delivered, and he was assured, would continue to deliver him, vs. 8–11.

1. 2. Paul, an apostle of Jesus Christ by the will of God, and Timothy (our) brother, unto the church of God which is at Corinth, with all the saints which are in all Achaia: Grace (be) to you, and peace, from God our Father, and (from) our Lord Jesus Christ.

The sense in which the word *apostle* is to be here taken, the force of the expression *by the will of God*, the scriptural meaning of the words *church* and *saints*, are all stated in the remarks on the first verse of the former epistle. In the first epistle Paul associates Sosthenes with himself in the salutation; here it is Timothy who is mentioned. In neither case is there any community of office or authority implied. On the contrary, a marked distinction is made between Paul the apostle and Sosthenes or Timothy the brother, i. e. the Christian companion of the apostle. From 1 Cor. 4, 17 it appears that Timothy was in Macedonia, on his way to Corinth, when the first epistle was written. From the form of expression (if Timothy come) in 1 Cor. 16, 10, and from the absence of any intimation in this epistle that Paul had received from him the information from Corinth which he was so desirous to obtain, it is doubtful whether Timothy had been able to reach that city. At any rate he was now with the apostle at Nicopolis or some other city in Macedonia. *With all the saints which are in all Achaia.* This epistle was not intended exclusively for the Christians in Corinth, but also for all the believers scattered through the province who were connected with the church in Corinth. These believers were probably not collected into separate congregations, otherwise the apostle would have used the plural form, as when writing to the *churches* of Galatia, Gal. 1, 3. Achaia was originally the name of the northern part of the Peloponnesus including Corinth and its isthmus. Augustus divided the whole country into the two provinces, Macedonia and Achaia; the former included Macedonia proper, Illyricum, Epirus and Thessaly;

and the latter all the southern part of Greece. It is in this wide sense *Achaia* is always used in the New Testament. From this it appears that the converts to Christianity in Greece were at this time very few out of Corinth, as they were all members of the church in that city. *Grace* and *peace*, the favour of God and its fruits, comprehend all the benefits of redemption. The apostle's prayer is not only that believers may be the objects of the love of God our Father and of Jesus Christ our Lord, but that they may have the assurance of that love. He knew that the sense of the love of God would keep their hearts in perfect peace. God is our Father, Jesus Christ is our Lord. Every one feels the distinction in this relationship, whether he reduces it to clear conceptions in his own mind or not. God, as God, is our father because he is the father of all spirits, and because, if believers, we are born again by his Spirit, and adopted as his children, made the objects of his love and the heirs of his kingdom. Jesus Christ, the eternal Son of God clothed in our nature, is our Lord, for two reasons: first, because as God he is our absolute sovereign; and secondly, because as Redeemer he has purchased us by his own most precious blood. To him, therefore, as God and Redeemer, our allegiance as Christians is specially due.

3. Blessed (be) God, even the Father of our Lord Jesus Christ, the Father of mercies, and God of all comfort.

This richness and variety of designations for the object of his reverence and gratitude, shows how full was the apostle's heart, and how it yearned after fellowship with God, to whom he places himself in every possible connection by thus multiplying the terms expressive of the relations which God bears to his redeemed people. *Blessed.* The word εὐλογητός (*blessed*) is used in the New Testament only of God. (In Luke 1, 28, where the Virgin Mary is spoken of, εὐλογημένη is used.) It expresses at once gratitude and adoration. Adored be God! is the expression of the highest veneration and thankfulness. It is not God merely as God, but as *the Father of our Lord Jesus Christ* who is the object of the apostle's adoration and gratitude. The expression does not refer to the miraculous conception of our Lord, but the person addressed is he whose eternal Son assumed our nature, who, as invested with that nature, is our Lord Jesus Christ. It is he who so loved the world that he gave his only-begotten Son, that whoso believeth in him might not perish but have everlasting life. It is therefore the peculiar, characteristic Christian designation of God, as it presents him as the God of redemption. Rom. 15, 6. 2 Cor. 11, 31. Col. 1, 3. 1 Pet. 1, 3. This God who has revealed himself as the God of love in sending his Son for our redemption, the apostle still further designates as *the Father of mercies*, i. e. the most merciful Father; he whose characteristic is mercy. Comp. Ps. 86, 5. 15. Dan. 9, 9. Micah 7, 18. The explanation which makes the expression mean *the author of mercies* is inconsistent with the signification of the word οἰκτιρμός, which always means *mercy* as a feeling. *The God of all comfort.* This most merciful Father is the God, i. e. the author of all, i. e. of all possible, consolation. God is the author of consolation not only by delivering us from evil, or by ordering our external circumstances, but also, and chiefly, by his inward influence on the mind itself, assuaging its tumults and filling it with joy and peace in believing. Rom. 15, 13.

4. Who comforteth us in all our tribulation, that we may be able to comfort them which are in any trouble, by the comfort wherewith we ourselves are comforted of God.

Us here refers to the apostle himself. Throughout this chapter he is speaking of his own personal trials and consolations. He blessed God as the author of comfort, because he had experienced his consolations. And the design, he adds, of God in afflicting and in consoling was to qualify him for the office of a consoler of the afflicted. In this design Paul acquiesced; he was willing to be thus afflicted in order to be the bearer of consolation to others. A life of ease is commonly stagnant. It is those who suffer much and who experience much of the comfort of the Holy Ghost, who live much. Their life is rich in experience and in resources. *In all our tribulation*, i. e. on account of (ἐπί). His tribulation was the ground or reason why God comforted him. The apostle was one of the most afflicted of men. He suffered from hunger, cold, nakedness, stripes, imprisonment, from perils by sea and land, from robbers, from the Jews, from the heathen, so that his life was a continued death, or, as he expressed it, he died daily. Besides these external afflictions he was overwhelmed with cares and anxiety for the churches. And as though all this were not enough, he had "a thorn in the flesh, a messenger of Satan," to buffet him. See 11, 24–30, and 12, 7. In the midst of all these trials God not only sustained him, but filled him with such a heroic spirit that he actually rejoiced in being thus afflicted. "I take pleasure," he says, "in infirmities, in reproaches, in necessities, in persecutions, in distresses for Christ's sake; for when I am weak, then am I strong," 12, 10. This state of mind can be experienced only by those who are so filled with the love of Christ, that they rejoice in every thing, however painful to themselves, whereby his glory is promoted. And where this state of mind exists, no afflictions can equal the consolations by which they are attended, and therefore the apostle adds, that he was enabled to comfort those who were in any kind of affliction by the comfort wherewith he was comforted of God.

5. For as the sufferings of Christ abound in us, so our consolation aboundeth by Christ.

This is a confirmation of what precedes. 'We are able to comfort others, *for* our consolations are equal to our sufferings.' *The sufferings of Christ*, do not mean 'sufferings on account of Christ,' which the force of the genitive case does not admit; nor sufferings which Christ endures in his own members; but such sufferings as Christ suffered, and which his people are called upon to endure in virtue of their union with him and in order to be like him. Our Lord said to his disciples, "Ye shall indeed drink of my cup, and be baptized with the baptism wherewith I am baptized with," Matt. 20, 23. Paul speaks of his *fellowship*, or participation in the sufferings of Christ, Phil. 3, 10; and the apostle Peter calls upon believers to rejoice, inasmuch as they are "partakers of Christ's sufferings," 1 Peter 4, 24. Comp. Rom. 8, 17. Col. 1, 24. Gal. 6, 17. In many other passages it is taught that believers must share in the sufferings, if they are to be partakers of the glory of Christ. *So*, i. e. in equal measure, *our consolation aboundeth through Christ*. As union with Christ was the source of the afflictions which Paul endured, so it was the source of the abundant consolation which he enjoyed. This makes the great difference between the sorrows of believers and those of unbelievers. Alienation from Christ does not secure freedom from suffering, but it cuts us off from the only source of consolation. Therefore the sorrow of the world worketh death.

6, 7. And whether we be afflicted, (it is) for your consolation and salvation, which is effectual to the enduring of the same sufferings which we also suffer: or whether we be comforted, (it is) for your consolation and salvation. And our hope of you (is) stedfast, knowing that as ye are partakers of the sufferings, so (shall ye be) also of the consolation.

Although the ancient manuscripts differ very much in the order in which the several clauses of these verses are arranged, yet the sense expressed in all is substantially the same. The text adopted by Beza, Griesbach, Knapp, Meyer, &c., on the authority of the manuscripts A, C, and several of the ancient versions, reads thus, " Whether we be afflicted, (it is) for your consolation and salvation; whether we are comforted, (it is) for your consolation, which is effectual in enduring the same sufferings which we also suffer; and our hope of you is stedfast, knowing that as ye are partakers of the suffering, so also (shall ye be) of the consolation." The reading adopted by Lachmann, Tischendorf, Rückert and others, differs from the common text in placing the clause *our hope of you is stedfast*, immediately after the first member of the sentence, and before the words, *whether we are comforted.* For this arrangement are the MSS. B, D, E, F, G, I. The reading of Beza gives the text in its simplest and most perspicuous form. In either way the main idea is, ' Whether we be afflicted, it is for your good; or whether we be comforted, it is for your good.' All the rest is subordinate. The relation in which the apostle stood to the Corinthians was such that he felt assured that they would share both in his sufferings and in his consolation, and therefore experience the benefit of both. It was not that Paul's constancy in suffering set them a good example; nor simply that Paul suffered in behalf of the Gospel, and therefore for the benefit of others; nor does he mean merely that the experience of the Corinthians would correspond to his, if they were similarly afflicted, they would be similarly comforted; but the main idea is that such was the intimate bond between them and him that he had a firm hope they would be partakers both of his affliction and of his consolation. Though this appears to be the primary idea of the passage, the others are not to be excluded. Paul no doubt felt, and intended to intimate, that his diversified experience would redound to their advantage by qualifying him more abundantly for his work, and especially for the office of consoling them in the afflictions which they, as well as he, would be called to endure. *Whether we be afflicted* (it is) *for your consolation and salvation;* i. e. my afflictions will contribute to your consolation and salvation. To the former, because those whom God afflicts, or, who suffer for Christ's sake and with Christ's people, God never fails to console; to the latter, because suffering and salvation are so intimately connected. "If we suffer with him we shall also be glorified together," Rom. 8, 17. It is not of suffering as suffering that the apostle here speaks. There is no tendency in pain to produce holiness. It is only of Christian suffering and of the sufferings of Christians, that is, of suffering endured for Christ and in a Christian manner, that the apostle says it is connected with salvation, or that it tends to work out for those who suffer an eternal weight of glory. *Or whether we be comforted it is for your consolation.* That is, our consolation is also yours. If we are consoled, so are you. If we suffer together, we rejoice together. Or, if you suffer as I do, you will enjoy similar consolation. My being consoled enables me to console you. According to the common text the reading here is, "your consolation *and salvation.*" But the repetition of the words *and salvation* is not sustained by some of the oldest manuscripts, and they do not cohere so well with the following clause; as it can hardly be said that "salvation is effectual in enduring affliction." On these grounds, as before remarked, Beza and many other editors omit the words in question. *Which is effectual;* that is, which consolation is operative or efficacious, not *to* the enduring, as in our version, but *in* the enduring (ἐν ὑπομονῇ). This consolation shows its efficacy in the patient endurance of suffering. According to another interpretation ἐνεργουμένης is taken passively, *which is wrought out.* The sense would then be good, 'This consolation is wrought out or experienced in patient endurance.' But as Paul always uses this word actively, the rendering adopted in our version is generally and properly preferred. *The same sufferings which I also suffer.* The sufferings of the Corinthians were the same with those of the apostle, because they sympathized in his afflictions, because they in a measure suffered as he did, and because their sufferings were "the sufferings of Christ," in the same sense that his were. They were not only such sufferings as Christ endured, but they were incurred because those who suffered were Christians. *And our hope of you is stedfast.* That is, 'we have a stedfast hope that you will be partakers of our consolation.' *Knowing,* i. e. because we know, *that as ye are partakers of the sufferings, so also of the consolation.* The two go together. Those who share in our sorrows, share in our joys. There are two ideas apparently united here as in the preceding context. The one is that the sufferings of the apostle were also the sufferings of the Corinthians because of the union between them. The other is, that his readers were in their measure exposed to the same kind of sufferings. In this twofold sense they were the κοινωνοί, the communicants or joint-partakers of his joys and sorrows.

8. For we would not, brethren, have you ignorant of our trouble, which came to us in Asia, that we were pressed out of measure, above strength, insomuch that we despaired even of life.

The apostle confirms from the facts of his recent history, what he had said of his afflictions. *Asia* is probably to be understood here in reference to proconsular Asia, which comprehended the western provinces of Asia Minor, viz., Mysia, Lydia, Caria, and part of Phrygia. What afflictions and dangers the apostle here refers to is uncertain. It is generally assumed that he alludes to the uproar in Ephesus, of which mention is made in Acts 19, 23–41. But to this it is objected that Paul does not appear to have been in personal danger during that tumult; that instead of saying *in Asia* he would probably have said *in Ephesus*, had he referred to that special event; and that the language used seems obviously to imply a succession and continuance of severe trials. Others think that the reference is to some severe illness. But there is nothing in the context to indicate that particular form of affliction. Neither could *illness* naturally be included under the "afflictions of Christ," under which head the apostle com-

prehends all the afflictions to which in this connection he refers. The probability is that he alludes to trials of different
kinds, and especially to plots and attempts against his life.
He was surrounded by enemies, Jews and heathen, who thirst-
ed for his blood. And we know, as remarked above, that the
Acts of the Apostles contains the record of only a small portion of his afflictions. *That we were pressed,* ἐβαρήθημεν, *we
were burdened.* The allusion is to a wearied animal that sinks
in despair under a burden beyond its strength. *Out of measure, above strength;* if thus separated, the former of these
phrases refers to the character of his afflictions in themselves,
'they were excessive;' and the latter, expresses their relation
to his ability to bear them. Absolutely, they were too great,
relatively, they were above his strength. Many commentators make the former qualify the latter, "We were burdened
far beyond our strength" (καθ᾿ ὑπερβολὴν ὑπὲρ δύναμιν). *Insomuch that we despaired even of life.* The expression is intensive, ἐξαπορηθῆναι, *to be utterly at a loss,* or, absolutely
without a way (πόρος) of escape. It seemed impossible to the
apostle that he could escape from the enemies who beset him
on every side. These enemies were not only men, but perils
and trials of all kinds.

9. But we had the sentence of death in ourselves,
that we should not trust in ourselves, but in God who
raiseth the dead.

So far from expecting to live, the apostle says, *on the contrary* (ἀλλά) he had in himself *the sentence of death.* This
may mean that he was as one who was actually condemned to
die. God appeared to have passed upon him the sentence of
death, from which there could be no reprieve. This supposes
ἀπόκριμα to have the sense of κατάκριμα. This meaning of the
word is very doubtful. It properly signifies *response, answer.*
'We had in ourselves the answer of death.' That is, when he
put to himself the question, whether life or death was to be
the issue of his conflicts, the answer was, Death! In other
words, he did not expect to escape with his life. God brought
him into these straits *in order that* he might not trust in himself, but in God who raiseth the dead. These two things are
so connected that the former is the necessary condition of the
latter. There is no such thing as implicit confidence or reli-

ance on God, until we renounce all confidence in ourself.
When Paul was convinced that no wisdom nor efforts of his
own could deliver him from death, then he was forced to rely
on the power of God. God is here described as he *who raiseth the dead*, because the apostle's deliverance was a deliverance from death. It was only that Being who could call
the dead to life who could rescue him from the imminent peril
in which he was placed. So when Abraham's faith was put
to the severe trial of believing what was apparently impossible, it is said, "He believed God who quickeneth the dead,
and calleth those things which be not as though they were,"
Rom. 4, 17. Comp. Heb. 11, 19. No man until he is tried
knows how essential the omnipotence of God is as a ground
of confidence to his people. They are often placed in circumstances where nothing short of an almighty helper can give
them peace.

10. Who delivered us from so great a death, and
doth deliver : in whom we trust that he will yet deliver (us).

Paul's trust in God was not disappointed. He did deliver
him from *such a death*, i. e. one so fearful and apparently so
inevitable. It is evident from the whole context that the
apostle had not only been in imminent peril, but exposed to a
more than ordinarily painful death. Whether this was from
disease or from enemies is a matter of conjecture. The latter
is the more probable. Though he had been delivered from
the instant and fearful death with which he was threatened,
the danger was not over. The machinations of his enemies
followed him wherever he went. He therefore says that God
had not only delivered, but that he continued to deliver him.
He was still beset with danger. He was however confident
for the future. For he adds, *in whom we trust*, εἰς ὃν ἠλπίκαμεν,
*on whom we have placed our hope that he will also henceforth
deliver*. He did, he does, he will, deliver, ἐρρύσατο, ῥύεται,
ῥύσεται. The experience of past deliverances and mercies is
the ground of present peace and of confidence for the future.
These words of Paul sound continually in the ears of the people of God in all times of emergency.

11. Ye also helping together by prayer for us, that

for the gift (bestowed) upon us by the means of many persons, thanks may be given by many on our behalf.

Intercessory prayer has great power, otherwise Paul would not so often solicit it on his own behalf, and enjoin the duty on his readers. His confidence in his safety for the future was not founded simply on the experience of God's past mercy, but also on the prayers of Christians in his behalf. God will yet deliver me, he says, *you also helping together by prayer.* That is, provided you join your prayers with those of others for my safety. *Helping together* probably refers to their co-operation in the work of intercession with other churches, rather than with the apostle himself. The design of God in thus uniting his people in praying for each other when in affliction or danger, is that the deliverance may be matter of common gratulation and praise. Thus all hearts are drawn out to God and Christian fellowship is promoted. This is expressed in the latter part of this verse; *that,* i. e. in order that *the gift being bestowed on us by means of many* (διὰ πολλῶν) *thanks may be rendered by many* (ἐκ πολλῶν). In the Greek it is ἐκ πολλῶν προσώπων, which most commentators render as our translators do, *by many persons.* The word πρὸσωπον, however, always elsewhere in the New Testament means *face* or *presence,* which sense many retain here. 'That thanks may be rendered from many (upturned) faces.' According to the interpretation given above, the words διὰ πολλῶν are connected with τὸ χάρισμα, "the favour to us by means of many;" and ἐκ πολλῶν προσώπων with εὐχαρεσθῇ, 'thanks may be rendered by many persons (or faces).' This gives a good sense, and is perhaps better suited to the force of the prepositions ἐκ and διά. It is more correct to say that the 'favour was (διά) by means of many,' i. e. by means of their prayer, than that it 'was (ἐκ) *out of,* or *by,'* as expressing the efficient cause. The order of the clauses, however, favours the connection adopted by our translators. 'The favour was by many persons, and the thanks to be rendered by means of many.' This construction of the sentence is also sanctioned by the majority of commentators.

The apostle's defence against the charge of inconstancy
Vs. 12–24.

Paul had informed the Corinthians that it was his purpose

to go direct from Ephesus to Corinth, thence into Macedonia, and back again to Corinth, v. 16. This plan he had been induced to modify before the former epistle was sent, as in 1 Cor. 16, 5 he tells them he would not visit them until he had passed through Macedonia. On this slight ground his enemies in Corinth represented him as saying one thing and meaning another. They seem also to have made this an occasion for charging him with like inconsistency in doctrine. If his word could not be depended on in small matters, what dependence could be placed on his preaching? Paul shows there was no levity or insincerity involved in this change of his plans, and no inconsistency in his preaching; but that to spare them he had deferred his visit to Corinth, vs. 12–24.

12. For our rejoicing is this, the testimony of our conscience, that in simplicity and godly sincerity, not in fleshly wisdom, but by the grace of God, we have had our conversation in the world, and more abundantly to you-ward.

The connection between this verse and what precedes, as indicated by the particle *for*, is, 'I look for your sympathy in my afflictions, and for your prayers in my behalf, *for* my conscience bears testimony to the simplicity and sincerity of my conversation among you.' Unless we are conscious of integrity towards others, we cannot be assured of their confidence in us. *Our rejoicing*, says Paul, *is this, the testimony of our conscience*. This may mean that the testimony of conscience was the *ground* of his rejoicing. This assumes a metonymical sense of the καύχησις, a meaning which is often attributed to the word. But as the word may express the inward feeling of exultation as well as the outward expression of it, which latter is its proper sense, the meaning may be (without assuming any metonomy), 'My joyful confidence consists in the consciousness of sincerity.' The testimony of the conscience is consciousness; and that of which Paul was conscious was integrity. And that consciousness sustained and elevated him. It was in its nature a joy. What follows is explanatory. His conscience testified that *in simplicity and godly sincerity*, &c. The word ἁπλότης means *singleness of mind*, the opposite of duplicity. The ancient manuscripts A, B, C, read ἁγιότης, *purity* or *sanctity*, which the recent editors generally adopt. The former word is much more common in Paul's writings, and is better suited to the following term, εἰλικρίνεια, which means *translucence*, clearness, sincerity of mind. It is called the *sincerity of God*, which our translators explain as meaning *godly sincerity*, either in the sense of religious, as distinguished from mere natural sincerity as a moral virtue; or in the sense of *divine*, what comes from God. The latter is the true explanation. It is the sincerity which God gives. The Bible often uses such expressions as "the peace of God," "joy of the Spirit," &c., meaning the peace or joy of which God or the Spirit is the author. There is a specific difference between moral virtues and spiritual graces, although they are called by the same names. Simplicity, sincerity, meekness, long-suffering, when the fruits of the Spirit differ from the moral virtues designated by those terms, as many external things, though similar in appearance, often differ in their inward nature. A religious man and a moral man may be very much alike in the eyes of men, though the inward life of the latter is human, and that of the former is divine. What Paul means here to say is, that the virtues which distinguished his deportment in Corinth were not merely forms of his own excellence, but forms of the divine life; modes in which the Spirit of God which dwelt in him manifested itself. This is expressed more clearly in what follows. *Not in fleshly wisdom*, that is, not in that wisdom which has its origin in our own nature. The familiar meaning of the word *flesh* in the New Testament, especially in the writings of St. Paul, is human nature as it now is, as distinguished from the Spirit of God. " Ye are not in the flesh," says this apostle, "but in the Spirit, if so be that the Spirit of God dwell in you," Rom. 8, 9. As our nature is corrupt, natural or fleshly necessarily involves more or less the idea of corruption. The natural man, carnal mind, fleshly wsdom, all imply that idea more or less, according to the context. *Fleshly wisdom*, therefore, is that kind of wisdom which unrenewed men are wont to exhibit, wisdom guided by principles of self-interest or expediency. It stands opposed to *the grace of God*. Paul was not guided by the former, but by the latter. The grace of God controlled his conduct; and by grace is here meant, as so often elsewhere, the gracious influences of the Spirit. *We have had our conversation ;* ἀνεστράφημεν, *we moved about*, we conducted ourselves. The expression includes all the manifestations of his inward life. *In the world*, i. e. among men generally; *and more especially to you-ward*. That is, the evidence of my sincerity is much more abundant to you than to others. The Corinthians had enjoyed more opportunities of learning the character of the apostle, and of seeing his simplicity and integrity, than the world, or men outside of the church, had possessed. He could therefore the more confidently assume that they confided in him.

13. 14. For we write none other things unto you, than what ye read or acknowledge, and I trust ye shall acknowledge even to the end; as also ye have acknowledged us in part, that we are your rejoicing, even as ye also (are) ours in the day of the Lord Jesus.

The same sincerity and honesty marked his correspondence that characterized his life. He never wrote one thing and meant another. The connection with the preceding verse is, 'We are perfectly honest, *for* we write none other things than what ye read.' The simple, obvious meaning of my letter, is the true meaning. *I write*, i. e. I mean none other things than what you understand me to intend when you read my letters, *or know* from other sources. The word ἐπιγινώσκετε may be rendered as in our version, *ye acknowledge*. The sense would then be, 'I mean nothing else but what you read or acknowledge to be my meaning.' But this is not so clear. The design of the apostle is to show that his purposes really were what his letters indicated, or what the Corinthians, by other means, had been led to understand them to be. The words are, " Ye read, *or also* (ἢ καί) know," *and I trust ye shall acknowledge to the end*. This clause may be connected with what precedes. 'I mean what you know, and I trust shall continue to acknowledge, to be my meaning.' That is, 'I have confidence that you will not misunderstand or misinterpret my intentions until we all come to the end;' ἕως τέλους, *to the end*, either of life, or of the world. A much better sense is obtained by connecting this clause with what follows, so that the clause (ὅτι καύχημα ὑμῶν ἐσμεν), *that we are your rejoicing*, is the object of the verb (ἐπιγνώσεσθε) *ye shall acknowledge.* 'I trust ye shall acknowledge unto the end (as ye have acknowledged us in part), that we are your rejoicing.' The verb ἐπιγινώσκειν combines the ideas of recognition and of complete knowledge. The words *in part* are most naturally referred to the Corinthians, *ye in part,* i. e. a part of you. Paul knew that there were some in Corinth who did not rejoice in him. Others understand them to qualify the verb. It was only a partial recognition of him that the Corinthians had as yet manifested. Compare 1 Cor. 13, 12, "I know in part." This, however, would give a tone of reproach to the language which is foreign to the character of the passage. *We are your rejoicing,* i. e. the ground of your exultation and delight. *As ye also ours, in the day of the Lord Jesus.* Paul believed that in the day of the Lord Jesus the Corinthians would rejoice over him as he would rejoice over them. In that day they would appreciate the blessedness of having had him for their teacher, as he would rejoice in having had them for his converts. The joy, however, which he anticipated in its fulness when Christ should come, was in a measure already theirs. 'We are, and shall be, your rejoicing, as ye are and shall be ours, in the day of the Lord Jesus.' Instead of rendering ὅτι in the above clause *that* many commentators render it *because.* This gives a different sense to the whole passage. 'We hope you will acknowledge—*because* we are your rejoicing, as ye are ours.' This, however, leaves the verb *acknowledge* without an object. What were they to acknowledge? We may indeed supply from the context the words *our sincerity,* but it is more natural so to construe the passage as to avoid the necessity of supplying any thing. The sense also is better according to the common interpretation. Paul does not design to prove that the Corinthians confided in him because he was their rejoicing, which would be to prove a thing by itself.

15. 16. And in this confidence I was minded to come to you before that ye might have a second benefit; to pass by you into Macedonia, and to come again out of Macedonia unto you, and of you to be brought on my way to Judea.

And in this confidence, that is, in the confidence that we are your rejoicing, Paul was not afraid to go to Corinth. He did not doubt that the great majority of the church would receive him with confidence and affection. The change in the plan of his journey arose, as he afterwards states, from very different motives. Paul says *he was minded*, i. e. intended to come to them *before*, i. e. before going to Macedonia; *that ye might have a second benefit*, i. e. the benefit of seeing me twice, once before going to Macedonia, and again after my return. The other explanation of this passage is, that *second* here refers to his first visit to Corinth. The first benefit was their conversion, the second would be the good effects to be anticipated from another visit. But it appears from 12, 14 and other passages that Paul had already been twice in Corinth, and therefore he could not speak of his intended visit as the second; and the word *second* here evidently refers to the word *before*. He was to see them *before* and *after* going to Macedonia. *Benefit*, χαρίν, *grace*, a term generally in the New Testament used of religious blessings. The word sometimes signifies *joy*, so the sense here may be, 'That ye might have the pleasure of seeing me twice.' The former explanation is not only better suited to the common use of the word, but also gives a higher sense. *And of you to be brought on my way to Judea.* Προπεμϑῆναι, *to be brought on my way*, i. e. to be aided in my journey. The word often, and perhaps most frequently, means *to escort* on a journey, or to furnish with the means of travelling. Acts 15, 3. 20, 38. &c. In ancient times when there were no established modes of travelling, it was customary for the friends of the traveller in one city to send him forward to the next, or at least to escort him on his way. This office of friendship Paul was willing and desirous to receive at the hands of the Corinthians. He was not alienated from them. And his purpose to seek this kindness from them was a proof of his confidence in their affection for him.

17. When therefore I was thus minded did I use lightness? or the things that I purpose, do I purpose according to the flesh, that with me there should be yea, yea, and nay, nay?

Paul did not execute the plan of his journey above indicated. His having changed his purpose was made the ground of a twofold charge against him; first, of levity, and secondly, of inconsistency; saying one thing, and doing another; or saying one thing at one time, and the opposite at another, so that he was utterly untrustworthy either as a man or as a teacher. This was indeed a slight foundation on which to rest such a charge. It is no wonder therefore that it excited the apostle's indignation. The first charge is that he *used lightness*, i. e. that in purposing to visit Corinth and in announcing his purpose he had no serious intention of doing what he promised. It was a careless, inconsiderate avowal such as none but a man of levity would make. In the Greek the article is used ($\tau \hat{\eta} \, \dot{\epsilon}\lambda\alpha\phi\rho\dot{\iota}\alpha$) *the* lightness, which may mean, *the* lightness with which they charged him; or that which belongs to our nature; or it may have no more force than when used in other cases before abstract nouns. *Or the things that I purpose, do I purpose according to the flesh?* The first charge related to the past, *did* I use lightness? This relates to his general character. 'Am I habitually governed in my plans by the flesh,' i. e. am I influenced and controlled by those considerations which govern ordinary men, who have nothing to guide them but their own corrupt nature? The word *flesh* here, as in v. 12, stands for our whole nature, considered as distinguished from the Spirit of God. All who are not *spiritual* (governed by the Spirit) are, according to the Scripture, *carnal* (governed by the flesh). What Paul therefore intends to deny in these two questions, is that his original purpose of visiting Corinth was formed in levity, and secondly, that his plans in general were controlled by worldly or selfish considerations. *That with me there should be yea, yea, and nay, nay.* That ($\ddot{\iota}\nu\alpha$) here expresses the result, not the design. 'Do I so act after the flesh that the consequence is,' &c. The repetition of the particles *yea, yea*, and *nay, nay*, is simply intensive, as in Matthew 5, 37, "Let your communication be yea, yea, and nay, nay." The meaning, therefore, is, 'Do I affirm and deny the same thing? Do I say both yes and no at the same time and in reference to the same subject? Is no dependence to be placed on my word?' This is the common interpretation and the one demanded by the context. Many commentators from Chrysostom downwards give a very different view of the passage. They understand the apostle to defend himself for his change of plan by saying that he was not like men of the world who obstinately adhered to their purposes, without regard to the manifested will of God, so that with him a yea should be yea, and a nay, nay, let what would be the consequence. But in the 18th v. this interpretation is impossible, because it is there simply "yea and nay." That verse therefore determines the meaning of this. Besides, what he goes on to defend himself against is not a charge of obstinacy, but of saying first one thing and then another. Luther's translation assumes still another interpretation. "Are my purposes carnal? *Not so*, but my yea is yea, and my nay is nay." But this arbitrarily introduces into the text what is not expressed, and thus changes the whole sense.

18. But as God is true, our word towards you was not yea and nay.

That is, 'My preaching, or the doctrine which I preached, was not inconsistent and contradictory. I did not preach first one thing and then another.' This sudden transition from the question as to his veracity as a man to his consistency as a preacher, shows two things; first, that his enemies had brought both charges against him, founding the latter on the former; and secondly, that Paul was much more concerned for the gospel than for his own reputation. They might accuse him, if they pleased, of breaking his word; but when they charged him with denying Christ, that was a very different affair. He therefore drops the first charge and turns abruptly to the second. 'Whatever you may think of my veracity as a man, as God is true, my preaching was not yea and nay,' i. e. unworthy of confidence. *As God is true.* The words are, *God is faithful, that*, &c. Comp. 1 Cor. 1, 9. 10, 13. 1 Thess. 5, 24. They may be understood as an appeal to the fidelity of God as the ground and evidence of the truth and reliableness of his preaching. 'God is faithful, *that* our preaching is not yea and nay.' That is, his fidelity secures the trustworthiness of the gospel. It is his word and therefore is unchangeably true. It abideth forever. 'If,' says the apostle, 'there is no dependence to be placed on my word, God is trustworthy. My preaching, which is his word, is to be relied upon. That is not yea and nay, but firm and true.' It must be admitted, however, that this interpretation is constrained; it is not the simple meaning of the words. The passage must be paraphrased to get this sense out of it. It is perhaps better with our translators, after Calvin, Beza, and many other commentators, ancient and modern, to take the words as an asseveration. *So true as God is faithful*, so true is it, *that*, &c. Comp. 11, 10, ἔστιν ἡ ἀλήθεια Χριστοῦ ἐν ἐμοί, ὅτι. Rom. 14, 11, ζῶ ἐγώ—ὅτι, *as I live—every knee shall bow to me.* Judith 12, 4, ζῇ ἡ ψυχή σου—ὅτι. It is therefore according to the usage of the language to understand πιστὸς ὁ θεός—ὅτι as an oath, and the sense given is much more natural. An oath is an act of worship. To predict that men shall everywhere swear by the name of Jehovah, Is. 65, 16, is to predict that Jehovah shall everywhere be worshipped. Men may, therefore, appeal to God for the truth of what they say on any solemn occasion, if they do it devoutly as an act of worship. It is a formal recognition of his being, of his omniscience, of his holiness and power, and of his moral government. Our Lord himself did not refuse to answer when put upon his oath, Matt. 27, 63; and the apostles often call on God to witness the truth of their declarations. When, therefore, our Saviour commands us, "Swear not at all," he must be understood to forbid profane swearing, that is, calling on God in an irreverent manner and on trivial occasions. *That our word towards you was not yea and nay;* ὁ λόγος ἡμῶν. This may mean *our preaching*, 1 Cor. 1, 17. 2, 1. 4, and often; or, *our word* generally, i. e. what I said. The apostle may be understood to assert the truth and consistency of his instructions as a teacher, or the trustworthiness of his declarations and promises as a man. The decision depends on the context. In favour of the latter it is urged that the charge against him, as intimated in v. 17, was that of breaking his promise, and therefore to make this verse refer to his preaching is to make him evade the point entirely. But the following verses, which are intimately connected with the one before us, clearly refer to matters of doctrine, and therefore this verse must have the same reference. The sudden transition from the charge of levity in v. 17, to that of false doctrine in v. 18, as before remarked, is sufficiently accounted for from the association of the two charges in the minds of his enemies. They said he was not to be depended upon as a preacher, because he had shown himself to be untrustworthy as a man. "As God is true, my preaching is true." The one is as true as the other. Hence in Gal. 1, 8 he pronounces an angel accursed should he preach another gospel. Paul's confidence in the truth of the gospel as he preached it was one and the same with his confidence in God. To tell him that his preaching was not to be depended upon, was in his mind the same as to say that God was not to be believed; for he knew that he was the infallible organ of God in all his teaching. 1 John 5, 10.

19. For the Son of God, Jesus Christ, who was preached among you by us, (even) by me and Silvanus and Timotheus, was not yea and nay, but in him was yea.

My preaching is true, for Christ is true. There is no contradiction, no yea and nay, in him, therefore there is no contradiction in my doctrine. There was no room in Paul's mind for doubt as to his preaching being a trustworthy exhibition of the person and work of Christ, and therefore if Christ be one and the same, i. e. self-consistent truth, so was his doctrine or teaching. With such self-evidencing light and irresistible conviction does the Spirit attend his communications to the human mind. Even in ordinary religious experience, the testimony of the Spirit becomes the testimony of consciousness. Much more was this the case when plenary inspiration was combined with the sanctifying power of the truth. *The Son of God, Jesus Christ;* that is, Christ, who is the Son of God, the same in nature with the eternal Father, and because he is the Son, and, therefore, eternally and immutably true, *was not yea and nay.* There was nothing in him contradictory or untrustworthy. This Christ *was* preached in Corinth by Paul, Silvanus and Timotheus. These persons are mentioned because the apostle probably refers to his first visit to Corinth when they were his companions. Acts 18, 5. His appeal is to the experience of his readers. They had found Christ to be the way, the truth and the life. He had been made unto them wisdom, righteousness, sanctification and redemption. 1 Cor. 1, 32. By *Christ* here the apostle does not mean the doctrine of Christ. He does not intend to assert simply that there was perfect consistency in his own preaching, and that it agreed with the preaching of his associates. The truth asserted is that Christ, the Son of God, had not been manifested among them, or experienced by them to be unsatisfying or uncertain, but *in him was yea.* That is, he was simple truth. *In him,* i. e. in Christ, was truth. He proved himself to be all that was affirmed of him. He was and continued to be (γέγονεν) all that they had been led to expect. Let, therefore, what will become of me and of my reputation for veracity, Christ is the same yesterday, to-day, and forever.

20. For all the promises of God in him are yea, and in him amen, unto the glory of God by us.

This verse is the confirmation of what precedes. Christ was, and is, not yea and nay, not uncertain and inconsistent, for in him all the promises of God were fulfilled. All that God had promised relative to the salvation of man met its full accomplishment in him. Instead of, *all the promises*, the Greek is, *as many promises*. That is, as many promises as had from the beginning been made as to what the Messiah was to be and to do. *In him were the yea*. That is, in him they found their affirmation or accomplishment. The article (τὸ ναί), *the* yea, has reference to the promises. Christ, as regards the promises of God, was *the* yea, i. e. their affirmation and accomplishment. *And in him the Amen.* This is saying in Hebrew what had just been said in Greek; *Amen* being equivalent to *yea*. It is not unusual with the sacred writers to give solemn or impressive formulas in both languages. The promises of God are amen in Christ, because he is the sum and substance of them. He says in a sense which includes the idea here expressed, "I am the truth," John 14, 6; and in Rev. 3, 7 he is designated as "He that is true;" and in Rev. 3, 14 he is called, "The Amen, the faithful and true witness." The common text, which is expressed in our version, has the support of the manuscripts D, E, I, K, which read καὶ ἐν αὐτῷ, *and in him*. A, B, C, F, G have διὸ καὶ δι αὐτοῦ, *wherefore also through him* the Amen. This reading, which most recent editions adopt, was preferred by Calvin, who renders the passage, *quare et per ipsum sit Amen.* The Vulgate has the same reading, *ideo et per ipsum Amen.* The sense thus expressed is certainly better and fuller. The verse then teaches not only that the promises of God receive their confirmation in Christ, but also that we experience and assent to their truth. We say Amen, it is even so, to all God had promised, when we come to know Christ. *To the glory of God by us.* As these words are commonly pointed the natural interpretation is, that by us, i. e. by the preaching of the apostles, men are brought thus to say Amen to the divine promises, to the glory of God. God is glorified by the faith

in his promises thus expressed. The words, however, admit
of a different construction. *By us* may be connected with
the first part of the clause. 'The Amen is said by us to the
glory of God.' This may mean, 'We Christians render a glad
assent to the promises thus ratified in Christ.' But *us* in the
immediate context refers to the apostles, and therefore cannot
be naturally here made to refer to Christians generally. Or,
the meaning may be, 'By us apostles testimony is given to the
truth of the promises, to the glory of God.' This last-mentioned interpretation, however, is inconsistent with the scriptural use of the expression "to say Amen," which means simply to assent to, or to sanction. 1 Cor. 14, 16. The apostles
did not say Amen to the promises by preaching the gospel;
but through their preaching men were brought to say Amen;
that is, they were led to the joyful experience and avowal of
faith in what God had promised. In Christ, therefore, the
promises were fulfilled; and in him also men were brought,
through the apostles, joyfully to assent to them. Bengel's
pithy comment on this verse is: *Nae* respectu Dei promitten-
tis, *amen* respectu credentium. "He that hath received his
testimony, hath set to his seal that God is true." John 3, 33.
1 John 5, 9. 10. To receive God's testimony concerning his
Son, to say Amen, and to believe, all mean the same thing.

21. 22. Now he which stablisheth us with you in
Christ, and hath anointed us, (is) God; who hath also
sealed us, and given the earnest of the Spirit in our
hearts.

In the preceding verse the apostle had spoken of Christ as
the truth and substance of all the divine promises, and of the
cordial assent which believers gave to those promises; he here
brings into view God as the author and preserver of their
faith, who would assuredly grant them the salvation of which
he had already given them the foretaste and the pledge. *Now
he*; or, *but he who stablisheth us with you in Christ.* The
word is ὁ βεβαιῶν, *who renders firm* or *stedfast ;* i. e. who
causes us with you to stand firm, εἰς Χριστόν, in reference to
Christ, so that we adhere to him with unshaken constancy.
As by the pronouns *we* and *us*, in what precedes, the apostle
had meant himself and Silas and Timothy, here where he has

reference to all believers he unites them with himself, *us with you*. The constancy in faith which God gave was not a gift peculiar to teachers, but common to all true Christians. *And hath anointed us*. Kings, prophets, and priests were anointed when inaugurated in their several offices ; *to anoint* may therefore mean to qualify by divine influence, and thereby to authorize any one to discharge the duties of any office. In Luke 4, 18 our Lord applies to himself the language of Isaiah 61, 1, "The Spirit of the Lord is upon me, because he hath anointed me to preach the gospel to the poor." Acts 4, 27. 10, 38. "God anointed Jesus of Nazareth with the Holy Ghost." In like manner Christians are spoken of as anointed, because by the Spirit they are consecrated to God and qualified for his service. 1 John 2, 20. 27. When Paul says here, *hath anointed us*, he means by *us* all Christians, and of course the anointing to which he refers is that which is common to all believers. This is plain, 1. Because the object of the two participles, βεβαιῶν and χρίσας, here used, must be the same ; 'who establisheth *us*, and hath anointed *us*.' But with the former Paul expressly associates the Corinthians. He says, *us with you*. They as well as he were the subjects of the confirmation, and therefore also of the anointing. 2. What follows of sealing and receiving the earnest of the Spirit, cannot with any propriety be restricted to ministers. 3. In the New Testament *official* anointing is spoken of only in relation to Christ, never of apostles or preachers ; whereas believers are said to receive the unction of the Holy Spirit. The design of the apostle is not, as some of the later commentators say, to assert that God had given to him the assurance of the Spirit as to his fidelity in preaching the gospel ; but to show that believers were indebted to God for their faith, and that he would certainly cause them to persevere. *Is God ;* God it is who confirms and anoints his people. Comp. 5, 5 for a similarly constructed passage. This is the common and natural explanation. Billroth and Olshausen render it thus : 'God, who establishes and anointed us, also sealed us.' But this makes the first part of the verse too subordinate ; the *sealing* is not the dominant idea. It is only one of the several benefits specified. It is God who establishes, anoints, seals and gives the earnest of the Spirit. *Who also hath sealed us.* A seal is used, 1. To indicate proprietorship. 2. To authenticate or prove to be genuine. 3. To preserve safe or inviolate.

The Holy Spirit, which in one view is an unction, in another view is a seal. He marks those in whom he dwells as belonging to God. They bear the seal of God upon them. Rev. 7, 2. 2 Tim. 2, 19. *Act. Thom.* § 26, ὁ ϑεὸς διὰ τῆς αὐτοῦ σφραγῖδος ἐπιγινώσκει τὰ ἴδια πρόβατα, *God knows by his seal his own sheep.* He also bears witness in the hearts of believers that they are the children of God. He authenticates them to themselves and others as genuine believers. And he effectually secures them from apostasy and perdition. Eph. 1, 3. 4, 30. This last idea is amplified in the next clause; and hath *given the earnest of the Spirit in our hearts.* The Holy Spirit is itself *the earnest,* i. e. at once the foretaste and pledge of redemption. The word ἀῤῥαβών, *pledge,* is a Hebrew word, which passed as a mercantile term, probably from the Phenician, into the Greek and Latin. It is properly that part of the purchase money paid in advance, as a security for the remainder. The indwelling of the Holy Spirit in the hearts of his people, is that part of the blessings of redemption, which God gives them as a pledge of their full and final salvation. So certain, therefore, as the Spirit dwells in us, so certain is our final salvation. "If any man have not the Spirit of Christ, he is none of his... But if the Spirit of him that raised up Jesus from the dead dwell in you, he that raised up Christ from the dead shall also quicken your mortal bodies by his Spirit that dwelleth in you," Rom. 8, 9–11. The indwelling of the Spirit is therefore called the first-fruits of redemption. Rom. 8, 23. Comp. Eph. 1, 14. 2 Cor. 5, 5. There is but one thing stated in these verses, and that is that God establishes or renders his people firm and secure in their union with Christ, and in their participation of the benefits of redemption. How he does this, and the evidence that he does it, is expressed or presented by saying he hath anointed, sealed, and given us the earnest of the Spirit. The indwelling of the Spirit, therefore, renders the believer secure and steadfast; it is his anointing; it is the seal of God impressed upon the soul, and therefore the pledge of redemption. The fruits of the Spirit are the only evidence of his presence; so that while those who experience and manifest those fruits may rejoice in the certainty of salvation, those who are destitute of them have no right to appropriate to themselves the consolation of this and similar declarations of the word of God. The perseverance of the saints is a perseverance in holiness.

23. Moreover, I call God for a record upon my soul, that to spare you I came not as yet unto Corinth.

Paul here returns to the original charge. The complaint against him for not having executed his purpose of going at once from Ephesus to Corinth, he had left on one side to meet the more serious charge of inconsistency in his teaching. Having answered that accusation, he here says, *But I sparing you*, i. e. for the sake of avoiding giving you pain, *came not again to Corinth*. The obvious implication is, that such was the state of things in Corinth that had he gone there immediately on leaving Ephesus, as he had originally intended, he would have been obliged to appear among them with a rod. 1 Cor. 4, 21. It was to avoid that necessity, and to give them the opportunity to correct abuses before he came, that he had deferred his visit. As there was no available testimony by which the apostle could prove that such was his motive, he confirms it by an oath. *I invoke God as a witness*, i. e. I call upon the omniscient God, who is the avenger of all perjury, to bear testimony to the truth of what I say. "An oath for confirmation is the end of all strife," Heb. 6, 16. All the bonds of society are loosened, and all security of life and property is lost, if men are not to be believed upon their oaths. This shows that human society depends on the sanctity of an oath; and as the oath derives all its sacredness from faith in God, as the providential and moral governor of the world, it is obvious that society cannot exist without religion. Superstition and false religion, although great evils, are far better than atheism. The words ἐπὶ τὴν ἐμὴν ψυχήν, rendered *on my soul*, may mean *against* my soul; or, I summon God *to* me as a witness. The latter idea includes the former, for, as Calvin says, "He who uses God as a witness, cites the punisher of falsehood."

24. Not for that we have dominion over your faith, but are helpers of your joy: for by faith ye stand.

This is intended to moderate and explain what precedes. 'When I speak of sparing you, I do not wish to intimate that I consider myself the lord over your faith.' *Not for that*, οὐχ ὅτι, equivalent to, *I do not say that* we have dominion over your faith. Some say *faith* is here used for believers, (the abstract for the concrete,) we have not dominion over believers; or, as

St. Peter says, are not lords over God's heritage. 1 Pet. 5, 3. Others say *faith* here means faith-life; we have not dominion over your Christian life. Both of these interpretations are unnatural and unnecessary. The word is to be taken in its ordinary sense. Paul disclaims all authority over their faith, either as a man or as an apostle. It was not for him, and if not for him, surely for no other man or set of men, to determine what they should believe. He called upon the Galatians to denounce him, or even an angel from heaven, as accursed, if he preached another gospel. Gal. 1, 8. Faith rests not on the testimony of man, but on the testimony of God. When we believe the Scriptures, it is not man, but God whom we believe. Therefore faith is subject not to man but to God alone. This is perfectly consistent with the plenary inspiration of the apostles, and with our confidence in them as the infallible witnesses of the truth. When a man speaks through a trumpet, it is the man and not the trumpet that we believe. Or when we read a printed page, we have confidence in the trustworthiness of the words as symbols of thought, but it is the mind expressed by those symbols with which we are in communion. So the apostles were but the organs of the Holy Ghost; what they spoke as such, they could not recall ·or modify. What they should communicate was not under their control; they were not the lords, so to speak, of the gospel, so that they could make it what they pleased. Not at all; they were as much subject to the communication which they received, and as much bound to believe what they were made the instruments of teaching, as other men. Paul therefore places himself alongside of his brethren, not over them as a lord, but as a joint-believer with them in the gospel which he preached, and *a helper of their joy.* That is, his office was to co-operate with them in the promotion of their spiritual welfare. It was not the end of the apostleship to give pain or to inflict punishment, but to promote the real happiness of the people. *For by faith ye stand.* The meaning of this clause is doubtful. Taken by themselves the words may mean, 'Ye stand firm or independently as to faith.' This would suit the connection as indicated by *for.* 'We are not lords over your faith, but merely helpers, for you stand independently as to faith.' Or the meaning may be what is expressed in our version, 'Ye stand *by* faith.' Then the connection, as explained by Calvin, is, 'Since it is the effect and nature of faith to sustain or cause you to stand, it is absurd that it should be subject to man, or that we should have dominion over your faith.' This, however, is rather an obscure argument. According to Meyer the connection is with the immediately preceding words, 'We are helpers of your joy, because ye are steadfast as to faith.' That is, steadfastness in faith is necessary to joy. The most natural interpretation probably is that given by Erasmus: fidei nomine nullum habemus in vos. dominium, in qua perseveratis; sed est in vita quod in vobis correctum volebam. 'Over your faith I have no dominion, for in that ye stand; but, when I speak of not sparing, I had reference to your conduct.' He had authority in matters of discipline, but not in matters of faith. As to the latter, he and they were equally under subjection to the revelation of God. He indeed, as the organ of the Spirit, could declare infallibly what that revelation was, but he could not go counter to it, and was to be judged by it. If the inspired apostles recognised not only their subjection to the word of God, but also the right of the people to judge whether their teachings were in accordance with the supreme standard, it is most evident that no church authority can make any thing contrary to Scripture obligatory on believers, and that the ultimate right to decide whether ecclesiastical decisions are in accordance with the word of God, rests with the people. In other words, Paul recognises, even in reference to himself, the right of private judgment. He allowed any man to pronounce him anathema, if he did not preach the gospel as it had been revealed and authenticated to the church. Quum eorum fidei dominari se negat, significat injustam hanc esse et minime tolerandam potestatem, imo tyrannidem in ecclesia. Fides enim prorsus ab hominum jugo soluta, liberrimaque esse debet. Notandum autem, quis loquatur: nam siquis omnino sit mortalium qui jus habeat tale dominium sibi vindicandi, Paulus certe dignus hac praerogativa fuit, fatetur autem sibi non competere. Itaque colligimus, fidem non aliam subjectionem agnoscere, quam verbi Dei: hominum imperio minime esse obnoxiam. CALVIN.

CHAPTER II.

The first paragraph, vs. 1–4, relates to the change of his plan of going immediately to Corinth. In vs. 5–11 he refers to the case of discipline mentioned in his former letter. In vs. 12–14 he states why he did not remain in Troas. And in vs. 14–17 he pours out his heart in gratitude to God for the continued triumph of the gospel.

The true reason why the apostle did not go immediately to Corinth, and his views in reference to the offender whose excommunication he had insisted upon in his former letter.

THERE is no change of subject in this chapter. The apostle after defending himself from the charge of levity in conduct and inconsistency in doctrine, had said, in v. 23 of the preceding chapter, that he did not go to Corinth before giving the church time to comply with the injunctions contained in his former letter, because he did not wish to appear among them as a judge. He here says, in amplification, that he had determined not again to visit Corinth under circumstances which could only give pain to the Corinthians and to himself. He knew that he could not give them sorrow without being himself grieved, and he was assured that if he was happy they would share in his joy, vs. 1–4. The sorrow occasioned by the incestuous person was not confined to the apostle, but shared by the church. He was satisfied with the course which the church had pursued in reference to that case, and was willing the offender should be restored to their fellowship if they were, vs. 5–11. His anxiety about them was so great that not finding Titus, from whom he expected to receive intelligence, he was unable to remain at Troas, but passed over into Macedonia to meet him on his way, vs. 12. 13. The intelligence which he received from Titus being favourable, the apostle expresses in strong terms his gratitude to God who always caused him to triumph, vs. 15–17.

1. But I determined this with myself, that I would not come again to you in heaviness.

The connection is with what immediately precedes. 'I deferred my visit in order to spare you, not that I assume to be a lord over your faith, but a helper of your joy. *But* the true reason for my not coming was that I did not wish to come with heaviness.' The words ἔκρινα ἐμαυτῷ, rendered *I determined with myself*, may mean simply *I determine as to myself*. I had made up my mind; or, 'I determined *for myself*,' i. e. for my own sake. This perhaps is to be preferred.. The apostle thus delicately intimates that it was not merely to spare them, but also himself, that he put off his visit. The word *this* refers to the purpose which the apostle had formed, and which is explained by the following infinitive, μὴ ἐλθεῖν, *not to come*. Two explanations are given of the following clause. According to the one, the meaning is, 'I determined that my second visit should not be with sorrow;' according to the other, 'I determined not a second time to visit you in sorrow.' In the one case the implication is that Paul had, at this time, been only once in Corinth; in the other, the passage implies that he had already (i. e. after his first visit) been to Corinth under circumstances painful to himself and to the church. There are two reasons for preferring this latter view. The first is, that according to the position of the words, as given in all the older manuscripts, (μὴ πάλιν ἐν λύπῃ πρὸς ὑμᾶς ἐλθεῖν,) the πάλιν, *again*, belongs to the whole clause and not exclusively to ἐλθεῖν. The sense, therefore, is that he determined not a second time to come with sorrow, (he had done that once.) The other reason is, that there is evidence from other passages that Paul had been twice to Corinth before this letter was written. See 12, 14. 21. 13, 1. That there is no mention in the Acts of this intermediate journey, is no sufficient reason for denying it, as the passages referred to are so explicit. To make the second visit one by letter, as Calvin (venerat enim semel per epistolam) and others have done, is evidently unnatural. Having gone once to correct abuses and to exercise severity, he was anxious not to have a second painful interview of the same kind, and therefore, instead of going to them, as he had intended, directly from Corinth, he waited to learn through Titus what had been the effect of his letter. *With heaviness*, ἐν λύπῃ, *with sorrow*, i. e. causing sorrow to you. This explanation is required by the following verse, otherwise the meaning would more naturally be *in sorrow*, i. e. in a sorrowful state of mind, as the word λύπη everywhere else with Paul means a state of grief.

2. For if I make you sorry, who is he that maketh me glad, but the same that is made sorry by me?

This is the reason why he did not wish to come bringing sorrow with him; 'For if,' says he, 'I make you sorry, who is there to make me glad? How can I be happy, if you are afflicted? Unless my visit cause you joy, it can bring no joy to me.' As inspiration leaves full play to all the characteristic peculiarities of its subject, in reading the writings of inspired men we learn not only the mind of the Spirit, but also the personal character of the writers. The urbanity of the apostle Paul, his refinement and courtesy, are just as plainly revealed in his epistles as his intellectual power and moral courage. The passage before us is one of many illustrations of the truth of this remark, furnished by this epistle. *Who is he that maketh me glad, but the same that is made sorry by me.* The singular is used, not because a particular individual, much less because the incestuous person, is specially referred to, but because the case is stated in the form of a general proposition. 'I cannot expect joy from one to whom I bring sorrow.' Such was the apostle's love for the Corinthians that unless they were happy he could not be happy. This is the natural and commonly received interpretation of the passage. Chrysostom, and many of the ancient commentators, and some also of the moderns, give a different view of its meaning. ' Who gives me joy, but he who allows himself ($\lambda\upsilon\pi o\acute{\upsilon}\mu\epsilon\nu o\varsigma$ as middle and not passive) to be grieved by me.' That is, no one causes me so much joy as he who is brought to repentance by me. But this is obviously inconsistent with the context. The verse, as thus explained, gives no reason why Paul did not wish to go to Corinth bringing sorrow. On the contrary, the more of that kind of sorrow he brought with him, or was occasioned by his visit, the better. This interpretation would make the apostle say, ' I will not come with sorrow, for nothing gives me so much pleasure as to cause (godly) sorrow.' To avoid this incongruity Olshausen says the connection is to be thus understood: Paul determined that he would not come with sorrow, because he feared that few of the Corinthians would give him the happiness of seeing that they had been made sorry by his former reproofs. But this makes the passage itself a reproof, an insinuation that they had not profited by his first letter. This is contrary to the whole spirit of the passage, which is overflowing with confidence and affection.

3. And I wrote this same unto you, lest, when I

came, I should have sorrow from them of whom I ought to rejoice; having confidence in you all that my joy is (the joy) of you all.

Having said that his motive for not coming at once to Corinth was to avoid giving them sorrow, he here adds, 'And I wrote what I did in my former letter that, when I came, I might not have sorrow.' Instead of going in person to correct the evils which existed in the church of Corinth, he wrote to them that those evils might be corrected before he came, and thus his coming would be a source of joy to both parties. It is evident from the preceding context, and from vs. 4 and 9, that ἔγραψα here refers not to this epistle, but to the former one. *This same,* τοῦτο αὐτό, *that very thing,* that is, the very thing which I did write respecting the incestuous person. The expression seems to have special reference to that case, because that is evidently the case to which the following verses relate. It appears that the point about which the apostle was most anxious was, how the Corinthians would act in regard to his command, 1 Cor. 5, 13, to put away from among them "that wicked person." He seems to have feared that his enemies might have had influence enough with the church, to prevent their executing his command. He therefore waited in painful suspense to learn the issue. And when Titus, on his return from Corinth, informed him that they had not only promptly obeyed his directions, but that the offender himself and the whole church had been brought to deep and genuine repentance, his heart was filled with gratitude to God, and with love to the people who had manifested such a Christian spirit. All this is plain from what is said in ch. 7. Erasmus and several other commentators render τοῦτο αὐτό *hac eadem de causa,* for this very reason. The sense would then be, 'I determined I would not come to you with sorrow, *and for that very reason* I wrote to you that I might not.' This, although it suits the preceding context, is not so consistent with what follows as the common interpretation; for in the following verses the apostle states the reasons for his writing as he had done in his former letter.

Lest when I came I should have sorrow from them of whom I ought to rejoice. That is, 'I wrote what I did that I might not have sorrow from those, who should be to me a source of joy.' He wished all painful questions settled before he came. *Having confidence in you all that my joy is the joy of you all.* Paul in saying that he wished all causes of painful collision might be removed out of the way before he went to Corinth, did not isolate himself from the people, as though concerned only for his own peace of mind, but was satisfied that what made him happy would make them happy. My joy will be the joy of you all. This does not mean merely that it would give them pleasure to see him happy, but also that obedience on their part, and the consequent purity and prosperity of the church, were as necessary to their happiness as to his. Paul says he had this confidence in them *all*, although it is abundantly evident that there were men among them who were his bitter opponents. These latter he here leaves out of view, and speaks of the majority, probably the great body, of the church as though it were the whole.

4. For out of much affliction and anguish of heart I wrote unto you with many tears; not that ye should be grieved, but that ye may know the love which I have the more abundantly towards you.

The connection is either with the immediately preceding clause, 'I have confidence in you, for otherwise it would not have given me so much pain to write as I did;' or, what is more natural because more direct, the reference is to the motives which dictated his letter. 'I was influenced by the desire of promoting your happiness, for to me it was a most painful duty.' *Out of* (ἐκ) indicates the source. His letter flowed from a broken heart. *Affliction and anguish* refer to his inward feelings, not to his outward circumstances, for both are qualified by the word *heart.* . It was out of an afflicted, an oppressed heart, that he wrote. *With many tears*, (διά,) *through* many tears. The union of fidelity and love which renders parental discipline peculiarly effective, gives also peculiar power to ecclesiastical censures. When the offender is made to feel that, while his sin is punished, he himself is loved; and that the end aimed at is not his suffering but his good, he is the more likely to be brought to repentance. Every pastor must see in the apostle's love for the Corinthians, and in the extreme sorrow with which he exercised discipline in the case of offenders, an instructive example for his imitation. *Not that ye should be grieved*, my object in writing was not to cause you sorrow, *but that ye may know the love that I have the more abundantly towards you.* The ends which the apostle desired to accomplish by his former letter were numerous, and he therefore sometimes specifies one, and sometimes another. Here, he says, it was to manifest his love; in v. 9 he says it was to test their obedience; in ch. 7 he says it was to bring them to repentance. These are not incompatible ends, and therefore there is no inconsistency between these several statements. *The love which I have the more abundantly towards you.* This naturally means *the special* love which I have for you. His love for them was more abundant, or greater, than that which he had for any other church. This view is borne out by numerous other passages in these two epistles, which go to show that Paul's love for the Corinthian church was, for some reason, peculiarly strong. As vs. 5–11 have direct reference to the case of the incestuous person, it is the more probable that all that he says in the preceding verses as to his reasons for not coming sooner to Corinth, and as to the sorrow and anxiety which he felt about the state of the church there, had special reference to that case.

5. But if any have caused grief, he hath not grieved me, but in part, that I may not overcharge you all.

The connection between this paragraph, vs. 5–11, and what precedes is natural and obvious. Paul had been speaking of his motives for writing his former letter. It was not intended to give them sorrow. If sorrow had been occasioned, it had not come from him. This led him to speak more particularly of the case which had occasioned so much distress. The proper interpretation of this particular verse is, however, a matter of great doubt. The translation is of necessity, in this case, an exposition, and therefore the grounds of doubt do not appear to the English reader. Our translators, after Luther, assume that ἀπὸ μέρους, *in part*, are to be connected with the preceding clause, and πάντας ὑμᾶς, *you all*, with ἐπιβαρῶ, *overcharge*. Thus construed the sense can only be, 'If any one has caused grief, he has not grieved me, but in part, that is, I am not the only person aggrieved. I say this, lest I should bear hard upon you all. It would be a severe reflection on you to say that you did not feel any sorrow for the offence in question.' According to this view, the design of the passage is to guard against the impression that he meant to charge them with indifference. But to this it is objected that to express this sense εἰ μή, and not ἀλλά, would be required. "He hath not grieved me *except* in part." And secondly, that the idea thus expressed is not suited to the context. The main idea evidently is, 'He hath not grieved me but you.' The subordinate words and clauses therefore must be accommodated to that idea. Hence ἀλλ' ἀπὸ μέρους must be connected with what follows, and πάντας ὑμᾶς with λελύπηκεν. Then the sense will be, 'He hath not grieved me, but in part, or, to a certain extent, (lest I should bear too hard *on him*,) you all.' The design of the passage, according to this view, is to soften the charge against the penitent offender of having been the cause of sorrow. This the apostle does, first, by saying, "he did not grieve me," i. e. it was no personal offence against me that he committed ; and second, that all the Corinthians were not afflicted, it was not a universal sorrow that he caused. This substantially is the interpretation given by Calvin after Chrysostom, and is the one adopted by the great majority of modern commentators. It has the advantage of being not only suited to the meaning of the words, but to the whole tone of the following context, which is eminently mild and conciliatory. The apostle's heart was overflowing with the tenderest feelings towards his Corinthian brethren, and he was evidently solicitous to heal the salutary wounds inflicted by his former letter. There is still another view of the passage which should be mentioned. It may be pointed so as to read thus: 'He hath not grieved me, but in part (that I may not overcharge all) you.' This, however, unnaturally separates the words πάντας ὑμᾶς, *you all.*

6. Sufficient to such a man is this punishment, which (was inflicted) of many.

I do not wish to be severe towards him, for the punishment which he has received is sufficient. The word ἡ ἐπιτιμία, rendered *punishment*, occurs only in *Wisdom* 3, 10 in this sense, and therefore many assume that it here does not mean punishment, but *reproof.* The word rendered *sufficient*, ἱκανόν, is used substantively. "This punishment is a sufficiency, or a satisfaction." Comp. Matt. 6, 34 for a similar construction. Paul says the punishment or reproof was administered ὑπὸ τῶν πλειόνων, *by the majority*, intimating that all did not concur in it. This, however, is not a necessary inference, because οἱ πλειόνες may mean *the many*, the whole body considered as many, because composed of many members. There are three views taken of this verse in connection with what follows. In his former letter the apostle had not only commanded the church to excommunicate the person here referred to, but declared his own determination to deliver him to Satan for the destruction of the flesh. 1 Cor. 5, 5. Grotius supposes that in consequence of that judgment he was seized with some bodily malady, for delivery from which Paul, in this connection, declares his willingness that the Corinthians should pray. Of this, however, the passage gives no intimation. A second view is that the sentence of excommunication had not been carried into effect, but as the reproof administered by many had had the effect of leading the offender to repentance, the apostle here intimates his satisfaction with what the church had done, although his injunctions had not been fully complied with. This is the view of Calvin, Beza, and of many others. In favour of this explanation it is urged that the expression "*this* punishment" naturally refers to that punishment or reproof which the Corinthians had administered as distinguished from that which he had enjoined; and his saying "*this* punishment," of which he had heard, was enough, implies that he did not wish them to proceed any further, but rather that they should console the penitent by the assurance of their love. On the other hand, however, v. 9 (as well as ch. 7) clearly intimates that the church had rendered a prompt obedience to the apostle's directions. The great majority of commentators, therefore, understand the passage to mean that Paul did not wish the excommunication to be continued any longer. As it had produced its desired effect, he was willing that the offender should be restored to the communion of the church. The whole passage indicates that Paul was more lenient than the church, for he exhorts his readers not to be too severe in their treatment of their offending brother. A passage, says Calvin, himself a severe disciplinarian, well to be observed, as it teaches with what equity and clemency the discipline of the church is to be attempered; *qua æquitate et clementia temperanda sit disciplina ecclesiæ.* Paul, he adds, was satisfied with the repentance of the offender; whereas the ancient bishops gave forth their canons requiring a penance of three, or seven years, or even for a life-time, without regard to the contrition of the unhappy victims of their severity.

7. So that contrariwise ye (ought) rather to forgive (him) and comfort (him), lest perhaps such a one should be swallowed up with overmuch sorrow.

The consequence of what is expressed in v. 8 is indicated by the words *so that.* 'The punishment being sufficient, the consequence is that, instead of its being increased or continued, you should forgive and comfort the offender.' As the apostle seems to indicate what *ought* to be done, most commentators supply before the infinitives χαρίσασθαι καὶ παρακαλέσαι the word δεῖ or δεῖν, '*it is necessary* to forgive and comfort.' The infinitive itself, however, often expresses, after verbs of saying, and the like, not what is, but what should be, e. g. λέγοντες περιτέμνεσθαι, *saying you ought to be circumcised.* Acts 15, 24. 21, 4. 21. *Winer,* p. 371, says that neither of these modes of explanation is necessary, as the infinitives may be connected immediately with ἱκανόν, 'The reproof is sufficient —in order to your pardoning and comforting him.' The delicacy of the apostle towards this offender is indicated by his abstaining either from naming him, or designating him as he had before done, 1 Cor. 5, 13, as *that wicked person.* He refers to him simply *as such an one,* without any appellation which could wound his feelings. The apostle combined, therefore, the strictest fidelity with the greatest tenderness. As long as the offender was impenitent and persisted in his offence, Paul insisted upon the severest punishment. As soon as he acknowledged and forsook his sin, he became his earnest advocate. *Lest he should be swallowed up with overmuch sorrow,* that is, lest he should be driven to despair and thus destroyed. Undue severity is as much to be avoided as undue leniency. The character which Paul here exhibits reflects the image of our heavenly Father. His word is filled with denunciations against impenitent sinners, and at the same time with assurances of unbounded pity and tenderness towards the penitent. He never breaks the bruised reed or quenches the smoking flax.

8. Wherefore I beseech you that ye would confirm (your) love towards him.

The connection is either with v. 6, 'His punishment is sufficient—*wherefore* confirm your love towards him;' or with what immediately precedes. 'There is danger of his being

swallowed up with overmuch sorrow unless you forgive him,
wherefore confirm your love to him.' The latter method is
to be preferred, though the sense is substantially the same.
I beseech you, παρακαλῶ, the same word which in the preceding verse is used in the sense of consoling. Paul not unfre-
quently uses the same word in the immediate connection in
different senses. 1 Cor. 3, 17. 11, 23. *That ye would confirm,* literally, *to confirm,* κυρῶσαι. The word properly means
to ratify with authority by some public or formal act. Gal.
3, 15. And this sense is generally adopted here. The apostle
is understood to call upon them by a formal act to reinstate
the offender in the communion of the church, to assure him
of their love, so that he might not have to infer it merely
from their treatment of him. The word, however, may mean
nothing more than is expressed in our version. 'I exhort you
to make your love towards him a matter of certainty.' But
as the implication is that they had already begun to manifest
their brotherly affection for him, the probability is that the
apostle wished them to give their love a formal ratification.

9. For to this end also did I write, that I might know the proof of you, whether ye be obedient in all things.

Verses 9 and 10 are sometimes regarded as a parenthesis,
so as to connect the 11th verse with the 8th. 'Confirm your
love towards him, lest Satan get an advantage over us.' But
a parenthesis is never to be assumed where the grammatical
construction continues unbroken, and the logical connection is
uninterrupted. The 11th verse is naturally connected with
the 10th, and the 9th with the 8th. 'Confirm your love to
him, for the object of my writing to you to exclude him from
your fellowship, has been accomplished.' *To this end* means
the end specified in the latter part of the verse. *I wrote,*
ἔγραψα, a form of the verb which is often in the epistolary style
used of the letter in the process of being written. Rom. 15,
15. 1 Cor. 9, 15. 1 Pet. 5, 12, &c. The whole context, however, shows that Paul refers to his former letter. See vs. 3. 4.
He did not write this letter to test their obedience, though
that was one of the objects of his former epistle. Paul says,
'I *also* wrote.' This *also* may indicate that it was the object
of his former letter as well as of the exhortation which he had
just given them, to test their obedience. But such was not

the object of that exhortation. It is better therefore to un-derstand the (καί) *also*, as simply intended to give prominence to the words *I wrote*, as something additional to other things which he had done with the same general object. 'To this end I also wrote, as well as did many other things,' &c. The end (although not the only one), which the apostle had in view in enjoining on the church the excommunication of the person here referred to, was, as he says, *that I might know the proof of you.* The word used is δοκιμή, which means *trial*, 8, 2, "trial of affliction;" or, *proof, test,* 13, 3, "As ye seek a proof of Christ speaking in me;" or, the result of trial, what is ap-proved, *integrity that has been tested.* Phil. 2, 22, "Ye know his tried integrity." The last meaning is the best suited to this place. 'That I might know your integrity, i. e. your true Christian temper.' This is explained by saying he wished to see whether they would be *obedient in all things*, εἰς πάντα, *in reference to all things.* These latter words stand first, 'Whether as to all things ye are obedient,' which is more em-phatic. Obedience to legitimate authority is one of the fruits and evidences of Christian sincerity. A rebellious, self-willed, disobedient spirit is a strong indication of an unsanctified heart. As the Corinthians had proved themselves obedient to the apostle's directions, and as the offender was truly peni-tent, the object of his letter, both as it related to them and to him, had been attained, and therefore there was no reason for the continuance of the punishment.

10. To whom ye forgive any thing, I (forgive) also : for if I forgave any thing, to whom I forgave (it),* for your sakes (forgave I it) in the person of Christ.

The apostle having exhorted the Corinthians to forgive their repentant brother, says he was ready to join in that for-giveness. *To whom ye forgive any thing, I also.* Although this is stated generally, as though he meant to say that he would forgive any one whom they were ready to forgive, yet it is obvious from the context that he intended to be under-

---

* The received text here reads καὶ γὰρ ἐγὼ εἴ τι κεχάρισμαι, ᾧ κεχάρισμαι, *for also I if I have forgiven any thing, to whom I forgave.* Griesbach, Lach-mann, Tischendorf, Rückert, Meyer, and others, after the majority of ancient MSS. read, καὶ γὰρ ἐγὼ ὃ κεχάρισμαι, εἴ τι κεχάρισμαι, *for also I what I have forgiven, if I have forgiven any thing.*

stood as referring to that particular case. He was satisfied with their course, and also with the evidence of the repentance of the offender, and therefore he was ready to sanction his restoration to their communion. His reason for this is stated in what follows, he did it for their sake. His forgiving, however, was suspended upon theirs. He would not interfere to restore the person in question unless they were satisfied to receive him. He therefore says, *If I have forgiven any thing*, that is, if the forgiveness expressed in the foregoing clause is to take effect and to be considered as already done, I have done it for your sake. He was influenced by no personal consideration either in the censure originally pronounced, or in his present course, but solely by a desire to promote their best interests. *In the person of Christ*, or, *in the presence* of Christ. This latter interpretation is the more consistent with usage, and is generally adopted. The meaning is that he acted in this matter as in the presence of Christ, i. e. as though Christ were looking on. The other explanation, which is preferred by Luther and many others, is consistent with the meaning of the words, and gives a good sense. He acted in the person of Christ, i. e. as his representative and by his authority. This idea, however, is commonly expressed by the phrase *in the name* of Christ. 1 Cor. 5, 4. Calvin prefers the former view, and adds, Christ is to be placed before us, or we "are to act as in his presence, for nothing is better adapted to incline us to mercy." No man can be severe in his judgment who feels that the mild eyes of Christ are fixed upon him.

The word χαρίζομαι, rendered *to forgive* in this verse, is a deponent verb, but is, in several of its forms, used in a passive sense. It is so taken here by Rückert and Meyer, who give an entirely different explanation of the passage. They adopt the reading of Griesbach, given in the margin, and render it thus: 'I forgive—for what I have been forgiven, if I have been forgiven anything, it is for your sake.' That is, if God has really pardoned my great sin in persecuting Christ, it was for your sake. Comp. 1 Tim. 1, 16. But this interpretation is inconsistent with the common use of the word, with the whole context, and with Paul's manner of speaking. His humility manifested itself in deep remorse and repentance for his past conduct, but not in doubting whether he had been forgiven. Besides, this interpretation would require a very unnatural explanation of the following clause. 'If I have been forgiven for your sake *in the presence of Christ*,' that is, Christ is the witness of my being forgiven. This is contrary to all scriptural representations. God is said to forgive for Christ's sake; and Christ is said to forgive, but he is never represented as the mere witness or spectator of our forgiveness.

11. Lest Satan should get an advantage of us : for we are not ignorant of his devices.

This verse, as above remarked, is by some made to depend on v. 8, the vs. 9 and 10 being parenthetical. 'Confirm your love towards him—lest Satan should get an advantage of us.' Others make it depend on the preceding words, 'We should act (or, I was pardoned) in the presence of Christ, lest,' &c. The most natural connection is with the first clause of v. 10, which contains the main idea of the context. 'I will join you in pardoning the offender lest Satan get an advantage of us,' i. e. make a gain of us. The expression is μὴ πλεονεκτηθῶμεν ὑπὸ τοῦ σατανᾶ, *lest we should be made gain of, or defrauded, by Satan*. It was a gain to Satan if either an individual soul could be driven to despair, or the peace of the church could be disturbed. Both of these evils were to be apprehended if discipline were carried too far. This dread of Satan was not chimerical or unreasonable, for he really does seek to turn every thing to the disadvantage of Christ and his kingdom. *We are not ignorant*, says the apostle, *of his devices*. This and similar passages of the Word of God teach that Satan is a personal being; that he exerts great influence over the minds of men; that although finite, and, therefore, not ubiquitous, he is nevertheless represented as operating on the minds of men generally, and not merely on those in any one place. His powers of intelligence and agency therefore must be great beyond our conceptions. No individual and no community can ever be sure that he is not plotting their destruction. Paul might have said to the Romans or the Ephesians, as he did to the Corinthians, that they must take heed lest Satan make a gain of them, and in some way secure them as his own.

12. 13. Furthermore, when I came to Troas to (preach) Christ's gospel, and a door was opened to me of the Lord, I had no rest in my spirit because I found

not Titus my brother; but taking my leave of them, I went from thence into Macedonia.

Furthermore, when I came; literally, *But having come.* The particle δέ (*but*) serves to resume the connection broken by the digression, vs. 5–11. In v. 4 he said he had written his former letter in great anguish and distress of heart, to manifest his love for them. And as a still further proof of the deep interest which he took in their welfare, he refers to the incident mentioned in these verses. In execution of his plan of going from Ephesus through Macedonia to Corinth, 1 Cor, 16, 5, Paul came *to Troas,* literally, *to the Troad* (εἰς τὴν Τρωάδα), a name given to the whole district around the site of ancient Troy. The city itself was on the coast of Mysia opposite to the island of Tenedos. It had been made a Roman colony by Augustus, and was a ·place of considerable importance, in constant commercial intercourse with the cities of Macedonia and Greece. Paul did not intend to make a rapid journey to Corinth, but a regular missionary tour; he therefore says he came to Troas to preach *Christ's gospel,* i. e. the gospel of which Christ is the author. It is also called the gospel of God, and Paul speaks of it as his gospel, i. e. the gospel which he preached. When spoken of as the gospel *of the kingdom of God,* Matt. 4, 23, the gospel *of salvation,* Eph. 1, 13, *of peace,* Eph. 6, 15, the genitive expresses either the subject of which the gospel treats or the effects which it produces. *And a door was opened to me,* i. e. a way of access, an opening to labour with effect. *Of the Lord,* according to this interpretation the words, ἐν κυρίῳ, are to be connected with the immediately preceding participle, "door opened by the Lord." See 1 Cor. 15, 58. Gal. 5, 10. Eph. 2, 21. It is, however, more in accordance with Paul's style, who so frequently uses these words in such expressions as 'work in the Lord,' 'temple in the Lord,' 'fellow-labourer in the Lord,' to refer them to the whole clause. "There was an open door in the Lord." The kind of door is thus indicated, or the sphere of labour pointed out. It was an opportunity for labouring successfully in the Lord's service. Though the prospects were so favourable, Paul says, *I had no rest in my spirit;* τῷ πνεύματι μου, *for my spirit.* The word *spirit* is here used because it is the highest term to designate the soul, Rom. 8, 16, and the anxiety or distress which the apostle experienced concerned the highest feelings of his nature. *Be-*

cause I found not Titus my brother.　He calls Titus his brother, both because of his relation to him as a fellow-Christian,
and because he was a joint labourer with him in the gospel.
He expected to meet Titus at Troas, and to learn from him the
state of things in Corinth, and especially the effect produced
by his former letter.　It seems that he regarded this as a
turning point in the history of that church.　If they submitted
to his authority and corrected the abuses which he had pointed out, and especially if they excommunicated the member
guilty of the unheard-of offence so often referred to in this
chapter, then he had hopes of their stability in faith and prog-
ress in holiness.　But if they refused to regard his injunctions,
and persisted in the course on which they had entered, then he
foresaw their speedy destruction.　So much was at stake that
he could not endure the state of suspense which he was in;
and therefore, *taking leave of them,* that is, of the brethren in
Troas, he passed over into Macedonia.　On his first visit to this
city, Paul was prevented from remaining by a vision, from which
he gathered that the Lord called him to preach the gospel in
Macedonia.　Acts 16, 8.　And on his return from his present
journey, it is said, he sailed from Philippi and came in five days
to Troas, and abode there seven days.　Acts 20, 6.　From the
circumstances connected with this last visit it is evident that
there was an established church at that time in Troas.　The
word ἀποτάσσομαι, *to take leave of,* means *to separate oneself
from,* to bid farewell to.　Luke 16, 61. Acts 18, 18. 21.　*I
went from thence into Macedonia;* ἐξῆλθον, *I went forth.*
He crossed over the northeastern corner of the Mediterranean
sea to one of the ports of Macedonia; the same voyage which
he made on his return, which then required five days.　As
Titus was to return from Corinth through Macedonia to Troas,
Paul thus went to meet him on his journey.

14. Now thanks (be) unto God, which always causeth us to triumph in Christ, and maketh manifest the
savour of his knowledge by us in every place.

Agreeably to the impulsive character of this epistle, instead of stating what was the intelligence which he received
from Titus, the apostle breaks out into a thanksgiving to God,
which assumes a form which might be taken for self-commendation, which he, however, disclaims, and humbly acknowl-
edges that all his qualifications for his work, and all his success

in it, are to be attributed to God. This leads him to speak of the ministry of the gospel, which he contrasts with that of the law, and himself with Moses, so that it is not until the seventh chapter that he pauses, as it were, to take breath, and resumes the narrative here broken off. The thing for which the apostle gives thanks is his success; which includes both his triumph over obstacles and enemies, and his efficiency in spreading abroad the knowledge of the truth. The word θριαμβεύειν, rendered here to *cause to triumph*, means *to triumph over*, *to lead in triumph*. This is its uniform sense in the classics, and it is so used by Paul in Col. 2, 5. Meyer and others so render the word here. 'Thanks be to God who triumphs over us,' i. e. who disappoints our fears and puts our anxieties to shame. But this is evidently incongruous. Paul does not represent himself as humbled and conquered, but just the reverse. Calvin and others retain the literal meaning of the word, and say the sense is, 'Thanks be to God who leads us in triumph, not as captives, but as sharers of his victory.' This gives a suitable meaning, but is not so consistent with the use of the word, which means *to triumph over*, not, to make one a sharer in our triumph. The great majority of commentators therefore modify the sense of the word as is done by our translators. This they justify by referring to the fact that many verbs which in ordinary Greek are neuter, in the Hellenistic dialect are used in a causative sense (*Winer*, p. 304), as μαθητεύειν, *to be a disciple*, in Matt. 28, 19 and elsewhere, means *to make disciples;* βασιλεύειν, *to reign*, in 1 Sam. 8, 22, and often in the Septuagint, means *to cause to reign;* and thus θριαμβεύειν, *to triumph*, may in obedience to the context be fairly rendered, *to cause to triumph*. *In Christ*, in virtue of union with Christ, or, as united to him. These words determine the nature of the triumph of which the apostle speaks. It was the triumph of a Christian minister in the service of Christ.

And maketh manifest the savour of his knowledge, i. e. diffuses or spreads abroad his knowledge, which is compared to the savour of a sacrifice (Gen. 8, 21. Eph. 5, 2. Phil. 4, 18), or to incense. *His* knowledge; the pronoun *his* is commonly referred to God, but as this clause is explanatory of the former, or an amplification of the idea therein expressed, it is perhaps better to refer it to Christ. 'He causes us to triumph in Christ, and to spread abroad the savour of his knowledge,' i. e. the knowledge of Christ. That Christ should be known was the great end of Paul's mission, and is of all things the most acceptable to God. Knowledge here, as so often elsewhere in Scripture, means not merely intellectual cognition, but spiritual apprehension and recognition. That men should know the Lord Jesus Christ in the sense of recognizing, loving and worshipping him as God manifest in the flesh, is the consummation of redemption; the sum of all blessedness and excellence. *In every place.* Wherever Paul went, there the knowledge of Christ was spread abroad. Comp. Rom. 15, 19. Can this be said of us?

15. For we are unto God a sweet savour of Christ, in them that are saved, and in them that perish.

We as ministers, and our work of preaching Christ, are acceptable to God, whatever may be the result of our labours. This idea is connected with the preceding as an amplification and confirmation. 'God by us diffuses the knowledge of Christ everywhere as a savour; *for* (ὅτι, *because*) it is well pleasing to God whatever be the effect which it produces.' There is, as is so common in Paul's epistles, a slight change in the figure. In v. 14 the knowledge of Christ is declared to be a savour as of incense, here the apostle is the sweet savour. But it is the apostle not as a man, not the purity or devotion of his life; but the apostle as a preacher of the gospel, and therefore the gospel which he preached; so that the thought remains the same. In both verses the diffusion of the knowledge of Christ is said to be well pleasing to God. *Savour of Christ*, does not mean a savour of which Christ is the author. The idea is not that Christ rendered Paul or his life acceptable to God. That indeed is true, but it is not what is intended. When we speak of the perfume of the rose, or of the violet, we mean that perfume which the rose or the violet emits and which is characteristic of it. When Paul says, "We are a sweet smelling savour of Christ," he means we are the means of diffusing the knowledge of Christ. When a man's garments are perfumed with myrrh or frankincense, he fills with the fragrance every place he enters. So Paul, wherever he went, diffused abroad the fragrance of the name of Christ, and that was acceptable to God. *In them*, i. e. among them, that are saved; *and in* (among) *them that perish*. This does not mean among them predestined to be saved, and those predestined to perish. The idea of predestination is not included. The two classes are designated *ab eventu*. The gospel and those who preach it are well pleasing to God, whether men receive it and are saved, or reject it and are lost. The light is inestimably precious, whether the eye rejoices in it, or through disease is destroyed by it. Comp. 1 Cor. 1, 18. 2 Thess. 2, 10.

16. To the one (we are) the savour of death unto death; to the other the savour of life unto life. And who is sufficient for these things?

The words *we are* are not in the text, but are necessarily implied. The apostle and all faithful ministers are to God an εὐωδία, *a sweet savour*, to men an ὀσμή, *a savour*, salutary or destructive according to circumstances. *We are*, i. e. we as preachers. The idea is the same whether we say that preachers of the gospel, or the gospel itself, or Christ, are the cause of life to some, and of death to others. As Christ is to some a tried corner stone, elect and precious, the rock of their salvation, to others he is a stone of offence. 1 Pet. 2, 7. 8. So the gospel and its ministers are the cause of life to some, and of death to others, and to all they are either the one or the other. The word of God is quick and powerful either to save or to destroy. It cannot be neutral. If it does not save, it destroys. "This is the condemnation, that light is come into the world, and men loved darkness rather than light," John 3, 19. "If I had not come and spoken unto them they had not had sin," John 15, 22. If a man rejects the gospel, it had been far better for him never to have heard it. It will be more tolerable for Sodom and Gomorrah in the day of judgment than for him. This, which is the doctrine of the Bible, is plainly the doctrine of this passage. The gospel and those who preach it, are either a savour of life or a savour of death. If not the one, they must be the other. In the phrase "a savour of death unto death," *of death* expresses the quality, *unto death*, the effect. It is a deadly savour, and it produces death. And so of the corresponding clause, "a savour of life unto life," is a salutary savour producing life. The Rabbins often use a similar expression in reference to the Law, which they say is either an odour of life or of death.

On the authority of two of the older MSS. (A and C), and several of the more modern ones, Lachmann, Tischendorf and Meyer read ἐκ θανάτου and ἐκ ζωῆς instead of the simple genitive. It is then not a savour *of death* or *of life*, but a savour arising from death, and a savour arising from life. To the one class Christ is dead and yields only a savour of death; to the other, he is alive, and yields a savour of life. According to either reading the main idea is the same. Christ and his gospel, and therefore his ministers, are to believers the source of life, and to unbelievers the source of death. See Matt. 21, 44. Luke 2, 34. John 9, 39. The common text has more external authority, and certainly gives a simpler sense, and is therefore preferred by the majority of editors.

And who is sufficient for these things? Καί (*and*) before a question often indicates a consequence of what precedes. It is frequently in our version in such cases rendered *then.* " Who then can be saved ? " Mark 10, 26. " How is he then David's son ? " Luke 20, 44. So here, Who then is sufficient for these things? If the work is so great, if eternal life or eternal death must follow the preaching of the gospel, who then is sufficient (ἱκανός) for so responsible a calling? The most natural answer to this question would seem to be, ' No one in himself.' The following verse, however, which begins with (γάρ) *for,* and is designed to confirm the implied answer, requires that answer to be, " I am." ' I am sufficient for this work, *for* I do not handle the word of God deceitfully.' " My sufficiency," however, the apostle immediately adds, 3, 5, " is of God." Of himself he was not fit or able to do any thing. There is, as Calvin remarks, an implied antithesis. ' The object of preaching is the diffusion of the knowledge of Christ ; the effect of that diffusion is life to some and death to others. Who then is competent to this work? Not your false teachers who corrupt the word of God, but I and others who preach the pure gospel from pure motives.' This view is sustained by what follows, for the apostle immediately proceeds to vindicate his claim to this sufficiency or fitness, which he denies to the false teachers.

17. For we are not as many, which corrupt the word of God; but as of sincerity, but as of God, as in the sight of God, speak we in Christ.

The connection indicated by *for* is obvious. ' We are competent to this work, for we are not like the false teachers, but are sincere.' We are not *as many,* οἱ πολλοί, *the* many.

This some understand to mean the mass or majority of those who preach the gospel. The apostle would thus be made to condemn, as corrupters of the faith, the great body of the ministers of the apostolic church. This, however, is unnecessary. *The* many, means the definite many known to the Corinthians as false teachers, to whom in the course of this epistle the apostle so often refers. *Which corrupt the word of God.* The word used is καπηλεύω, *to be a huckster*, and then *to act as one.* Paul says, We do not act as hucksters in reference to the word of God. The word is frequently used in the Greek writers in a figurative sense, to express the ideas of adulterating, and of making merchandise of any thing for the sake of gain. Both ideas may be united, for both are included in the disclaimer of the apostle. He neither adulterated the word of God, by mixing it with Judaism or false philosophy (i. e. with his own speculations), nor did he use it for any selfish or mercenary purpose. *But as of sincerity.* The (ὡς) *as*, is not redundant. The meaning is, 'We speak as those who are sincere,' i. e. those whose characteristic is εἰλικρίνεια, *transparent purity*, or integrity; who can bear being looked through and through; all whose motives will sustain inspection. *As of God*, not merely sent of God, but godly, influenced by God, and belonging to God, and therefore like him. Our Lord said to the Jews, "He which is of God, heareth God's words: ye therefore hear them not because ye are not of God," John 8, 47. *As in the sight of God*, i. e. as in his presence and conscious of his inspection. We speak *in Christ ;* not of Christ, nor, according to Christ, but in communion with him, as a member of his body and actuated by his Spirit. We have here then Paul's description of a faithful minister, of one who is (ἱκανός) *sufficient*, or qualified for the fearful responsibility of being a savour of life or of death. He does not corrupt the word of God by any foreign admixtures, nor use it as a means of his own advancement by dispensing it so as to please men; but he is governed by pure motives, is of God, and speaks as in the presence of God, and as a true Christian man.

CHAPTER III.

The apostle shows that he does not need to commend himself or to be commended by the Corinthians; that God had qualified him for the work of a minister of the new, and not of the old covenant, vs. 1–11. He exercised his ministry in accordance with the peculiar character of the new dispensation, vs. 12–18.

Proof of the Apostle's fitness for his work, and its nature.
Vs. 1–11.

ALTHOUGH the concluding paragraph of the preceding chapter contained a strong assertion of the integrity and fidelity of the apostle, he says, it was not written for the purpose of self-commendation. He needed no commendation from any source, v. 1. The Corinthians themselves were his commendation. Their conversion was an epistle of Christ authenticating his mission and his fidelity, which all men could read, vs. 2. 3. His fitness or sufficiency for his work was due in no measure to himself, but to God, who had endowed him with the qualifications of a minister of the new covenant, vs. 4–6. This covenant and its ministry are far superior to the old covenant and the ministry of Moses, because the one was a ministry of death, the other of life; the one was of condemnation, the other of righteousness; the glory of the one was transient, the glory of the other is abiding, vs. 7–11.

1. Do we begin again to commend ourselves? or need we, as some (others), epistles of commendation to you, or (letters) of commendation from you?

Many of the peculiarities of this epistle are due to the fact that at the time of writing it the apostle's mind was filled with conflicting feelings. On the one hand, he was filled with gratitude to God and love to the Corinthians on account of their repentance and ready obedience; and on the other, with feelings of indignation at the perverse and wicked course adopted by the false teachers in Corinth. Hence even in the expression of the former class of feelings, he is interrupted or turned aside by the thought that his opponents were on the watch to turn every thing to his disadvantage. Thus although there was nothing of a spirit of self-commendation in his thanking God for causing him to triumph, or in the assertion of his sincerity, in 1, 15–17, yet he knew that his enemies would put that construction on what he had said. He seems to hear them say, 'He is commending himself again.' It is plain from the use of the word *again* in this connection, that the charge of praising himself had before been made against the apostle, whether founded on his former epistle or what he said on other occasions, is uncertain and unimportant.

The authorities are divided as to whether ἢ μη or εἰ μη is the true reading in the following clause. If the former, the sense is, "Or do we need," &c.; if the latter, "Unless we need," &c. The latter gives an ironical turn to the passage. The apostle sets it forth as certain that his apostolic mission and authority were so authenticated, that he did not need, as certain people did, letters of commendation either to them or from them. These false teachers had no doubt gained access to Corinth on the strength of certain letters of recommendation. They were so little known and had so little character, that when they went elsewhere, they would need to be commended by the Corinthians. With Paul the case was different.

2. Ye are our epistle written in our hearts, known and read of all men.

Ye are our epistle, &c., or, *The epistle which we have ye are.* You as Christians, your conversion is, as it were, a letter from Christ himself authenticating our mission and fidelity. *Written in our hearts.* The plural form, *our hearts*, may be explained either on the assumption that the apostle is speaking of Timothy as well as of himself; or on the ground that he says *hearts* instead of *heart* for the same reason that he says *We* instead of *I;* or that the word is used figuratively for the affections. It is not Paul's manner to make his associates the joint authors of his letters, and in no one of his epistles does he speak more out of the fulness of his personal feelings than he does in this. It was not Timothy who was accused of self-commendation, who needed no letters of commendation, and it was not of Timothy's mission that the conversion of the Corinthians was the authentication, and therefore it was not in Timothy's heart that the epistle referred to was written. Paul is speaking of himself. A thing is said to be written in the heart when it is a matter of consciousness;

when it is a matter of subjective, as distinguished from objective knowledge. Thus the law of God is said to be written on the heart when the knowledge of it is inward and not merely outward. Jer. 31, 33. Heb. 8, 10. Rom. 2, 15. Any thing of which a man is certain, or of which he has a conviction founded upon his inward experience, may be said to be written on his heart. That the Corinthians were his epistle was to the apostle a matter of consciousness. It was a letter written on his heart which he could neither misunderstand nor be ignorant of. Comp. Rom. 10, 8. Any thing also that is very dear to us is said to be written on the heart, or to be in the heart. So Paul says to the Corinthians, "Ye are in our hearts," 7, 3. The apostle therefore may be understood to mean either that he was perfectly certain that the conversion of the Corinthians was for him a letter of commendation; or that it was most dear to him. A letter cherished in his heart. The context is in favour of making the former idea the prominent one. This letter, however, was not only well known to the apostle, it was *known and read of all men.* It was a palpable evidence of his divine mission, which no one could be ignorant of, and which no one could gainsay. Men could not doubt its genuineness, nor could they question its import. He expresses the same idea when he says, "The seal of my apostleship are ye in the Lord," 1 Cor. 9, 2.

3. (Forasmuch as ye are) manifestly declared to be the epistle of Christ ministered by us, written not with ink, but with the Spirit of the living God; not in tables of stone, but in fleshly tables of the heart.

The fact that the Corinthians were to Paul an epistle of commendation, is here confirmed; ὑμεῖς—φανερούμενοι ὅτι ἐστέ, *ye are conspicuous or publicly known as the epistle of Christ.* That is, an epistle of which Christ is the author. *Ministered by us.* The conversion of the Corinthians was the work of Christ, effected by the ministry of Paul. Considered as a letter, they were a letter of Christ written by the hand of Paul as Christ's instrument. The importance or superior worth of this epistle is set forth in what follows by a twofold contrast or comparison. First, it was not a letter written with ink, but by the Spirit of the living God. Any man could write with ink; Christ alone can write with the Spirit of God.

This is a figurative way of expressing the idea that the conversion of the Corinthians was a divine, supernatural work, and therefore an irrefragable proof that Paul, by whose instrumentality the work was effected, was the minister of Christ. This was a letter, therefore, infinitely above any ordinary letter written with ink. Secondly, it was not an outward, but an inward, spiritual work. The decalogue, written on tables of stone by the finger of God, was indeed a divine work, and proved the divine mission of Moses'; but what was that to writing the law upon the fleshly tables of the heart! The work of regeneration and sanctification is always represented in the Scripture as a much higher manifestation of divine power and grace than any mere external miracle. In predicting the new dispensation in contrast with the old, God says, "Behold the days come when I will make a new covenant with the house of Israel—not according to the covenant that I made with their fathers,—but I will put my law in their inward parts, and write it in their hearts," Jeremiah 31, 31–33. To this the apostle evidently refers to show that the evidence of his mission was of a higher character than that of Moses, and that his ministry was far more exalted and glorious.

Instead of the genitive, καρδίας, the great body of ancient MSS. have the dative, καρδίαις; *on tables which are hearts of flesh*, instead of fleshly tables *of the heart*. The majority of editors adhere to the common text on the authority of the Greek fathers. The sense is the same.

4. And such trust have we through Christ to God-ward.

This confidence in the divinity and glory of his mission, and in his sufficiency for the apostleship he had from Christ and in the presence of God. It was a confidence so strong (and yet so humble) that it did not quail even under the eye of God; much less therefore under the scrutiny of the bleared eyes of his opponents. *Such confidence*, not merely confidence in the fact that the Corinthians were to him a letter of commendation, but the confidence expressed in the whole context, and especially in 2, 15–17. This confidence he had *through Christ*. It was not self-confidence. It was not the consciousness of superior excellence; but a conviction of the truth of the gospel and of the reality of that vocation which he had received from Christ. This confidence of the apostle that he was what God had called him to be, an able or fit minister of the gospel, was not a trait of natural character; it was not a conclusion from his inward and outward experience; it was one of the forms in which the Spirit of God which was in him manifested itself; just as that Spirit manifested itself in his humility, faith, courage, or constancy. It is easy to determine whether such confidence is self-inflation, or the strength of God in the soul. If the former, it has its natural concomitants of pride, arrogance, indifference, contempt of others. If the latter, it is attended by self-abhorrence, meekness, long-suffering, a willingness to be the least and lowest, and by all other graces of the Spirit. *To God-ward*, πρὸς τὸν Θεόν. This may mean in reference to God, i. e. a confidence exercised toward God as its object. Or, πρός may be used here as in Rom. 4, 2. Abraham, it is there said, had no καύχημα, *ground of boasting*, πρὸς Θεόν, *before God;* that is, none that could stand his inspection. Paul says he had a confidence before God; that is, one which could endure in his sight.

5. Not that we are sufficient of ourselves to think any thing as of ourselves; but our sufficiency (is) of God.

The apostle had strongly asserted his sufficiency or fitness for his work. He here tells us what was not, and then what was, the source of his sufficiency. *Not that*, i. e. I do not say, or, I do not mean, that we are sufficient of ourselves. In most of the older MSS. the words ἀφ' ἑαυτῶν, *of ourselves*, stand after λογίζασθαί τι, "sufficient to think any thing of ourselves," instead of, as in the common text, 'sufficient of ourselves to think any thing.' The former order of the words has greater authority, and gives perhaps the better sense. There is a difference in the prepositions in Greek which is not expressed in the English. Paul says his sufficiency or ability to think any thing was not ἀφ' ἑαυτῶν ὡς ἐξ ἑαυτῶν, not *from* himself as *out of* himself. He was not the source of this sufficiency either remotely or immediately. We should express much the same idea by saying, 'Our sufficiency is not in or of ourselves.' Comp. Gal. 1, 1. What he disclaims is sufficiency or ability *to think any thing;* the implication is any thing right or good. He had no power of himself to accomplish any thing. His fitness for his work, whether consisting in knowledge, or grace, or fidelity, or efficiency, did not arise out of any thing he was in or of himself. The word λογίζασθαι does not here mean *to judge*, or *to think out* or *determine*. The idea is not that Paul was of himself unable to judge what was best and right, i. e. to think out the means of rendering his ministry successful. The word is to be taken in its simplest sense, *to think*. Thought is the lowest form of our efficiency, in so far as it is much easier to think good, than either to will or to do it. Paul means to say that so far as the subject in hand is concerned, he could do nothing, not even think. He was in himself absolutely empty and powerless. *Our sufficiency is of God.* All our fitness for our work—all our knowledge, holiness and power are of God. They are neither self-acquired nor self-sustained. I am nothing, the apostle would say; God in me is every thing. The same truth and feeling are expressed in 1 Cor. 15, 10.

6. Who also hath made us able ministers of the new testament; not of the letter, but of the spirit: for the letter killeth, but the spirit giveth life.

This verse is a confirmation of the preceding. The relative ὅς is here used as in Luke 8, 13, and elsewhere, as implying the cause or reason. Our sufficiency is of God, *who;* equivalent to *for he* hath made us able ministers. The same radical word is retained, ἱκάνωσε, hath rendered us ἱκανούς, *sufficient*, able, well qualified, *ministers of the new testament*, καινῆς διαθήκης, *of the new covenant*, as the word διαθήκη always means in the New Testament, unless Heb 9, 16 be an exception. The covenant formed between God and the Hebrews at Mount Sinai is called the Old Covenant; the gospel dispensation as distinguished from the Mosaic is called the New Covenant. Matt. 26, 28. 1 Cor. 11, 25. Heb. 8, 8. 9, 15. &c. As, however, the promises of the gospel, and especially the great promise of redemption by the blood of Christ, underlay both the patriarchal and Mosaic dispensations, the plan of salvation or the covenant of grace, is also called the New Covenant, although older than the Mosaic covenant, to distinguish it from the covenant of works formed with Adam. This gives rise to no little obscurity. It is not always easy to determine whether the words "new covenant" refer to the gospel dispensation introduced by Christ, or to the covenant of grace inaugurated in the first promise made to our fallen parents. And in like manner it is not easy always to decide whether the words the "old covenant" designate the Mosaic covenant or the covenant of works. The context must in every case be our guide in deciding these questions. In the present case it is plain that by the New Covenant the apostle means the gospel as distinguished from the Law,—the Christian as distinguished from the Mosaic dispensation. It was of that he was made a minister, and it is that which he contrasts with the Old Testament economy. *Not of the letter, but of the spirit.* These words admit of two constructions. They may depend on the word covenant. 'Covenant not of the letter, but of the spirit.' They thus determine the nature of the New Covenant as being not of the letter but of the spirit. This is the construction adopted by perhaps the majority of modern commentators. The older interpreters, followed by our translators, make the words in question depend on *ministers.* "Ministers not of the letter, but of the spirit." This latter is not only more familiar to the readers of the English version, but is favoured by the whole context. Paul contrasts two dispensations; one he calls the letter, the other the spirit. He says he is minister of the one, not of the other, and afterwards, vs. 7. 8, he speaks of the ministry of death and ministry of the spirit; the ministry of condemnation and the ministry of righteousness. That the words *letter* and *spirit* as here used mean the law and the gospel is plain, first, because it is the law and the gospel which he proceeds to compare in the following verses; and secondly, because these are terms which he elsewhere uses in the same sense. Thus in Rom. 7, 6 he speaks of the oldness of the letter and newness of the spirit. In Rom. 2, 27 he characterizes the Jew as being of the letter, i. e. as having the law. Comp. also Gal. 3, 3. If it be asked what is the ground of these designations, why the law is called *letter*, and the gospel *spirit*, it may be answered in the first place, that the law is called γράμμα, letter, for the same reason that it is called γράφη, *scripture*. It was something written. Not only was the decalogue, the kernel of the Mosaic economy, originally written on stones, but the whole law was a volume known as *the writings*. And in the second place, the law as written was something external and objective. It was addressed to the eye, to the ear, to the under-

standing. It was not an inward principle or power. It held
up the rule of duty to which men were to be conformed, but
it could not impart the disposition or ability to obey. It was,
as it were, a mere writing or book. On the other hand, the
gospel is spiritual, as distinguished from what was external
and ritual. It is the power of God, Rom. 1, 6; the organ
through which the Spirit works in giving life to the soul.
These words therefore express concisely the characteristic difference between the law and the gospel. The one was external, the other spiritual; the one was an outward precept, the
other an inward power. In the one case the law was written
on stone, in the other on the heart. The one therefore was
letter, the other *spirit*.

For the letter (i. e. the law) *killeth*, but the spirit (i. e. the
gospel) *giveth life*. This is the reason why God hath made
Paul the minister of the spirit. 'God had made us able ministers not of the law but of the gospel, *for* the law kills, but
the gospel gives life.' This passage and the following context
present two important questions. First, in what sense does
the law kill? And second, How is it that the apostle attributes to the Mosaic system this purely legal character, when
he elsewhere so plainly teaches that the gospel was witnessed
or taught both in the law and the prophets? As to the former of these questions, the answer furnished by the Scriptures
is plain. The law demands perfect obedience. It says, "Do
this and live," Rom. 10, 5. Gal. 3, 12, and "Cursed is every
one who continueth not in all things written in the book of
the law to do them," Gal. 3, 10. As no man renders this
perfect obedience, the law condemns him. It pronounces on
him the sentence of death. This is one way in which it kills.
In the second place, it produces the knowledge or consciousness of sin, and of course of guilt, that is, of just exposure to
the wrath of God. Thus again it slays. And thirdly, by presenting the perfect standard of duty, which cannot be seen
without awakening the sense of obligation to be conformed to
it, while it imparts no disposition or power to obey, it exasper-
ates the soul and thus again it brings forth fruit unto death.
All these effects of the law are systematically presented by
the apostle in the 6th and 7th chapters of his epistle to the
Romans, and in the 3d chapter of the epistle to the Galatians.

The second question is more difficult. Every reader of
the New Testament must be struck with the fact that the
apostle often speaks of the Mosaic law as he does of the moral

law considered as a covenant of works; that is, presenting the promise of life on the condition of perfect obedience. He represents it as saying, Do this and live; as requiring works, and not faith, as the condition of acceptance. Rom. 10, 5–10. Gal. 3, 10–12. He calls it a ministration of death and condemnation. He denies that it can give life. Gal. 3, 21. He tells those who are of the law (that is, Judaizers) that they had fallen from grace; that is, had renounced the gratuitous method of salvation, and that Christ should profit them nothing. Gal. 5, 2. 4. In short, when he uses the word law, and says that by the law is the knowledge of sin, that it can only condemn, that by its works no flesh can be justified, he includes the Mosaic law; and in the epistle to the Galatians all these things are said with special reference to the law of Moses. On the other hand, however, he teaches that the plan of salvation has been the same from the beginning; that Christ was the propitiation for the sins committed under the old covenant; that men were saved then as now by faith in Christ; that this mode of salvation was revealed to Abraham and understood by him, and taught by Moses and the prophets. This view is presented repeatedly in Paul's epistles, and is argued out in due form in Rom. 3, 21–31. Rom. 4, and Gal. 3. To reconcile these apparently conflicting representations it must be remembered that the Mosaic economy was designed to accomplish different objects, and is therefore presented in Scripture under different aspects. What, therefore, is true of it under one aspect, is not true under another. 1. The law of Moses was, in the first place, a re-enactment of the covenant of works. A covenant is simply a promise suspended upon a condition. The covenant of works, therefore, is nothing more than the promise of life suspended on the condition of perfect obedience. The phrase is used as a concise and convenient expression of the eternal principles of justice on which God deals with rational creatures, and which underlie all dispensations, the Adamic, Abrahamic, Mosaic and Christian. Our Lord said to the lawyer who asked what he should do to inherit eternal life, "What is written in the law? How readest thou? And he answering said, Thou shalt love the Lord thy God with all thy heart, and with all thy soul, and with all thy strength, and with all thy mind; and thy neighbour as thyself. And he said unto him, Thou hast answered right, this do and thou shalt live," Luke 10, 26–28. This is the covenant of works. It is an immutable principle that where there is no sin there is no condemnation, and where there is sin there is death. This is all that those who reject the gospel have to fall back upon. It is this principle which is rendered so prominent in the Mosaic economy as to give it its character of law. Viewed under this aspect it is the ministration of condemnation and death. 2. The Mosaic economy was also a national covenant; that is, it presented national promises on the condition of national obedience. Under this aspect also it was purely legal. But 3, as the gospel contains a renewed revelation of the law, so the law of Moses contained a revelation of the gospel. It presented in its priesthood and sacrifices, as types of the office and work of Christ, the gratuitous method of salvation through a Redeemer. This necessarily supposes that faith and not works was the condition of salvation. It was those who trusted, not those free from sin, who were saved. Thus Moses wrote of Christ, John 5, 46; and thus the law and the prophets witnessed of a righteousness of faith, Rom. 3, 21. When therefore the apostle spoke of the old covenant under its legal aspect, and especially when speaking to those who rejected the gospel and clung to the law of Moses as law, then he says, it kills, or is the ministration of condemnation. But when viewing it, and especially when speaking of those who viewed it as setting forth the great doctrine of redemption through the blood of Christ, he represented it as teaching his own doctrine. The law, in every form, moral or Mosaic, natural or revealed, kills. In demanding works as the condition of salvation, it must condemn all sinners. But the gospel, whether as revealed in the promise to Adam after his fall, or in the promise to Abraham, or in the writings of Moses, or in its full clearness in the New Testament, gives life. As the old covenant revealed both the law and the gospel, it either killed or gave life, according to the light in which it was viewed. And therefore Paul sometimes says it does the one, and sometimes the other. *But the spirit giveth life.* The spirit, or the gospel, gives life in a sense correlative to that in which *the letter* (i. e. the law) kills. 1. By revealing a righteousness adequate to our justification, and thus delivering us from the sentence of death. 2. By producing the assurance of God's love and the hope of his glory in the place of a dread of his wrath. 3. By becoming, through the agency of the Holy Spirit, an inward principle or power transforming us into the image of God; instead of a mere outward command.

7. 8. But if the ministration of death, written (and) engraven in stones, was glorious, so that the children of Israel could not steadfastly behold the face of Moses for the glory of his countenance ; which (glory) was to be done away : how shall not the ministration of the Spirit be rather glorious ?

It was the design and effect of the law to kill. This is true, so far as the work of salvation is concerned, of the law in all its forms, whether the moral law as revealed in the Scriptures, or as written in the heart, or as the Mosaic law. In all these forms it was designed to bring men to the knowledge of sin and helplessness; to produce a sense of guilt and misery, and a longing for redemption, and thus be a schoolmaster to bring men to Christ. Gal. 3, 24. This was a necessary office, and therefore glorious. But how can it compare with the gospel? How can that which only makes us know that we are sinful and condemned, be compared with that which delivers us from sin and condemnation? This is the idea which the apostle expands, and, as it were with exultation, turns over as though he could not let it go, in vs. 7–11. *But if the ministration of death, written* (and) *graven in stones.* The Greek is, ἐι δὲ ἡ διακονία τοῦ θανάτου ἐν γράμμασιν ἐντετυπωμένη ἐν λίθοις, *but if the ministration of death in letters engraven in stones.* The simplest interpretation of these words is that the ministration of death was in letters, i. e. by means of letters, engraven on stone; which is the sense expressed by the free translation given in our common version. According to this view ἐν γράμμασιν are connected with what follows. But more commonly they are connected with what precedes; *the ministration of death in letters*, which Luther makes to mean, "the ministration which by means of letters (i. e. the written law) produces death." This certainly gives a good sense and consistent with the context; but it is not so simple or natural as the one first mentioned. It will be observed that Paul says that the *ministration* was engraven on stone. It was, however, of course not the ministration (the office of a minister) but the law itself that was thus engraven. There are two things here stated. First, that Moses was the minister of a covenant that produced death; and secondly, that that covenant was an external economy or system. These two ideas are combined at the expense of mere verbal accuracy in a single clause. The word διακονία, *ministration,* means either *the service,* i. e. the act of ministering, or the office of a διάκονος or minister. Commonly the former. In what sense the ministry of the law was a ministry of death, and the reason why the law is described as engraven on stone, have already been stated. The law is thus exhibited as external, as opposed to what is spiritual.

Was glorious, ἐγενήθη ἐν δόξᾳ, *existed in glory;* was surrounded, as it were, by a halo. The reference here is only indirectly to the brightness of Moses's face, which was but a symbol of the glory of his ministration. The glory which pertained to the old dispensation was not the illumination of the countenance of Moses, which was merely an incident. It was of the same kind, though less in degree, as the glory of the gospel. The one dispensation was indeed glorious, but the other was more so. *So that the children of Israel could not steadfastly behold the face of Moses.* The whole service was so glorious that even the face of Moses was so bright that the people could not look upon it. This brightness of the face of Moses was in two respects a symbol of the glory of the old dispensation. In the first place, it was an outward brightness. So too the glory of the Mosaic dispensation was derived in large measure from its pompous ritual, its temple, its priesthood, its sacrifice, and, above all, its Shekinah, or visible symbol of the divine presence. But what was all this to the glory of the gospel? What was a bright cloud overhanging the cherubim, to the light of God's presence filling the soul? And secondly, the brightness of the face of Moses was transient. The participle καταργουμένην may be taken as imperfect —They could not behold it as *it was vanishing away;* or as present, *which is evanescent,* or *perishable.* It was in its own nature a mere transient brightness, analogous to the temporary splendour of the service committed to him. *How shall not the ministration of the Spirit be rather glorious?* If the one was glorious, how much more the other! The future *shall* is not to be understood in reference to the future world. The idea is not that hereafter, when Christ's kingdom is consummated, the ministration of the gospel shall be found more glorious than that of the law. The future expresses the certain sequence. If the ministration of death was glorious, the ministration of the Spirit shall assuredly, if rightly considered, be regarded as glorious. This is plain from the fact that the things compared are the ministration committed to Moses and the ministration committed to Paul; and also from the reason assigned for the superiority of the latter, which is not what is to be realized in the future, but what is experienced in the present. It was because it is *the ministration of the spirit* that it is more glorious than the ministration of death. The ideas of life and life-giving are inseparable from that of spirit. Hence the Holy Ghost in the ancient creeds of the church is designated as τὸ πνεῦμα τὸ ἅγιον, τὸ κύριον, τὸ ζωοποιόν. And hence the gospel as the source of life is called spirit. It is doubtful, however, whether the word *spirit* here refers to the Holy Spirit, or to the gospel. Luther renders the phrase ἡ διακονία τοῦ πνεύματος, *das Amt, das den Geist giebt*, i. e. the office which gives the Spirit; because it is by the ministration of the gospel the Holy Spirit is imparted to men. This view is perhaps commonly adopted. But as in v. 6, *spirit*, as opposed to *letter*, evidently means the gospel as opposed to the law, and as the things compared are the law and gospel, or the ministry of the one and the ministry of the other, the probability is that Paul intended the word to be so understood here. The gospel is *spirit* because it is the source of life. Instead of being something external and powerless, it is inward and saving; and this is the ground of its superiority to the law.

9. For if the ministration of condemnation (be) glory, much more doth the ministration of righteousness exceed in glory.

This verse is a confirmation of the preceding. The gospel is more glorious than the law, for the ministration of righteousness is more glorious than the ministration of condemnation. *The ministration of condemnation* is that ministration which brings men into a state of conscious condemnation; that is, which makes them know and feel that they are condemned. *The ministration of righteousness* is that ministration which reveals a righteousness by which men are justified, and thus freed from the condemnation pronounced upon them by the law. As much better therefore as justification is than condemnation to eternal death, so much better is the gospel than the law. Although the words κατάκρισις, *condemnation*, and δικαιοσύνη, *righteousness*, are here in antithesis, it does not follow that the latter means *justification*, which is a sense it

never has in the New Testament.   It retains its proper meaning, *righteousness*, i. e. that which the law demands.   It is
not justification, but the ground of it; that on account of
which a man is justified or pronounced righteous.   The gospel, being the ministration of the spirit, is the ministration of
righteousness, because as what is spirit is life-giving, the gospel must reveal a righteousness which satisfies the demands
of the law, and thus free us from judicial death, or it could
not be the source of life.   It is true that the life of which the
gospel is the source is more than mere justification; but as
justification is the necessary condition of spiritual life, Paul
here exalts the gospel by making it the means of securing
that righteousness which is necessary to sanctification and inseparable from it.   The use of the present tense, περισσεύει,
doth abound, in this verse, serves to confirm the explanation
given of v. 8.   Paul in both instances is speaking of the glory
which now belongs to the ministry of the gospel, not of what
is to be hereafter.

10. For even that which was made glorious hath
no glory in this respect, by reason of the glory that
excelleth.

For even, καὶ γάρ, *for moreover*.   Too little was said in
simply asserting that the gospel excelled the law.   The law,
though glorious in itself, ceased to be glorious in the presence
of the gospel, as the moon loses its brightness in the presence
of the sun.   *That which was made glorious*, τὸ δεδοξασμένον,
that which was and is glorious, viz. the ministry of Moses, and,
by implication, the law or dispensation of which he was the
minister.   *Hath no glory*, οὐ δεδόξασται, *is not glorious*, ἐν
τούτῳ τῷ μέρει, *in this particular*.   This is explained by what
follows.   *Because of the glory that excelleth*.   The ministry
of the gospel so much excels the ministry of the law, that the
latter ceases in the comparison to be glorious at all.   This is
the common and natural interpretation of the text.   Two other
explanations have been proposed.   First, the words ἐν τούτῳ
τῷ μέρει are connected with δεδοξασμένον, *that which was glorious* (viz. the ministry of Moses), in this particular, viz. that the
face of Moses was rendered luminous.   This gives a very insignificant sense.   The shining of the face of Moses was not
the glory of his ministry or of the old economy.   It was but

a symbol of it. Second, Meyer and others, retaining the ordinary construction of the passage, make the apostle say, that the general truth that the lesser glory is eclipsed by the greater, was illustrated *in this case*, i. e. in the case of Moses and his ministry. This brings out the same sense as that given by the ordinary interpretation, but in a less natural way. *That which was made glorious*, τὸ δεδοξασμένον, naturally refers to the definite subject of which the context treats, which is the ministry of Moses.

11. For if that which was done away (was) glorious, much more that which remaineth (is) glorious.

A new ground of superiority. The old dispensation and its ministry were temporary, the new is permanent. There is nothing to intervene, no new revelation, no new economy, between the gospel and its ministry, and the final consummation. Whoever are to be converted, whatever nations are to be brought in, it must be by the preaching of the gospel, *which remaineth*, or is to continue, according to Christ's promise, until the end of the world. In the former clause the apostle says the law was διὰ δόξης, *with glory*, in the latter, that the gospel was ἐν δόξῃ, *in glory*. This is a mere variation of expression without any difference of meaning. Comp. Rom. 3, 30. 5, 10. That the binding authority of the law ceased on the introduction of the gospel, is a doctrine which the apostle had to sustain against the Judaizing tendency of the early Christians, on many occasions. To this point the epistles to the Galatians and to the Hebrews are principally directed. As Paul's opponents in Corinth were of this class, there is little doubt that what he here says of the inferiority and temporary character of the old economy had a special reference to them; while his strong assertion of his divine mission, of the dignity and superiority of the ministry which he had received, was intended to counteract the influence of their invidious attacks upon his authority. No less clear is the inculcation of the other great truth here presented. The gospel did away the law, but is itself never to be superseded. These are "the last times," the last dispensation, which is to continue until the consummation of all things.

The clearness and freedom of the Gospel as contrasted with the obscurity of the Law. Vs. 12–18.

The apostle having referred to the transient brightness of Moses's face, as a symbol of the passing glory of his ministry, here employs the fact that Moses veiled his face as a twofold illustration. In the first place, it is symbolical of the obscurity of the revelation made under the old dispensation. As the brightness of Moses's face was covered, so spiritual or evangelical truth was of old covered under the types and shadows of the Mosaic economy. In the second place, it is symbolical of the blindness which rested on the minds of the Jews, which prevented their seeing the true import of their own institutions, vs. 12–15. Nevertheless, as Moses removed the veil from his face when he turned to the Lord, so both the obscurity which rests on the law, and the blindness which rests upon the mind of the Jew, are dispelled when he turns towards Christ. The vision of his glory transforms the soul into his likeness, vs. 16–18.

12. Seeing then that we have such hope, we use great plainness of speech.

Seeing then that we have such hope, literally, *Having then such hope,* i. e. because we have it. The hope to which he refers must be that mentioned in the context, v. 14, that the gospel and its ministry were, and would prove themselves to be, far superior to the law and to the ministry of Moses. What in v. 4 he calls πεποίϑησις, *confidence,* he here calls ἐλπίς, *hope,* because the confidence which he felt had reference not only to the present, but also to the future. *We use great plainness of speech,* i. e. παῤῥησία, *outspokenness.* This stands opposed to all concealment, whether from timidity or from a desire to deceive; and also to all fear of consequences. It is a frank, open, courageous manner of speech. Paul therefore says that in his case it was the result of his firm conviction of his divine mission and of the truth and glory of the gospel which he preached, that he proclaimed it fully, intelligibly, and without regard to consequences. Its being to the Greeks foolishness, and to the Jews a stumblingblock, did not prevent his declaring the whole counsel of God. The same cause will ever produce the same effect. If Paul's experience of the truth and excellence of the gospel led him to declare it with-

out reserve, a similar experience will produce a similar openness and boldness in other ministers of the gospel. This indeed is one of the glories of Christianity. It is characteristic
of error to practise reserve and to seek concealment. In all
the religions of antiquity there was an esoteric and exoteric
doctrine; one for the people and the other of the initiated.
They all had mysteries carefully concealed from the public
eye. So in the Romish church, just in proportion as it is in-
fected with the spirit of heathenism the doctrine of reserve is
avowed and practised. The gospel is not preached with
openness, so that all may understand it. The people are kept
in ignorance. They are told they need not know; that faith
without knowledge, a blind confidence in rites which they do
not understand, is all-sufficient. But if a man in a church has
the conviction that the gospel is of God, that it is unspeakably
glorious, adapted to all and needed by all in order to salvation, then the word will be preached openly and without
reserve.

13. And not as Moses, (which) put a veil over his
face, that the children of Israel could not steadfastly
look to the end of that which is abolished.

And not as Moses, that is, we do not do what Moses did.
Paul had just said that he used great plainness of speech, that
he practised no concealment or reserve. Of course he means
that Moses did the reverse. He did use concealment and
practise reserve. This is no impeachment of the character
of Moses. Paul is not speaking of his personal character, but
of the nature of his office. The truth concerning man's redemption was not "in other ages made known unto the sons
of men as it is now revealed unto the holy apostles and
prophets by the Spirit," Eph. 3, 5. It was not consistent
with the nature of the ministry of Moses to use the παῤῥησία,
the openness, in communicating the doctrines of redemption,
which it is the glory of the Christian ministry to be permitted
to employ. He was sent to speak in parables and in types, to
set forth truth in the form of significant rites and ceremonies.
He put a veil over the glory, not to hide it entirely from
view, but to obscure its brightness. The people saw the
light, but only occasionally and imperfectly. Paul had already spoken of the brightness of Moses's face as a symbol of his

ministry, and therefore he represents him as veiling himself, to express the idea that he communicated the truth obscurely. Paul was sent to let the truth shine forth clearly; he did not put a veil over it as Moses did, and was commanded to do. *That the children of Israel could not steadfastly look to the end of that which is abolished.* That is, to prevent their seeing the end or fading away of the brightness of his face. The word καταργούμενος (*that which is abolished*) is used, v. 7, in reference to the glory of the face of Moses, and v. 11 in reference to his ministry and the dispensation to which it belonged. Here the reference is to the former, because his face is spoken of, and its brightness was veiled, and therefore, it was the brightness the end of which the Israelites were prevented from seeing. If this be so, then τέλος, *the end,* must mean the termination, and not the design or scope. In Rom. 10, 4, Christ is said to be the end of the law, not only as abrogating it, but as being the object towards which it tended. He was that which it was intended to reveal. Those commentators who make καταργούμενον (*that which is abolished*) refer to the old law and its ministry, give τέλος the sense of end or object. They understand the apostle to say that Moses put a veil over his face to prevent the children of Israel seeing Christ, who was the end of the law. But this gives a most incongruous meaning. How could Moses's veiling his face prevent the Israelites seeing Christ? The first part of the verse cannot be taken literally, and the latter part figuratively. If the veiling was a literal covering of the face, that which the veil hid must be something which a literal veil could cover. The majority of commentators, therefore, understand the words, *that which is abolished,* to refer to the visible brightness of the face of Moses, and *the end* to mean the termination of that brightness. The whole clause therefore means that Moses veiled his face in order to prevent the Israelites seeing how soon its brightness faded. But what has this to do with the point in hand? In answering this question it must be remembered that the apostle had referred to the brightness of the face of Moses as a fit symbol of his ministry, inasmuch as it was external and transient. To say, therefore, that Moses veiled his face that the people might not see the end of its brightness, is a figurative way of saying that Moses hid the light, or taught obscurely, that the people might not understand the true nature and intent of his ministry. But how is it consistent with the character of God that he should commission Moses to teach

obscurely in order that he might not be understood? Some
endeavour to obviate this difficulty by saying that πρὸς τὸ μὴ
ἀτενίσαι expresses the result and not the design. 'He put a
veil over his face, *so that* (not, *in order that*) the children of
Israel did not see the end of that which is abolished.' Or, to
drop the figure, 'He taught obscurely, *so that* the people did
not understand him.' This explanation, however, is forbidden
by the force of the preposition πρός, which in such connections
properly expresses the design or intention. There is no special difficulty in the matter. Whatever is, God intended
should be. If Moses taught obscurely or in types, God intended that he should do so. If, in point of fact, the Jews
misunderstood the nature of their own economy, regarding as
ultimate and permanent what was in fact preparatory and
temporary, this was included in the divine purpose. It was
evidently the plan of God to make the revelation of the
scheme of redemption gradually. The whole was by slow
degrees evolved from the original promise made to our first
parents. Perhaps the object of their faith was the simple
promise of redemption. To Abraham it was revealed that
the Redeemer was to be one of his descendants. To Moses it
was made known that he was to be a prophet like himself, and
the nature of his work was obscurely set forth in the priesthood and sacrifices which he ordained. This was enough for
salvation, so long as nothing more had been revealed. It was
in accordance with this plan that Moses spoke in such a way
that the people did not understand the full import of his
teaching, God having purposed "that they without us should
not be made perfect," Heb. 11, 40. The passage before us is
parallel, in a measure, to Mark 4, 11, where our Lord says,
"Unto you it is given to know the mysteries of the kingdom
of God; but unto them that are without all these things are
done in parables; that seeing they may see, and not perceive." There is, therefore, as just remarked, no special difficulty in this passage, even if it is understood to teach that
Moses was commissioned so to veil his teachings that they
should not be clearly understood. There is another difficulty
connected with this verse. It does not seem to agree with
Exodus 34, 30. There it is said that the people were afraid
to approach Moses on account of the brightness of his face,
and the implication (according to the English version, at least)
is, that it was to calm their fears he put on a veil. Whereas
here it is said that he put a veil over his face that the people

might not see the transient nature of that brightness. There
is no inconsistency between the two accounts. The veiling
had both effects; it calmed the fears of the people, and it prevented their seeing how fleeting the brightness was. As both
effects followed, both were intended. Paul in this epistle assigns in different places three or four reasons why he commanded the Corinthians to excommunicate the incestuous
member of their church. That it was meant as a test of their
obedience, 2, 9, is not incompatible with its being a proof of
his care for them, 7, 12. There is, however, not even the appearance of discrepancy between what the apostle here says
and Exodus 34, 30–33, as it is rendered both in the Septuagint
and Vulgate. The English version of that passage is, "And
when Aaron and all the children of Israel saw Moses, behold,
the skin of his face shone; and they were afraid to come nigh
him. And Moses called unto them; and Aaron and all the
rulers of the congregation returned unto him: and Moses
talked with them. . . . And *till* Moses had done speaking
with them, he put a veil on his face." According to this
Moses put a veil over his face when he spoke to the people,
and the implication is that he did it because they were afraid
on account of the brightness of his countenance. But the
Hebrew, in v. 33, is simply, "Moses ceased to speak with
them, and put a veil over his face." The natural meaning of
which is that he did not veil his face until he had ceased
speaking. The Septuagint therefore renders the passage,
"And when he ceased speaking with them, he put a veil over
his face." And the Vulgate, *impletisque sermonibus, posuit
velamen super faciem suam.* It appears from the following
verses that when Moses went in before the Lord, he removed
the veil; and when he came out his face shone, and he spake
to the people, and again resumed the veil. According to this
interpretation of the original, the object of putting on the veil
was not to calm the fear of the people, but, as Paul says, to
prevent their seeing how the brightness of his face vanished.

14. But their minds were blinded; for until this
day remaineth the same veil untaken away in the reading of the Old Testament; which (veil) is done away
in Christ.

In the preceding verse Paul was speaking of his ministry;

the same subject is resumed in the following chapter. Verses 14–18 are therefore a digression, although intimately connected with what precedes and follows. The particle ἀλλά either introduces something just the reverse of what precedes, and means *on the contrary*, or simply something different, and is to be rendered *but*. This verse admits of two modes of connection with what precedes. 'The Jews did not understand the ministry of Moses, *on the contrary*, their minds were blinded.' Or, the connection may be with the main idea of the preceding context. 'We use great plainness of speech, *but* their minds are blinded.' That is, notwithstanding the clearness with which the gospel is presented as the substance and true meaning of the old economy, still the Jews were so blinded they did not perceive it. In either way the sense is good. But as it is so much the habit of the apostle to connect what follows with what immediately precedes, and as the figure of the veil, which is not mentioned in v. 12, is continued in v. 14, it is most natural to make the connection with v. 13, where that figure is introduced, especially as Paul's immediate object in v. 12 is not to exhibit his plainness of speech in opposition to the hebetude of the Jews. It is the general fact that under the new dispensation the truth is exhibited plainly which he asserts. The blindness of the Jews is only incidentally introduced. *Their minds,* νοήματα, *thoughts, affections.* It means the whole inner man. *Were blinded,* ἐπωρώθη, properly *were rendered hard* or *callous.* The word is used both of the understanding and of the feelings. It expresses an inaptitude both of seeing and feeling. They neither understood nor felt the power of the truth. *For until this day remaineth untaken away the same veil.* This is a confirmation derived from experience of the fact previously stated. That the minds of the Israelites were thus blinded and hardened, is proved from the fact that until this day they do not understand the law. *The same veil,* i. e. the same obscurity. A veil was thrown over the truth as first revealed by Moses, and that same veil is there still. The Israelites of Paul's day understood their Scriptures as little as their fathers did. They remained satisfied with the external, ritual and ceremonial, without penetrating to what was beneath, or asking the real import of the types and shadows of the old economy. *In the reading of the Old Testament,* that is, when the Old Testament (covenant) is read. This metonymical use of the word *covenant* for the books in which that covenant is

contained, is perfectly familiar to our ears, as we are accustomed to call the two great divisions of the Scriptures the Old
and New Testaments or covenants; but this is the only instance of this use of the word in the New Testament. The
English version does not in this passage follow the order of
the Greek, which reads, "For until this day the same veil in
the reading of the old covenant remains." Here the sense is
complete. The following clause, μὴ ἀνακαλυπτόμενον ὅτι ἐν
Χριστῷ καταργεῖται, admits of three interpretations. 1. The
first is that adopted by our translators; μὴ ἀνακαλυπτόμενον is
referred to the preceding clause (*remains untaken away*),
and ὅτι (*because*, or *that*) is read as two words, ὅ τι, *which*, i. e.
which veil is done away in Christ. So Luther, in his free
translation: Denn bis auf den heutigen Tag bleibet dieselbige
Decke unaufgedeckt über das Alten Testament wenn sie es
lesen, welche in Christo aufhöret. The great majority of
editors, however, read ὅτι. 2. The word ἀνακαλυπτόμενον, *untaken away*, is, as before, referred to κάλυμμα, *veil*, and ὅτι is
rendered *because*. 'The veil remains untaken away, *because*
it is removed (only) in Christ.' 3. ἀνακαλυπτόμενον is taken
absolutely, and ὅτι is rendered *that*. 'The veil remains, it being unrevealed *that* it (viz. the old covenant) is done away
in Christ.' In favour of this last-mentioned interpretation it is
urged, that the old covenant was in fact done away in Christ,
and that ignorance of that fact prevented the Jews understanding their own Scriptures. The sense therefore is good.
Besides, the word καταργεῖται, *is done away*, is the proper term
to express the abrogation of the law, but not so suitable to
express the idea of the removal of a veil, for which, in v. 16,
Paul uses the word περιαιρεῖται, *is removed*. The word καταρ-
γέω is used in verses 7. 11 and 13, to express the passing away
of the brightness of the face of Moses, and of his ministry and
dispensation, of which that brightness was the symbol, and
therefore it is the more probable that it has the same reference here. On the other hand, however, it must be admitted
that ἀνακαλυπτόμενον naturally agrees with κάλυμμα, *the veil remains untaken away*, and that ἀνακαλύπτω, to *uncover* or *un-
veil*, is not the common word to express the idea of making
known or revealing. See v. 18, ἀνακαλυπτομένῳ προσώπῳ, *with
unveiled face*. The second interpretation, therefore, above
mentioned, is on the whole to be preferred. 'The veil which
hid the meaning of the Old Testament remained unremoved,
because it is done away in Christ, whom the Jews rejected.'

The Old Testament Scriptures are intelligible only when understood as predicting and prefiguring Christ. The present καταργεῖται (*is done away*) is used as expressing the certain consequence. The knowledge of Christ, as a matter of fact and as a matter of course, removes the veil from the Old Testament.

15. But even unto this day, when Moses is read, the veil is upon their heart.

But, ἀλλά, *on the contrary*, i. e. so far from being taken away, the veil remains until this day. *When Moses is read.* The word ἡνίκα, *when*, is used in the New Testament only here and in v. 16. As it occurs often in the Septuagint, and is used in Exodus 34, 34, it is the more probable that the language of that version was before the apostle's mind, and determined the mode in which he presents the incident of Moses veiling his face, which, as shown above, accords better with the view which the Septuagint gives of the original than with that presented in the English version. In Acts 15, 21, Moses, it is said, was read every sabbath day in the synagogues. *The veil*, or, as the article is wanting, *a veil*, was, however, over his face. The apostle presents the idea that the Jews did not understand their Scriptures in two forms. He says, in v. 14, that a veil rests on the Old Testament, and here that a veil was over the hearts of the Jews. The true source of the want of knowledge was subjective. The revelation of Christ, even in the writings of the Old Testament, though obscure when compared with that contained in the writings of the apostles, was sufficiently clear to be understood if the Jews had only been in a right state of mind. Hence our Lord upbraided his disciples, saying, " O fools and slow of heart to believe all that the prophets have spoken," Luke 24, 25. Compare Acts 13, 27–29. The darkness was not so much in the Scriptures, as in their minds.

16. Nevertheless, when it shall turn to the Lord, the veil shall be taken away.

According to the narrative in Ex. 34, 29–35, as understood by the Septuagint, and as expounded by the apostle, the face of Moses was made to shine by speaking with the Lord; when among the people (except when delivering his message) he

wore a veil; when he turned to the Lord he removed the
veil. To this allusion seems to be here made. So long as the
people were turned from the Lord, the veil was on their heart;
they could not understand the Scriptures; as soon as they
turn to the Lord, the veil is removed, and all is bright and
intelligible. *When it shall turn to the Lord;* ἡνίκα δ᾽ ἂν ἐπιστρέψῃ, *when it has turned,* i. e. when that conversion is accomplished, and as often as it occurs. The most natural subject
of the verb ἐπιστρέψῃ (*turned*) is καρδία (*heart*). A veil is on
the heart, but when it turns to the Lord, the veil is removed.
As, however, the apostle is speaking of the heart of the Jews,
and as the turning of their heart is their turning, so the sense
is the same if the word Israel be supplied. The veil is on the
heart of the people, but when the people turn to the Lord the
veil is taken away. Calvin and others supply *Moses* as the
nominative. By Moses, however, Calvin understands the
Law. 'When Moses is read, a veil is on the heart of the
Jews; but when he, i. e. the law, is directed to Christ, who is
the end of the law, then the veil is removed.' That is, as
soon as the Jews see that their law relates to Christ, then
they understand it. This, however, is obviously an unnatural
interpretation, as ἐπιστρέψῃ expresses the turning of the heart
or of the people to God, and not giving the law a particular
interpretation. Stanley, who also says that *Moses* must be
the nominative of the verb, makes him, however, the representative, not of the law, but of the people. 'When Moses
turns to the Lord he strips off the veil.' The word περιαιρεῖται
he gives an active sense, according to its common use in the
Septuagint. This too is less simple and natural than the common interpretation given above. The veil was on the heart
of the people, and when *it,* i. e. their heart, turns to the Lord,
it is stripped off; περιαιρεῖται is the word used in Ex. 34, 34.
By *Lord* here, as the context shows, we are to understand
Christ. He is the Lord whom Moses saw face to face on
Mount Sinai, and to whom the Jews and all others must turn
if they would enjoy the light of salvation.

17. Now the Lord is that Spirit: and where the Spirit of the Lord (is), there (is) liberty.

The first point to be determined with regard to this difficult passage, is the relation in which it stands to what precedes. It may be either an explanation or an inference. If

the former, then it is designed to show why turning to the Lord secures the removal of the veil from the heart. It is because the Lord is the Spirit, and where the Spirit is, there is liberty, freedom from the law, from its bondage and obscurities. If the latter, then the idea is, that since the veil is removed by turning to the Lord, it follows as a further consequence that by thus turning we have liberty. The force of the particle δέ, which so often introduces an explanation, and the whole structure of the passage is in favour of the first interpretation. 2. It is plain that *the Lord* here means Christ. This is clear not only because the word *Lord*, as a general rule, in the New Testament, refers to Christ, but also because the context in this case demands that reference. In v. 14 it is said that the veil is done away in Christ, and in v. 16 that it is removed when the heart turns to the Lord, and here that the Lord is the Spirit. The main idea of the whole context is, that the recognition of Jesus Christ as Lord, or Jehovah, is the key to the Old Testament. It opens all its mysteries, or, to use the figure of the apostle, it removes the veil which hid from the Jews the true meaning of their own Scriptures. As soon as they turn to the Lord, i. e. as soon as they recognize Jesus Christ as their Jehovah, then every thing becomes bright and clear. It is plain, therefore, that the Lord spoken of is Christ. This also determines another point, viz. that *Lord* is here the subject, and *Spirit* the predicate. Paul says that "The Lord is the Spirit," and not "The Spirit is the Lord." The latter view of the passage is taken by many of the Fathers, who regard it as a direct assertion of the divinity of the Holy Ghost. Although the words would admit of this interpretation, it is evidently inconsistent with the context. It also follows from the fact that "Lord" here means Christ, that it must designate his person and not his doctrine. The apostle does not mean to say that the doctrine of Christ, or the gospel, or new covenant, is the Spirit. It is true that in v. 6, when contrasting the law and the gospel, he calls the one the letter and the other the spirit; but this does not authorize us to make *Lord* mean the gospel because the Lord is said to be the Spirit. As in the preceding verses Christ and Lord refer to Christ as a person; the word Lord must have the same reference here. 3. When Paul says "The Lord is *the* Spirit," he does not mean to say that 'the Lord is *a* spirit,' agreeably to the analogy of John 4, 24, where it is said "God is a spirit." This is not only opposed to the force of the article τὸ before πνεῦμα, *the* Spirit, but also to the connection, as Paul is speaking of Christ's office rather than of his nature. It is not his object to say that Christ is a spiritual being. Neither is the idea that he is replenished with the Holy Spirit, so as to be in that sense and on that account called the Spirit. This is not the meaning of the words, nor is the idea demanded by the context. The two interpretations which the words admit are either, first, that which our translators probably intended to indicate when they rendered τὸ πνεῦμα *that Spirit.* "The Lord is that Spirit," that is, the spirit spoken of in v. 6; the spirit which stands opposed to the letter, that which gives life and righteousness; the inner sense of the law, the saving truth and power hidden under the types and forms of the Mosaic economy. Christ, says Calvin, is the life of the law. Accedat anima ad corpus: et fit vivus homo, praeditus intelligentia et sensu, ad vitales actiones idoneus: tollatur anima a corpore, et restabit inutile cadaver, omnique sensu vacuum. Thus if Christ is present in the Mosaic law, it is living and life-giving; if he is absent from it, it is dead and death-dispensing. Christ is therefore *that* spirit which animates the law or institutions of Moses, and when this is recognized, the veil which hides their meaning is removed. True as all this is, it can hardly be expressed by the simple words ὁ κύριος τὸ πνεῦμά ἐστι, *the Lord is the Spirit.* The words τὸ πνεῦμα, "the Spirit," have in the New Testament a fixed and definite meaning, which is not to be departed from unless the context renders such departure necessary. Besides, this interpretation requires that "the Spirit" should mean one thing, and "the Spirit of the Lord" another, in the same verse. This, however, can hardly be admitted. If "the Spirit of the Lord," in the last clause, means the Holy Spirit, which will not be questioned, "the Spirit," in the first clause, must have the same meaning. The other interpretation, therefore, must be adopted. "The Lord is the Spirit," that is, Christ is the Holy Spirit; they are one and the same. Not one and the same person, but one and the same Being, in the same sense in which our Lord says, "I and the Father are one." It is an identity of essence and of power. Christ is the Holy Spirit, because, being the same in substance, where Christ is, there the Spirit is, and where the Spirit is, there is Christ. Therefore this same apostle interchanges the three forms of expression as synonymous, "the Spirit of Christ," "Christ," and "the Spirit." Rom. 8, 9. 10. The Holy Ghost is everywhere in the Bible recognized as the source of all life, truth, power, holiness, blessedness and glory. The apostle, however, had in the context spoken of Christ as the source of life, as delivering from the death and bondage of the law. He is and does this because he and the Spirit are one; and therefore wherever Christ is, or in other words, wherever the Spirit of Christ is, or in other words still, wherever the Spirit is, *there is liberty*. By turning unto Christ we become partakers of the Holy Spirit, the living and life-giving, because he and the Spirit are one, and Christ dwells in his people, redeeming them from the law and making them the children of God, by his Spirit. *The Spirit of the Lord*, as a designation of the Holy Ghost, shows that the Spirit stands in the same relation to the Son that he does to the Father. Therefore he is called the "Spirit of Christ," Rom. 8, 10, and "Spirit of His Son," Gal. 4, 6. And, therefore, also the Son is said to send and give the Spirit. John 16, 7. All this of course supposes the supreme divinity of our Lord. *The liberty* of which the apostle here speaks, must be that liberty which is consequent on the indwelling of the Holy Spirit, that is, which flows from the application to us of the redemption purchased by Christ. We have not received, says the apostle, the Spirit of bondage again to fear, but the Spirit of adoption. Rom. 8, 15. The liberty here intended is the glorious liberty of the children of God. Rom. 8, 21. It is the liberty wherewith Christ has made us free. Gal. 5, 1. This includes, 1. Freedom from the law in all its forms, Mosaic and moral, Rom. 6, 14. 7, 4, i. e. freedom from the obligation to fulfil the law as the condition of our justification before God; which involves freedom from condemnation and from a legal, slavish spirit. 2. Freedom from the dominion of sin, Rom. 7, 6, and from the power of Satan. Heb. 2, 14. 15. 3. Freedom from the bondage of corruption, not only as to the soul, but as to the body. Rom. 8, 21–23. This liberty, therefore, includes all that is involved in being the sons of God. Incidental to this liberty is freedom from all ignorance and error, and all subjection to the authority of men, except so far as it represents the authority of Christ, and therefore liberty of conscience or freedom from all authority in matters of religion other than that of the Spirit of God. There is not only no reason for restricting the idea of the liberty of which the apostle speaks to any one of these forms, but the context requires that it should include all that liberty of which the presence of the Spirit is the source and the assurance. As no

man in this life is perfectly and at all times filled with the
Spirit of Christ, he is never in this life a partaker of the full
liberty of which Christ is the author.

18. But we all, with open face beholding as in a
glass the glory of the Lord, are changed into the same
image from glory to glory, (even) as by the Spirit of
the Lord.

This verse is connected with the preceding by the simple
particle of transition δέ, *but*. The natural consequence of the
liberty mentioned in v. 17 is what is here stated. *We all*, i. e.
all whom the indwelling of the Spirit of the Lord has made
free. They are delivered from the bondage of the law, the
veil has been removed from their face, and being turned to
the Lord, they behold his glory *with open face*, ἀνακεκαλυμμένῳ
προσώπῳ, i. e. with a face which has been, and which remains
unveiled. The darkness arising from alienation, ignorance,
misconception and prejudice has been dissipated, so that we
can see clearly. *Beholding as in a glass or mirror.* This is
probably the proper interpretation of the word here used.
Κατοπτρίζω, in the active voice, means *to show in a mirror*,
and in the middle, (the form here used,) it generally means,
to see one's self in a mirror. This is its constant use in the
classics. But in Philo it is used to express the idea of seeing
by means of a mirror. As this sense is perfectly suited to this
passage it is generally adopted by commentators, because the
other explanations given to the word are either contrary to
usage or to the context. Some render it simply *beholding*.
But to this it is objected that it overlooks the special etymo-
logical signification of the word, and that ἀτενίζω, which occurs
twice in this chapter, vs. 7 and 13, is the proper term for that
idea. Besides, this interpretation loses sight of the figure involved in the passage. It is an *image* we see, and therefore
we see, as it were, by reflection, or as in a glass. Luther,
after Chrysostom, renders the word, *reflecting as in a mirror*.
This explanation is adopted by Bengel, Billroth, Olshausen
and others. They understand the apostle to say that Christians reflect, with an unveiled face, the glory of the Lord.
They suppose that allusion is had to the glory of God as reflected from the face of Moses, which was transient and veiled;
whereas, in the case of Christians, the glory of the Lord is

constantly and clearly manifested in them and by them. They reflect his image wherever they go. But, in the first place, this explanation is inconsistent with the signification of the word, which never means to reflect; secondly, it is contrary to the context. The contrast is not between Moses and Christians, but between the Jews, or the unconverted, and Christians. The former were blinded by a veil, the latter see with an unveiled face. The one see and the others do not. This is obviously the antithesis implied, and not that the one class do, and the other do not reflect the glory of the Lord. In the third place, the relation in which this verse stands to the preceding forbids this interpretation. We have here the effect of turning to the Lord. We are delivered from the law, we are made free, we are introduced into the presence of the Lord, and enabled to behold his glory. And, finally, this interpretation overlooks the causal relation between the two clauses of this verse. We are transformed into the image of the Lord by beholding it, not by reflecting it. The common interpretation is therefore to be preferred; *beholding as in a mirror*. Though in comparison with the unconverted those who are turned to the Lord see clearly, or with an unveiled face, still it is only as in a mirror. 1 Cor. 13, 12. It is not the immediate, beatific vision of the glory of the Lord, which is only enjoyed in heaven, but it is that manifestation of his glory which is made in his word and by his Spirit, whose office it is to glorify Christ by revealing him to us. John 16, 14.

The object which we behold is *the glory of the Lord*, i. e. as the context evidently demands, of Christ. The glory of Christ is his divine excellence. The believer is enabled to see that Jesus is the Son of God, or God manifested in the flesh. This is conversion. Whoever shall confess that Jesus is the Son of God, God dwelleth in him, and he in God. 1 John 4, 15. The turning unto the Lord mentioned in the preceding verse is recognizing Christ as Jehovah. This is not only conversion, it is religion. It is the highest state of the human soul. It is eternal life. John 17, 3. Hence our Lord prays that his disciples may behold his glory, as the consummation of their blessedness. John 17, 24. And the apostle John says of all who received Christ, that they beheld "his glory as of the only begotten of the Father," John 1, 14. The idea here presented is more fully unfolded in the beginning of the following chapter.

Beholding his glory *we are changed into the same image;*

τὴν αὐτὴν εἰκόνα μεταμορφούμεθα, *we are transformed into the same image*. The verb is commonly construed with εἰς, *into*, or κατά, *after*, but sometimes, as here, with the simple accusative. *The same image*, that is, the same which we are by the Spirit enabled to behold. 'Beholding we are transformed;' there is a causal relation between the one and the other. This is a truth everywhere recognized in the word of God. While, on the one hand, it is taught that the natural man cannot see the things of the Spirit, because they are spiritually discerned, 1 Cor. 2, 14, and that this blindness is the cause of alienation and pollution, Eph. 4, 18; on the other hand, it is no less clearly taught that knowledge is the source of holiness, Eph. 5, 9; that spiritual discernment implies and produces congeniality. We shall be like Christ, because we shall see him as he is. 1 John 3, 2. The conformity to the image of Christ, as it arises from beholding his glory, must of course begin here. It is the vision of that glory, although only as in a glass, which has this transforming power. As the vision is imperfect, so the transformation is imperfect; when the vision is perfect, the conformity will be perfect. Rom. 8, 29. 1 John 3, 2. Only they are Christians, who are like Christ. The conformity of which the apostle speaks, although it is spiritual, as here presented, is not confined to the soul. Of the body it is said, since we have borne the image of the earthy, we shall bear the image of the heavenly. 1 Cor. 15, 49. Phil. 3, 21. *From glory to glory*. This may mean that the transformation proceeds *from glory* (i. e. from the glory of Christ as apprehended by us), and results in glory. This explanation is adopted by the Greek fathers. Or the expression indicates progression from one stage of glory to another. Comp. Ps. 84, 7, "They go from strength to strength." This is the common and most natural interpretation. The transformation is carried forward without intermission, from the first scarce discernible resemblance, to full conformity to the image of Christ, both as to soul and body. *As by the Spirit of the Lord*. *As*, i. e. as might be expected from such an agent. It is a work which corresponds to the nature of its author. *By;* the preposition is ἀπό, *from*, as indicating the source whence this glorious effect flows. *The Spirit of the Lord*. The Greek is κυρίου πνεύματος, which the Vulgate renders *Domini Spiritu*, an explanation which is adopted by Augustin, Calvin and many others, as well as by our translators. But this inverts the order of the words, and

is the more unnatural here because in the immediately preceding verse the apostle had said τὸ πνεῦμα κυρίου, *Spirit of the
Lord;* he would therefore hardly express the same idea in the
same connection by κυρίου πνεύματος. Others render the words
the Lord Spirit, i. e. the Spirit who is Lord. We have in the
Old Testament and in the apocalypse the familiar phrase, "the
Lord God;" but this is only the translation of יְהֹוָה אֱלֹהִים Je-
hovah Elohim, Jehovah who is God, which the Septuagint ren-
der κύριος ὁ θεός, the Vulgate Dominus Deus, and the English,
"Lord God." More analogous to the passage in the text is the
Hebrew אֲדֹנָי יְהֹוָה, which the Septuagint render κύριος κύριος,
the Vulgate Dominus Deus, and the English Lord God. In
Joshua 22, 22, we have the unusual combination, אֵל אֱלֹהִים יְהֹוָה;
Septuagint, ὁ θεὸς θεὸς κύριός ἐστι; and immediately after ὁ
θεὸς θεός; Vulgate, Fortissimus Deus Dominus; the English,
"The LORD God of gods." As then in Hebrew אֲדֹנָי יְהֹוָה, in
Greek κύριος κύριος (or κύριος ὁ θεός), in Latin, Dominus Deus,
and in English, Lord God, all meaning *God who is Lord,* so
κύριος πνεῦμα may mean *the Spirit who is Lord,* i. e. the divine
Spirit. This is the explanation adopted by Chrysostom, Theodoret and some of the moderns, in accordance with the interpretation which they give of the first clause of v. 17, which,
as stated above, they understand to mean, *the Spirit is Lord,*
πρὸς τὸ Πνεῦμα ἐπιστρέφων, πρὸς Κύριον ἐπιστρέφεις κύριος γὰρ τὸ
Πνεῦμα, καὶ ὁμόθρονον, ὁμοπροσκύνητον καὶ ὁμοούσιον Πατρὶ καὶ υἱῷ.
But as in v. 17 Paul does not say the Spirit is the Lord, but
on the contrary that the Lord is the Spirit, so it would be
unnatural to make him here say we are transformed by *the
Spirit who is the Lord.* If *Lord* is the subject in the one
case, it must be in the other. According to others, the phrase
in question should be rendered *Lord of the Spirit,* i. e. Christ,
who may be said to be Lord of the Spirit, in a sense analogous
to that in which God is said to be the God of Christ. That
is, as God sent Christ, and was revealed by him, so Christ
sends the Spirit and is revealed by him. This is the interpretation of Billroth, Olshausen, Meyer and others. But the
"Lord of the Spirit" is an expression without any scriptural
authority or analogy. It is only of the incarnate Son of God
that the Father is said to be his God. There is no grammatical necessity for this interpretation, and it does not accord
with v. 17. Luther, Beza and others render the phrase ἀπὸ
κυρίου πνεύματος, *the Lord who is the Spirit.* In favour of this
interpretation is, first, the analogy of such expressions as ἀπὸ

θεοῦ πατρός, *from God who is Father*, Gal. 1, 3 ; and secondly, the authority of v. 17. There the apostle had said, 'The Lord is the Spirit,' and here he says, the transforming power by which we are made like Christ flows from 'the Lord who is the Spirit.' The former passage determines the meaning of the latter. The Lord who is the Spirit means, the Lord who is one with the Spirit, the same in substance, equal in power and glory; who is where the Spirit is, and does what the Spirit does.

CHAPTER IV.

In vs. 1–6 the apostle resumes the theme of 3, 12, viz. the open and faithful manner in which he preached the gospel. In vs. 7–15 he shows that his own personal insufficiency and suffering served to manifest more clearly the power of God, who rendered such a feeble instrument the means of producing so great effects. Therefore, vs. 16–18, he was not discouraged or faint-hearted, but exultingly looked above the things seen to those unseen.

As Paul had been made a minister of the new covenant, intrusted with the ministration of righteousness and life, he acted as became his high commission. He was neither timid nor deceitful. He doubted not the truth, the power, or the success of the gospel which he preached; nor did he in any way corrupt or conceal the truth, but by its open proclamation commended himself to every man's conscience, vs. 1. 2. If, notwithstanding this clear exhibition of the truth, the gospel still remained hid, that could only be accounted for by the god of this world blinding the eyes of men. Nothing short of this can account for the fact; for, says the apostle, we preach Christ and not ourselves, and Christ is the image of God. In him there is a revelation of the glory of God to which there is nothing analogous but the original creation of light out of darkness, vs. 3–6. This treasure, however, is in earthen vessels. The gospel is the revelation of God. It is to do for the world what the creation of light did for the chaotic earth. But we ministers are to have none of the glory of the work. We are nothing. The whole power is of God;

who so orders events as to make his power apparent. I am so perplexed, persecuted, down-trodden and exposed to death, as to render it evident that a divine power is exercised in my preservation and continued efficiency. My continuing to live and labour with success is a proof that Jesus lives. This he tells the Corinthians is for their benefit. vs. 7–12. Having the same faith that David had, he spoke with equal confidence, assured that God, who raised up Christ, would not only preserve him while in this world, but also raise him hereafter from the dead. As all Paul endured and did was for the benefit of the Church, thanks would be rendered by the people of God for his preservation and success, vs. 13–15. Therefore, adds this great apostle, I do not faint; although my outward man perishes, my inward man is renewed day by day; for I know that my present afflictions are not only temporary, but that they are to be succeeded by an eternal weight of glory, vs. 16–18.

1. Therefore, seeing we have this ministry, as we have received mercy, we faint not.

Therefore, i. e. on this account. This is explained by what follows; *seeing we have this ministry*, that is, because we have it. In the former chapter he had proclaimed himself a minister of the new covenant, not of the letter, but of the spirit, 3, 6 ; a ministry far more glorious than that of the law, inasmuch as the law could only condemn, whereas the gospel conveys righteousness and life. The possession of such an office he assigns as the reason why he does not *faint ;* οὐκ ἐκκακοῦμεν, *we do not turn out bad*, or prove recreant. That is, we do not fail in the discharge of duty, either through weariness or cowardice. *As we have received mercy.* The position of these words in the text admits of their being connected either with what precedes or with what follows. In the former case, the sense is, having through the mercy of God obtained this ministry; in the latter, the meaning would be, as we have obtained mercy we faint not. The former is almost universally preferred, both because his not fainting is referred to his having so glorious an office, and because he so often refers to his call to the apostleship as a signal manifestation of the mercy and grace of God. Rom. 15, 15. 16. 1 Cor. 15, 9. 10. Eph. 3, 8. 'Having through the mercy of God obtained such a ministry, we faint not.'

2. But have renounced the hidden things of dishonesty, not walking in craftiness, nor handling the word of God deceitfully; but by manifestation of the truth commending ourselves to every man's conscience in the sight of God.

But, ἀλλά, on the contrary, i. e. so far from proving recreant to his duty as a minister of the new covenant he acted in the manner set forth in this verse. The apostle in the description which he here gives of his official conduct, evidently intends to describe the false teachers in Corinth. What he denies of himself he impliedly affirms of them. First, Paul says, *we have renounced,* declared off from, *the hidden things of dishonesty,* τὰ κρυπτὰ τῆς αἰσχύνης. The word αἰσχύνη (from αἰσχρός, *ugly*), means either *shame* as a feeling, or the cause of shame, any thing disgraceful or scandalous. The above phrase therefore may mean either those things which men conceal, or do in secret, because they are ashamed of them, or, secret scandals or crimes. It may be taken in a general sense, as including any course of conduct which men conceal from fear of being disgraced; or in a specific sense for secret immoralities, or for secret machinations and manœuvres. The last is probably the true view, because the emphasis is rather on *secret* than *shame.* It was secrecy or concealment, the opposite of openness and honest frankness, that the apostle charges on his opponents. In the preceding context he had spoken of his openness of speech and conduct, and in the latter part of this verse he speaks of the manifestation of the truth, i. e. of its open proclamation. What therefore he says he renounced, that which he represents as characteristic of false teachers, is the want of openness, adopting secret methods of accomplishing their ends, which they would be ashamed to avow openly; *pudendas latebras,* as Beza says, *minime convenientes iis, qui tantæ dignitatis ministerium tractant. Not walking in craftiness,* this is an amplification of what precedes. A πανοῦργος is a man who can do every thing, and is willing to do any thing to accomplish his ends; and hence πανουργία includes the ideas of shrewdness or acuteness in seeing how things can be done, and unscrupulousness as to the character of the means to be employed. It is the quality manifested by Satan when he beguiled Eve, 2 Cor. 11, 3; which the Jews exhibited when they endeavoured to entrap our Lord, Luke 20, 23; and

which false teachers are wont to exercise when they would
seduce the unwary into heresy. Eph. 4, 14. All such cunning,
all such sly and secret ways of accomplishing his purposes Paul
renounced. *Nor handling the word of God deceitfully.* The
word δολόω means not only *to deceive,* but also *to falsify.* The
latter is its meaning here. Not falsifying or corrupting the
word of God, i. e. not adulterating it with the doctrines or
traditions of men. Comp. 2, 17. The gospel which Paul
preached was the word of God; something divinely revealed,
having therefore a divine, and not merely human authority.
The apostles always thus speak with the consciousness of being the mouth of God or organs of the Spirit, so that we cannot deny their inspiration without denying not only their authority but their integrity. *But by the manifestation of the
truth.* This stands opposed to the preceding clauses. Instead of availing ourselves of secret and cunning arts, and
corrupting the word of God, we declared it openly and purely. *The truth,* therefore, here is not moral truth or integrity,
nor truth in general, but revealed truth, i. e. the word of God.
Commending ourselves to every man's conscience. Paul's opponents endeavoured to recommend themselves and to secure
the confidence of others by cunning, and by corrupting the
gospel; but he relied simply on the manifestation of the truth.
He knew that the truth had such a self-evidencing power that
even where it was rejected and hated it commended itself to
the conscience as true. And those ministers who are humble
and sincere, who are not wise in their own conceit, but simply
declare the truth as God has revealed it, commend themselves
to the consciences of men. That is, they secure the testimony
of the conscience even of wicked men in their favour. *In the
sight of God,* that is, he acted thus in the sight of God.
This is an assertion of the purity of the motives which governed his official conduct. He acted as in the sight of that
God before whose eye nothing unholy or selfish could stand.
The assertion of conscious integrity is not self-praise.

3. But if our gospel be hid, it is hid to them that
are lost.

Although the gospel is thus glorious in itself, and although
it was clearly set forth, yet to some it remained hid. That is,
its true character and excellence as a revelation from God and
of God was not apprehended or recognized. The reason or

cause of this fact was not to be sought either in the nature of
the gospel, or in the mode of its exhibition, but in the state
and character of those who rejected it. The sun does not
cease to be the sun although the blind do not see it. And if
any man cannot see the sun on a clear day at noon, he must
be blind. So Paul does not hesitate to say that if any man
does not receive the gospel when clearly presented, he is lost.
If our gospel be hid, it is hid to them that are lost, ἐν τοῖς
ἀπολλυμένοις, *among*, or *before* them who are lost. See 1 Cor.
1, 18, where it is said that the gospel is foolishness to them
that perish. *The lost* are those who are in a state of perdition
and who are certain (if they continue to reject the gospel) to
perish forever. Nothing can be plainer than the doctrine of
this passage. A man's faith is not a matter of indifference.
He cannot be an atheist and yet be saved. He cannot reject
the gospel and yet go to heaven when he dies. This is not an
arbitrary decision. There is and must be an adequate ground
for it. Atheism implies spiritual death, the absence of all that
constitutes the true life of the soul, of all its highest and best
aspirations, instincts and feelings. The rejection of the gospel
is as clear a proof of moral depravity, as inability to see the
light of the sun at noon is a proof of blindness. Such is the
teaching of the Bible, and such has ever been the faith of the
church. Men of the world cry out against this doctrine.
They insist that a man is not accountable for his opinions.
He is, however, accountable for the character by which those
opinions are determined. If he has such a character, such an
inward moral state, as permits and decides him to believe that
there is no God, that murder, adultery, theft and violence are
right and good, then that inward state which constitutes his
character, and for which he is responsible, (according to the
intuitive perception and universal judgment of men,) is reprobate. A good infidel is, according to the Bible, as much a
contradiction as good wickedness or sweet bitterness. It is
not for nothing that infinite truth and love, in the person of
our Lord, said, "He that believeth not shall be damned."

4. In whom the god of this world hath blinded the
minds of them which believe not, lest the light of the
glorious gospel of Christ, who is the image of God,
should shine unto them.

In this verse the apostle assigns the reason why those who are lost do not see the truth and excellence of the gospel. It is that the god of this world hath blinded their minds. *In whom* (ἐν οἷς). The relative is used here as implying a cause or reason. ' Our gospel is hid to them who are lost, *because* in them,' &c. See 3, 6. *The god of this world,* i. e. Satan, who is called the god of this world because of the power which he exercises over the men of the world, and because of the servile obedience which they render to him. They are taken captive by him at his will. 2 Tim. 2, 26. It is not necessary in order that men should serve Satan, and even worship him, that they should intend to do so, or even that they should know that such a being exists. 1 Cor. 10, 20. It is enough that he actually controls them, and that they fulfil his purposes as implicitly as the good fulfil the will of God. Not to serve God, is to serve Satan. There is no help for it. If Jehovah be not our God, Satan is. He is therefore called the prince of this world. John 12, 31. 14, 30. Comp. Matt. 4, 8. 9. Eph. 2, 2. 6, 12. This was one of the designations which the Rabbins applied to Satan. The true God, they said, is Deus primus, Satan, Deus secundus. Or as old Calovius said, *Diabolus est simia Dei.* As the Arians argued from the fact that Satan is called god of this world, that Christ's being called God is no proof of his true divinity; and as the Manicheans quoted the passage in favour of their doctrine of two eternal principles, the one good and the other evil, many of the fathers, including even Chrysostom and Augustine, in violation of its obvious construction, make it to mean, " God hath blinded the minds of this world, i. e. of unbelievers." On which Calvin remarks, We see how far the spirit of controversy can lead men in perverting Scripture. The word *god* may be used figuratively as well as literally. That we say mammon is the god of the world, or that Paul said of certain men, " their belly is their god," does not prove that calling Jehovah God is no assertion of his divinity. And as to the Manichean argument, unless it can be shown that when Baal is called god of the Syrians, eternity and self-existence are ascribed to him, it cannot be inferred that these attributes belong to Satan because he is called the god of this world. Satan is said to *blind the minds of those that believe not;* that is, he exerts such an influence over them as prevents their apprehending the glory of the gospel. This control of Satan over the human mind, although so effectual, is analogous to

the influence of one created intellect over another in other
cases, and therefore is perfectly consistent with free agency
and responsibility. It should, however, make us feel our danger and need of divine assistance, seeing that we have to contend not only against the influence of evil men, but against
the far more powerful influence of the rulers of darkness; the
pantocrators of this world. Eph. 6, 12. The grammatical
construction of this clause is somewhat doubtful. The words
are ἐν οἷς ἐτύφλωσε τὰ νοήματα τῶν ἀπίστων. The common explanation makes the genitive, τῶν ἀπίστων, virtually in apposition with ἐν οἷς. 'In whom, i. e. in unbelievers, he had blinded the minds.' The simple meaning then is, 'The gospel is
hid to them who are lost, because Satan hath blinded their
eyes.' The *lost* and the *unbelieving* are identical. According
to this view unbelief is the effect of the blinding. The same
idea is expressed if, according to Fritzsche and Billroth, τῶν
ἀπίστων be taken proleptically. 'Whose minds Satan hath
blinded so that they believe not.' Comp. 1 Thess. 3, 13, "To
establish your hearts unblamable," i. e. so that they may be
unblamable; and Phil. 3, 21, (according to the corrected
text,) "changed like," i. e. changed so as to be like. According to Meyer this would require the accusative, τὰ νοήματα
ἄπιστα, as the genitive of adjectives taken substantively is
never thus proleptically used. His explanation is, 'Blinding
the eyes of unbelievers is the business of Satan, and this he
has done in them who are lost.' According to this view,
blindness does not precede, but follows unbelief. Those who
will not believe, Satan blinds so that they cannot see. Comp.
Rom. 1, 21, "Their foolish heart was darkened." Their inex-
cusable folly was the ground of their judicial blindness. The
doctrine thus taught is one clearly recognized in Scripture.
Those who resist the truth, God gives up to a reprobate mind.
Rom. 1, 24. 28. The logical connection, however, is here opposed to this interpretation. Paul had said that the gospel
was hid to the lost. This he accounts for by saying that Satan had blinded their minds. The blindness therefore precedes the unbelief and is the cause of it.

*Lest the light of the glorious gospel of Christ, who is the
image of God, should shine unto them.* This is both the design and effect of the blindness spoken of. Satan intends by
the darkness which he spreads over the minds of men, to prevent their seeing the glory of Christ. *Lest the light*, φωτισμός,
a word which does not occur in common Greek, but is used

in the Septuagint, Ps. 44, 3, in the phrase rendered, "in the light of thy countenance," and Ps. 78, 14, "He led them all night with a light of fire." The word therefore signifies the brightness emitted by a radiant body. *Of the glorious gospel of Christ*, literally, *the gospel of the glory of Christ*, i. e. that gospel which reveals the glory of Christ. The word δόξης, *glory*, is not to be taken as a merely qualifying genitive of εὐαγγελίον, *gospel*. It is the genitive of the object. The glory of Christ is the sum of all the divine and human excellence which is centred in his person, and makes him the radiant point in the universe, the clearest manifestation of God to his creatures, the object of supreme admiration, adoration and love, to all intelligent beings, and especially to his saints. To see this glory is to be saved; for we are thereby transformed into his likeness from glory to glory, 3, 18. Therefore it is that Satan, the great adversary, directs all his energy to prevent men becoming the subjects of that illumination of which the gospel, as the revelation of the glory of Christ, is the source. *Who is the image of God*, i. e. who being God represents God, so that he who hath seen the Son hath seen the Father also. John 14, 9. 12, 45. Christ, as to his divine nature, or as the Logos, is declared to be the brightness of the Father's glory, Heb. 1, 3, to be in the form of God and equal with God, Phil. 2, 6, and perhaps also Col. 1, 15; but here it is the incarnate Logos, the exalted Son of God clothed in our nature, who is declared to be the image of God, because in him dwells the fulness of the Godhead bodily. Col. 2, 9.

5. For we preach not ourselves, but Christ Jesus the Lord; and ourselves your servants for Jesus' sake.

The connection indicated by the particle *for* is with the main idea of the preceding verse. 'Our gospel,' says Paul, 'is the gospel of the glory of Christ, *for* we do not preach ourselves, but him.' To preach one's self is to make self the end of preaching; that is, preaching with the design to attract to ourselves the admiration, the confidence or homage of men. This Paul declares he did not do, but he preached *Christ Jesus the Lord*. His object in preaching was to bring men to recognize Jesus the son of Mary as Christ, i. e. as him whom Moses and the prophets designated as the Messiah, and consequently that this Jesus was, had done, is doing, and would hereafter do, all that had been asserted or predicted of the Messiah; and further that he is LORD in that sense in which every tongue in heaven, and on earth, and under the earth shall confess that he is Lord.   The great end of Paul's preaching, therefore, was to bring men to receive and acknowledge Jesus of Nazareth as the Messiah and as the supreme Lord, the maker of heaven and earth.   This is the only proper end of preaching.   It is the only way by which men can be made either virtuous or religious.   It is the only way in which either the true interests of society or the salvation of souls can be secured.   To make the end of preaching the inculcation of virtue, to render men honest, sober, benevolent and faithful, is part and parcel of that wisdom of the world that is foolishness with God.   It is attempting to raise fruit without trees.   When a man is brought to recognize Jesus Christ as Lord, and to love and worship him as such, then he becomes like Christ.   What more can the moralist want?   Paul cared little for the clamour of the Greeks that he should preach wisdom and virtue.   He knew that by preaching Christ he was adopting the only means by which men can be made wise and virtuous here and blessed hereafter.

And ourselves your servants (slaves) *for Jesus' sake.* Paul presented Christ as Lord; himself as a servant.   A servant is one who labours, not for himself, but for another. Paul did not labour for himself, but for the Corinthians.   *For Jesus' sake.*   The motive which influenced him to devote himself to the service of the Corinthians was the love of Christ. Here again the wisdom of the world would say the proper motive would be a desire for their good.   Paul always puts God before man.   A regard for the glory of Christ is a far higher motive than regard for the good of men; and the former is the only true source of the latter.   The ideal of a Christian minister, as presented in this pregnant passage, is, that he is a preacher of Christ, and a servant of the church, governed and animated by the love of Jesus.

6. For God, who commanded the light to shine out of darkness, hath shined in our hearts, to (give) the light of the knowledge of the glory of God in the face of Jesus Christ.

There are two different views taken of the meaning of this verse.   First, it may be understood to assign the reason why

Paul was the servant of the Corinthians. He devoted himself to their service, because God had revealed to him the knowledge of Christ, in order that he might communicate that knowledge to others. According to this view the connection is with the last clause of v. 5. "I am your servant, ὅτι, *because*," &c.; "in our hearts," means in Paul's heart; and πρὸς φωτισμόν (for the light) is equivalent to πρὸς τὸ φωτίζειν, *to diffuse the light.* Second, it may be understood to state the reason why Paul preached Christ. 'We preach not ourselves, but Christ Jesus the Lord, ὅτι, *because* in him is revealed the glory of God.' In this case the connection is with the first clause of v. 5, and not with the last; "in our hearts" means in the hearts of believers; and πρὸς φωτισμόν (for light) means, as our version expresses it, *to give us the light.* The end or design of God's shining into our hearts is that we should apprehend the glory of God in the face of Jesus Christ. The latter of these interpretations is adopted by Calvin, the former by Luther and by almost all the modern commentators. With regard to the former it must be admitted that the sense is good and consistent with the meaning of the words. It accords also with Gal. 1, 16, where the apostle says that God had revealed his Son in him that he might preach him among the Gentiles. The following considerations, however, are in favour of the other view of the passage. 1. The connection is better. The main idea of the context is that Paul preached Christ, and therefore it is more natural to understand him to give the reason for so doing, than why he served the Corinthians, which is a subordinate matter. 2. The phrase "in our *hearts*" is much more naturally understood to mean "in the hearts of believers" than in Paul's own heart. It is indeed possible that here, as in 3, 2, the plural (hearts) may be used in reference to the apostle himself. Still this is admissible only when the context requires it. Had Paul meant himself he would probably have said "in our heart," as in the parallel passage in Galatians 1, 16 he says, ἐν ἐμοί, *in me.* To explain the plural form here by assuming that Paul means himself and Timothy is contrary to his uniform habit of speaking for himself. His epistles are his and not Timothy's. 3. The former interpretation supposes φωτισμός to have a different meaning here from what it has in v. 4. There it means *light,* here it is made to mean *the act of communicating light.* But if φωτισμὸς τοῦ εὐαγγελίου means the light which flows from the gospel (or the gospel itself as luminous), then φωτισμός τῆς γνώσεως means the light of which the knowledge of Christ is the source, (or that knowledge as light.) In v. 4, it is said that Satan hath blinded the eyes of unbelievers so that they cannot see the light of the gospel of the glory of Christ. Here it is said that God has enlightened us so that we do see it. In Test. XII. Patr. p. 578, it is said, τὸ φῶς τοῦ κόσμου, τὸ δοθὲν ἐν ὑμῖν πρὸς φωτισμὸν παντὸς ἀνθρώπου, *the light of the world deposited in you, for the (subjective) illumination of every man.* 4. It is an additional reason in favour of this interpretation that it suits the antithesis between vs. 4 and 6. The gospel is hid to one class of men, but God has opened the eyes of another class to see its glory. Here, as elsewhere, particularly in 1 Cor. 2, 14, the apostle recognizes a twofold illumination, the one external by the word, to which Satan renders unbelievers blind; and the other internal by the Spirit, whereby we are enabled to see the glory which is objectively revealed.

The literal translation of this passage is, 'God who commanded the light to shine out of darkness, who shined into our hearts.' Something must be supplied to complete the sense. We may read either ' *It is* God who commanded, &c., who shined into our hearts;' or, 'God who commanded the light to shine out of darkness, *is he* who shined,' &c. There is an obvious reference to the work of creation as recorded in Genesis. Darkness originally brooded over chaos, until God said, Let there be light. So spiritual darkness broods over the minds of men, until God shines into their hearts. *Shined into our hearts.* The word λάμπω, means either, *to be luminous;* or as here, to *illuminate,* or *cause light,* as the analogy with the physical creation, just referred to, requires. The idea is not that God becomes luminous in us, but that he produces light in our hearts. The design of this inward illumination is expressed by the words πρὸς φωτισμὸν τῆς γνώσεως, which, according to the former of the two interpretations mentioned above, means, *to the shining abroad of the knowledge,* &c. He illuminates us that we may diffuse light, and thus illuminate others. According to the second interpretation, the meaning is, *to give us the light of the knowledge.* God illuminates our minds so that we apprehend that light which flows from the knowledge of *the glory of God,* or which consists in that knowledge. By *the glory of God* is of course meant the divine majesty or excellence, which is the proper object of admiration and adoration. *In the face of Jesus*

Christ; the position of these words and the sense require that they should be connected with the word *glory,* notwithstanding the omission in the Greek of the connecting article (τῆς). It is the glory of God as revealed in Christ that men are by the illumination of the Holy Ghost enabled to see. There are two important truths involved in this statement. First, that God becomes in Christ the object of knowledge. The clearest revelation of the fact that God is, and what he is, is made in the person of Christ, so that those who refuse to see God in Christ lose all true knowledge of him. "No man hath seen God at any time; the only begotten Son, who is in the bosom of the Father, he hath declared him," John 1, 18. "Neither knoweth any man the Father, save the Son, and he to whomsoever the Son will reveal him," Matt. 11, 27. "Whosoever denieth the Son, the same hath not the Father," 1 John 2, 23. 2 John 9. John 15, 23. Insignis locus, says Calvin, unde discimus Deum in sua altitudine non esse investigandum (habitat enim lucem inaccessibilem), sed cognoscendum quatenus se in Christo patefacit. Proinde quicquid extra Christum de Deo cognoscere appetunt homines, evanidum est, vagantur enim extra viam. . . . Nobis utilius est Deum conspicere, qualis apparet in Filio unigenito, quam arcanam ejus essentiam investigare. The other truth here taught is, that this knowledge of God in Christ is not a mere matter of intellectual apprehension, which one man may communicate to another. It is a spiritual discernment, to be derived only from the Spirit of God. God must shine into our hearts to give us this knowledge. Matt. 16, 17. Gal. 1, 16. 1 Cor. 2, 10. 14. As the glory of God is spiritual, it must be spiritually discerned. It is therefore easy to see why the Scriptures make true religion to consist in the knowledge of Christ, and why they make the denial of Christ, or want of faith in him as God manifest in the flesh, a soul-destroying sin. If Christ is God, to know him, is to know God; and to deny him, is to deny God.

7. But we have this treasure in earthen vessels, that the excellency of the power may be of God, and not of us.

This treasure is not the light or inward illumination spoken of in v. 6, but the ministry of the gospel which Paul had received, and of which he had spoken in such exalted terms. It was a ministration of life, of power, and of glory. It revealed the grandest truths. It produced the most astonishing effects. It freed men from the condemnation and power of sin; it transformed them into the image of Christ; it delivered them from the power of the god of this world, and made them partakers of eternal life. These are effects which infinitely transcend all human power; and to render this fact conspicuous God had committed this treasure *to earthen vessels.* By earthen vessels is not meant frail bodies, but weak, suffering, perishing men, because it is not on account of the frailty of the body merely that ministers are so incompetent to produce the effects which flow from their ministrations. The apostle means to present the utter disproportion between the visible means and the effects produced, as proof that the real efficiency is not in man, but in God. *The excellency of the power,* i. e. the exceedingly great power, the wonderful efficiency of the gospel. *May be,* i. e. may be known and acknowledged to be, *of God,* i. e. to flow from him as its source, and not from us. Although what the apostle here says is true of all ministers, yet he had, no doubt, special reference to himself and to his own peculiar circumstances. He had magnified in the highest degree his office, but he himself was a poor, weak, persecuted, down-trodden man. This, he says, only renders the power of God the more conspicuous, not only in the success of my ministry, but in my preservation in the midst of dangers and sufferings which it seems impossible any man could either escape or bear. It is to show, on the one hand, how weak he is, how truly a mere earthen vessel, and, on the other, how great and manifest God's power is, that in the following verses he contrasts his trials and his deliverances.

8. 9. (We are) troubled on every side, yet not distressed; (we are) perplexed, but not in despair; persecuted, but not forsaken; cast down, but not destroyed.

Our version supplies the words *we are,* turning the participles into verbs, which, in the Greek, are all connected with the verb ἔχομεν (*we have*) in the preceding verse. 'We, troubled, perplexed, persecuted and cast down, have, &c.' *On every side,* ἐν παντί, in every way and on every occasion.

These words belong to all the clauses, and not merely to the first. He was not only troubled, but perplexed and persecuted, ἐν παντί, *in every way.* *Troubled, but not distressed,* θλιβόμενοι, ἀλλ' οὐ στενοχωρούμενοι, "pressed for room, but still having room." The figure is that of a combatant sore pressed by his antagonist, but still finding room to turn himself. *Perplexed, but not in despair,* constantly doubtful what way to take, and yet always finding some way open. The word ἀπορέω (ἄπορός εἰμι) means to be at a loss what to say or do; ἐξαπορέω is intensive, to be absolutely shut up so as to have no way or means available. *Persecuted, but not forsaken;* that is, although God allowed men to persecute him, and seek to destroy his life and usefulness, yet he never deserted him or gave him up to the power of those who thus followed him. *Cast down, but not destroyed.* The allusion is still to a combat. Paul was not only persecuted or pursued by his enemies, but actually overtaken by them and cast to the ground, but not killed. When they seemed to have him in their power, God delivered him. This occurred so often, and in cases so extreme, as to make it manifest that the power of God was exerted on his behalf. No man from his own resources could have endured or escaped so much. There is in these verses an evident climax, which reaches its culmination in the next succeeding sentence. He compares himself to a combatant, first hardly pressed, then hemmed in, then pursued, then actually cast down. This was not an occasional experience, but his life was like that of Christ, an uninterrupted succession of indignities and suffering.

10. Always bearing about in the body the dying of the Lord Jesus, that the life also of Jesus might be made manifest in our body.

We constantly illustrate in our person the sufferings of Christ. We are treated as he was treated; neglected, defamed, despised, maltreated; oppressed with hunger and thirst, and constantly exposed to death. *Always bearing about.* Wherever he went, among Jews or Gentiles, in Jerusalem and Ephesus; in all his journeyings, he met everywhere, from all classes of persons, the same kind of treatment which Christ himself had received. *In his body.* This is said because the reference is to his external trials and sufferings, and not to his internal anxieties and sorrows. *The dying of* [the Lord] *Jesus.* The word κυρίου, *of the Lord,* is not found in the majority of the ancient manuscripts, and is therefore omitted in the later editions of the Greek Testament. If this word be left out, the two clauses more nearly correspond. *The dying of Jesus* then answers to *the life of Jesus* in the following clause. The word νέκρωσις is used figuratively in Rom. 4, 19, "the deadness of Sarah's womb." Here it is to be taken literally. It means properly *a slaying* or *putting to death,* and then violent death, or simply death. *The death of Jesus* does not mean death on his account; but such death as he suffered. Comp. 1, 5. Though the reference is principally to the dying of Christ, and the climax begun in the preceding verse is here reached, yet his other sufferings are not to be excluded. "The mortification of Jesus," says Calvin, "includes every thing which rendered him (i. e. Paul) despicable before men." Paul elsewhere refers to his constant exposure to death in terms as strong as those which he here uses. In Rom. 8, 36 he says, "We are killed all the day long," and 1 Cor. 15, 31, "I die daily." Compare also 1 Cor. 4, 9. 2 Cor. 11, 23. The death or sufferings of Christ were constantly, as it were, reproduced in the experience of the apostle. In the use of another figure he expresses the same idea in Gal. 6, 17. "I bear in my body the marks of the Lord Jesus." The scars which I bear in my body mark me as the soldier of Christ, and as belonging to him as my divine Master, and as suffering in his cause.

That the life also of Jesus might be made manifest in our body. This expresses the design of God in allowing Paul to be thus persecuted and involved in the constant danger of death. The treasure of the gospel was committed not to an angel, but to Paul, an earthen vessel, and he was pressed, persecuted, cast down, and beset with deadly perils, in order that his preservation, his wonderful efficiency and astonishing success, should be a constant proof that Jesus lives, and not only exercises a providential care over his servants, delivering them out of all their perils, but also attends their labours with his own divine efficiency. Paul's deliverances, and the effects of his preaching, made it manifest that Jesus lives. In Rom. 15, 18 the apostle says, "I will not dare to speak of those things which Christ hath not wrought by me, to make the Gentiles obedient, by word and deed;" and in Gal. 2, 8, "He that wrought effectually in Peter to the apostleship of the cir-

cumcision, the same was mighty in me towards the Gentiles."
As the life of every believer is a manifestation of the life of
Christ, (for it is not we that live, but Christ liveth in us, Gal.
2, 20,) so also was the apostolic life of Paul. As the life of
Christ, however, is not only manifested in the spiritual life of
his followers, and in the deliverance and success of his ministers, as it is not only made known in rescuing them from
deadly perils, but is hereafter to be more conspicuously revealed in delivering them from death itself, it seems from v.
14 that Paul includes the resurrection in the manifestation of
the life of Jesus of which he here speaks. We die (daily, and
at last, literally) in order that the life of Christ may be revealed. This passage is thus brought into unison with Rom.
8, 17, "If so be that we suffer with him, that we may be also
glorified together;" and with 2 Tim. 2, 11, "If we be dead
with him, we shall live with him." See 1 Peter 4, 13. 14.
Rom. 6, 8. 9. John 14, 19, "Because I live, ye shall live also."
The association is natural between deliverance from the danger of death, and the ultimate deliverance from death itself.
The following verses show that this association actually existed in the apostle's mind, and that both were regarded as
manifestations of the life of Christ, and therefore proofs that
he still lives. *In our body ;* this does not mean simply *in me.*
A special reference is made to the body, because Paul was
speaking of bodily sufferings and death.

11. For we which live are always delivered unto
death for Jesus' sake, that the life also of Jesus might
be made manifest in our mortal flesh.

This is a confirmation and explanation of what precedes.
Paul constantly bore about the dying of Jesus, *for* he was always delivered to death for Jesus' sake. He was, as he says
1 Cor. 4, 9, ὡς ἐπιθανάτιος, *as one condemned,* and constantly
expecting death. *We which are alive ;* ἡμεῖς οἱ ζῶντες, *we the
living,* i. e. although living, and therefore, it might seem, not
the subjects of death. Death and life are opposed to each
other, and yet in our case they are united. Though living we
die daily. The words in this connection do not mean 'as long
as we live,' or, 'we who are alive,' as in 1 Thess. 4, 17, where
they designate the living as a class distinguished from the
dead. They mark the peculiarity of Paul's condition as living
although constantly delivered to death.

That the life also of Jesus might be made manifest in our mortal flesh. The only variation between this and the corresponding clause of the preceding verse is, that here the phrase *in our mortal flesh* is substituted for *in our body.* The word *body* does not of itself involve the idea of weakness and mortality, but the word *flesh* does. Hereafter we are to be clothed with bodies, but not with flesh and blood. The contrast, therefore, between the power of the life of Christ, and the feebleness of the instrument or organ through which that life is revealed, is enhanced by saying it was manifested in our mortal flesh. In himself Paul was utter weakness; in Christ he could do and suffer all things.

12. So then death worketh in us, but life in you.

This verse expresses the conclusion or the result of the preceding exhibitions. *So then* I have the suffering and you the benefit. I am constantly dying, but the life of Jesus manifested in me is operative for your good. The death and life here spoken of must be the same as in vs. 10. 11. The death is Paul's sufferings and dying; the life is not his physical life and activity by which the life of Christ is represented, but the divine life and efficiency of Jesus. Death and life are personified. The one is represented as operative in Paul; the other in the Corinthians. The divine power manifested in the support of the apostle, and in rendering his labours so successful, was not primarily and principally for his benefit, but for the benefit of those to whom he preached. It was, however, to him and to them a consolation that his labours were not in vain. There is no analogy between this passage and 1 Cor. 4, 8–10, where the apostle in a tone of irony contrasts his own condition with that of the Corinthians, " Now ye are full, now ye are rich, ye have reigned as kings without us," &c., and therefore there is no propriety in understanding the apostle here to represent the Corinthians as living at their ease while he was persecuted and afflicted. According to this view, *life* here signifies a state of enjoyment and prosperity, and *death* the opposite. But it is plain from the connection that the life spoken of is " the life of Jesus " which was manifested in the apostle, the fruits of which the Corinthians enjoyed.

13. We having the same spirit of faith, according

as it is written, I believed, and therefore have I spoken; we also believe, and therefore speak.

The afflictions and dangers to which the apostle was exposed, were adapted to discourage and even to drive him to despair. He, however, was not discouraged; but having the same faith which of old animated the Psalmist, he also, as David did, proclaimed his confidence in God. Our version omits the connecting particle, δέ, which expresses the contrast between what follows and what precedes. 'We are delivered unto death, *but* having,' &c. *The same spirit of faith.* "The spirit of faith" may be a periphrase for faith itself; or the word spirit may refer to the human spirit, and the whole mean 'having the same believing spirit.' It is more in accordance with scriptural usage, and especially with Paul's manner, to make spirit refer to the Holy Spirit, who is so often designated from the effects which he produces. He is called the Spirit of adoption, Rom. 8, 15; the Spirit of wisdom, Eph. 1, 17; Spirit of grace, Heb. 10, 29; Spirit of glory, 1 Pet. 4, 14. The apostle means to say that the same blessed Spirit which was the author of faith in David he also possessed. *According as it is written,* i. e. the same faith that is expressed in the passage where it is written, 'I believed, therefore have I spoken.' This is the language of David in Ps. 116, 10. The Psalmist was greatly afflicted; the sorrows of death compassed him, the pains of hell gat hold of him, but he did not despair. He called on the Lord, and he helped him. He delivered his soul from death, his eyes from tears, and his feet from falling. David's faith did not fail. He believed, and therefore, in the midst of his afflictions, he proclaimed his confidence and recounted the goodness of the Lord. Paul's experience was the same. He also was sorely tried. He also retained his confidence, and continued to rely on the promises of God. The apostle follows the Septuagint in the passage quoted. The Hebrew expresses the same idea in a rather different form. "I believed *for* I speak." In either way, *speaking* is represented as the effect and proof of faith. See ALEXANDER on the Psalms.

We also believe, therefore we also speak. As Paul's faith was the same, its effect was the same. The faith of David made him proclaim the fidelity and goodness of God. The faith of Paul made him, despite all the suffering it brought upon him, proclaim the gospel with full assurance of its truth and of his own participation of its benefits. This clause, "we also believe," depends on the participle at the beginning of the verse. 'Having the Holy Spirit, the author of faith, we speak.' The interpretation here given of this passage is the common one. Calvin and many other commentators take a very different view. They say that by the *same* faith is to be understood, not the same the Psalmist had, but the same that the Corinthians had. Paul, says Calvin, is to be understood as saying, 'Although there is a great difference between my circumstances and yours; although God deals gently with you and severely with me, yet, notwithstanding this difference, we have the same faith; and where the faith is the same, the inheritance is the same.' But this supposes that the design of the preceding part of the chapter is to contrast the external condition of Paul with that of the Corinthians; and it supposes that by *we* is meant *we* Christians, whereas the apostle evidently means himself. 'We are persecuted, cast down, and delivered to death, but we, having the same faith with David, do as he did. We retain our confidence and continue to confess and to proclaim the gospel.' It is his own experience and conduct, and not those of the Corinthians, that Paul is exhibiting.

14. Knowing, that he which raised up the Lord Jesus, shall raise up us also by Jesus, and shall present (us) with you.

That this is to be understood of the literal resurrection, and not of a mere deliverance from dangers, is evident, 1. Because wherever a figurative sense is preferred to the literal meaning of a word or proposition, the context or nature of the passage must justify or demand it. Such is not the case here. There is nothing to forbid, but every thing to favour the literal interpretation. 2. Because the figurative interpretation cannot be carried through without doing violence to the passage and to the analogy of Scripture. "To present us with you" cannot be made to mean, 'to exhibit us with you as rescued from danger.' 3. The figurative interpretation rests on false assumptions. It assumes that Paul confidently expected to survive the second coming of Christ, and therefore could not say he expected to be raised from the dead. In this very connection, however, he says he longs to be absent from the body and to be present with the Lord; as he said to the Philippians, at a later period of his career, that he had a desire to depart and to be with Christ. Again, it is said that according to the true reading of the passage, Paul says he knows we shall be raised up *with* (not *by*) Christ, and therefore he cannot refer to the literal resurrection. But admitting the reading to be as assumed, to be raised up *with* Christ does not mean to be raised contemporaneously with him, but in fellowship with him, and in virtue of union with him. This figurative interpretation, therefore, although at first adopted by Beza and advocated by many of the most distinguished modern commentators, is generally and properly rejected.

The apostle here indicates the ground of the confidence expressed in the preceding verse. He continued to speak, i. e. to preach the gospel, notwithstanding his persecutions, *knowing*, i. e. because he was sure that he and his fellow-believers should share in its glorious consummation. The word *to know* is often used in the sense of being convinced or sure of. Rom. 5, 3. 1 Cor. 15, 58. It is assumed as a fact which no Christian did or could doubt, that God had raised up Jesus from the dead. What Paul was fully persuaded of is, that God would raise us (i. e. him, for he is speaking of himself) *with* or *by Jesus.* The majority of the ancient manuscripts and versions here read σύν, *with*, instead of διά, *by*, and that reading is adopted in most critical editions. Both forms of representation occur in Scripture. Believers are said to be raised up *by* Christ and *with* Christ. Our Lord often says, "I will raise him up at the last day;" and in 1 Cor. 15, 21, the resurrection is said to be (διά) *by* man, i. e. *by* Christ. On the other hand, believers are said to be raised up *with* or *in* him. 1 Cor. 15, 22. Eph. 2, 6. Col. 3, 3. 4. 1 Thess. 5, 10. The two modes of statement are nearly coincident in meaning The believer is united to Christ, as a member of his body, and therefore a partaker of his life. It is in virtue of this union, or of this participation of life, which, the apostle expressly teaches, extends to the body as well as to the soul, Rom. 8, 8–11. 1 Cor. 6, 13–20. 15, 21. 22, that our bodies are raised from the dead. It is therefore immaterial whether we say we are raised by him, i. e. by the power of his life, or, we are raised with, i. e. in union with him, and in virtue of that union. As our resurrection is due to this community of life, our bodies shall be like his glorious body. Phil. 3, 21. And this congeniality and conformity are included in the idea which is expressed by saying, we shall be raised up with him, i. e. in his fellowship and likeness. The resurrection, there-fore, was the one great, all-absorbing object of anticipation and desire to the early Christians, and should be to us. It is then that we shall be introduced into the glorious liberty of the sons of God; it is then that the work of redemption shall be consummated, and Christ be admired in his saints. *And present us together with you.* To present, παρίστημι, is to cause to stand near or by, to offer to. We are required to present our members (Rom. 6, 13,) or our bodies (Rom. 12, 1,) unto God; Paul says he desired to present the Corinthians as a chaste virgin unto Christ, 11, 2; God is said to have recon-cilèd us to present us holy in his sight, Col. 1, 22; and Jude (v. 24) gives thanks to him who is able to present us faultless before the presence of his glory with exceeding joy. This is the idea here. It is true that in the following chapter it is said that we must all appear before the judgment seat of Christ, whence many suppose that the apostle means here that having been raised from the dead, believers shall be presented before the tribunal of the final judge. But the idea of judg-ment is foreign from the connection. It is a fearful thing to stand before the judgment seat of Christ, even with the cer-tainty of acquittal. The apostle is here exulting in the assur-ance that, however persecuted and down-trodden here, God, who had raised up Jesus, would raise him up and present him with all other believers before the presence of his glory with exceeding joy. This it was that sustained him, and has sus-tained so many others of the afflicted of God's people, and given them a peace which passes all understanding.

The resurrection of Christ here, as in other passages, is represented as the pledge of the resurrection of his people. "He that raised Christ from the dead shall also quicken your mortal bodies," Rom. 8, 11. "God hath both raised up the Lord, and will also raise us up by his own power," 1 Cor. 6, 14. "Christ is risen from the dead and become the first fruits of them that slept; for . . . in Christ shall all be made alive," 15, 19–22. "For if we believe that Jesus died and rose again, even so them also which sleep in Jesus will God bring with him," 1 Thess. 4, 14. See also John 11, 25. Eph. 2, 6. Col. 2, 12. In the view of the sacred writers, therefore, the glori-ous resurrection of believers is as certain as the resurrection of Christ, and that not simply because God who has raised up

Jesus has promised to raise his followers, but because of the union between him and them. They are in him in such a sense as to be partakers of his life, so that his life of necessity secures theirs. If he lives, they shall live also. Now as the fact of Christ's resurrection was no more doubted by the apostles, who had seen and heard and even handled him after he rose from the dead, than their own existence, we may see how assured was their confidence of their own resurrection to eternal life. And as to us no event in the history of the world is better authenticated than the fact that Christ rose from the dead, we too have the same ground of assurance of the resurrection of those who are Christ's at his coming. Had we only the faith of the apostle, we should have his constancy and his joy even in the midst of the greatest afflictions.

15. For all things (are) for your sakes, that the abundant grace might through the thanksgiving of many redound to the glory of God.

In the preceding verse Paul had expressed his confident hope of being delivered even from the grave and presented before God in glory with his Corinthian brethren, *for* all things are for your sakes. They were to be partakers of the salvation which he proclaimed and for which he suffered. All he did and all he suffered was for them. According to this interpretation the *all things* are limited to all things of which he had been speaking, viz. his sufferings, his constancy, and his deliverance. In 1 Cor. 3, 21, however, he says in a much more comprehensive sense, 'All things are yours, whether things present or things to come.' Hence some understand the expression with the same latitude in this passage: 'I expect to be presented *with you*, for all things are for your sakes.' But this does not agree with the latter part of the verse. He evidently means all that he did, and suffered, and experienced. 'They are for your sake, *that* (ἵνα, in order that) the abundant grace or favour manifested to me, might, through the thanksgiving of many, i. e. through your gratitude, called forth by your experience of the blessings flowing from my labour and sufferings, as well as from my deliverance, redound to the glory of God.' This is the sense of the passage, according to the construction of the original, adopted by our translators. Paul says that the favour shown him re-

dounds the more to the glory of God, because others besides
himself are led to give thanks for it. This supposes that in
the Greek, διὰ τῶν πλειόνων, κ.τ.λ. are to be connected with
περισσεύσῃ, *might abound through.* Those words, however,
may be connected with πλεονάσασα, *the grace rendered abundant by many.* This may mean either that the favour shown
the apostle was the more abundant because so many interced-
ed in his behalf. Comp. 1, 11, and Phil. 1, 19. "I know that
this shall turn to my salvation through your prayer." Or the
meaning may be, 'The favour shown me, rendered abundant,
or greatly multiplied, through the participation of many.' In
the one case, Paul says the grace was the greater because so
many prayed for him; in the other, it was the greater because
so many enjoyed the fruits of it. The passage admits of either
of these constructions and explanations; and whichever is preferred the general idea is the same. The church is one. If
one member be honoured, all the members rejoice with it.
If Paul was redeemed from his enemies, all the church gave
thanks to God. A favour shown to him was a favour shown
to all, and was thereby multiplied a thousand-fold and rendered a thousand-fold more prolific of thanksgiving unto God.
Whichever construction be adopted, περισσεύσῃ is to be taken
transitively, as in Eph. 1, 8. 1 Thess. 3, 12. 'Grace causes
thanksgiving to abound.'

16. For which cause we faint not ; but though our
outward man perish, yet the inward (man) is renewed
day by day.

For which cause, that is, because we are sure of a glorious
resurrection, and are satisfied that our present sufferings and
labours will advance the glory of God. *We faint not,* we do
not become discouraged and give up the conflict. On the
contrary, though his outward man, his whole physical constitution, *perish,* διαφθείρεται, be utterly worn out and wasted
away by constant suffering and labour, yet *the inward man,*
the spiritual nature, is renewed, i. e. receives new life and
vigour, day by day. By 'inward man' is not meant simply
the soul as distinguished from the body, but his higher nature
—his soul as the subject of the divine life. Rom. 7, 22.
Eph. 3, 16. Of no unholy man could it be said in the sense
of the apostle that his inward man was daily renewed. It is

not of renewed supplies of animal spirits or of intellectual vigour that the apostle speaks, but of the renewal of spiritual strength to do and suffer. This constant renewal of strength is opposed to fainting. 'We faint not, but are renewed *day by day*,' ἡμέρᾳ καὶ ἡμέρᾳ. This is a Hebraism, Gen. 39, 10. Ps. 68, 19, familiar to our ears but foreign to Greek usage. The supplies of strength came without fail and as they were needed.

17. For our light affliction, which is but for a moment, worketh for us a far more exceeding (and) eternal weight of glory.

This is the reason why we faint not. Our afflictions are light, they are momentary, and they secure eternal glory. Every thing depends upon the standard of judgment. Viewed absolutely, or in comparison with the sufferings of other men, Paul's afflictions were exceedingly great. He was poor, often without food or clothing; his body was weak and sickly; he was homeless; he was beset by cruel enemies; he was repeatedly scourged, he was stoned, he was imprisoned, he was shipwrecked, robbed, and counted as the off-scouring of the earth; he was beyond measure harassed by anxieties and cares, and by the opposition of false teachers, and the corruption of the churches which he had planted at such expense of time and labour. See 1 Cor. 4, 9–13, and 2 Cor. 11, 23–29. These afflictions in themselves, and as they affected Paul's consciousness, were exceedingly great; for he says himself he was pressed out of measure, above strength, so that he despaired even of life. 1, 8. He did not regard these afflictions as trifles, nor did he bear them with stoical indifference. He felt their full force and pressure. When five times scourged by the Jews and thrice beaten with rods, his physical torture was as keen as that which any other man would have suffered under similar inflictions. He was not insensible to hunger, and thirst, and cold, and contempt, and ingratitude. His afflictions were not light in the sense of giving little pain. The Bible does not teach, either by precept or example, that Christians are to bear pain as though it were not pain, or bereavements as though they caused no sorrow. Unless afflictions prove real sorrows, they will not produce the fruits of sorrow. It was only by bringing these sufferings

into comparison with eternal glory that they dwindled into
insignificance. So also when the apostle says that his afflictions were for a moment, it is only when compared with eternity. They were not momentary so far as the present life
was concerned. They lasted from his conversion to his mar-
tyrdom. His Christian life was a protracted dying. But
what is the longest life to everlasting ages? Less than a single second to threescore years. The third source of consolation to the apostle was that his afflictions would secure for
him eternal glory, i. e. the eternal and inconceivable excellence and blessedness of heaven. This is all the words κατεργάζεται ἡμῖν express. Afflictions are the cause of eternal glory.
Not the meritorious cause, but still the procuring cause. God
has seen fit to reveal his purpose not only to reward with exceeding joy the afflictions of his people, but to make those
afflictions the means of working out that joy. This doctrine
is taught in many passages of Scripture. Matt. 19, 29. Rom.
8, 17. 2 Tim. 2, 12. 13. 1 Pet. 1, 6. 4, 13. Rev. 7, 14. It is
not, however, suffering in itself considered which has this effect; and therefore not all suffering; not self-inflicted suffering, not punishment, but only such sufferings which are either
endured for Christ's sake, or which when imposed for the trial
of our faith are sustained with a Christian spirit. We are,
therefore, not to seek afflictions, but when God sends them
we should rejoice in them as the divinely appointed means of
securing for us an eternal weight of glory. Our Lord calls on
those who were persecuted to rejoice and be exceeding glad,
Matt. 5, 12; so does the apostle Peter, 4, 13; and Paul often
asserts that he gloried or rejoiced in his afflictions. Phil. 2, 17.
Col. 1, 24.

The expression τὸ παραυτίκα ἐλαφρὸν τῆς θλίψεως, the momentary lightness of affliction, exhibits the adverb (παραυτίκα)
used as an adjective, and the adjective (ἐλαφρόν) used as a substantive. Comp. 8, 8. 1 Cor. 1, 25. Wetstein and other col-
lectors furnish abundant illustrations of this usage from the
Greek writers. In this carefully balanced sentence, ἐλαφρόν,
light, stands opposed to βάρος, weight, and παραυτίκα, momentary, to αἰώνιον, eternal. In Hebrew the same word signifies
to be heavy, and to be glorious, and the literal meaning of the
Hebrew word for glory is weight, which may have suggested
the peculiar expression " weight of glory." The words καθ᾽
ὑπερβολὴν εἰς ὑπερβολήν, according to excess unto excess, in the
sense of exceeding exceedingly, (one of Paul's struggles with

the impotency of language to express his conceptions,) may be taken as an adjective qualification of βάρος δόξης, *weight of glory*. This is the explanation adopted by our translators, who render the phrase, "far more exceeding, *and* eternal weight of glory." There is, however, no καί (*and*) in the text. If this view be adopted, it would be better therefore to take "eternal weight of glory" as one idea. The eternal glory exceeds all limits. The words in question, however, may be connected adverbially with κατεργάζεται, as proposed by Meyer and De Wette. 'Our light afflictions work exceedingly, i. e. are beyond measure efficacious in securing or producing an eternal weight of glory.'

18. While we look not at the things which are seen, but at the things which are not seen : for the things which are seen (are) temporal ; but the things which are not seen (are) eternal.

The participial clause with which this verse begins (μὴ σκοπούντων ἡμῶν) may have a causal force. 'Our light afflictions are thus efficacious *because* we look not at the things which are temporal.' This, however, is hardly true. The afflictions of Christians do not work out for them eternal glory, *because* their hearts are turned heavenward. It is therefore better to understand the apostle as simply expressing the condition under which the effect spoken of in v. 17 is produced. This is the idea expressed in our version by the word *while*. Afflictions have this salutary operation while (i. e. provided that) we look at the things which are eternal. This clause thus serves to designate the class of persons to whom even the severest afflictions are light, and for whom they secure eternal glory. It is not for the worldly, but for those whose hearts are set on things above. The word translated *look*, σκοπέω, is derived from σκοπός (*scopus, scope*), meaning the mark or goal on which the eye is fixed, as in Phil. 3, 14, κατὰ σκοπὸν διώκω, *I press toward the mark.* Therefore *looking* here means making things unseen the goal on which our eyes are fixed, the end toward which the attention, desires and efforts are directed. As is usual with the apostle, he states both what is not, and what is, the absorbing object of the believer's attention. Not *the visible*, but *the invisible ;* i. e. not the world and the things of the world, but the things which pertain to that state which is to us now invisible. The reason why the latter, and not the former class of objects do thus engross the believer, is that the things seen are *temporal*, or rather, *temporary*, lasting only for a time; whereas the things unseen are eternal. Few passages in Paul's writings exhibit so clearly his inward exercises in the midst of sufferings and under the near prospect of death. He was, when he wrote what is here written, in great affliction. He felt that his life was in constant and imminent danger, and that even if delivered from the violence of his enemies, his strength was gradually wearing away under the uninterrupted trials to which he was subjected. Under these circumstances we see him exhibiting great sensibility to suffering and sorrow; a keen susceptibility in reference to the conduct and feelings of others towards him; a just appreciation of his danger, and yet unshaken confidence in his ultimate triumph; a firm determination not to yield either to opposition or to suffering, but to persevere in the faithful and energetic discharge of the duty which had brought on him all his trials, and a heroic exultation in those very afflictions by which he was so sorely tried. He was sustained by the assurance that the life of Christ secured his life; that if Jesus rose, he should rise also; and by the firm conviction that the more he suffered for the sake of Christ, or in such a way as to honour his divine master, the more glorious he would be through all eternity. Suffering, therefore, became to him not merely endurable, but a ground of exceeding joy.

CHAPTER V.

The confidence expressed in the preceding chapter is justified by showing that the apostle was assured of a habitation in heaven, even if his earthly tabernacle should be destroyed, vs. 1–10. His object in what he had said of himself was not self-commendation. He laboured only for the good of the church, impelled by the love of Christ, whose ambassador he was, in exhorting men to be reconciled to God, vs. 11–21.

The state of believers after death. Vs. 1–10.

PAUL did not faint in the midst of his sufferings, because he knew that even if his earthly house should be destroyed, he

had a house in heaven—not like the present perishable tabernacle, but one not made with hands, and eternal, v. 1.   He
looked forward to the things unseen, because in his present
tabernacle he groaned, desiring to enter his heavenly habitation.   He longed to be unclothed that he might be clothed
upon with his house which is from heaven, vs. 2–4.   This confidence he owed to God, who had given him the Holy Spirit
as a pledge of his salvation, v. 5.   Having this indwelling of
the Spirit he was always in good courage, knowing that as
soon as he should be absent from the body, he would be present with the Lord, vs. 6–8.   Therefore his great desire was to
please him, before whose tribunal he and all other men were
to appear to receive according to their works, vs. 9. 10.

1. For we know that if our earthly house of (this)
tabernacle were dissolved, we have a building of God,
a house not made with hands, eternal in the heavens.

The connection between this passage and the preceding
chapter is plain.   Our light afflictions, Paul had said, work
out for us an eternal weight of glory, *for* we know that even
if our earthly house perishes, we have an everlasting habitation in heaven.   The general sense also of the whole of the
following paragraph is clear.   The apostle expresses the assurance that a blessed state of existence awaited him after
death.   There is, however, no little difficulty in determining
the precise meaning of the figurative language here employed.
Few passages in Paul's writings have awakened a deeper or
more general interest, because it treats of the state of the soul
after death; a subject about which every man feels the liveli-
est concern, not only for himself, but in behalf of those dear
to him.   Where are those who sleep in Jesus before the resurrection?   What is the condition of a redeemed soul when it
leaves the body?   These are questions about which no Christian can be indifferent.   If Paul here answers those inquiries,
the passage must have peculiar value to all the people of God.
This, however, is the very point about which the greatest difficulty exists.   There are three views taken of the passage;
that is, three different answers are given to the question,
What is that building into which the soul enters when the
present body is dissolved?   1. The first answer is, that the
house not made with hands is heaven itself.   2. That it is the

resurrection body. If this be the correct view, then the passage throws no light on the state of the soul between death and the resurrection. It treats solely of what is to happen after Christ's second coming. 3. The third opinion is, that the house into which the soul enters at death is, so to speak, an intermediate body; that is, a body prepared for it and adapted to its condition during the state intermediate between death and the resurrection. This, however, is not a scriptural doctrine. Many philosophers indeed teach that the soul can neither perceive nor act unless in connection with a body; nay, that an individual man is nothing but a revelation of the general principle of humanity in connection with a given corporeal organism, as a tree is the manifestation of the principle of vegetable life through a specific material organization. As therefore vegetable life is, or exists, only in connection with vegetable forms, so the soul exists only in connection with a body. Thus Olshausen in his Commentary, 1 Cor. 15, 42–44, says, Wie ohne Leib keine Seele, so ohne Leiblichkeit keine Seligkeit; Leiblichkeit und die dadurch bedingte Persönlichkeit ist das Ende der Werke Gottes. "As without body there is no soul, so without a corporeal organization there can be no salvation; a corporeal organization, as the necessary condition of personality, is the end of God's work." Still more explicitly, when commenting on verses 19 and 20 of the same chapter, he says, Ein Fortleben als reiner Geist ohne körperliches Organ erkennt der Apostle gar nicht als Möglichkeit an; die Lehre von der Unsterblichkeit der Seele ist der ganzen Bibel, ebenso wie der Name, fremd—und zwar mit vollem Recht, indem ein persönliches Bewusstseyn im geschaffenen Wesen die Schranken des Leibes nothwendig voraussetzt. "The continued existence of the soul as a pure spirit without a body is to the apostle an impossibility. The Bible knows nothing of the doctrine of the immortality of the soul; the very expression is strange to it. And no wonder, for self-consciousness in a created being necessarily supposes the limitation of a bodily organization." Of course all angels must have bodies, and of course also if the soul exists between death and the resurrection it must have a body. Strange to say, however, Olshausen, despite his maxim, "no body no soul," admits the existence of the soul during the interval between death and the resurrection, and yet denies that it has a body. His utterly unsatisfactory attempt to reconcile this contradiction in his theory is, first, that self-consciousness in departed spirits is very obscure—a mere dreamy state of existence; and secondly, that it must be assumed that a relation continues between the soul and the elements of its decaying body in the grave. This is a perfect collapse of the theory. If it involves either of these consequences, that the soul is unconscious after death, or that its life is in connection with its disorganized body, and conditioned by that connection, then it comes in direct conflict with the Scripture, and is exploded as a mere product of the imagination. If the Bible teaches or assumes that a body is necessary to the self-consciousness of the soul, or even to its power to perceive and to express, to act and to be acted upon, then it would be not only natural but necessary to understand the apostle to teach in this passage that the moment the soul leaves its present body it enters into another. Then it would follow either that the only resurrection of which the Scriptures speak takes place at the moment of death, or that there is a body specially fitted for the intermediate state, differing both from the one which we now have, and from that which we are to have at the resurrection. The former of these suppositions contradicts the plain doctrine of the Bible that the resurrection is a future event, to take place at the second advent of Christ; and the latter contradicts this very passage, for Paul says that the house on which we enter at death is eternal. Besides, the Bible knows nothing of any body except the σῶμα ψυχικόν, *the natural body,* which we have now, and the σῶμα πνευματικόν, *the spiritual body,* which we are to receive at the resurrection. We are therefore reduced to the choice between the first and second of the three interpretations mentioned above. The building of which the apostle here speaks must be either a house in heaven, or the resurrection body. If the latter, then Paul teaches, not what is to happen immediately after death, but what is to take place at the second coming of Christ. In opposition to this view, and in favour of the opinion that the house here mentioned is heaven itself, it may be argued, 1. Heaven is often in Scripture compared to a house in which there are many mansions, John 14, 2; or to a city in which there are many houses, Heb. 11, 10. 14. 13, 14. Rev. 21, 10; or more generally to a habitation, Luke 16, 9. 2. The figure in this case is peculiarly appropriate. The body is compared to a house in which the soul now dwells, heaven is the house into which it enters when this earthly house is dissolved. Our Lord told his sorrowing disciples that they should soon be with him, that in his Father's house, whither he went, there were many mansions, and that he would receive them unto himself. 3. The description here given of the house of which the apostle speaks agrees with the descriptions elsewhere given of heaven. It is a building of God; compare Heb. 11, 10, where heaven is said to be a city whose builder and maker is God. It is not made with hands, i. e. not of human workmanship or belonging to the present order of things. In the same sense the true tabernacle in heaven is said to be "not made with hands," Heb. 9, 11. It is eternal, because the state on which the soul enters at death is unchanging. And finally, this house is said to be "in heaven," or, we are said to have it "in heaven." This last clause is not consistent with the assumption that the house spoken of is the resurrection body. That body is not now in heaven awaiting our arrival there, nor is it to be brought down to us *from* heaven. But the mansion which Christ has gone to prepare for his people is in heaven; and therefore the apostle in raising his eyes heavenward could appropriately say, 'If this tabernacle be dissolved I have a house in heaven.' 4. The principal argument in favour of this interpretation is that the house spoken of is one on which the soul enters immediately after death. This is plain because Paul says, that if our earthly house be dissolved *we have*, i. e. we have at once, a house in heaven. The whole context requires this explanation to be given to ἔχομεν, *we have*. The apostle is speaking of the grounds of consolation in the immediate prospect of death. He says in effect that the dissolution of the body does not destroy the soul or deprive it of a home. His consolation was that if unclothed he would not be found naked. While at home in the body he was absent from the Lord, but as soon as he was absent from the body he would be present with the Lord. It is so obvious that the apostle is here speaking of what takes place at death, that those who maintain that the building referred to is the resurrection body, propose various methods of getting over the difficulty. Some, as Usteri, assume that Paul, when he wrote the first epistle to the Corinthians, believed that the resurrection was not to take place until the second advent of Christ, but changed his view and here teaches that it takes place at death. That is, that the soul when it leaves the present body is furnished with that spiritual body which in the former epistle he taught was not to be received until Christ comes the second time. To those who proceed on the assumption of the inspiration of Scripture, this unnatural explanation needs no refutation. In his epistle to the Philippians, written still later, he teaches the same doctrine that we find in First Corinthians. He must, therefore, have reverted to his former view. Paul was not thus driven about by every wind of doctrine. Even those who deny his inspiration must admit his consistency. Others say that as the apostle confidently expected to survive the second advent, he here speaks of what he anticipated in his own case. He believed he would not die, but be changed at once as described in 1 Cor. 15, 51. 52. But even admitting that Paul at this time did expect to survive the coming of the Lord, that is not the expectation here expressed. On the contrary, he is speaking of what would take place ($\dot{\varepsilon}\dot{\alpha}\nu$) even in case he should die. If, worn out by his sufferings, his earthly house should be dissolved before Christ came, still he knew he should have a house in heaven. Others again say that the interval between death and the resurrection is not taken into account, but that the apostle, after the manner of the prophets, speaks of events as chronologically coincident which in fact are separated by a long period of time. But this does not meet the difficulty. As the apostle is speaking of the ground of consolation in the prospect of death, he must be understood to refer, not to what might be expected at an indefinite period after that event, but to its immediate consequence. He did not glory in his afflictions because when his earthly house should be dissolved he would sink into a state of unconsciousness until the resurrection; but because he would have another and unspeakably better habitation. This is evident, because he speaks of his being absent from the body as the immediate antecedent of his being present with the Lord; which is only another form of saying he would be clothed upon with his house which is from heaven. 5. A fifth consideration in favour of the interpretation in question, is derived from the analogy of Scripture. The Bible in other places teaches that the souls of believers do at their death immediately pass into glory. Our Lord in refuting the Sadducees, who denied the existence of spirits, said, "Have ye not read that which was spoken unto you by God, saying, I am the God of Abraham, the God of Isaac, and the God of Jacob? God is not the God of the dead, but of the living," Matt. 22, 32. Abraham, Isaac and Jacob therefore are living, and not in a dreamy state of semi-conscious existence. In the parable of the rich man and Lazarus, we are told that when Lazarus died he was carried by angels into Abraham's bosom, i. e. to heaven. On the mount of transfiguration, Moses and Elias appeared talking with Christ. Our Lord said to the dying thief, "This day shalt thou be with me in paradise," and paradise, as we learn from 2 Cor. 12, 2 and 4, is the third heaven. In Phil. 1, 22–24, Paul says that although he had a desire to depart and be with Christ, yet his abiding in the flesh was more needful for them. This clearly implies that as soon as he departed from the flesh he expected to be present with the Lord. This flows from the perfection of Christ's work. As his blood cleanses from all sin, there is no process of expiation or purification to be endured or experienced by believers after death. And as we know, as our Lord says, that they still live, they must enter on the blessedness secured by his merits. Accordingly the apostle says that the saints on earth and the saints in heaven form one communion. "We are come unto Mount Zion—and unto the spirits of just men made perfect," Heb. 12, 23.

The considerations above presented appear decisive in favour of understanding the apostle to mean by the house not made with hands, a mansion in heaven into which believers enter as soon as their earthly tabernacle is dissolved. It is, however, objected to this view of the passage, that as the earthly house is the present body, the heavenly house must also be a body. This, however, does not follow. The comparison is not of one body with another; but of one house with another. We dwell now in an earthly tabernacle; after death, we shall dwell in a heavenly house. This is all that the figure demands. In the second place, it is urged that in v. 2 it is said our house is "from heaven," and if from heaven it is not heaven itself. But our resurrection body is not *from* heaven in the local sense. It is from heaven only in the general sense of being heavenly, and in this sense our house is of heaven. It is not of the earth, does not belong to the present state of existence, but to that on which we enter in heaven. Besides, it is not heaven considered as a state, nor even as a place, (in the wide sense of the word heaven,) that is our house, but the mansion which the Lord has gone to prepare for his people in heaven. The simple idea is that the soul, when it leaves its earthly tabernacle, will not be lost in immensity, nor driven away houseless and homeless, but will find a house and home in heaven. This is the consoling doctrine here taught. The soul of the believer does not cease to exist at death. It does not sink into a state of unconsciousness. It does not go into purgatory; but, being made perfect in holiness, it does immediately pass into glory. As soon as it is absent from the body, it is present with the Lord. This is all that is revealed, and this is enough. What Paul learnt more than this when he was caught up into the third heaven, he was not permitted to make known.

As Paul is speaking of himself in this whole connection, when he says *we know*, he does not refer to a knowledge common to all men, nor to other Christians, but he expresses his personal conviction—*I know*. *That if*, ἐάν, *if as it may;* (not *although*). The apostle is speaking of his afflictions, which were wearing away his strength; and says, 'Even if my sufferings should prove fatal, and my earthly house be dissolved, I have another habitation.' *Our earthly house of this tabernacle*, i. e. our earthly house which is a tabernacle, ὁ σκῆνος, a frail, temporary abode, as opposed to a stable, permanent building. See 2 Peter 1, 13. 14. *Is dissolved*, i. e. its component parts separated either by violence or decay, so that it falls in pieces. *We have*, i. e. I have, as he is speaking of himself. The present tense, ἔχομεν, is used because the one event immediately follows the other; there is no perceptible interval between the dissolution of the earthly tabernacle and entering on the heavenly house. As soon as the soul leaves the body it *is* in heaven. *A building of God*, οἰκοδομὴν ἐκ θεοῦ, a building from God, one provided by him, and of which he is the builder and maker, Heb. 11, 10, and therefore is said to be *not made with hands*, i. e. not like the buildings erected by man. Comp. Heb. 9, 11 and Col. 2, 11. The latter passage refers to the circumcision of the heart as the immediate work of God; it is therefore said to be ἀχειροποίητος. The soul therefore at death enters a house whose builder is God. This is said to exalt to the utmost our conceptions of its glory and excellence. Being made by God it is *eternal*. It is to last forever; and we are never to leave it. We dwell in our present bodies only for a little while, as in a tent; but heaven is an abode which, once entered, is retained forever. The words *in the heavens* may be connected with *house*, in the sense of heavenly, i. e. a celestial house. This construction is assumed in our version where the words "eternal in the heavens" are made to qualify or describe the house spoken of. The natural connection of the words, however, is with (ἔχομεν) *we have.* 'If our earthly house be dissolved, we have in heaven a house of God, not made with hands, and eternal.'

2. For in this we groan, earnestly desiring to be clothed upon with our house which is from heaven.

This verse must, from the force of the connecting particle (γάρ) *for*, be a confirmation of what precedes, but whether of what is said in v. 1, or at close of preceding chapter, is doubtful. The words καὶ γάρ may mean either *for also*, or *for even*. If the former, this verse is condinate with v. 1, and assigns an additional reason why the apostle looked at the things unseen and eternal. He thus looked *for* he knew he had in heaven a house not made with hands, and *because* he earnestly desired to enter that house. If the latter explanation of the particles be preferred, the sense is, 'I know I have a house in heaven, *for even* in this I groan, desiring to be clothed with my house which is from heaven.' In this case the argument would be, 'There is such a house, for I long for it.' This, however, is hardly a scriptural argument. Paul's confidence in a state of blessedness beyond the grave was not founded on the obscure aspirations of his nature, but on express revelation from God. Rom. 8, 22 is not parallel, for there the groaning of the creation is presented, not as a proof of future blessedness, but to show that the creature is subject to vanity, *not willingly* nor finally. *In this*, i. e. in this tabernacle, as the word σκῆνος is used in v. 1, and also v. 4. *We groan earnestly desiring*, i. e. we groan because we desire. The groaning is the expression of this longing after his heavenly home; and not, as in v. 4, of suffering caused by afflictions. The ἐπί in ἐπιποθοῦντες is either intensive, *earnestly* desiring, or it expresses the tendency of the desire. The word and its cognates are always used in the New Testament to express strong desire or longing. What the apostle thus longed for was, ἐπενδύσασθαι, *to be clothed upon*, i. e. to put on over, as an outer garment. *With our house which is from heaven.* As the body is familiarly compared sometimes to a house in which the soul dwells, and sometimes to a garment with which it is clothed, the two figures are here combined, and the apostle speaks of putting on a house as though it were a garment. Both are a covering and a protection. *Our house*, οἰκητήριον, i. e. *dwelling*, more specific than the general term οἰκία, *a building*. *Which is from heaven*, ἐξ οὐρανοῦ, i. e. heavenly, as distinguished from a dwelling which is ἐκ γῆς, *of the earth.* 1 Cor. 15, 47. It is not "of this building," ταύτης τῆς κτίσεως, Heb. 9, 11. Those who understand this whole passage to treat of the change which is to take place in those believers who shall be alive when the Lord comes, and which is described in 1 Cor. 15, 51–54, lay special stress on this verse. They urge that this house being *from* heaven cannot be heaven; and that the verb ἐπενδύω, meaning *to put on over,* evidently refers to the putting on of the new body, as it were, over the old one; and therefore can be understood only of those who, being in the body when Christ comes, are thus clothed *upon* without being unclothed. It has already been remarked that there is no force in the former of these arguments, because the new body is not *from* heaven. It is ἐξ οὐρανοῦ only in the sense of being heavenly, and in that sense the expression suits the idea of a building as well as that of a body. As to the second argument, it may be admitted, that if the context demanded, or even naturally admitted of our understanding "the house not made with hands" to be the resurrection body, there would be a peculiar propriety in the use of the word ἐπενδύσασθαι, (to be clothed *upon,*) instead of the simple verb ἐνδύσασθαι, *to be clothed.* But the use of this word is not sufficient to determine the interpretation of the whole passage. 1. Because nothing is more common than the use of compound verbs in the same sense as the corresponding simple ones. 2. Because in 1 Cor. 15, 53. 54, Paul uses the simple verb (ἐνδύσασθαι) four times to express the very thing which it is here urged he must refer to because he uses the compound ἐπενδύσασθαι. That is, he uses the two words in the same sense. He makes no difference between "putting on" and being "clothed *upon.*" We are not required, therefore, by the use of the latter expression, to infer that the apostle speaks of the change which those who are in the body should experience at the coming of Christ. This view, as remarked above, is out of keeping with the whole context. Paul was daily exposed to death, his outward man was perishing. His consolation was that if his earthly tabernacle were dissolved, he had a better house in heaven. He earnestly longed for that house; to be absent from the body and to be present with the Lord. All he says is said on the hypothesis of his dying, and therefore he cannot say he earnestly desired to escape death. What he longed for was, not that he might be alive when Christ came, and thus escape the pains of dissolution, but that he might quit his mud hovel and enter in that house not made with hands, eternal in the heavens.

3. If so be that being clothed we shall not be found naked.

Few verses in this epistle have been more variously explained than this. In the first place the reading is doubtful. The received text has εἴγε, which the great majority of the critical editions also adopt; Lachmann, on the authority of the manuscripts, B, D, E, F, G, reads εἴπερ. The latter (*if so be, provided*) expresses doubt; the former (*since*) expresses certainty. This distinction, however, is not strictly observed in Paul's writings. See 1 Cor. 8, 5. Gal. 3, 4. Col. 1, 23. 2 Thess. 1, 6. A more important diversity is that several ancient manuscripts and most of the Fathers read ἐκδυσάμενοι (*unclothed*) instead of ἐνδυσάμενοι (*clothed*). The former renders the passage much plainer. 'We earnestly desire to be clothed with our house from heaven, since (or, even if) being unclothed we shall not be found naked.' That is, 'Although despoiled of our earthly tabernacle we shall not be found houseless.' Mill, Semler and Rückert prefer this reading, but the weight of authority is in favour of the received text. There are three general modes of explaining this passage which have been adopted. 1. Calvin among the older commentators, and Usteri and Olshausen among the moderns, say that the words *clothed* and *naked* must be understood to refer to the moral or spiritual state of the soul; to its being clothed with righteousness or being destitute of that robe. Calvin says the apostle's design is to limit the blessedness spoken of in the preceding verses to the righteous. The wicked are to be despoiled of their bodies and will appear naked before God; but believers, being clothed in the righteousness of Christ, will stand before him in the glorious vesture of immortality. There are two garments, therefore, he says, referred to ; the one, the righteousness of Christ, received in this life; the other, immortal glory, received at death. The former is the cause and necessary condition of the latter. Calvin lays special stress on the καί, *also*, which is inserted for the sake of amplification, as though Paul had said, 'A new garment shall be prepared for believers at death if also (or already) in this life they were clothed.' This interpretation, however, is evidently out of keeping with the context. It is very unnatural to make the same words have such different meanings in the same connection. In v. 2 we are said to be clothed with our house from heaven; in v. 3 we are so clothed as not to be found naked, and in v. 4 Paul speaks of being unclothed. If in vs. 2 and 4 the word refers to a body or house, in v. 3 it cannot refer to the robe of righteousness. Being unclothed is evidently the opposite of being clothed. As the former refers to laying aside the earthly tabernacle, the latter must refer to our being invested with the house from heaven. Besides, any such distinction between the righteous and the wicked, or any caution that the unrighteous are not to be received into heaven, as this interpretation supposes, is foreign to the design of the passage. Paul is not speaking of the general destiny of men after death, but of his own personal experience and conviction. 'I know,' he says, 'that if I die I have a house in heaven, and being clothed with that house I shall not be found naked.' There is no room here for a warning to the unrighteous. They are not at all brought into view.

2. The second general view of this passage is founded on the assumption that v. 2 speaks of the change to be effected in those who shall be alive when Christ comes. According to Grotius the meaning is, 'We shall be clothed upon (i. e. invested with a new body over the present one), if so be that day shall find us clothed (i. e. in the body) and not *naked* (i. e. bodiless spirits).' That is, we shall experience the change mentioned in v. 2, provided we are alive when Christ comes. To this, however, it is objected, first, that as the event of Paul's being alive at that time was entirely uncertain, and is here so presented, the appropriate particle would be εἴπερ (*if so be*) and not εἴγε (*if*, as is sure to be the case); and second, that this interpretation is inconsistent with the force of the aorist participle ἐνδυσάμενοι. The sense given to the passage would require the perfect ἐνδεδυμένοι, *being then clothed*. According to Meyer the meaning is, 'If, as is certain to be the case, we in fact (καί) shall be found clothed, and not naked.' That is, 'If clothed upon with our house from heaven (i. e. the new body) we shall not be found bodiless when Christ comes.' This interpretation suits the words, but not the connection. As before remarked, the whole passage proceeds on the hypothesis of death. 'If I die,' says the apostle, 'so and so will happen.' This being the case, he cannot be understood to state what would happen if he did not die, but

survived the coming of the Lord.   Besides, the whole basis of
this interpretation is unsound.   Paul did not expect to survive
the second advent, as is plain from 2 Thess. 2, 1–6.   See the
comment on 1 Cor. 15, 51.

3. The third interpretation assumes that the apostle refers
not to the spiritual body but to a mansion in heaven.   In the
preceding verse he said that he earnestly desired to be clothed
upon with his house from heaven, "since," he adds, "being
clothed, we shall not be found (i. e. shall not be) naked."   As
the house from heaven is spoken of as a garment, being houseless is expressed by the word *naked*.   This interpretation
gives the same translation of the words as the preceding, but
a different exposition of their meaning; and it has the advantage of agreeing logically with the context and with the elevated tone of the whole passage.   'If I die,' says Paul, 'I
know I have a home in heaven, and I earnestly desire to enter
on that heavenly house, since when driven from this earthly
tabernacle I shall not be houseless and homeless.'   According
to this view the object of his desire was the glory and blessedness of heaven; according to the other, it was that he might
live until Christ came, and thus escape the pain of dying.
This was an object comparatively insignificant, and utterly
out of keeping with the heroic spirit which pervades the
whole context.

4. For we that are in (this) tabernacle do groan,
being burdened: not for that we would be unclothed,
but clothed upon, that mortality might be swallowed
up of life.

This verse gives the reason of the desire expressed in v. 2.
'We desire our house which is from heaven, *for* in this we
groan, &c.'   The words οἱ ὄντες mean *we who are*, not 'whilst
we are,' which would require the simple ὄντες without the article.   *In this tabernacle*, ἐν τῷ σκήνει, literally, in *the* tabernacle, i. e. the tabernacle mentioned in v. 1, and implied in v. 2.
Do groan being burdened, i. e. because burdened.   The burden meant may be the affliction by which Paul was overwhelmed; or the body itself; or the longing after a better
world.   As this passage is intimately connected with the preceding chapter, in which the apostle had spoken so freely of
his sufferings, and as his experience in view of death was de-

termined by those sufferings, it is perfectly natural to understand him to refer to the burden of sorrow. It was because
he suffered so much that he groaned to be delivered, i. e. to
be absent from the body and present with the Lord. *Not
that we would be unclothed.* The words are ἐφ' ᾧ, which in
Rom. 5, 12 mean *propterea quod*, 'because that;' but here
they more naturally mean *quare*, 'wherefore.' They introduce the reason of what follows, not of what precedes. 'On
which account,' i. e. because we are thus burdened we desire,
&c. If ἐφ' ᾧ be taken in the sense of *because that* the sense is
just the opposite. Then this clause states the nature of the
burden under which the apostle groaned. 'We groan *because that* we do not wish to be unclothed.' It was then the
dread of death, or the desire to be glorified without the necessity of dying, that was the object of the apostle's intense
desire. This is altogether unworthy of the man and inconsistent with the context. Paul says, 'We groan being burdened, *wherefore*, i. e. because thus burdened, we do not wish
to die; death is not that for which we long, but that which
comes after death. It is not mere exemption from the burden of life, from its duties, its labours or its sufferings, which
is the object of desire, but to be in heaven.' The passage is
in its spirit and meaning altogether parallel with v. 8. "Willing rather to be absent from the body and present with the
Lord." *To be unclothed* means to lay aside our earthly tabernacle. *To be clothed upon* means to enter the house not made
with hands. As the earthly house is compared to a garment,
so is the heavenly house. *That mortality* (τὸ θνητόν, *that
which is mortal*) *may be swallowed up of life,* i. e. absorbed
by it so that the one ceases to appear and the other becomes
dominant. Comp. 1 Cor. 15, 53. 54. This is the elevated object of the apostle's longing desire. It was not death, not
annihilation, nor mere exemption from suffering; but to be
raised to that higher state of existence in which all that was
mortal, earthly and corrupt about him should be absorbed in
the life of God, that divine and eternal life arising from the
beatific vision of God, and consisting in perfect knowledge,
holiness and blessedness.

5. Now, he that hath wrought us for the selfsame
thing (is) God, who also hath given unto us the earnest
of the Spirit.

It was something very heroic and grand for a poor, persecuted man to stand thus erect in the presence of his enemies
and in the immediate prospect of death, and avow such superiority to all suffering, and such confidence of a glorious immortality. The apostle, therefore, adds that neither the
elevated feelings which he expressed, nor his preparation for
the exalted state of existence which he so confidently expected, was due to himself. *He who hath wrought us for the
selfsame thing is God.* The words εἰς αὐτὸ τοῦτο, *to this very
thing*, naturally refers to what immediately precedes, the
being clothed upon so that mortality should be swallowed up
of life. For this elevated destiny God had prepared him;
not created him, but (ὁ κατεργασάμενος) made him fit by giving
the requisite qualifications. He was, as a believer, looking
forward with joyful expectation to his home in heaven, the
workmanship of God. *Who also hath given unto us the
earnest of the Spirit.* God had not only prepared him for
future glory, but had given him the assurance of a blessed
immortality, of which the indwelling of the Holy Ghost
was the earnest, i. e. a foretaste and pledge. 1, 22. Eph. 1,
13. 14. Rom. 5, 5. 8, 16. According to the view given
above of the context, the object of the apostle's desire was
not the resurrection, nor the change which the living believer is to experience at Christ's coming, but the state of
glory immediately subsequent to death. It is therefore of
that the Holy Spirit is here declared to be the earnest. Elsewhere, as in Rom. 8, 11, the indwelling of the Spirit is represented as the pledge of the future life of the body, because he
is the source of that life which the believer derives from
Christ, and which pertains to the body as well as to the soul.
Comp. 1 Cor. 6, 19. All therefore in whom the Spirit dwells,
i. e. manifests his permanent presence by producing within
them the Christian graces, have the pledge of immediate admission into heaven when they die, and of a glorious resurrection when the Lord comes.

6. Therefore (we are) always confident, knowing
that, whilst we are at home in the body, we are absent
from the Lord.

The grammatical construction in this and the following
verse, 8, is interrupted and irregular, which our translators

have helped out by inserting the words *we are*, thus turning the participle θαρροῦντες into a verb. The unfinished sentence in v. 6 is resumed and completed in v. 8. Omitting the words of resumption in v. 8, the whole sentence stands thus: " Being confident and knowing that whilst at home in the body, we are absent from the Lord, we are desirous (εὐδοκοῦμεν) rather to be absent from the body and present with the Lord." This verse is introduced as a consequence of what precedes. 'Having the earnest of the Spirit, *therefore* we are confident.' This confidence is not a mere temporary feeling due to some transient excitement; but a permanent state of mind. Being *always*, πάντοτε, on all occasions and under all circumstances, even in the midst of dangers and discouragements which, were it not for divine support, would produce despair. The ground of the boldness and confidence expressed by the word θαρροῦν-τες is not any thing in the believer; it is not his natural courage, not the strength of his convictions; but it is a state of mind produced by the indwelling of the Spirit, and the natural consequence of his presence. *Being confident and knowing ;* both these particles are grammatically constructed with the verb *we are willing*, εὐδοκοῦμεν, in v. 8, and together express the ground of the apostle's desire to be absent from the body. *Knowing that, whilst we are at home in the body, we are absent from the Lord.* The words ἐνδημέω, to be at home (literally, among one's people), and ἐκδημέω are opposed to each other. The figure is slightly changed from that used in the preceding verses. There it was a house, here a city, at least δῆμος, *people*, naturally suggests that idea. Comp. Phil. 3, 20. Heb. 11, 13. 13, 14.

7. (For we walk by faith, not by sight.)

This is a passing, parenthetical remark, intended as a confirmation of the preceding declaration. 'We are absent from the Lord, *for* we now, in this life, walk by faith.' The passage is parallel to Rom. 8, 24, " We are saved by hope (or in hope, i. e. in prospect)." Salvation is not a present, but a future good. So here, presence with the Lord is now a matter of faith, not of fruition. The condition of our present state of being is that of believing. The faith which is the evidence of things not seen and the substance (or assurance) of things hoped for, is the element in which we live, so long as we are not present with those things. Being the objects of faith they

are of course absent. The preposition, διά, may have its ordinary force, "We walk *by means of* faith;" it is by faith we
regulate our walk through life. Or it may be used here as in
Rom. 8, 25. Heb. 12, 1, and elsewhere, to mark the attending
circumstances, "we wait *with* patience," "let us run *with*
patience," "we walk *with* faith." *And not by sight.* The
word εἶδος does not mean the sense of sight, but the thing
seen, form, appearance, that which is the object of sight. In
Luke 3, 22, the Spirit is said to have descended σωματικῷ εἴδει,
in a bodily shape; in 9, 29 it is said of our Lord that the
εἶδος τοῦ προσώπου αὐτοῦ, *the fashion of his face was changed;*
and in John 5, 37 our Lord tells the Jews, speaking of the
Father, "Ye have never heard his voice or seen his (εἶδος)
shape." If this, the proper signification of the word, be retained, then εἶδος is the object of faith, the form and fashion
of the things believed. *Loco rei verbo acquiescimus,* as
Calvin expresses it. We are conversant with the report of
heavenly things, not with the things themselves. We are
absent, not present with them. In this case διά means *with.*
'We are not surrounded with the forms of things in heaven.'
It is no objection to this interpretation that the preposition
διά has a different force given to it in the second clause, from
that commonly given to it in the first clause of the verse.
'We walk *by* faith, and not *with,* or *in presence of* the objects
of our faith.' This change in the force of the same preposition in the same sentence is not unusual. See Heb. 9, 11. 12.
10, 20. The majority of commentators, however, depart from
the proper signification of the word εἶδος and take it in the
sense of ὄψις, because this agrees best with the antithesis to
πίστις (*faith*) and with the force of the preposition. "We
walk by faith, not by sight;" we believe, but do not see
things which govern our life. This, no doubt, is the idea
which the apostle intended, although not precisely the form
in which he has expressed it.

8. We are confident, (I say,) and willing rather to
be absent from the body, and to be present with the
Lord.

The sentence begun and left incomplete in v. 6 is here
resumed and carried out. Θαρροῦμεν δέ, *we are of good courage.*
The particle δέ may either serve to indicate the resumption of
what he had begun to say in v. 6, or be taken adversatively in

reference to v. 7. 'We walk by faith, not by sight, *nevertheless* we are not discouraged.' We are not only not despond-
ing, but are so confident as to prefer to be absent from the
body. Death is not an object of dread, but of desire. That
the phrase "to be absent from the body" means *to die* is evident, not only from the import of the expression and from
the parallel passage in Phil. 1, 23, but also from the whole
context, which treats of the apostle's experience in view of
death. He was surrounded by dangers; he could scarcely
bear up under the load of his sufferings; he was every day
exposed to a violent death, which he had escaped hitherto
only, as it were, by miracle; still he was not cast down. He
sustained his courage, and even desired to die. There can be
no doubt that this verse is parallel with v. 4, where the apostle
says he desired to be clothed upon, i. e. with his house which
is from heaven. The object of desire is the same in both.
It is also plain that in this verse it is absence from the body
and presence with the Lord, not the being changed from cor-
ruptible to incorruptible without dying, that he earnestly
longed for; and therefore this verse shows that the subject
treated of in the context is the change which the believer
experiences at death, and not that which those who are alive
shall experience at Christ's second coming. The words ἐκδημέω and ἐνδημέω, here used as in v. 6, are best rendered 'from
home' and 'at home.' 'We would be from home as to the
body, and at home with the Lord.' THE LORD is of course
Christ, the supreme Lord, who in virtue of the fulness of the
Godhead is the rightful sovereign and possessor of the universe, and in virtue of his dying for the redemption of his
people, in a peculiar sense the sovereign and possessor of believers. The Christian's heaven is to be with Christ, for we
shall be like him when we see him as he is. Into his presence
the believer passes as soon as he is absent from the body, and
into his likeness the soul is at death immediately transformed;
and when at the resurrection, the body is made like unto his
glorious body, the work of redemption is consummated.
Awaiting this consummation, it is an inestimable blessing to
be assured that believers, as soon as they are absent from the
body, are present with THE LORD.

9. Wherefore we labour, that, whether present or
absent, we may be accepted of him.

Wherefore, διὸ καί, *wherefore also,* i. e. because we desire to be with the Lord. Longing after communion with him produces the desire and secures the effort to be found acceptable to him. Those who have this hope purify themselves as he is pure. 1 John 3, 3. It is impossible that those who regard the presence of Christ, or being with him, as heaven, should not desire and labour to be pleasing to him, by living in obedience to his commandments. *We labour.* The word φιλοτιμεῖσθαι means more than to labour. It signifies literally, to love honour, to be ambitious; and then to make any thing a point of honour, or to set one's honour in doing or attaining something. So Paul says, he made it a point of honour not to build on another man's foundation. Rom. 15, 20. And here he intends to say that as ambitious men desire and strive after fame, so Christians long and labour to be acceptable to Christ. Love to him, the desire to please him, and to be pleasing to him, animates their hearts and governs their lives, and makes them do and suffer what heroes do for glory. *Whether present or absent.* These words may be variously explained. 1. The sense may be, 'Whether present *in the body,* or absent *from the body,*' i. e. whether living or dying. Comp. Rom. 14, 8, "Whether we live, we live unto the Lord; or whether we die, we die unto the Lord." 1 Thess. 5, 10, "Whether we wake or sleep, we live together with him." The connection is then either with φιλοτιμούμεθα, 'we strive whether in the body or out of the body; i. e. the desire in question is active as well in the living as the dead;' or, as is better, with εὐάρεστοι εἶναι, 'we strive to be acceptable whether in the body or absent from it.' 2. The sense may be, 'Whether present *with the Lord,* or absent *from the Lord.*' This is only expressing the same idea in a different form. Whether living or dead, as in Rom. 14, 8. 3. Meyer takes the words literally, 'Whether at home or abroad.' But this is utterly inconsistent with the context. The objection to the first interpretation, that the desire to be acceptable to the Lord when actually saved, must cease, inasmuch as the object is attained, is of no force. The thing desired, τὸ ζητούμενον, as Chrysostom says, is that we may be pleasing to Christ whether here or there, whether in this world or the next.

10. For we must all appear before the judgment-seat of Christ; that every one may receive the things

(done) in (his) body, according to that he hath done, whether (it be) good or bad.

In what precedes Paul had been speaking of himself. It was his own sufferings, hopes, and efforts which the occasion called upon him to exhibit. In all this, however, he spoke as a Christian, and therefore in the name of other Christians. In this verse he expressly comprehends others, and all others. 'I strive to be acceptable to the Lord, *for* we must all (I as well as all believers, and even all men) must, &c.' As Christ is to decide upon our eternal destiny, it is of infinite moment that we should be acceptable, or well-pleasing, in his sight. *We must all appear,* φανερωθῆναι. This means either nothing more than a judicial appearance, as when any one is said to appear in court before a judge; or, as Bengel explains it, *manifestos fieri cum occultis nostris,* 'we must all stand revealed in our true character before the judgment-seat of Christ.' 1 Cor. 4, 5. Col. 3, 4. As there can be no disguise, no deception before an omniscient judge, Paul was assiduous in his efforts to be prepared to stand the scrutiny of an all-seeing eye. *The judgment-seat of Christ;* βῆμα, literally, *step,* then a raised platform, or seat; most frequently used of the elevated seat on which the Roman magistrates sat to administer justice, an object of reverence and fear to all the people. As Christ is to be the judge, as all men are to appear before him, as the secrets of the heart are to be the grounds of judgment, it is obvious that the sacred writers believed Christ to be a divine person, for nothing less than omniscience could qualify any one for the office here ascribed to our Lord. *That every one may receive,* κομίζω, which in the active form means *to take up,* in the middle, as here, *to take for one's self,* properly to take or receive what is one's due, or what on some ground one is entitled to. Matt. 25, 27. Col. 3, 25. 2 Pet. 2, 13. The punishment which men are to receive will be what they have earned, and therefore what is in justice due to them. The reward of the righteous, although a matter of grace and not of justice, yet being, agreeably to the tenor of the covenant of grace, according to their works, it is of the nature of a reward. The pay of a faithful soldier is a matter of debt, titles and estates are matters of favour. There is no inconsistency, therefore, in the Scriptures denying all merit to believers, and yet teaching that they shall be rewarded according to their works. We are said to receive *the things*

done in the body, because the matter is conceived of, or is
here represented as an investment. Our acts are treasures
laid up for the future, whether treasures of wrath, or treasures
in heaven; and these (κομιζόμεθα) *we receive back*. The words
τὰ διὰ τοῦ σώματος may mean *things (done) through or by the
body*. Then bodily acts are taken for acts of all kinds. Compare Rom. 8, 13. Or the διά may be taken as in v. 7, (according to one interpretation of that verse,) as indicating the attending circumstance—*with the body*, i. e. while clothed with
the body. This is the sense expressed in our version, which
renders the clause "things (done) *in* the body," although διά
of course does not mean *in*. *According to that he hath done*,
πρὸς ἃ ἔπραξεν, indicating the rule according to which the
retributions of the final judgments are to be administered.
Both with regard to the wicked and the righteous, there is to
be a great distinction in the recompense, which different members of each class are to receive. Some will be beaten with
few stripes, and some with many. It will be more tolerable
in that day for Tyre and Sidon than for those who reject the
gospel; and on the other hand, those believers who suffer
most, will love most and be most blessed. *Whether good or
evil*, i. e. whether he did good or evil. Each shall receive
according to his deeds whether good or bad. It is from such
passages as this that some American theologians have inferred
that the only benefit which the believer receives from Christ
is the forgiveness of sin, and that being pardoned he is dealt
with according to the principles of justice. Others, especially
in Germany, have drawn from the same source the conclusion
that the doctrine of Paul is that the merit of Christ cleanses
only from the sins committed before conversion. If a Jew or
Gentile became a Christian his sins were blotted out, and then
he was rewarded or punished, saved or lost, according to his
works. The merit of Christ availed nothing for the pardon
of sin after conversion. And this again is very much the
ancient doctrine that there is no forgiveness for post-baptismal
sins. The benefits of Christ's work, according to many of the
ancients, are conveyed to the soul in baptism, but if once for-
feited by sin can never be reapplied. This gloomy doctrine,
which belonged to the transition period which preceded the
full development of the theology of the Papal church, has been
revived by the inchoate Romanists of the present day. But
according to the Scriptures and the doctrine of all Protestant
churches, the blood of Jesus Christ cleanses from all sin,

whether committed before or after baptism or conversion. It is a fountain to which we may daily come for cleansing. He is a priest who ever lives to make intercession for us, and who ever presents before God the merit of his sacrifice as a perpetual offering, typified by the morning and evening sacrifice under the law. According to the anti-scriptural views mentioned above, when a man first comes to Christ his sins are forgiven, and he then commences anew under the covenant of works, and stands in the same relation to God that Adam did before the fall. The condition of salvation is to him as it was to our first parent, "Do this and live." Christ henceforth profits him nothing. But according to the apostle we are not under the law, but under grace. Rom. 6, 14. On the ground of the one offering of Christ, by which those who believe are forever sanctified, (i. e. atoned for,) God does not impute to the penitent believer his sins unto condemnation. He is not judged by the law or treated according to its principles, for then no man could be saved. But he is treated as one for all whose sins, past, present, and future, an infinite satisfaction has been made, and who has a perpetual claim to that satisfaction so long as he is united to Christ by faith and the indwelling of his Spirit. Hence the Scriptures are filled with exhortations not merely to the unconverted, to Jews and Pagans, but to baptized Christians, to repent of sin and to believe in the Lord Jesus Christ; that is, to exercise trust in the merit of his sacrifice and the prevalence of his intercession for the pardon of their daily and manifold transgressions and shortcomings. The sacrifice of Christ avails for the sins committed from the foundation of the world to the final consummation. It affords a permanent and all-sufficient reason why God can be just and yet justify the ungodly.

Paul's defence of himself against the charge of self-commendation. Vs. 11–21.

He declares that he acted under a solemn sense of his responsibility to God, v. 11. This was not said with the view of commending himself; but rather to afford them the means of vindicating his character, v. 12. Whether his way of speaking of himself was extravagant or moderate, sane or insane, his motive in doing as he did was a sincere regard to the glory of God and the good of his church, v. 13. For the love of Christ constrained him to live, not for himself, but for

him who died for him and rose again, vs, 14. 15. Acting under the control of this elevated principle, he was raised above
the influence of external things.   He did not judge of men by
their external condition.   He was a new creature in virtue of
his union with Christ, vs. 16. 17.   This great change which he
had experienced was not self-wrought; it was of God, who is
the author of the whole scheme of redemption.   He is reconciled unto the world through Jesus Christ, and he has commissioned his ministers to proclaim this great truth to all
men, vs. 18. 19.   Therefore, the apostle, as an ambassador of
God, exhorted men to accept of this offer of reconciliation, for
which the most abundant provision had been made, in that
God had made Christ to be sin for us, in order that we might
be made the righteousness of God in him, vs. 20. 21.

11. Knowing therefore the terror of the Lord, we
persuade men; but we are made manifest unto God;
and I trust also are made manifest in your consciences.

This verse is an inference from what precedes, as is indicated by the particle (οὖν) *therefore.* Paul had asserted his
earnest desire to be acceptable to the Lord, and, therefore,
knowing the terror of the Lord, &c. In this version of the
clause, τὸν φόβον τοῦ κυρίου, the genitive is taken as the genitive of the subject. It is the terror which belongs to the
Lord. 'Knowing how terrible the Lord is.'   But this is
contrary to the constant use of the phrase. The fear of the
Lord is that fear or reverence which the Lord excites, or of
which he is the object. Hence it so often stands in Scripture
for true religion. "The fear of the Lord is the beginning of
wisdom."   So in Acts 9, 31, "Walking in the fear of the
Lord."   Rom. 3, 18, "The fear of God is not before their
eyes;" and in 7, 1 of this epistle, "perfecting holiness in the
fear of God." See also Eph. 5, 21, "Submitting yourselves
one to another in the fear of Christ."   In all these cases
(φόβος) *fear* means pious reverence. There is no reason for
departing from that sense in this place. Knowing, i. e. feeling or experiencing, the pious reverence for Christ, the earnest desire to meet his approbation, asserted in the context,
the apostle acted under the influence of that sentiment, and
not from selfish or unworthy motives, in all his conduct as a
man and as a minister. As the expression "fear of the Lord"

is so uniformly used to express that reverence and submission which are due only to God, it is clear from this and analogous passages that Christ was to the apostles the object of the religious affections; and that they felt themselves to be responsible to him for their moral character and conduct. The evidence of the divinity of the Lord is thus seen to pervade the New Testament, and is not confined to a few isolated passages. Influenced, says the apostle, by the fear of the Lord, *I persuade men.* What this means is somewhat doubtful. The word πείθειν expresses the endeavour to convince, as in Acts 18, 4, "He persuaded the Jews," i. e. endeavoured to convince them of the truth, and in Acts 28, 23, "Persuading them concerning Jesus." The apostle therefore may here mean that he endeavoured to convince men of the truth of the gospel, i. e. to convert them, or bring them to the obedience of faith. Or, he may mean that he endeavoured to convince them of his integrity, or that he was really governed by the fear of Christ, and was therefore sincere and honest, which in Corinth had been so unjustly called in question. This latter explanation is generally preferred, both because it suits the context, and because the following clause seems to require this idea. 'We seek to convince men of our integrity, but God we need not convince, to him our inmost soul is manifest.' The word (πείθειν), however, also signifies *to conciliate,* to seek to please, as in Gal. 1, 10, "Do we persuade (i. e. seek to please) men, or God." Matt. 28, 14. Acts 12, 20. 1 John 3, 19. Many prefer that sense here. Luther, in his idiomatic style, renders the clause, *fahren wir schön mit den Leuten.* The apostle is supposed to refer to the fact that he accommodated himself to all classes, and became all things to all men, that he might save some. 1 Cor. 9, 22. Though he thus acted still he was manifest unto God; i. e. God knew the purity of his motives. This, however, is an idea foreign to the connection. His accommodating himself to others was not the specific objection made against him by his enemies in Corinth, but, as appears from the previous chapters, his "lightness" or instability of purpose, and his consequent untrustworthiness as a man and as a teacher. Others again, take πείθειν in a bad sense. 'We deceive men, (as our enemies say,) but are manifest to God.' But this is utterly incongruous. How could Paul say in such a solemn connection, 'I deceive men,' and leave the saving clause, *as my enemies say,* to be supplied by the reader. The most natural interpretation is that given above. 'Under the influence of the fear of the Lord, we endeavour to convince men, i. e. as he had said in 4, 2, to commend himself to every man's conscience, and whether successful in this or not he was at least known to God.' *Made manifest unto God,* i. e. to God I am (φανερός) *apparent,* my true character is known. *And I trust also are made manifest in your conscience.* Although misunderstood and defamed by others, he trusted that the Corinthian Christians as a body had an inward conviction of his integrity. The evidence of his sincerity was his moral excellence, and therefore it addressed itself to their consciences. There may be many reports against a good man which we cannot contradict ; many charges which we cannot refute ; and yet the self-evidencing light of goodness will produce the conviction of his integrity in the consciences even of wicked men, and much more in the hearts of the good.

12. For we commend not ourselves again unto you, but give you occasion to glory on our behalf, that ye may have somewhat to (answer) them which glory in appearance, and not in heart.

His object in thus speaking of himself was not self-praise, nor to secure the confidence of the Corinthians, which he already possessed ; but to give them materials for a vindication of his character against the aspersions of his enemies. The connection, as indicated by *for,* is with the preceding verse, of which this is a confirmation. 'I am assured of your confidence, *for* the object of my self-commendation is not to recommend myself to you, but, &c.' In chapter 3, 1, Paul had had occasion to repel the charge of self-laudation, and hence he says, he was not about to commend himself *again,* as some said he had before done. *But give you,* literally, *giving* (διδόντες), and therefore a verb must be supplied, 'Giving you occasion *we say these things.' An occasion of glorying in our behalf,* ἀφορμὴν καυχήματος; καύχημα being taken in the sense of καύχησις. *On our behalf,* ὑπὲρ ἡμῶν, not simply *over* us, or *about* us, but for our benefit. That is, for our vindication. Some commentators suppose that there is something ironical in this whole passage. As though the apostle designed to taunt the Corinthians with their readiness to listen to the false representations of his opponents, and with the plea that they needed not the disposition, but the ability to defend him. This view, however, is inconsistent with the connection and with the whole drift of the epistle. In the immediately preceding verse he had expressed his assurance of their confidence in his integrity, and throughout the epistle his overflowing love for the faithful in Corinth is mingled with his severe denunciations of the false teachers and their followers. *That ye may have.* There is no object expressed to the verb (ἔχητε), *ye may have.* We may supply (τί) *something,* and insert the words *to answer,* as is done by our translators; or we may borrow from the context the word καύχημα; "That ye may have *some ground of boasting.*" *Against those who glory in appearance and not in heart.* This is evidently descriptive of the false teachers. The words ἐν προσώπῳ, *in face,* may, from the antithesis to ἐν καρδίᾳ, *in heart,* be taken, as in our version, for what is external as opposed to what is inward. Then the expression refers to the fact that those teachers gloried in their Hebrew descent, in their circumcision, their external religious privileges, their churchmanship, &c. It was in these things they placed their confidence, and of them they made their boast. Or the words may be taken literally, and according to their uniform use in other passages. Then the expression describes the sanctimoniousness and hypocrisy of the false teachers. They gloried, says Meyer, in the holiness, the zeal, and devotion which expressed themselves in the face. They wished to appear unto men to fast, to wear the look of sanctity, while their hearts, as our Lord describes the same class of men, were full of all uncleanness. The former explanation is commonly adopted, and is probably the true one, because regard for externals is elsewhere in this epistle represented as the prominent characteristic of Paul's opponents in Corinth. Their great boast was that they belonged to the true church or theocracy, and that Paul and his followers were dissenters and schismatics.

13. For whether we be beside ourselves, (it is) to God : or whether we be sober, (it is) for your cause.

This verse again is a confirmation of the preceding. 'You have good reason to glory on my behalf, *for,* &c.' *Whether we be beside ourselves.* The word ἐξίστημι, *to be out of one's mind,* and other words of like signification, are used either in their strict sense to express insanity or madness, or in a wider sense, to express undue excitement or extravagance. When Festus, Acts 26, 24, said to the apostle, "Paul, thou art beside thyself; much learning doth make thee mad," he did not mean that he was really insane. And when our Lord's zeal provoked his friends to say of him, "He is beside himself," Mark 3, 21, they certainly did not intend to charge him with insanity. There is therefore no necessity for taking the word here in its strict sense, and assuming that Paul's enemies had accused him of being out of his mind. It is the more natural to take the word in a wider sense here, because the opposite term, σωφρονέω, (*to be sober*, or *sane*,) and its cognates, are much more frequently used to express moderation and discretion than sanity in the strict sense of that word. The apostle means to say that whether he was extravagant or moderate, whether he exceeded the bounds of discretion, as his enemies asserted, or whether he was sober and discreet, it was not for himself; he had in view only the glory of God and the good of his church, and therefore the Corinthians might safely boast of him, i. e. vindicate him from the aspersions of the false teachers. Whether the extravagance or insanity here referred to, consisted in his self-commendation, or in his zeal and devotion, is matter of dispute. The former is the more probable, both because in the immediate context he had been speaking of that subject, and because in chapters 11 and 12 he speaks so much at large of his commending himself, although forced upon him, as a kind of folly or insanity. In those chapters the ἀφροσύνη, (*the want of mind*,) of which he accuses himself, was self-praise; and the σωφροσύνη (*soberness* or *sanity*) which he desired to exhibit was moderation in speaking of himself and of his labours. Paul, therefore, in this passage, is most naturally understood to mean, that whether he praised himself or whether he did not, whether the manner in which he had spoken of himself be considered as ἀφροσύνη or σωφροσύνη, as insanity or sobriety, he spoke not for himself, but for God and his people.

14. For the love of Christ constraineth us; because we thus judge, that if one died for all, then were all dead.

'In whatever I do,' says the apostle, 'I act for God and his church, *for* the love of Christ constraineth me.' The connection is thus plain. *The love of Christ* here means Christ's love for us, not the love of which he is the object. This is obvious, because the apostle goes on to illustrate the greatness of Christ's love to us, and not of our love to him. Comp. Gal. 2, 20, where the same idea is expressed by the words "who loved me." See Rom. 8, 35. Eph. 3, 19. *Constraineth us*, i. e. controls and governs us. The word συνέχω means also to *restrain*, a sense which many adopt here. 'The love of Christ restrains me from acting for myself.' This is a more limited sense, and is not required by the usage of the word, which is often used to express the idea of being pressed as by a crowd, or figuratively, by calamity or sorrow. There is no better version for it in this passage than that adopted by our translators. 'The love of Christ *constraineth* us.' It coerces, or presses, and therefore impels. It is the governing influence which controls the life. This is a trait of Paul's experience as a Christian, and is therefore common to all Christians. It is not benevolence which makes a man a Christian, for then all philanthropists would be Christians. Nor is it mere piety, in the sense of reverence for God, which makes a man a Christian, for then all devout Mussulmans and Jews would be Christians. Morality does not make us religious, but religion makes us moral. In like manner benevolence and piety (in the wide sense) do not make men Christians, but Christianity makes them benevolent and devout. A Christian is one who recognizes Jesus as the Christ, the Son of the living God, as God manifested in the flesh, loving us and dying for our redemption; and who is so affected by a sense of the love of this incarnate God as to be constrained to make the will of Christ the rule of his obedience, and the glory of Christ the great end for which he lives. The man who does this perfectly, is a perfect Christian. The man who does it imperfectly, yet with the sincere desire to be entirely devoted to Christ, is a sincere Christian. On the other hand, the man who lives supremely for himself, for his family, for science, for the world, for mankind, whatever else he may be, is not a Christian. Whosoever loveth father or mother, son or daughter, more than me, saith our Lord, is not worthy of me, Matt. 10, 37. He that hateth not his own life, cannot be my disciple, Luke 14, 26. The great question is, What constitutes a Christian? It is being so constrained by a sense of the love of our divine Lord to us, that we consecrate our lives to him. Hence faith in his divinity, faith in his love,

faith in his having died for us, is the principle or source of the
Christian life. And this is the only form in which true religion can now exist. That is, the only true religion now
possible is the worship, love, and service of the Lord Jesus
Christ. It is impossible for a man to turn his back on Christ
and worship the God of nature or the God of the Jews.
Should a man reveal himself to us first as an acquaintance,
then as a friend, and then as a father, filial reverence and devotion would be the only form in which sincere and true
regard for him could exist. To deny him as father, would be
to reject him as a friend and acquaintance. Since, therefore,
the same God who revealed himself first in nature, and then
as the Jehovah of the Hebrews, has revealed himself in the
flesh, loving us and dying for our redemption, to deny him in
this the clearest revelation of his being and perfection, is to
deny him altogether. "Whoso denieth the Son, the same
hath not the Father," 1 John 2, 23. It is the practical or ex-
perimental form of this great truth, which is presented in this
passage.

Because we thus judge. This clause assigns the reason
why the love of Christ exerted the constraining power referred to. It was because the apostle judged that the death
of Christ for his people not only placed them under the
strongest obligation to devote themselves to his service, but
it secured this devotion. They died in him. Rom. 6, 4. 5.
As the participle (κρίναντας) is in the aorist, it would be more
strictly rendered, *because we judged.* That is, 'I live for
Christ, because when I became a Christian I regarded his
dying for me as involving the obligation and necessity of my
living for him.' This was the aspect under which he em-
braced Christianity; the judgment which he formed of it
from the beginning. *That if one died for all.* The contrast
presented, especially in the epistle to the Hebrews, between
the priest and sacrifices of the old economy on the one hand,
and the high priest and sacrifice of the gospel on the other,
is that those were many, these are one. The ancient priests
could not continue by reason of death. Our high priest, being a divine person, and therefore possessed of an endless life,
ever lives to save. The sacrifices of the law were daily repeated, because it was impossible that they should take away
sin; Christ by the offering up of himself hath forever perfected them that are sanctified. His blood cleanses from all sin.
The apostle here presents him as the one priest and the one

sacrifice. *Died for all.* The words are ὑπὲρ πάντων. The preposition ὑπέρ, may have the general sense, *for the benefit of, in behalf of,* or the stricter sense, *in the place of,* as in v. 20 of this chapter. Philem. 13. Eph. 6, 20. In many places the choice between these senses depends on the context. In all those passages in which one person is said to die for another, as Rom. 5, 6. 7. 8. 14, 15. 1 Thess. 5, 10. Heb. 2, 9. Comp. Luke 22, 19. 1 Tim. 2, 6. Titus 2, 14. &c., &c., or in which the reference is to a sacrifice, the idea of substitution is clearly expressed. The argument does not rest on the force of the preposition, but on the nature of the case. The only way in which the death of the victim benefited the offerer, was by substitution. When, therefore, Christ is said to die as a sacrifice for us, the meaning is, he died in our stead. His death is taken in the place of ours so as to save us from death. That the preposition ὑπέρ, in this and similar passages, does mean *instead of,* is admitted by the great body of even Rationalistic commentators. See De Wette, Rückert, &c. Christ, it is said, died for *all,* i. e. for all the subjects of redemption. This limitation is not an arbitrary one, but arises of necessity out of the nature of the case, and is admitted almost universally. He did not die for all creatures; nor for all rational creatures; nor for all apostate rational creatures. The *all* is of necessity limited by what the Scriptures teach of the design of his death. If his death was merely didactic, intended to reveal and confirm some truth, then he may be said to have died for all benefited by that revelation, and therefore for angels as well as men. If designed to make it consistent with the interests of God's moral government for him to pardon the sins of men, then he may be said to have died equally for all men. But if his death was intended to save his people, then it had a reference to them which it had not to others. The true design of the death of Christ is to be learned from express assertions of Scripture, and from its effects. It is so obvious that the death of Christ was designed to save those for whom it was offered, that many of the recent as well as ancient commentators justify their explaining ὑπὲρ πάντων as meaning all men, by attributing to Paul the belief that all men are to be saved. This is an admission that the *all* for whom he died, are the all who are saved by his death. One of its effects is stated in the following clause; *Then were all dead,* or, *Then all died.* The word is ἀπέθανον. It is the same verb, and in the same tense. 'If one died, (ἀπέθανεν,) then all died, (ἀπέθανον).' The word must have the same sense in both clauses. It cannot mean *were* dead, because that is inconsistent with the force of the aorist. *All*, (literally, *the* all, οἱ πάντες,) i. e. *the* all for whom the one died. His death involved, or secured their death. This was its design and effect, and, therefore, this clause limits the extent of the word *all* in the preceding clause. Christ died for the all who died when he died. The meaning of this expression has, however, been variously explained. 1. It is made to mean, 'Then all died to themselves and sin.' His dying literally, secured their dying figuratively. 2. Others say the true meaning is, 'Then all *ought* to die.' But this is not included in the words. The aorist does not express obligation. 3. Chrysostom, Theodoret, Beza and others, give the same explanation which is implied in our version, 'If one died for all, then were all subject to death.' That is, the vicarious death of Christ proves that those for whom he died were in a state of condemnation. But this suits neither the meaning of the word nor the context. It was not to Paul's purpose to prove that men were in a state of death. It was not what they *were*, but what the death of Christ caused them to become, that he evidently intended to express. 4. The simple meaning of the passage is, that the death of one was the death of all. If one died for all, the all died. The Scriptures teach that the relation between Christ and his people is analogous to that between Adam and his posterity. Rom. 5, 12–21. 1 Cor. 15, 21. 22. The apostasy of Adam was the apostasy of all united to him; the work of Christ was the work of all united to him. In the one, all died; in the other, all are made alive. As the sin of Adam was legally and effectively the sin of his race; so the death of Christ was legally and effectively the death of his people. This doctrine underlies the whole scheme of redemption. It is, so to speak, the generic idea of the Epistle to the Romans. The apostle shows that man, ruined by the sin of Adam, is restored by the work of Christ. His people are so united to him that his death is their death, and his life is their life. "If we be dead with him, we shall also live with him," Rom. 6, 8. Hence believers are said to be crucified with Christ, to rise with him, to reign with him. Gal. 2, 20. Eph. 2, 5. 6. The simple meaning of the words, "If one died for all, then all died," therefore is, that Christ's death was the death of his people. This as we have seen is according to the analogy of Scripture; and is also entirely pertinent to the design of this passage. The apostle denied that he lived for himself. He asserts that he lived for God and his people. For, he adds, I died in Christ. This is precisely the argument which he uses in Rom. 6. Shall we continue in sin that grace may abound? Far from it, he says, How shall they who have died on account of sin live any longer therein? If united to Christ in his death, we must be united to him in his life. Another consideration in favour of this interpretation is that it comprehends the others. They are objectionable, not because they are erroneous, but because they are defective. Death on account of sin, is death to sin. Dying with Christ, involves death to self and sin; and of course includes the obligation so to die. The death of Christ reconciles us to God; and reconciliation to God secures a life of devotion to his service. This is the doctrine set forth in the Epistle to the Romans, ch. 7.

15. And (that) he died for all, that they which live should not henceforth live unto themselves, but unto him which died for them, and rose again.

This is a continuation of the preceding sentence, and is designed to express more fully the judgment or conviction ($\kappa\rho\iota\nu\alpha\nu\tau\alpha\varsigma$) which the apostle had formed of his relation to Christ. He judged that the death of Christ was the death of his people, and that the design with which he died for them was that they might live for him. This idea is expressed in various forms in the word of God. Sometimes our Lord is said to have died, the just for the unjust, to bring us near to God, 1 Pet. 3, 18; or, that we, being dead to sins, should live unto righteousness, 1 Pet. 2, 26; or, to purify to himself a peculiar people, zealous of good works, Titus 2, 14. In Rom. 14, 9, the mode of statement is exactly parallel to the passage before us. "To this end Christ both died and rose that he might be the Lord both of the dead and living." To say that Christ died that he might be the Lord of his people, is to say that he died that they might be his servants, i. e. belong to him and be devoted to him. The proximate design and effect of the death of Christ is the expiation of sin and reconciliation with God, and the design and effect of reconciliation with God are devotion to his service. Hence the death of Christ is sometimes presented in reference to its proximate, sometimes in reference to its ultimate design; i. e. sometimes he is said to have died to make a propitiation for sin, and sometimes, to bring us near to God. Here it is the latter. He died *that they which live should not henceforth live unto themselves.* "Those who live," οἱ ζῶντες, not, *those who survive his death;* nor, *those who are spiritually living;* nor, *the happy or blessed,* but, those who, although they died in Christ, are still living. Their death in him is not inconsistent with their being alive, for they died in one sense and they live in another. Those for whom Christ died, and on whom his death takes effect, thenceforth, i. c. from the time they apprehend their relation to him, and feel the power of his vicarious death, *do not live unto themselves,* i. e. self is not the object for which they live. This is the negative description of the Christian. He is a man who does not live unto himself. This is what he is not. The positive description is given in the next clause. He lives *for him who died for him and rose again.* This presents both the object and the ground of the Christian's devotion. He lives for him who died for him, and because he died for him. He is not a Christian who is simply unselfish, i. e. who lives for some object out of himself. He only is a Christian who lives for Christ. Many persons think they can be Christians on easier terms than these. They think it is enough to trust in Christ while they do not live for him. But the Bible teaches us that if we are partakers of Christ's death, we are also partakers of his life; if we have any such appreciation of his love in dying for us as to lead us to confide in the merit of his death, we shall be constrained to consecrate our lives to his service. And this is the only evidence of the genuineness of our faith. *And rose again.* We do not serve a dead Saviour. The resurrection of Christ is as essential to redemption as his death. He died for our sins and rose again for our justification. And it is to this risen Saviour, seated at the right hand of God, to whom all power in heaven and earth has been committed, and who ever lives to make intercession for us, who is the object of the supreme love of the believer, to whose service and glory the Christian consecrates his life.

16. Wherefore henceforth know we no man after the flesh : yea, though we have known Christ after the flesh, yet now henceforth know we (him) no more.

This is an inference, (ὥστε, *so that*). ‘Such is the nature of the change which I have experienced through the apprehension of the love of Christ, as just described, that I no longer see or judge of things according to the flesh.’ The *we* refers primarily to the apostle himself, as he is still engaged in self-vindication. He was acting from pure motives, he says, for a sense of the love of Christ constrained him not to live for himself but for Christ, and therefore he no longer judged of persons or things as he had been accustomed to do. Paul's experience, however, was his experience as a Christian, and therefore not peculiar to himself. It is true of all Christians that they do not know (i. e. estimate, judge, feel in reference to) *any man according to the flesh.* This may mean, that the judgment is not regulated or determined by a regard to what is external. It is not a man's outward circumstances, his birth, his station, his being rich or poor, Jew or Gentile, that determines our estimate of him. Or the meaning may be, that the judgment was not determined by carnal or selfish considerations. Paul was not led to approve or disapprove, love or hate any man from selfish or corrupt motives. This latter view would suit the context, for the apostle had just said that he lived not for himself but for Christ, and therefore his judgments of men were not determined by a regard to himself. It is also consistent with the usage of the word; for σάρξ means *corrupt nature*, as well as what is outward. The following part of the verse, however, is decisively in favour of the former interpretation. Comp. 11, 18. John 8, 15. Phil. 3, 4. Paul evidently contrasts himself as he now was (ἀπὸ τοῦ νῦν) with what he was before his conversion; and also himself with his Judaizing opponents in Corinth. *Yea, though we have known Christ after the flesh.* The words εἰ δὲ καί, *but even if*, are concessive. Paul admits that he had once done what he here condemns. *He had known or estimated Christ after the flesh.* Of course this does not mean that he had known Christ while in the flesh, as Olshausen supposes, because that would be saying nothing to the purpose, and because there is no evidence of Paul's ever having seen our Lord before his resurrection. Olshausen's idea is, that as he formerly regarded men as men, but now only as Christians, i. e. had reference only to what was spiritual, so also he no longer thinks of Christ as he once knew him on earth, but as he is glorified in heaven. But this does not suit the connection nor the facts of the case. The words κατὰ σάρκα must have the same sense in both parts of the verse; and in the former they do not designate the life before conversion, and therefore when spoken in reference to Christ are not to be understood of his earthly as opposed to his heavenly life. Paul had known Christ after the flesh in the sense of estimating him entirely according to the outward appearance of things. *Christ* does not here mean the Messiah, but is the historical designation of our Lord as an individual. Paul had despised and hated him because he judged him only according to his outward appearance as a poor suffering man, yet claiming to be the Christ the Son of the living God. His Jewish notions of what the Messiah was to be led him to regard with indignation the claims of Jesus to be the Christ. *Yet now henceforth know we (him) no more.* The order of the words in the original shows that the words κατὰ σάρκα are to be connected with the verb and not with its object; εἰ δὲ καὶ ἐγνώκαμεν κατὰ σάρκα Χριστόν. That is, we no longer judge *after the flesh* concerning Christ; we no longer estimate him according to appearance, but know him to be the Son of God, who loved us and gave himself for us. Gal. 2, 20.

17. Therefore, if any man (be) in Christ, (he is) a new creature: old things are passed away; behold, all things are become new.

A further inference from what precedes. What was true in Paul's case, must be true in all analogous cases. If the revelation of Christ, the apprehension of his glory and love, had wrought such a change in him, the same illumination must produce a like change in others. He therefore says, *If any man be in Christ he is a new creature.* The proposition is general; it applies to every man. To be in Christ is the common scriptural phrase to express the saving connection or union between him and his people. They are in him by covenant, as all men were in Adam; they are in him as members of his body, through the indwelling of his Spirit; and they are in him by faith, which lays hold of and appropriates him as the life and portion of the soul. Rom. 8, 1. 9. Gal. 5, 6, &c. This union is transforming. It imparts a new life. It effects a new creation. This expression indicates not only the greatness and radical nature of the change effected, but also its divine origin. It is a divine work, i. e. one due to the mighty power of God. It is therefore called a creation, the commencement of a new state of being. Eph. 1, 19. In Gal. 6, 15. Rom. 8, 9, and elsewhere, the same effects are ascribed to union with Christ. If we are united to him so as to be interested in the merits of his death, we must also be partakers of his life. This is the foundation on which the apostle builds his whole doctrine of sanctification as developed in the sixth and seventh chapter of his epistle to the Romans. The word καινός, *new, unimpaired, uncontaminated,* is an epithet of excellence; a new song, a new name, new heavens, new earth, the new Jerusalem, the new man, a new creature, are scriptural expressions which will occur to every reader. In the margin of the English Bible this clause is rendered, *Let him be a new creature.* This is in accordance with Calvin's view of the passage. "If any man would be in Christ, i. e. if he would be of consequence in Christ's kingdom, let him become a new creature." He supposes that the apostle refers to the ambition of the false teachers, whom he tells that if they wish to attain the influence to which they aspire, they must like him be entirely changed from selfishness to devotion to Christ. There is nothing in the words to require this, and every thing in the context is opposed to it. The apostle is detailing his own experience, unfolding the principles on which he acted, and showing the effect which the apprehension of the love of Christ had on him and must have on others. If any man is in Christ he is thereby made a new creature. In the Old Testament, Is. 43, 18. 19. 65, 17, the effects to be produced by the coming of the Messiah are described as a making all things new. The final consummation of the Redeemer's kingdom in heaven is described, Rev. 21, 5, in the same terms. "He that sat upon the throne said, Behold, I make all things new." The inward spiritual change in every believer is set forth in the same words, because it is the type and necessary condition of this great cosmical change. What would avail any conceivable change in things external, if the heart remained a cage of unclean birds? The apostle therefore says that if any man is in Christ he experiences a change analogous to that predicted by the prophets, and like to that which we still anticipate when earth shall become heaven. "Old things are passed away; behold, all things have become new." Old opinions, views, plans, desires, principles and affections are passed away; new views of truth, new principles, new apprehensions of the destiny of man, and new feelings and purposes fill and govern the soul.

18. And all things (are) of God, who hath reconciled us to himself by Jesus Christ, and hath given to
us the ministry of reconciliation.

All things are of God ; this is not spoken of the universe
as proceeding from God as its author ; nor does it refer to
the providential agency of God, by which all events are controlled.   The meaning of τὰ δὲ πάντα here is, *but all is of God,*
i. e. the entire change of which he had been speaking.   The
new creation experienced by those who are in Christ is ἐκ τοῦ
Θεοῦ, *is out of God,* proceeds from him as its efficient cause.
It is his work.   God effects this great moral and spiritual
revolution *by reconciling us unto himself.*   The word *us* is
not to be limited to the apostle, first, because the reconciliation
spoken of is not peculiar to him ; and secondly, because the
change or new creation effected by this reconciliation belongs
to all who are in Christ.   *Us,* therefore, must include all who
are in Christ.   The objection to this interpretation that *to us*
in the next clause of the verse must refer to the apostle, is
not a serious one, because the passage is perfectly perspicuous
even supposing ἡμᾶς, *us,* to refer to all believers, and ἡμῖν, *to
us,* to the apostle himself.   *To reconcile* is to remove enmity
between parties at variance with each other.   In this case
God is the reconciler.   Man never makes reconciliation.   It
is what he experiences or embraces, not what he does.   The
enmity between God and man, the barrier which separated
them, is removed by the act of God.   This is plain, 1. Because
it is said to be effected *by Jesus Christ,* that is, by his death.
The death of Christ, however, is always represented as reconciling us to God as a sacrifice ; the design and nature of a
sacrifice are to propitiate and not to reform.   2. In the parallel passage, Rom. 5, 9. 10, being " reconciled by the death of
the Son," is interchanged as equivalent with " being justified
by his blood," which proves that the reconciliation intended
consists in the satisfaction of the divine justice by the sacrifice
of Christ.   3. In this case our reconciliation to God is made
the source and cause of our new creation, i. e. of our regeneration and holiness.   God's reconciliation to us must precede
our reconciliation to him.   This, as remarked above, is the
great doctrine of the Bible.   So long as we are under the
wrath and curse of God, due to us for sin, we are aliens and
enemies, cut off from his favour and fellowship, which are the
life of the soul.   Therefore until God's wrath and curse are

removed, there is no possibility of holiness and love. It is vain to attempt to secure the favour of God by being holy; we must enjoy his favour before we can be holy. See Rom. 7, 56. As the apostle here ascribes our holiness to our being reconciled to God, he must of necessity refer to the reconciliation of God to us; i. e. to his being propitious, ready to receive us into his favour and to manifest to us his love. *And hath given to us,* i. e. to the apostle and to other preachers of the gospel, for the thing given was not something peculiar to the apostles but common to all preachers, viz., *the ministry of reconciliation,* i. e. the office and duty of announcing this reconciliation. It is therefore the peculiar duty or special design of the ministry to proclaim to men that God, justly offended by their sins, can be just and yet justify those who come to him by Jesus Christ. This is the εὐαγγέλιον, or glad tidings, which our blessed Lord has commissioned his disciples to announce to every creature under heaven.

19. To wit, that God was in Christ, reconciling the world unto himself, not imputing their trespasses unto them; and hath committed unto us the word of reconciliation.

This verse is an explanation and confirmation of what precedes. According to our version, and to the common interpretation, it is an explanation of the last clause of v. 18, i. e. of the "reconciliation" there spoken of. 'He hath given to us the ministry of reconciliation—because God was reconciling the world unto himself, &c.' To this it is objected by Meyer and others, that the position of the word θεός (*God*) requires the emphasis to be thrown on that word; and secondly, that the two following clauses must, in that case, explain the mode of that reconciliation. Paul would then say, 'God was reconciling the world unto himself, having committed to us the word of reconciliation.' But our reconciliation to God is not the ministry of reconciliation. The former does not consist in the latter; nor is the first the consequence of the second. This verse therefore is referred to the first clause of v. 18. 'All things are of God, &c., because God was reconciling, &c.' The words ὡς ὅτι, rendered *to wit,* mean here *seeing that,* or *because.* They are equivalent to the simple ὅτι. The expression is explained either as a pleonasm, or as the mixture of two constructions, ὡς θεοῦ ὄντος and ὅτι θεός ἐστι.

The principal difference among interpreters in the explanation of this verse relates to the question whether (ἦν) *was* is to be referred to (ἐν Χριστῷ) *in Christ*, or to (καταλλάσσων) *reconciling*. Our version favours the former mode of construction, which is adopted both by Luther and Calvin. The sense then is, 'God was in Christ, when he reconciled the world unto himself;' or, as Luther renders it, "God was in Christ, and reconciled the world with himself, and imputed not to them their sins, &c." This breaks up the verse into distinct propositions, turning all the participles into verbs. Calvin says that by *God* we are not to understand the divine nature, or "the fulness of the Godhead," but God the Father; and refers to John 10, 38, "The father is in me," as a parallel expression. He thinks the design of the apostle is to assure believers that in having Christ, they have the Father also; that Christ is the true Immanuel, whose advent is the approximation of God to man. But all this is foreign to the context. What follows is no proof that "God was in Christ," but it is a proof of his being engaged, so to speak, in the great work of reconciling the world unto himself. Most interpreters, therefore, adopt the other construction, 'God was reconciling the world unto himself in Christ.' As in v. 18 it is said that God reconciled us to himself διὰ Χριστοῦ (*through Christ*), here it is said to be ἐν Χριστῷ (*in Christ*). The imperfect ἦν καταλλάσσων, *was reconciling*, expresses either contemporary or continuous action. The sense may be, 'God was, when Christ died, reconciling the world unto himself;' that was what he was doing and designed to do when he gave his Son up for us all. So Meyer and others. Or, the reference is to what follows; 'He reconciled the world, not imputing unto men their sins, &c.' That is, 'While not imputing, &c.' But this is impossible, because the next clause, 'and given to us the word of reconciliation,' cannot express what was contemporaneous with the reconciling. Others say that the imperfect is used for the aorist. The first explanation is to be preferred. *God was reconciling the world unto himself*, means God was making atonement for the sins of the world. He set Christ forth as a propitiation. Theodoret explains ἦν καταλλάσσων by καταλλαγὰς ἐποιήσατο. By *the world* (κόσμος, without the article) is meant *man, mankind*. The reference or statement is perfectly indefinite; it merely indicates the class of beings towards whom God was manifesting himself as propitious. In the same sense our Lord is called the Saviour of the world, or, the Saviour of men, Jesus Salvator Hominum. *To reconcile unto himself*, does not mean to convert, or to render friendly to himself. This is plain first, because this reconciliation is said to be effected by the death of Christ as a sacrifice; and secondly, because what follows is not a proof of God's converting the world, but it is a proof of his being propitious. The proof that God was reconciling the world to himself in Christ (i. e. in his death) is that he does not impute to men their trespasses, and that he has established the ministry of reconciliation. The forgiveness of sin and the institution of the ministry are clear evidence that God is propitious. Not to impute sin, is to forgive it. Rom. 4, 5. 2 Tim. 4, 16. In Col. 2, 13, the same idea is expressed by saying, "hath forgiven you all trespasses." The participle μὴ λογιζόμενος, *not imputing*, is in the present because continuous action is intended; whereas in the next clause, θέμενος, *having committed*, is a past participle, because the institution of the ministry was done once for all. *To them*, i. e. to men, as included in the κόσμος, *world*. When God is said to forgive men it of course does not mean that all men, penitent and impenitent, believing and unbelieving, are forgiven; but here, as before, the class of beings is indicated towards whom forgiveness is exercised. God is propitious to men, as is manifest by his forgiving their trespasses. *And hath committed unto us*, καὶ θέμενος ἐν ἡμῖν, i. e. *having deposited in us*. This may mean, 'having put within us,' i. e. in our souls. Or the idea may be, 'having placed upon us.' If the former, then the following words, τὸν λόγον τῆς καταλλαγῆς, must mean 'the doctrine of reconciliation.' That is, God hath instructed us apostles in the doctrine of reconciliation. If the latter, then the clause just quoted means, 'the word of reconciliation,' i. e. the preaching of reconciliation, as in 1 Cor. 1, 18, ὁ λόγος τοῦ σταυροῦ means 'the preaching of the cross.' This latter view is to be preferred. The evidence that the death of Christ has been accepted as an expiation for sin, of infinite value and efficiency, is the fact that God hath commissioned his ministers to announce to all men that God is reconciled and ready to forgive, so that whosoever will may turn unto him and live.

20. Now then we are ambassadors for Christ, as though God did beseech (you) by us: we pray (you) in Christ's stead, be ye reconciled to God.

This is an inference from what precedes. *Now then* (οὖν, *therefore*). 'Seeing that God in Christ is reconciled, and that he has commissioned us to make known this great truth, it follows that we, as preachers of the gospel, are ambassadors of Christ.' An ambassador is at once a messenger and a representative. He does not speak in his own name. He does not act on his own authority. What he communicates is not his own opinions or demands, but simply what he has been told or commissioned to say. His message derives no part of its importance or trustworthiness from him. At the same time he is more than a mere messenger. He represents his sovereign. He speaks with authority, as accredited to act in the name of his master. Any neglect, contempt or injury done to him in his official character, is not a personal offence, but an offence to the sovereign or state by whom he is commissioned. All this is true of ministers. They are messengers. They communicate what they have received, not their own speculations or doctrines. What they announce derives its importance not from them, but from him who sends them. Nevertheless, as they speak in Christ's name and by his authority, as he hath ordained the ministry and calls men by his Spirit into the sacred office, the rejection of their message is the rejection of Christ, and any injury done unto them as ministers is done unto him.

For Christ, ὑπὲρ Χριστοῦ, this may mean either 'in Christ's stead,' as his substitute and representative; or, 'in Christ's behalf,' for his sake, to promote his interests by furthering the accomplishment of the object for which he died; as in Eph. 6, 20, the apostle, speaking of the gospel, says, ὑπὲρ οὗ πρεσβεύω, *for which I act as an ambassador*. The latter sense is good, and is in accordance with the common force of the preposition. The former, however, is better suited to the context. To act as an ambassador for any one, is to act in his name or as his representative. And in the following explanatory clause it is said, 'God beseeches you by us,' where the idea of substitution is clearly expressed. The clause, *as though God did beseech you by us*, is commonly connected with what precedes. 'We are ambassadors for Christ, as though God did beseech you by us.' That is, 'We are the ambassadors of Christ, because it is God that speaks through us; or, we speak in his name.' Beza and others connect the words with the following clause. 'We are the ambassadors of Christ,' here is the pause, and then follows as one clause, 'As though God did beseech you by us we pray, &c.' This is the more natural, because the latter words express the prayer, so to speak, which God through the ministry addresses to sinners. It will be noticed that to be an ambassador for Christ, and that God speaks through us, mean the same thing. Redemption is as much the work of the Father as of the Son. God reconciles the world unto himself in Christ. God gives us the word of reconciliation. We are acting for God, or in his name, when we appear as the ambassadors of Christ. *We pray you in Christ's stead.* Here again ὑπὲρ Χριστοῦ may be either *in Christ's stead*, or, *for Christ's sake.* The former is to be preferred as better suited to the uniformity of the passage. *Be ye reconciled unto God;* this does not mean, 'Reconcile yourselves unto God.' The word, καταλλάγητε, is passive. *Be reconciled*, that is, embrace the offer of reconciliation. The reconciliation is effected by the death of Christ. God is now propitious. He can now be just, and yet justify the ungodly. All we have to do is not to refuse the offered love of God. Calvin remarks that this exhortation is not directed exclusively to the unconverted. The believer needs daily, and is allowed whenever he needs, to avail himself of the offer of peace with God through Jesus Christ. It is not the doctrine of the Scriptures that the merits of Christ avail only for the forgiveness of sins committed before conversion, while for post-baptismal sins, as they were called, there is no satisfaction but in the penances of the offender. Christ ever lives to make intercession for us, and for every short-coming and renewed offence there is offered to the penitent believer, renewed application of that blood which cleanses from all sin.

21. For he hath made him (to be) sin for us, who knew no sin; that we might be made the righteousness of God in him.

This verse is designed to enforce the preceding. 'Be reconciled to God, *for* an abundant and trustworthy provision has been made for your reconciliation and acceptance.' It is indeed doubtful whether γάρ, *for*, belongs to the text, as it is omitted in many of the oldest manuscripts. Its omission only renders the transition more abrupt, the relation of the passage remains the same. The apostle states in this verse what God has done for the justification of men. The passage, therefore, is of special interest, as presenting in a concise form the testimony of the Spirit on that all important subject. *He made him who knew no sin to be sin for us.* The Greek here is, τὸν μὴ γνόντα ἁμαρτίαν ὑπὲρ ἡμῶν ἁμαρτίαν ἐποίησεν. Our Lord is presented as one whom God contemplated as free from sin and yet he made him sin. Others understand the μή γνόντα as referring to Christ himself, as one having no consciousness of sin. Others again, to the necessary judgment of believers, he whom we know was free from sin. One or the other of these modes of interpretation is supposed to be necessary, as the apostle uses μή and not οὐ; the one being, as the grammarians say, the subjective, the other the objective particle of negation; the one denying a thing as it appears to the mind, the other denying it simply as a fact. In either case the thing here asserted is that Christ was without sin. This was one of the indispensable conditions of his being made sin for us. Had he not been free from sin, he could not have taken the place of sinners. Under the old dispensation the sacrifices were required to be without blemish, in order to teach the necessity of freedom from all sin in him who was to bear the sins of the world. See Heb. 4, 15. 1 Pet. 2, 22. 1 John 3, 5. *He was made sin*, may mean either, he was made a sin-offering, or, the abstract being used for the concrete, he was made a sinner. Many of the older commentators prefer the former explanation; Calvin, and almost all the moderns adopt the latter. The meaning in either case is the same; for the only sense in which Christ was made sin, is that he bore the guilt of sin; and in this sense every sin offering was made sin. Hence in the Hebrew Scriptures the same word is used both for sin and a sin-offering. This is the principal ground on which the explanation of ἁμαρτία here in the sense of a sacrifice for sin is defended. The reasons, however, against this explanation are decisive. 1. In the Septuagint the Hebrew word for sin, when it means a sin-offering, is always rendered by ἁμαρτία in the genitive. It is always " of sin," or " for sin," (περὶ ἁμαρτίας), Lev. 5, 9. 14, 19. Num. 8, 8, and never simply " sin," as here. 2. The use of the word in the ordinary sense in this same clause, ' He made him to be sin who knew no sin.' It must have the same meaning in both cases. 3. The antithesis between " sin " and " righteousness." He was made sin, we are made " righteousness." The only sense in which we are made the righteousness of God is that we are in Christ regarded and treated as righteous, and therefore the sense in which he was made sin, is that he was regarded and treated as a sinner. His being made sin is consistent with his being in himself free from sin; and our being made righteous is consistent with our being in ourselves ungodly. In other words, our sins were imputed to Christ, and his righteousness is imputed to us. Justitia hic non pro qualitate aut habitu, says Calvin, sed pro imputatione accipitur, eo quod accepta nobis fertur Christi justitia. Quod e converso peccatum? reatus quo in Dei judicio obstringimur..... Personam enim nostram quodammodo suscepit, ut reus nostro nomine fieret, et tanquam peccator judicaretur, non propriis, sed alienis delictis, quum purus foret ipse et immunis ab omni culpa, pœnamque subiret nobis, non sibi debitam. Ita scilicet nunc justi sumus in ipso: non quia operibus propriis satisfaciamus judicio Dei, sed quoniam censimur Christi justitia, quam fide induimus, ut nostra fiat. In Gal. 3, 13, the apostle says that "Christ was made a curse for us," which is equivalent to saying that he was made sin for us. In both cases the idea is that he bore the punishment of our sins. God laid on him the iniquities of us all. His sufferings and death were penal, because inflicted and endured in satisfaction of justice. And in virtue of the infinite dignity of his person they were a perfect satisfaction; that is, a full equivalent for all the law's demands. In Rom. 8, 3, it is said, "What the law could not do, in that it was weak through the flesh, God, sending his own Son in the likeness of sinful flesh, and for sin, condemned sin in the flesh." Here again we have precisely the same doctrine. What in one passage is expressed by saying that Christ was made sin, in the other is expressed by saying, he was sent "for sin," i. e. as a sin-offering (περὶ ἁμαρτίας).

The apostle says Christ was made sin *for us*, ὑπὲρ ἡμῶν, i. e. *in our stead*, because the idea of substitution is involved in the very nature of the transaction. The victim was the substitute for the offender. It was put in his place. So Christ was our substitute, or, was put in our place. This is the more apparent from the following clause, which teaches the design of this substitution. He was made sin, that we might be made righteous. He was condemned, that we might be justified. The very idea of substitution is that what is done by one in the place of another, avails as though that other had done it himself. The victim was the substitute of the offerer, because its death took the place of his death. If both died there was no substitution. So if Christ's being made sin does not secure our being made righteousness, he was not our substitute. Righteousness does not here mean inward rectitude, or moral excellence. It is true that the word often has this sense; and it is true that the work of Christ does secure the holiness of his people, and was designed to produce that effect, as is often asserted in Scripture. But this was neither its only, nor its proximate design. Its immediate end was to reconcile us to God; to propitiate him, by the satisfaction of justice, so that he can be just and yet justify the ungodly. As the apostle is here speaking of the sacrificial effect of Christ's death, that is, of the proximate effect of his being made sin for us, the word righteousness must be understood in its forensic sense. It expresses our relation to the law, not our inward moral state. It is that which justifies, or satisfies the demands of the law. Those who have this δεκαιοσύνη are δίκαιοι, just in the sight of the law, in the sense that the law or justice is satisfied as concerns them. It is called *the righteousness of God*, either because it is from him as its author; or, because it renders us righteous in his sight. Those who possess this righteousness are δίκαιοι παρὰ τῷ Θεῷ, i. e. righteous before God. The former is the more common representation in Paul's writings. Rom. 1, 17. 3, 22. 10, 3. Phil. 3, 9, where "the righteousness of God," is explained by "the righteousness which is of God." In this view of the meaning of the phrase, the sense of the clause "we become the righteousness of God," is that we become divinely righteous. We are righteous with the righteousness of God, not with our own which is but as a filthy rag, but with that which he has provided and which consists in the infinitely meritorious righteousness of his own dear Son. All this is true; but the context here favours the other mode of representation. Christ was treated as a sinner, i. e. condemned, that we might be justified, i. e. regarded as just before God. The apostle uses the present tense, γινώμεθα, *we become* righteous, because this justification is continuous. We are introduced into a justified state. *In him*, that is, in Christ. It is by virtue of our union with Christ, and only as we are in him by faith, that we are righteous before God.

There is probably no passage in the Scriptures in which the doctrine of justification is more concisely or clearly stated than in this. Our sins were imputed to Christ, and his righteousness is imputed to us. He bore our sins; we are clothed in his righteousness. Imputation conveys neither pollution nor holiness. Christ's bearing our sins did not make him morally a sinner, any more than the victim was morally defiled which bore the sins of the people; nor does Christ's righteousness become subjectively ours, it is not the moral quality of our souls. This is what is not meant. What is meant is equally plain. Our sins were the judicial ground of the sufferings of Christ, so that they were a satisfaction of justice; and his righteousness is the judicial ground of our acceptance with God, so that our pardon is an act of justice. It is a justification; or, a declaration that justice is satisfied. We are set free by no mere act of sovereignty, but by the judicial decision of the infinitely just. As we, considered in ourselves, are just as undeserving and hell-deserving as ever, this justification is to us an act of infinite grace. The special consideration, therefore, by which the apostle enforces the exhortation, 'Be ye reconciled to God,' is that God can be just in the justification of sinners. There is nothing in the perfection of his character, nothing in the immutability of his law, nothing in the interests of his moral government, that stands in the way of our pardon. A full, complete, infinitely meritorious satisfaction has been made for our sins, and therefore we may come to God with the assurance of being accepted. This is a ground of confidence which an enlightened conscience, burdened with a sense of sin, absolutely needs. It is not mere pardon, but justification alone, that gives us peace with God.

CHAPTER VI.

The apostle continues the vindication of himself, vs. 1–10. Asserts his strong love for the Corinthians, and exhorts them to keep themselves free from all contaminating alliances, vs. 11–18.

The apostle's fidelity and love. Vs. 1–18.

As the occasion of writing this epistle was the false accusations of his opponents, a strain of self-vindication runs through the whole. In 5, 12 he said he spoke of himself to enable his friends in Corinth to defend him against his enemies. He was governed by the love of Christ, and acted as his ambassador; as such he was a fellow-worker with God, and exhorted men not to fail of the grace of God, vs. 1. 2. In the exercise of this office he avoided all offence, v. 3, proving his sincerity and fidelity as a minister of God, by the patient endurance of all kinds of trials, vs. 4. 5; by the exercise of all the graces and gifts of the Spirit, vs. 6. 7; and under all circumstances, whether of honour or dishonour, prosperity or adversity, whether understood or misunderstood by his fellow men, vs. 8–10. He thus unbosomed himself to the Corinthians, because his heart was enlarged. It was wide enough to take them all in. Whatever there was of the want of love or of due appreciation between them and him, the fault was on their side, not on his, vs. 11. 12. He begs them to be as large-hearted towards him as he was towards them, v. 13, and not to allow themselves to be involved in any intimate alliances with the wicked, vs. 13–18.

1. We then, (as) workers together (with him), beseech (you) also that ye receive not the grace of God in vain.

This verse is intimately connected with the preceding chapter by the particles δὲ καί, *but also*. He is still describing his manner of discharging his apostolic duties. He not only announced that God had made Christ sin for us, that we might become the righteousness of God in him, but also, as a co-worker with God, he exhorted men not to receive the grace of God in vain. In our version the apostle is made to say, "I beseech you also." This is wrong; the *also* belongs to the verb—"I also beseech you." That the word συνεργοῦντες, *co-operating*, refers to the apostle's co-operating with God, is plain from the connection, and from the nature of the work. He had just before, 5, 20, spoken of God's beseeching them; and now he says, we as co-workers beseech you. So in 1 Cor. 3, 9, he says, "We are co-workers with God." In the Vulgate the word is rendered *adjuvantes*, which favours the idea that he was co-operating with them, assisting them (i. e. the Corinthians) by his exhortations. Luther's version suggests the same meaning; Wir ermahen aber euch, als Mithelfer, *as joint-labourers or helpers we exhort you*. Compare 1, 24, where the apostle says, "We are helpers (συνεργοί) of your joy." This view of the passage is given by many commentators. It does not, however, so well, as just remarked, agree with the context; and it would require, to prevent ambiguity, the insertion of ὑμῖν, *with you.* As an apostle or minister of the gospel, Paul was a co-worker with God.

That ye receive not the grace of God in vain. What is it to receive the grace of God in vain? Some say that the meaning is to accept of the atonement of Christ, or reconciliation with God spoken of in the preceding chapter, and yet to live in sin. The favour of God is then accepted to no purpose. But this is an unscriptural idea. Justification and sanctification cannot be thus separated. A man cannot accept of reconciliation with God and live in sin; because the renunciation of sin is involved in the acceptance of reconciliation. Paul never assumes that men may accept one benefit of redemption, and reject another. They cannot take pardon and refuse sanctification. Others say that the apostle here exhorts his readers to guard against "falling from grace;" that having been graciously pardoned they should not, by a relapse into sin, forfeit the grace or favour which they had received. This is a very common interpretation. Olshausen says, "It is undeniable that the apostle assumes that grace when once received may be lost; the Scriptures know nothing of the dangerous error of the advocates of predestination, that grace cannot be lost; and experience stamps it as a lie." But in the first place, it is no argument in favour of this interpretation that the apostle uses the infinitive aorist (δέξασθαι), *have received,* because the aorist infinitive is very commonly used for the present after verbs signifying to command or exhort. See Rom. 12, 1. 15, 20. 2 Cor. 2, 8. Eph. 4, 1. Winer's Idioms of the New Testament, p. 386. In the second place, the "grace of God," here spoken of, does not mean the actual forgiveness of sin, nor the renewing, sanctifying influence of the Spirit, but the *favour* of which the apostle spoke in the preceding chapter. It is the infinite grace or favour of having made his Son sin for us, so that we may become the righteousness of God in him. This is the grace of God of which the apostle speaks. He exhorted men not to let it be in vain, as it regarded them, that a satisfaction for sin sufficient for all, and appropriate to all, had been made and offered to all who hear the gospel. In precisely the same sense he says, Gal. 2, 21, "I do not frustrate the grace of God." That is, 'I do not, by trusting to the works of the law, make it in vain that God has provided a gratuitous method of salvation.' That great grace or favour he did not make a thing of naught. In Gal. 5, 4, he says, " Whosoever of you are justified by the law, are fallen from grace." That is, ' ye have renounced the gratuitous method of salvation, and are debtors to do the whole law.' So in Rom. 6, 14, it is said, "We are not under law, but under grace." In no one of these cases does "grace" mean either the actual pardon of sin, or inward divine influence. It means the favour of God, and in this connection the great favour of redemption. The Lord Jesus Christ having died for our sins and procured eternal redemption for us, the apostle was most earnest in exhorting men not to allow this great favour, as regards them, to be in vain. It is the more evident that such is the meaning of the passage because it is not so much a direct exhortation to the Corinthians, as a declaration of the method in which the apostle preached. He announced the fact that God had made Christ who knew no sin to be sin for us, and he exhorted all men not to receive the grace of God in vain, that is, not to reject this great salvation. And finally, this interpretation is required by the following verse. "Behold, now is the accepted time; now is the day of salvation." This is appropriate as a motive to receive the offer of pardon and acceptance with God, but it is not appropriate as a reason why a renewed and pardoned sinner should not fall from grace. There is therefore no necessity to assume, contrary to the whole analogy of Scripture, that the apostle here teaches that those who have once made their peace with God and experienced his renewing grace can fall away unto perdition. If reconciled by the death of his Son, much more shall they be saved by his life. Nothing can ever separate them from the love of God which is in Christ Jesus. Whom he calls, them he also glorifies. They are kept by the mighty power of God through faith unto salvation.

2. (For he saith, I have heard thee in a time accepted, and in the day of salvation have I succoured thee; behold, now (is) the accepted time; behold, now (is) the day of salvation.)

The Scriptures contain abundant evidence that inspiration did not interfere with the natural play of the powers of the sacred writers. Although they spoke as they were moved by the Holy Ghost, yet they were probably in most cases unconscious of his influence, and acted as spontaneously as the believer does under the power of the Spirit in all his holy exercises. Hence we find that the sacred writings are constructed according to the ordinary laws of mind, and that the writers pass from subject to subject by the usual process of suggestion and association. So here the use of the word δέξασθαι brought up to the apostle's mind the word δεκτῷ, as it occurs in the beautiful passage, Is. 49, 8. Hence the quotation of that passage as it stands in the Greek version of the Old Testament. *I have heard thee in an accepted time.* In the Hebrew it is, *a time of grace;* and to this answers the equivalent expression, *the day of salvation.* It is on these expressions that the appropriateness of the citation rests. The Old Testament speaks of "a time of grace," and of "a day of salvation." That is, of a time and a day in which grace and salvation may be obtained. The apostle adds, by way of comment and application, "Behold, now is the accepted time; behold, now is the day of salvation." The connection between this verse and what precedes is thus clear. 'Receive not the grace of God in vain, *for* there is a time of grace and a day of salvation, and that day is now. Therefore, neglect not this great salvation.' The 49th chapter of Isaiah, whence this passage is taken, is addressed to the Messiah. He it was whom God chose to be his servant to restore Israel and to be a light to the Gentiles. He it was whom man despised and the nation abhorred, to whom kings should rise and princes worship. It was he to whom Jehovah said, "I have heard thee in an accepted time, and in the day of salvation have I succoured thee." This being the case, the use which the apostle makes of the passage may be explained either on the hypothesis adopted by Dr. J. A. Alexander, in his comment on this chapter, that the ideal person addressed is not the Messiah exclusively, but the Messiah and his people as represented in him. Therefore a promise of grace and salvation to the Messiah was at the same time a promise of grace and salvation to his people. This is the view which Bengel adopts. "*He saith,* the Father to Messiah, Is. 49, 8, embracing in him all believers." Or we may assume, in strict accordance with scriptural usage, that the apostle employs the language of the Old Testament to express his own ideas, without regard to its original application. God had in many ways, and on many occasions, promised to save sinners. To this promise the apostle appeals as a reason why men should accept the grace offered to them in Christ Jesus. He clothes this promise in scriptural language. He might have expressed it in any other equivalent form. But the language of the passage in Isaiah being brought to his mind by the principle of association, he adopts the form there given, without any intimation, expressed or implied, that the passage had not in the original a different application. Thus in Rom. 10, 18 he might have expressed the idea of the general proclamation of the gospel in his own words, but he chose to express it in the words of the nineteenth Psalm, "Their sound went into all the earth, and their words unto the ends of the world;" although that Psalm relates to an entirely different subject. We are accustomed, without hesitation and almost unconsciously, to make a similar use of scriptural language.

3. Giving no offence in any thing, that the ministry be not blamed.

The preceding verse is parenthetical, so that the connection is with v. 1. "We beseech—giving, &c." This and the following participles are all connected with the word (παρακαλοῦμεν) we beseech, or exhort, and are designed to show how the apostle discharged the duties of his office. This is his defence. *In nothing he gave offence.* He so acted that no one could fairly make his conduct a ground of rejecting the gospel. The word προσκοπή is properly the act of striking or stumbling; then metonymically, that at which or against which any one stumbles. In the figurative use of the word, as here employed, it means an occasion of unbelief. Paul, in preaching the gospel to those to whom it was previously unknown, and whose principal means of judging of it was the conduct of its preachers, was specially careful to avoid every thing which could prove a stumblingblock to his hearers. Although this motive has peculiar weight where the gospel is new, as among the heathen, yet every one knows that the moral power of a preacher depends almost entirely on the conviction which the people have of his sincerity and of the purity of his motives. This is a source of power for which neither learning nor talents can compensate. *That the ministry be not blamed;* or, as it is in many copies, *our ministry,* which gives the passage a most specific reference to himself, and is well suited to the whole connection.

Although in the following verses the apostle, as is his wont, gives his discourse free scope, allowing it, as it were, to flow on in its own impetuous and majestic course, without any attempt to reduce it to logical arrangement, yet in his mind order was so immanent that a certain method can always be detected even in his most impassioned utterances. So here, he first refers to the manifold trials, vs. 4. 5, then to the graces and gifts, vs. 6. 7, by which his sincerity had been tested and established; and then to the diverse circumstances of evil and of good report, under which he had maintained his integrity, vs. 8. 9. 10. Under these several heads there are the same number of specifications, nine in each. Under the two former, there is a ternary arrangement observable; three divisions, each with three specifications; and under the last, nine pairs of contrasts or antitheses, rising to that highest form of oratorical language, where truth is expressed in seeming contradictions. "Having nothing, yet possessing all things."

4. 5. But in all (things) approving ourselves as the ministers of God, in much patience, in afflictions, in necessities, in distresses, in stripes, in imprisonments, in tumults, in labours, in watchings, in fastings.

So far from causing the ministry to be blamed, Paul *in all things*, (ἐν παντί,) *in every relation, and on every occasion, approved* himself, i. e. commended himself, not by self-laudation, but by so acting as to force the conviction of his sincerity on all men. *As the ministers of God*, i. e. as the ministers of God commend themselves. This interpretation is required, as Paul uses διάκονοι, not διακόνους. It was as a minister he commended himself. *In much patience*, i. e. by patient endurance and constancy. Both ideas are expressed by the word ὑπομονή. Paul proved himself to be a true minister of Christ by the fortitude with which he endured sufferings, and by the constancy with which he adhered to his master under all these trials. In what follows in this and the next verse we have the trials enumerated to which he was subjected. These are arranged, as Bengel remarks, in three classes. The first, are general, *afflictions, necessities, and distresses ;* the second are specific, *stripes, imprisonments, and tumults ;* the third, voluntary, *labours, watchings, and fastings.* His constancy was exhibited in the cheerful endurance of all these kinds of trials.

As to the first, the terms used are often interchanged and often combined. Θλίψεις, *pressures*, from without or from within; including every thing which presses on the heart or tries the power of endurance or resistance; ἀνάγκαι, *necessities*, when a man is taxed to the utmost to know what to do or how to bear; στενοχωρίαι, *straits*, when one has no room to stand or turn, and therefore escape seems hopeless. It is opposed to largeness of place. "He brought my feet into a large place," as the Psalmist says. The preposition ἐν is to be rendered *by* before ὑπομονή, and *in* before all the other nouns in these two verses. He commended himself *by* patience, *in* afflictions, *in* necessities, &c., &c. *In stripes.* Paul, as we learn from 11, 24. 25, had already, at this period of his history, been eight times subjected to the ignominy and torture of the lash, five times by the Jews and thrice by the heathen. *In imprisonments.* How often the apostle was in prison we know not, as the Acts contain only a small part of his history. He was a prisoner at Philippi, at Jerusalem, at Cesarea, and at Rome; and when a prisoner his feet were in the stocks, or he was chained. The Holy Ghost testified that in every place "bonds and afflictions" awaited him. *In tumults.* The word is ἀκαταστασίαι, which may mean "tossings to and fro," and refer to Paul's being constantly driven from one place to another, so that he had no quiet abode. This he mentions as one of his sore trials in 1 Cor. 4, 11. The word, however, in the New Testament always elsewhere means either disorder or tumultuous outbreaks. Luke 21, 9. To these violent bursts of popular feeling the apostle was frequently exposed, as at Antioch in Pisidia, Acts 13, 50; at Lystra, 14, 19; at Philippi, 16, 19; at Ephesus, Acts 19, 29; at Jerusalem, 21, 30. Before these manifestations of wrath and power the bravest men often quail. Such tumults can neither be resisted by force, nor be stilled by the voice. What can one man do before an infuriated mob? He could as well resist a tornado. Yet he can be calm and adhere to his purpose. "It is often required," says Calvin, "of ministers of the gospel, that while they strive for peace, they should pass unbroken through tumults, and never deflect from the right course though heaven and earth should be mixed." Besides these trials which came upon the apostle against his will, or without his agency, there were painful sacrifices which he made voluntarily, and which were among the strongest proofs of his sincerity. These were his *labours, watchings, and fastings.* By labours are to be understood not only his working with his own hands to support himself while he made the gospel of no expense, but also the indefatigable exertions which he was constantly called to make, in travelling, and preaching, and in caring for the sick, the poor, and the interests of the church. *Watchings,* the sleepless nights which his constantly travelling, his anxieties and labours caused him to pass. *Fastings ;* this is often understood to refer to his suffering from hunger. But the word νηστεία is never used for involuntary abstinence from food, and as it occurs here in connection with labours and watchings, both of which were voluntary acts of self-denial, it is probably to be taken in its ordinary sense. Perhaps, however, the reference is to those cases of abstinence which were in a measure forced upon him, or which he chose to submit to rather than to omit some duty or to fail to take advantage of some opportunity of usefulness. There is nothing in the connection to demand a reference to religious fasting, as when prayers and fasting are mentioned together. Here it is labours and fastings.

6. 7. By pureness, by knowledge, by long-suffering, by kindness, by the Holy Ghost, by love unfeigned, by the word of truth, by the power of God, by the armour of righteousness on the right hand and on the left.

As the apostle commended himself *in* the various trials enumerated in the two preceding verses, so *by* the graces and gifts here specified, it was made manifest to all that he was a true apostle and faithful minister of God. *By pureness,* both of heart and life. This includes not merely freedom from the pollution of immoral acts, but disinterestedness and singleness of motive. *By knowledge ;* what kind or form of knowledge is here indicated can only be gathered from the context. Some say it is the knowledge of the fitness and propriety of things, which exhibits itself as discretion. But as the apostle is speaking of those things which commended him as a minister of God and preacher of the gospel, and as several of the other specifications in these two verses, refer to gifts as distinguished from graces, it is more probable that the reference is to evangelical knowledge; that knowledge which he manifested in his teaching. Comp. Eph. 3, 4, where he speaks of his knowledge of the mystery of Christ, as patent to all his readers. And in Gal. 1, 12, *et seq.*, he appeals to his possession of this knowledge, without any human teaching, as an undeniable proof of his divine mission. *By long-suffering*, i. e. patiently submitting to injustice and undeserved injuries. *By kindness*, i. e. χρηστότης (from χρηστός, *useful*) benevolence; a disposition to do good; as God is said to be kind to the unthankful and the evil, Luke 6, 35. *By the Holy Ghost;* that is, by the manifestation of the Holy Ghost as dwelling in me. It is the doctrine of the Scriptures, and specially of Paul's writings, that the Spirit of God dwells in all believers, and that besides those manifestations of his presence common to all, there is given to each one his special gift, whether ordinary or extraordinary; to one wisdom, to another knowledge, to another the gift of teaching, to another the working of miracles, &c. 1 Cor. 12, 7–11. In proof of his being a true minister of God, Paul appeals to the evidence of the presence of the Spirit in him, which evidence was to be found in those graces and gifts of the Holy Ghost with which he was replenished; and in the divine power which attended and rendered successful his preaching. He could appeal to his converts and say, "Ye are the seal of my apostleship in the Lord," 1 Cor. 9, 2. *By love unfeigned.* As in the preceding clause he referred to kindness or benevolence, here *love* must be taken in the restricted sense of Christian love—not that affection which is exercised towards the just and the unjust, but that which springs from the peculiar relations of the believer to God and to his brethren. It is brotherly love, or the love of the brethren as such. *By the word of truth*, that is, by the preaching of the truth, or preaching the contents of which is truth. The reference is not to veracity, but to the exhibition of the truth in his preaching. In a previous chapter, 4, 2, he had said, "By the manifestation of the truth I commend myself to every man's conscience in the sight of God." *By the power of God.* The power of God was manifested in various ways in Paul's ministry. "He that wrought in Peter," he says, "to the apostleship of the circumcision, the same was mighty in me towards the Gentiles," Gal. 2, 8. By these various manifestations of divine power in his conversion, in his preparation for his work, and in the exercise of his apostleship, he was proved to be a true servant of God. *By the armour of righteousness.* The word "righteousness" is used in Scripture in two senses. It means either rectitude, uprightness, honesty, in the comprehensive sense of the terms; or it means justifying righteousness, the righteousness of faith, so often called the righteousness of God. Calvin and many others take it in the former sense here, and understand by the "armour of righteousness," that armour which integrity affords, or those arms which are consistent with moral rectitude. Others prefer the latter sense of the word, and understand the armour of righteousness to be that which is secured by our justification before God. This interpretation is not only more in keeping with Paul's usage of the word, but more consistent with the context. It was not Paul's honesty which was his armour, or by which he established his claim to be a minister of God, but the supernatural gifts and graces of the Spirit. In Eph. 6, 14, he compares this righteousness to a breastplate; here to the whole panoply, *on the right hand and on the left*, offensive and defensive, because he who is justified, or clothed with the righteousness of Christ, has every thing at command. He has the shield of faith, and the helmet of salvation, and the sword of the Spirit.

8-10. By honour and dishonour, by evil report and good report; as deceivers, and (yet) true; as unknown, and (yet) well known; as dying, and behold, we live; as chastened, and not killed; as sorrowful, yet always rejoicing; as poor, yet making many rich; as having nothing, and (yet) possessing all things.

These verses are intimately connected, forming a distinct division of the apostle's discourse. In vs. 4. 5, we had the preposition ἐν in its local sense. Paul commended himself by patience *in* afflictions, *in* necessities, &c. In vs. 6. 7 the same preposition is used in its instrumental sense, *by* pureness, *by* knowledge, &c. Here the preposition διά has a local sense, *through, in the midst of*. He maintained his consistency and integrity under all circumstances, through honour and dishon-. our, through evil report and good report. He was always the same—preached the same doctrine, urged the same duties, maintained the same principles, whether his preaching was approved or disapproved, whether it secured for him admiration or brought down upon him reproach. This is the common and most natural interpretation. Many, however, prefer the instrumental sense of the preposition. ' *By means of* honour which we receive from the friends of God, and by means of the dishonour heaped upon us by our enemies.' That the good honoured him, and the wicked defamed him, was proof of his integrity. This requires too much to be supplied in order to bring out the sense. The former interpretation is more simple, and gives a meaning quite as pertinent. The figure which he uses is that of a road, along which he marches to victory, through all obstacles, disregarding what is said or thought by others. This last clause serves as the transition to a new mode of representation. He no longer speaks of what he did, but of the judgment of others concerning him. *As deceivers, and yet true.* These and the following adjectives and participles, as they are in Greek, though translated in some cases as substantives, are parallel with συνιστῶντες in v. 4. 'We beseech you, *commending* ourselves, &c., and we beseech you, *as deceivers, yet true*, &c.' That is, we go steadily on in the discharge of our duty whatever men may think or say. *As deceivers*, (πλάνοι,) not merely false pretenders, but seducers, men who lead others astray, and themselves wander from the truth. Matt. 27, 63. 1 Tim. 4, 1. 2 John 7. It is here the opposite of ἀληθεῖς, in the sense of *truthful*, loving and speaking the truth. Matt. 22, 16. Mark 12, 14. 'Regarded as seducers, we are the advocates of the truth.' *As unknown, yet well known*, (ὡς ἀγνοούμενοι, καὶ ἐπιγινωσκόμενοι,) regarded with contempt as obscure and ignoble, yet recognised and famous. The antithesis is either that expressed in our version, between being unknown and being well known, or, between being misunderstood and being duly appreciated. The latter of the two words used by the apostle may well express that sense, as ἐπιγινώσκω often means to recognize, or acknowledge one to be what he is, or professes to be, 1, 13. 14. Matt. 17, 12, and although the former word does not elsewhere occur precisely in the sense of being misunderstood, yet to be unknown and to be unrecognized are ideas so nearly related, that it is not unnatural to take the word in that sense here, if the antithesis and context require it. Paul was unknown to the mass of the people; he was taken to be what he was not; and yet he was duly appreciated, and recognized in his true character by others. *As dying*, i. e. regarded by others as certain to perish, *and behold we live.* This is one interpretation. It is, however, more in harmony with what follows to understand the apostle to refer to actual facts. He was, as he says, 4, 11 and 1 Cor. 15, 31, constantly exposed to death. He died daily, and yet he lived. God always interposed to rescue him from destruction when it seemed inevitable, and to sustain him under calamities which to all appearance no man could bear. *As chastened, but not killed.* To chasten (παιδεύειν) is properly to treat as a child, and as children are often made to suffer by their parents for their good, to chasten is to correct by suffering. The word, however, is often used to express simply the idea of infliction of pain without any reference to the end of the infliction. God never punishes his people. That is, their sufferings are never designed to satisfy justice; nor are they always even chastisements in the proper sense of the word. They are not in all cases sent to correct evils, to repress pride, or to wean from the world. God often afflicts his people and his church simply to enable them the better to glorify his name. It is an unchristian disposition, therefore, which leads us always to ask, when afflictions are sent upon ourselves or others, Why is this? What have we or they done to call forth this expression of parental displeasure or solicitude? What does God mean to rebuke? It may be that our sufferings are chastisements, that is, that they are designed to correct some evil of the heart or life, but this is not to be inferred from the simple fact that they are sufferings. The greater part of Paul's sufferings were not chastisements. They were designed simply to show to all ages the power of the grace of God; to let men see what a man could cheerfully endure, and rejoice that he was called upon to endure, for the sake of the Lord Jesus. In this case *chastened* means simply afflicted. There is no reference to the design of God in sending the sufferings which the apostle was called to endure. There is another view of the meaning of this passage, which supposes the words to be uttered from the stand-point of Paul's enemies. "Chastised, but not killed." 'Regarded as an object of divine displeasure, as smitten of God, (which may be true,) yet I am not killed.' It is, however, more in keeping with what follows to understand the apostle as referring to his actual experience. He was greatly afflicted, but not killed; cast down, as he says in 4, 9, but not destroyed. Compare Ps. 118, 18, "The Lord hath chastened me sore; but he hath not delivered me over unto death." Let believers therefore regard their afflictions, when they can, not as indications of God's disapprobation, but rejoice in them as opportunities graciously afforded them to glorify his name. *As sorrowful, yet always rejoicing.* This again may mean, 'Looked upon as sorrowful, yet in fact always rejoicing;' or, 'Although overwhelmed with sorrow, yet full of joy.' The latter interpretation is to be preferred. This is one of the paradoxes of Christian experience. The believer has more true joy in sorrow, than the world can ever afford. The sense of the love of God, assurance of his support, confidence in future blessedness, and the persuasion that his present light afflictions shall work out for him a far more exceeding and an eternal weight of glory, mingle with his sorrows, and give the suffering child of God a peace which passes all understanding. He would not exchange his lot with that of the most prosperous of the children of this world. *As poor, yet making many rich.* Poor in this world's goods, yet imparting to many the true riches; *as having nothing,* i. e. of earthly treasure, *yet possessing all things,* in the sense in which in 1 Cor. 3, 21, he tells the Corinthians, "All things are yours." The real property in any thing vests in him for whose benefit it is held and used. And as all things, whether the world, or life or death, or things present or things to come, are held and disposed by God for the benefit of his people, for their present good and future glory, they are the real proprietors of all things. Being joint heirs with Christ, Rom. 8, 17, they possess all things.

11. O (ye) Corinthians, our mouth is open unto you, our heart is enlarged.

This and the two following verses are an epilogue to the preceding vindication of himself, and an introduction to the following exhortations. *O Corinthians.* This direct address is unusual with the apostle, and is expressive of strong feeling. Gal. 3, 1. *Our mouth is open* (ἀνέωγε, 2 perfect, as present and intransitive, see John 1, 52.) To open the mouth is a common scriptural expression, meaning to begin to speak, or, to speak, as in Matt. 5, 2. Acts 8, 32. 35. Here, as the context shows, it is used emphatically, and means, to speak freely and openly. Compare Eph. 6, 19. *Our heart is enlarged.* See 1 Kings 4, 29. Ps. 119, 32. Is. 60, 5. Any joyful, generous feeling is said to enlarge the heart. A large-hearted man is one of generous and warm affections. The apostle had poured out his heart to the Corinthians. He has spoken with the utmost freedom and openness, and in doing so his heart was expanded towards them. He was ready to embrace them all, and to take them to his arms as his dear children.

12. Ye are not straitened in us, but ye are straitened in your own bowels.

The apostle abides by his figure. A large heart is one expanded by love; a straitened heart is one void of generous affections. To be straitened (στενοχωρέω) is to want room; στενοχωρία is want of room, straits, distress, anguish of mind. Hence to enlarge, to give one a wide place, is to deliver, to bless. Ps. 4, 1. 118, 5. *Ye are not straitened in us,* i. e. there is no lack of room for you in our heart; *but ye are straitened in your own bowels,* i. e. your heart is too narrow to admit me. *Straitened in your own bowels,* means, not that you are inwardly afflicted, or that the cause of your trouble is in yourselves, but, as the context requires, ' Your bowels (hearts) are narrow or contracted.' There is not room in them to receive me. Without a figure the meaning is, ' The want of love is on your side, not on mine.'

13. Now for a recompense in the same, (I speak as unto (my) children,) be ye also enlarged.

The exhortation or request is, ' Be ye also enlarged, i. e. open your hearts to receive me, which is only a proper recompense for my love to you. I speak as to children, who are expected to requite the love of their parents with filial affection.' The words τὴν δὲ αὐτὴν ἀντιμισθίαν are explained as a concise expression for τὸ δὲ αὐτό, ὅ ἐστιν ἀντιμισθία, ' as to the same thing, which is a recompense, be ye also enlarged.' The accusative is the accusative absolute.

14. Be ye not unequally yoked together with unbelievers : for what fellowship hath righteousness with unrighteousness ? and what communion hath light with darkness ?

After the exhortation to requite his love by loving him, he exhorts them to keep aloof from all intimate association with the evil. The exhortation is general, and is not to be confined to partaking of heathen sacrifices, nor to intermarriage with

the heathen, much less to association with the opponents of
the apostle. It no doubt had a special reference or application to the peculiar circumstances of the Corinthians, and was
intended to guard them against those entangling and dangerous associations with the unconverted around them, to which
they were specially exposed. And as we know that their
special danger was from idolaters, (see 1 Cor. ch. 8, and 10,
14–33,) whose festivals they were constantly urged to attend,
it is to be presumed that it was from all association with the
heathen in their worship that the apostle intended to warn
them.   But this is only one application of the principle here
laid down, viz., that intimate associations ought not to be
formed by the people of God with those who are not his people. The same remark may be made in reference to the persons here intended by *unbelievers*. It is no doubt true that
by unbelievers (οἱ ἄπιστοι) Paul meant the heathen. (See 1
Cor. 6, 6.) But it does not follow from this that intimate association with the heathen is all that is here forbidden. The
principle applies to all the enemies of God and children of
darkness.   It is intimate, voluntary association with the
wicked that is forbidden. The worse a man is, the more
openly he is opposed to Christ and his gospel, the greater the
danger and evil of connection with him. It is not so much
his profession as his real character and influence that is to be
taken into account. If it be asked whether the marriage of
professors of religion with non-professors, in the modern (or
American) sense of those terms, is here expressly prohibited?
The answer must be in the negative. There were no such
classes of persons in the apostolic age, as professing and non-
professing Christians. The distinction was then between
Christians and heathens. Persons born within the pale of the
Christian Church, baptized in the name of Christ, and relig-
iously educated, do not belong to the same category as the
heathen. And the principle which applied to the latter therefore does not apply to the former. Still it is to be remembered that it is the union of incongruous elements, of the
devout and undevout, of the spiritual and the worldly, of the
good and the evil, of the children of God and the children of
the evil one, that the apostle exhorts Christians to avoid. *Be
not unequally yoked.* The word is ἑτεροζυγέω, *to be yoked
heterogeneously*, i. e. with an animal of another kind. The
allusion is evidently to the Mosaic law which forbade the
uniting animals of different kinds in the same yoke. Deut. 22,

10. In Lev. 19, 19, ἐτερόζυγος, in the Septuagint, means an animal of a different kind. It is the union of incongruous, uncongenial elements or persons that is forbidden. *With unbelievers ;* as the dative, ἀπίστοις, cannot depend on the preceding word, it is explained by resolving the concise phrase of the apostle into the full form, μὴ γίνεσθε ἐτεροζυγ. καὶ οὕτως ὁμιζυγοῦντες ἀπίστοις. Winer, p. 252. By unbelievers, as above remarked, are to be understood the heathen, those who did not profess faith in the gospel. The exhortation is enforced by the following questions, which are designed to show the incongruity of such unions. *For what fellowship hath righteousness with unrighteousness ?* This is stronger than asking, What fellowship have the righteous with the unrighteous? because there are many bonds of sympathy between good and bad men, arising from the participation of a common nature, and from the fact that in this life, the good are not wholly good, nor the bad wholly bad. The apostle, therefore, contrasts the characteristic and opposing principles by which the two classes are distinguished. By righteousness as opposed to unrighteousness, (δικαιοσύνη to ἀνομία,) is meant goodness, or moral excellence in general, conformity to the law of God as opposed to opposition to that law. It does not mean justifying righteousness, as though the contrast were, as some explain it, between the justified and the not justified. The opposition intended is that which exists between the righteous and the wicked. What *fellowship,* (μετοχή,) partnership. That is, what have they in common ? What bond of union or sympathy is there between them? *And what communion* (κοινωνία), see Acts 2, 42. 1 Cor. 1, 9. 10, 16. Parties are said to be in communion when they are so united that what belongs to the one belongs to the other, or when what is true of the one is true of the other. Believers are in communion, or have fellowship one with another, when they recognize each other as having a joint interest in the benefits of redemption, and are conscious that the inward experience of the one is that of the other. Incongruous elements cannot be thus united, and any attempt to combine them must destroy the character of one or the other. *Hath light with darkness. Light* is the common scriptural emblem of knowledge, holiness and blessedness. Hence Christians are said to be the children of light. Luke 16, 8. 1 Thess. 5, 5. Paul was sent "to turn men from darkness to light," Acts 26, 18. Rom. 13, 12. Eph. 5, 8. 9. *Darkness,* on the other hand, is the emblem of error, sin and

misery. Satan's kingdom is called the kingdom of darkness,
and the wicked are the children of darkness; and the state of
final perdition is " outer darkness." Nothing can be more incongruous than light and darkness, whether in the literal or
figurative meaning of the terms. The attempt, therefore, of
Christians to remain Christians and retain their inward state
as such, and yet to enter voluntarily into intimate fellowship
with the world, is as impossible as to combine light and darkness, holiness and sin, happiness and misery.

15. And what concord hath Christ with Belial? or what part hath he that believeth with an infidel?

What concord, (συμφώνησις,) " harmony of voice." How
discordant or opposite are Christ and Belial? How then can
their followers agree? The proper orthography of the word
according to the Hebrew is Belial, as here in the received
text. Many MSS. read Beliar, (agreeably to a common
change of the l for r by the Jews who spoke Greek,) others
Beliam. The word is properly an abstract noun signifying
worthlessness, then *wickedness.* Hence the wicked are called
" sons of Belial," i. e. *worthless.* It is used as a concrete noun
in 2 Sam. 23, 6. Job 34, 18. " Wicked one," and hence, by
way of eminence, for Satan, who is ὁ πονηρός, the evil one.
Compare 1 Cor. 10, 21, where the impossibility of uniting the
service of Christ and the service of Satan is presented in much
the same terms as it is here. Christ is God manifest in the
flesh; Satan is the prince of darkness. How can they, or their
followers agree? *Or what part* (μερίς, in the sense of *participation, fellowship.* Col. 1, 12) *hath he that believeth with an
infidel.* In modern usage an *unbeliever* often means one destitute of saving faith; and an *infidel* one destitute even of
speculative faith, one who denies the gospel to be a revelation
from God. This is a distinction unknown to the Bible. The
word here rendered *infidel* is in v. 14 rendered *unbeliever.*
In the apostolic age all who professed faith of any kind were
called believers, and unbelievers were infidels. It was assumed that the faith possessed was genuine; and therefore it
was assumed that all believers were truly the children of God.
A mere speculative believer and an infidel may agree well
enough in their tastes, character and pursuits. There is no
such incompatibility or antipathy between them, as the apostle assumes to exist between the (πιστός and ἄπιστος) believer

and unbeliever. It is taken for granted that faith changes the whole character; that it makes a man move in an entirely different sphere, having different feelings, objects, and principles from those of unbelievers; so that intimate union, communion or sympathy between believers and unbelievers is as impossible as fellowship between light and darkness, Christ and Belial. And it must be so. They may indeed have many things in common; a common country, common kindred, common worldly avocations, common natural affections, but the interior life is entirely different; not only incongruous, but essentially opposed the one to the other. To the one, Christ is God, the object of supreme reverence and love; to the other, he is a mere man. To the one, the great object of life is to promote the glory of Christ and to secure his favour; to the other, these are objects of indifference. Elements so discordant can never be united into a harmonious whole.

16. And what agreement hath the temple of God with idols? for ye are the temple of the living God; as God hath said, I will dwell in them, and walk in (them); and I will be their God, and they shall be my people.

In this and the following verses we have, 1. The assertion of the incongruity between the temple of God and idols. 2. The reason assigned for presenting this incongruity, '*For* ye are the temple of God.' 3. The proof from Scripture that believers are God's temple. 4. The duty which flows from this intimate relation to God; and 5. The gracious promise made to all those who live in accordance with the relation which they bear to God. *What agreement* (συγκατάθεσις, see Luke 23, 51,) *hath the temple of God with idols?* A building consecrated to the true God is no place for idols. Men cannot combine the worship of God and the worship of devils. Idolatry is everywhere in Scripture represented as the greatest insult the creature can offer the Creator; and the grossest form of that insult is to erect idols in God's own temple. Such was the indignity which those Corinthians offered to God, who, while professing to be Christians, joined in the religious services of the heathen. And such, in its measure, is the offence committed when the people of God become associated with the wicked in their inward and outward life. It is the introduction of idols into God's temple. *For ye are the temple of the living God.* There would be no propriety in the preceding illustration if believers were not God's temple. This, therefore, the apostle first asserts and then proves. The text is here uncertain. The majority of MSS. read with the common text, ὑμεῖς, *ye;* Lachmann, Meyer and some other editors, on the authority of a few MSS. and of the context, read ἡμεῖς, *we.* The sense is substantially the same. The common text is to be preferred both on external and internal grounds. The apostle is addressing the Corinthians, and properly therefore says, *Ye are the temple of God.* A temple is not a building simply consecrated to God, but one in which he dwells, as he dwelt by the visible manifestation of his glory in the temple of old. Hence heaven, as God's dwelling place, is called his temple. Ps. 11, 2. Habak. 2, 20. Christ's body is called a temple, because in him dwelt the fulness of the Godhead. John 2, 19. Believers collectively, or the church, is God's temple, because inhabited by his Spirit, Eph. 2, 21, and for the same reason every individual believer, and every believer's body is a temple of God. 1 Cor. 3, 16. 6, 19. To prove that they were the temple of God, individually and collectively, he therefore cites the declaration of the Scriptures that God dwells in his people. "I will dwell in them and walk in them." God is said to dwell wherever he specially and permanently manifests his presence. And since he thus specially and permanently manifests his presence in his people collectively and individually, he is said to dwell in all and in each. *To walk in them* is simply a parallelism with the preceding clause, expressing the idea of the divine presence in another form. The nearest approach to the words here cited is Lev. 26, 11. 12, where the same thought is expressed, though in somewhat different words. Instead of, "I will set my tabernacle among you," the apostle expresses the same idea by saying, "I will dwell in them." *In them*, is not simply among them, because the presence of God by his Spirit is always represented as internal, in the heart. "If Christ be in you," says the apostle, "the body is dead, &c." "If the Spirit of Him who raised Christ from the dead dwell in you, &c." Rom. 8, 10. 11. So of every believer our Lord says, "If a man love me, he will keep my words, and my Father will love him; and we will come unto him, and make our abode with him," John 14, 23. Every thing is full of God. An insect, a flower, is a constant manifestation of his presence and power. It is what it is because God is in it. So of the human soul, it is said to be full of God when its inward state, its affections and acts, are determined and controlled by him, so as to be a constant manifestation of the divine presence. Then the soul is pure, and glorious, and free, and blessed. This is what God promises to accomplish in us, when he says, "I will dwell in you and walk in you." It is only a variation of form whem it is added, *I will be their God, and they shall be my people.* This is the great promise of the covenant with Abraham and with all the true Israel. It is one of the most comprehensive and frequently repeated promises of the Scriptures. Gen. 17, 8. Deut. 29, 13. Jerem. 31, 33. Heb. 8, 10, &c., &c. There is unspeakably more in the promises of God than we are able to understand. The promise that the nations should be blessed in the seed of Abraham, as unfolded in the New Testament, is found to comprehend all the blessings of redemption. So the promise, I will be their God, and they shall be my people, contains more than it has ever entered into the heart of man to conceive. How low are our conceptions of God! Of necessity our conceptions of what it is to have a God, and that God, Jehovah, must be entirely inadequate. It is not only to have an infinite protector and benefactor, but an infinite portion; an infinite object of love and confidence; an infinite source of knowledge and holiness. It is for God to be to us what he designed to be when he created us after his image, and filled us with his fulness. *His* people, are those whom he recognizes as his peculiar property, the objects of his love, and the recipients of his favours.

17. Wherefore come out from among them, and be ye separate, saith the Lord, and touch not the unclean (thing); and I will receive you.

This is a free citation from Is. 52, 11. 12, where the same exhortation to separate themselves from the wicked, and specially from the heathen, is addressed to the people of God. The words *and I will receive you* have nothing to answer to them in the passage in Isaiah, unless it be the words "God shall be your rere-ward;" literally, "he that gathereth you." In Judges 19, 18 the same word is rendered *to receive*, "There is no one receiveth me to house." It is more probable, however, that they are borrowed from Ezekiel 20, 34, as

it is rendered in the Septuagint. The exhortation is founded
on the preceding passage. God is most intimately related to
his people. They are his temple. He dwells in them. Therefore they are bound to keep themselves unspotted from the
world. Their being God's temple, his presence in them, and
his regarding them as his people, depends upon their separa-
tion from the world. For if any man love the world, the love
of the Father is not in him. 1 John 2, 15. In this whole context the apostle clothes his own exhortation to the Corinthians
in the language of God himself, that they might see that what
he taught was indeed the word of God.

18. And will be a Father unto you, and ye shall be my sons and daughters, saith the Lord Almighty.

This is a continuation of the promise commenced in the
preceding verse. God declares that he will not only receive
into his favour those who regard themselves as his temple and
keep themselves aloof from all contaminating associations with
the wicked, but that he will be a father to them. It is not
with the favour of a master to a servant that he will regard
them, but with the favour which a father exercises to his sons
and daughters. This is the language of the Lord Almighty;
of the omnipotent God. To be his sons and daughters is a
dignity and blessedness before which all earthly honours and
all worldly good disappear. It is doubtful what particular
passage of the Old Testament the apostle had in his mind in
this citation. Some think it was 2 Sam. 7, 14, but there
God merely says to David in reference to his promised seed,
"I will be his father, and he shall be my son." There is
too little similarity in form, and too remote an analogy of
sentiment, to render it probable that that passage was the
one referred to. Is. 43, 6 is more in point. "Bring my
sons from far, and my daughters from the ends of the earth."
Here the people of God are said to be his sons and daughters;
which is all that the citation of the apostle asserts. The concluding verses of this chapter are an instructive illustration of
the way in which the New Testament writers quote the Old.
1. They often quote a translation which does not strictly adhere to the original. 2. They often quote according to the
sense and not according to the letter. 3. They often blend
together different passages of Scripture, so as to give the sense
not of any one passage, but the combined sense of several.

4. They sometimes give the sense not of any particular passage or passages, but, so to speak, the general sense of Scripture. That is, they quote the Scriptures as saying what is nowhere found in so many words, but what nevertheless the Scriptures clearly teach. There is no such passage, for example, as that contained in this verse in the Old Testament, but the sentiment is often and clearly therein expressed. 5. They never quote as of authority any but the canonical books of the Old Testament.

CHAPTER VII.

An exhortation founded on what is said in the preceding chapter, v. 1. Paul's consolation derived from the favourable account which he had received from Corinth, vs. 2–16.

The effect produced on the church in Corinth by the apostle's former letter, and his consequent satisfaction and joy.

AFTER in v. 1 exhorting them to live as became those to whom such precious promises had been given as he had just recited from the word of God, he in vs. 2. 3 repeats his desire before expressed, 6, 13, that they would reciprocate his ardent love. So far as he was concerned there was nothing in the way of this cordial reconciliation. He had not injured them, nor was he alienated from them. He had great confidence in them. His apprehensions and anxiety had been in a great measure removed by the account which he had received from Titus of the feelings of the Corinthians towards him, vs. 4–7. It is true that he did at one time regret having written that letter respecting the incestuous person; but he no longer regretted it, because he found that the sorrow which that letter occasioned was the sorrow of true repentance, redounding not to their injury, but to their good, vs. 8. 9. It was not the sorrow of the world, but true godly sorrow, as was evident from its effects, vs. 10–12. Therefore the apostle was comforted, and delighted to find how much Titus had been gratified by his visit to Corinth. All that the apostle had told him of the good dispositions of the Corinthians had proved to be true, vs. 13–16.

1. Having therefore these promises, dearly beloved, let us cleanse ourselves from all filthiness of the flesh and spirit, perfecting holiness in the fear of God.

This verse properly belongs to the preceding chapter. It is the appropriate conclusion of the exposition there made. The promises referred to are, 1st. Of the indwelling of God, 6, 16. 2d. Of his favour, v. 17. 3d. That they should be his sons and daughters. *Therefore*, says the apostle, having these promises of intimate association with God, and this assurance of his love, *let us purify ourselves;* i. e. not merely keep ourselves pure by avoiding contamination, but, as already defiled, let us strive to become pure. Though the work of purification is so often referred to God as its author, Acts 15, 9. Eph. 5, 26, this does not preclude the agency of his people. They are to work out their own salvation, because it is God who worketh in them both to will and to do. If God's agency in sanctification does not arouse and direct ours; if it does not create the desire for holiness, and strenuous efforts to attain it, we may be sure that we are not its subjects. He is leaving us undisturbed in our sins. *From all filthiness of the flesh and spirit.* All sin is a pollution. There are two classes of sin here recognized; those of the flesh, and those of the spirit. By the former we are to understand those sins which defile the body, as drunkenness and debauchery; and by the latter those which affect only the soul, as pride and malice. By filthiness of the flesh, therefore, is not to be understood mere ceremonial uncleanness, nor the participation of the body in sinful acts, such as bowing down to an idol, or offering incense to false gods, but the desecration of the body as the temple of the Holy Ghost. See 1 Cor. 6, 19. *Perfecting holiness.* This expresses or indicates the way in which we are to purify ourselves. It is by perfecting holiness. The word ἐπιτελέω does not here mean simply *to practise*, but to complete, to carry on to perfection. Comp. 8, 6. 11. Phil. 1, 6. It is only by being completely or perfectly holy that we can attain the purity required of us as the temples of God. *Holiness* (ἁγιωσύνη, Rom. 1, 3. 1 Thess. 3, 13) includes not only the negative idea of purity, or freedom from all defilement, but also, positively, that of moral excellence. *In the fear of God.* This is the motive which is to determine our endeavours to purify ourselves. It is not regard to the good of others, nor our own happiness, but reverence for God. We are to be holy, because he is holy.

2. Receive us; we have wronged no man, we have corrupted no man, we have defrauded no man.

Receive us ; literally, *make room for us,* i. e. in your heart. It is a repetition or resumption of the request, "Be ye also enlarged," contained in 6, 13. Then follow the reasons, at least those of a negative kind, why they should thus receive the apostle. *We have wronged no man,* (ἠδικήσαμεν,) *we have treated no one unjustly.* The expression is perfectly general. It may refer either to his conduct as a man, or to the exercise of his apostolical authority. There is nothing to limit it, or to determine the kind of injustice which had been laid to his charge, or which he here had specially in view. *We have corrupted no man.* The word φθείρω, rendered *to corrupt,* means to injure or destroy, either in a moral or physical sense. It is used in a moral sense, 11, 3. 1 Cor. 15, 33. Eph. 4, 22, and in 1 Cor. 3, 17, it is used first in the one sense and then in the other. "If any defile the temple of God, him shall God destroy." Which sense should be adopted here is uncertain. Paul may mean to say that he had corrupted no one's morals by his example or arts of seduction; or that he had corrupted no man's faith by his false teaching; or that he had ruined no man as to his estate. The only reason for preferring the latter interpretation is that the other words with which it is associated express external injuries. There is no ground for the assumption that Paul refers to his former letter and intends to vindicate himself from the charge of injustice or undue severity in his treatment of the incestuous person. That matter he has not yet adverted to; and the expressions here used are too general, and the last ("we have defrauded no man") is inapplicable to that case. By *defrauding* he probably means acting unfairly in pecuniary affairs. The word πλεονεκτέω, in the New Testament, means either to have or take advantage of any one, 2, 11, or, *to make gain of, to defraud.* The usage of the word and of its cognates is in favour of the latter sense. 12, 17. 18. 1 Cor. 5, 10. 6, 10. Paul was specially careful to avoid all occasion of suspicion as to the disposition of the money which he raised from the churches for the relief of the poor. 8, 19. 20, and no doubt his enemies were ready enough to insinuate that he appropriated the money to his own use. He had therefore occasion to show that he had never made gain of them, that he had defrauded no man.

3. I speak not (this) to condemn (you): for I have said before, that ye are in our hearts to die and live with (you).

I speak not this to condemn you; i. e. In defending myself I do not mean to condemn you. This may mean either, 'In saying that I have wronged no man, I do not intend to imply that you have wronged me;' or, 'I do not mean to imply that you think of me so unjustly as to suppose that I have wronged, injured or defrauded any one.' In other words, 'I do not mean to question your love.' *For.* What follows assigns the reason or proof that he had no unkind feeling towards them which would lead him to condemn them. *I said before,* viz., in 6, 12, *that ye are in our hearts.* That is, that I love you. He had said that his heart was enlarged towards them, which was proof enough that he did not now mean to upbraid them. *To die and live with you,* εἰς τὸ συναποθανεῖν καὶ συζῆν, *so as to die and live together.* That is, 'Ye are so rooted in my heart that I would gladly live and die with you,' or, 'so that neither death nor life can separate us.' As remarked above, Paul's love for the Corinthians seems to have been extraordinary, having something of the nature of a passion, being more ardent than either their good qualities or their conduct towards him could account for. This is often the case in men of warm and generous feeling, who have frequently to say, 'The more abundantly we love, the less we are loved.'

4. Great (is) my boldness of speech toward you, great (is) my glorying of you: I am filled with comfort, I am exceeding joyful in all our tribulation.

So far from having any disposition to upbraid or to recriminate, his heart was overflowing with far different feelings. He had not only confidence in them, he was proud of them; he was not only comforted, he was filled with exceeding joy.

There is a climax here, as Calvin says: Gradatim procedit amplificando: plus enim est gloriari, quam securo et quieto esse animo: liberari vero a moerore ex multis afflictionibus concepto, utroque majus. His boasting of them was more than having confidence in them; and his rejoicing in the midst of his afflictions was more than being comforted. *Great is my boldness of speech towards you.* The word is παῤῥησία, which here, as in many other places, Eph. 3, 12. Heb. 3, 6. 1 John 2, 28. 3, 21. 4, 17. 5, 14, instead of its primary sense of freedom of speech, expresses the idea of joyful confidence; i. e. the state of mind from which freedom of utterance, or boldness of speech, flows. Paul means to say that so far from wishing to condemn the Corinthians he had joyful confidence in them. And not only that, he adds, but, *Great is my glorying of you,* (καύχησις,) i. e. *my boasting over you.* The accounts which the apostle had just received of the state of things at Corinth, and especially of the effect produced by his former letter, had not only obliterated his feelings of anxiety and doubt concerning them, but made him boast of them. He gloried on their account. He was disposed to tell every one how well his dear Corinthians had behaved. He thus, as it were, unconsciously lays bare the throbbings of his warm and generous heart. *I am filled with comfort,* literally, 'with *the* comfort,' i. e. the comfort to which he afterwards refers; or the comfort which his situation specially demanded. Such was the apostle's anxiety about the effect of his former letter that, as he says, 2, 13, "he had no rest in his spirit," and therefore left Troas and hastened into Macedonia that he might meet Titus on his way back from Corinth. This anxiety was now all gone. His mind was at rest. He was full of consolation. *I am exceedingly joyful,* (ὑπερπερισσεύομαι τῇ χαρᾷ,) *I more than abound in joy,* or *the* joy. Comp. Rom. 5, 20. He was more than merely comforted, he was overflowing with joy, and that too in spite of all the troubles which still pressed upon him, for he adds, *in all our tribulation.* The favourable accounts which Paul had received from Corinth, although they had removed some of the causes of his anxiety and suffering, left others in their full force. So that even when he wrote he was in great trouble. He therefore uses the present tense. 'I am overflowing with joy in the midst of tribulation.' Another proof that joy and sorrow may coexist in the mind. The martyr at the stake, in the midst of his agony, has often been filled with ecstatic joy.

5. For, when we were come into Macedonia, our flesh had no rest, but we were troubled on every side; without (were) fightings, within (were) fears.

The connection is with the last clause of the preceding verse. I was comforted in tribulation, *for also* (καὶ γάρ) *having come into Macedonia, our flesh had no rest.* Paul did not leave his troubles behind him in Troas, 2, 12, but *also* in Macedonia his flesh had no rest. By *flesh* he does not mean his body, for the sufferings, which he immediately specifies, were not corporeal, but mental. It stands for his whole sensitive nature considered as frail. It is equivalent to saying, 'my feeble nature had no rest.' The same idea is expressed in 2, 13, by saying, "I had no rest in my spirit." *But,* so far from having rest, *we were troubled* (θλιβόμενοι, either ἤμεθα is to be supplied, or a slight departure from the regular construction is to be assumed) *on every side, ἐν παντί, in every way.* This is amplified and explained by saying, *without* (were) *fightings, within fears.* Calvin and many other commentators understand *within* and *without* to mean within and without the church. Paul's troubles were partly from his contentions with the Jews and heathen, and partly from his anxieties about the conduct and welfare of Christians. It is more common and natural to understand the distinction to be between inward and outward troubles. He had to contend with all kinds of outward difficulties, and was oppressed with an inward load of anxieties. *Fears,* painful apprehensions lest his labours should be vain, lest his enemies should at last prevail, lest his disciples should apostatize and perish, or the peace and purity of the church be disturbed.

6. Nevertheless God, that comforteth those that are cast down, comforted us by the coming of Titus.

The order of the words is inverted in the English version. In the Greek the order is, He who comforteth those who are cast down, comforted us, even God, by the coming of Titus. The fact that it is the characteristic work of God, or, so to speak, his office, to comfort the dejected, is thus made more prominent. All the miserable are thus encouraged, because they are miserable, to look to that God who proclaims himself as the comforter. It is to be remarked that the objects of his compassion, those who call forth the exercise of his power as a consoler, are described not by a term expressive of moral excellence, but by a word which simply designates them as sufferers. The ταπεινοί are properly simply the low, those who are in depressed circumstances. As, however, it is the tendency of such circumstances to render men fearful, or meek, or humble, the word often expresses one or the other of these states of mind. In 10, 1 it means *timid* as opposed to *bold;* in 1 Pet. 5, 5, it is the opposite of *proud.* Here, however, it has its simple, proper sense—those who are low, i. e. cast down by suffering so as to be the proper objects of compassion. Luke 1, 52. James 1, 9. Ps. 18, 27. Paul says God comforted him by the coming of Titus, whom he had sent to Corinth to know the state of the church there.

7. And not by his coming only, but by the consolation wherewith he was comforted in you, when he told us your earnest desire, your mourning, your fervent mind toward me; so that I rejoiced the more.

It was not the pleasure of seeing Titus, so much as the intelligence which he brought, which comforted the apostle. By the consolation wherewith he was comforted *in you,* (ἐφ' ὑμῖν,) in reference to, or, as concerns you. The fact that Titus was comforted in Corinth was a great consolation to the apostle, and he was made to share in the comfort which Titus had experienced, as the latter *reported* to him (ἀναγγέλλειν, *to bring back word, to recount,* Acts 14, 27. 16, 38,) *your earnest desire,* i. e. either your earnest desire to see me and to secure my approbation; or, your earnest desire to correct the evils existing among you. The former is to be preferred, both on account of the context and the signification of the word ἐπιπόθησις, which means strong affection. *Your mourning,* (ὀδυρμός, i. e. *wailing, lamentation,* Matt. 2, 18,) either, mourning on account of their sins, or on account of having offended and pained the apostle. The latter is the more probable on account of what follows. *Your fervent mind toward me,* (ζῆλος ὑπὲρ ἐμοῦ,) *zeal for me,* i. e. the great interest which you took in me. Gal. 4, 17. 18. As the zeal of which the apostle speaks is expressly said to be a zeal of which he was the object, it is probable that the preceding words (*earnest desire* and *mourning*) express their feeling and conduct in reference to him. What was so specially gratifying to him was that in a church in which he had met with so much opposition, and in which the false teachers had exerted so great and so evil an influence, the mass of the people proved themselves devoted to him. Devotion to Paul, however, involved devotion to the truth and holiness, just as zeal for the false teachers involved the opposite. *So that I rejoiced the more*, i. e. I had more joy than the mere coming of Titus and the satisfaction which he experienced in Corinth were able to impart.

8. For though I made you sorry with a letter, I do not repent, though I did repent: for I perceive that the same epistle hath made you sorry, though (it were) but for a season.

This and the following verses assign the reason why he rejoiced. It was because the letter which he had written them, although it made them sorry, yet did them good. Though I made you sorry (i. e. caused you grief) *with a letter*, rather, *by the letter*, i. e. the letter which related to the incestuous person. *I do not repent, though I did repent.* That is, he regretted writing as he had done until he learned through Titus the good effect his letter had produced. Calvin says the word μεταμέλομαι must not be taken here to express repentance, for that would imply that his former letter was written under the influence of human feeling, and not by the direction of the Holy Spirit. He thinks that all Paul meant to say is, that he was grieved at having given the Corinthians pain. This, however, is not the meaning of the word. See Matt. 21, 29. 32. We must accommodate our theory of inspiration to the phenomena of Scripture, and not the phenomena to our theory. Inspiration simply rendered its subject infallible in writing and speaking as the messenger of God. Paul might doubt whether he had in a given instance made a wise use of his infallibility, as he might doubt whether he had wisely exercised his power of working miracles. He never doubted as to the truth of what he had written. There is another thing to be taken into consideration. Inspiration did not reveal itself in the consciousness. It is perfectly conceivable that a man might be inspired without knowing it. Paul was no doubt impelled by the Spirit to write his former epistle as well as divinely guided in writing; but all he was conscious of was his own thoughts and feelings. The believer is not conscious of the operations of grace, neither were the apostles conscious of inspiration. As the believer, however, may know that he is the subject of divine influence, so the apostles knew that they were inspired. But as the believer may doubt the wisdom of some of his holiest acts, so the apostles might doubt the wisdom of acts done under divine guidance. Such acts are always wise, but the agent may not always see their wisdom.

For I perceive that the same epistle made you sorry. This gives the reason why he at first regretted having written. He knew that his letter had excited much feeling in Corinth, and until he learned the nature and effects of that feeling, he repented having written. *Though but for a season.* That is, although the sorrow which he had occasioned was only temporary, yet it made him regret his former letter. This interpretation supposes a different punctuation of the passage from that found either in the common editions of the Greek text, or in the English version. It supposes that the proper place for the period or colon is after "I did not repent," and not after the following clause, "I did repent." In this latter case the whole sense is different, and the latter clause of the verse (βλέπω γάρ) is connected with the first clause, and is intended to give the reason why he said he had made them sorry, and not the reason why he regretted having done so. The sense of the whole would then be, 'I made you sorry . . . . . for I perceive from what I hear from Titus, that my former letter did, although only for a while, grieve you.' The next verse then begins a new sentence. But this is an unnatural construction; it requires the verse to be paraphrased in order to bring out the sense; and after all it amounts to little to say, 'I made you sorry, for I see I made you sorry.' The construction is simpler and the sense better if we put a colon or semi-colon after "I do not repent," and make v. 9 a part of the same sentence. 'Though I made you sorry I do not repent: although I did repent, (for I see that my letter made you sorry, though only for a time,) I now rejoice.' The meaning is, 'Though I did repent, I now rejoice.' Thus the passage is printed in the Greek of STIER and THIELE'S Polyglott, and, so far as the pointing is concerned, (omitting the marks of parenthesis,) in Tischendorf's Greek Testament. In the Vulgate the same sense is expressed. "Quoniam etsi contristavi vos in epistola, non me pœnitet; et si pœniteret, videns quod epistola illa (etsi ad horam) vos contristavit, nunc gaudeo, &c." So also Luther.

9. Now I rejoice, not that ye were made sorry, but that ye sorrowed to repentance : for ye were made sorry after a godly manner, that ye might receive damage by us in nothing.

He rejoiced, not in their grief, but that their grief led them to repentance. A parent, when he sees a child mourning over his sins, sincerely rejoices, however much he sympathizes in his grief. *Sorrowed unto repentance,* (εἰς μετάνοιαν,) i. e. change of mind, sometimes in the restricted sense of the word mind, (or purpose,) as in Heb. 12, 17 ; generally, in the comprehensive sense of the word as including the principles and affections, the whole soul, or inward life. Matt. 3, 8. Luke 5, 32. Acts 5, 31. Repentance, therefore, in its religious sense, is not merely a change of purpose, but includes a change of heart which leads to a turning from sin with grief and hatred thereof unto God. Such is the repentance here intended, as appears from what follows. *For* (this shows they sorrowed unto repentance) *they were made sorry* (they grieved) *after a godly sort,* (κατὰ θεόν,) i. e. in a manner agreeable to the mind and will of God ; so that God approved of their sorrow. He saw that it arose from right views of their past conduct. *That,* (ἵνα, *in order that,*) as expressing the design of God in making their sorrow a sorrow unto repentance. *Ye might receive damage by us in nothing.* God had so ordered that Paul's letter, instead of producing any injury, had resulted in the greatest spiritual good.

10. For godly sorrow worketh repentance to salvation not to be repented of ; but the sorrow of the world worketh death.

The connection is with the last clause. 'Ye were not injured by us, *for* the sorrow we occasioned worked repentance.' Sorrow in itself is not repentance ; neither is remorse, nor self-condemnation, nor self-loathing, nor external reformation. These all are its attendants or consequences ; but repentance itself (μετάνοια) is a turning from sin to holiness, from a state of sin to a holy state. It is a real change of heart. It is a change of views, feelings and purposes, resulting in a change of life. Godly sorrow *worketh* repentance, i. e. that sorrow on account of sin, which arises from proper apprehensions of God and of our relation to him, necessarily leads to that entire change in the inward life which is expressed by the word repentance, and which is connected with salvation. It is not the ground of our salvation; but it is a part of it and a necessary condition of it. Those who repent are saved; the impenitent perish. Repentance therefore is *unto salvation.* Comp. Acts 11, 18. It is that inward change in which salvation largely consists. *Never to be repented of.* This may belong either to the *repentance* or to *salvation.* If to the latter, the word ἀμεταμέλητος may be taken in the sense of *unchangeable.* See Rom. 11, 29. So the Vulgate explains it, *ad salutem stabilem;* or it may mean *not to be regretted.* Repentance leads to a salvation which no one ever will regret. So Luther and many of the moderns. The position of the words is in favour of connecting "not to be repented of" with "salvation." Had Paul intended the other connection, he would have probably said εἰς μετάνοιαν ἀμετανόητον, and not have chosen (ἀμεταμέλητον) a word of an entirely different root. Still, as "not to be repented of" seems to be an unsuitable epithet when applied to salvation, the majority of commentators prefer the other connection, and consider the apostle as designating true repentance as that which no one will regret notwithstanding the sorrow with which it is attended. *But the sorrow of the world worketh death.* By the sorrow of the world is not meant worldly sorrow, i. e. sorrow arising out of worldly considerations, but the sorrow of men of the world. In other words, κόσμου is the genitive of the subject, not a qualifying genitive. "The world" means men, the mass of mankind as distinguished from the church. 1 Cor. 1, 20, Gal. 4, 3. John 7, 7. 14, 7. &c. What therefore the apostle means is the sorrow of unrenewed men, the sorrow of the unsanctified heart. Of this sorrow, as opposed to godly sorrow, he says, *it works death,* not physical death, nor specifically eternal death as opposed to salvation, but evil in the general sense of the word. The effects of godly sorrow are salutary; the effects of worldly sorrow (the sorrow of worldly men) are evil. It is a great mistake to suppose that the natural tendency of pain and sorrow is to good. They tend rather to excite rebellion against God and all evil feelings. It is only when they are sanctified, i. e. when they are experienced by the holy, and

are made by the Spirit of God to call into exercise the resig-
nation, patience and faith of the sufferer, that they bring forth
fruit unto righteousness.   The natural element of holiness is
happiness, and misery is the natural element of sin.   They
stand severally in the relation both of cause and effect.   The
more miserable you make a bad man, the worse you make
him.   The wicked are said to curse God while they gnaw
their tongues with pain, and they repent not of their deeds.
Rev. 16, 10. 11.

11. For behold this self-same thing, that ye sorrowed after a godly sort, what carefulness it wrought
in you, yea, (what) clearing of yourselves, yea, (what)
indignation, yea, (what) fear, yea, (what) vehement desire, yea, (what) zeal, yea, (what) revenge! In all
(things) ye have approved yourselves to be clear in
this matter.

The question may be asked whether Paul means here to
describe the uniform effects of genuine repentance, so as to
furnish a rule by which each one may judge of his own experience.   This, to say the least, is not the primary design of
the passage.   If it affords such a rule it is only incidentally.
The passage is historical.   It describes the effects which godly
sorrow produced in the Corinthian church.   It shows how
the church felt and acted in reference to a specific offence,
when roused to a sense of its enormity.   *For, behold!*   The
connection is with what precedes.   'Godly sorrow is salutary,
for, see what effects it wrought for you.'   *This self-same
thing*, i. e. this very thing, viz., *being sorry after a godly
sort*.   *What carefulness it wrought in you* (ὑμῖν, *for you*, for
your advantage).   *Carefulness*, (σπουδήν,) literally, haste; then
the inward feeling which leads to haste; then any outward
manifestation of that earnestness of feeling.   Here it means
earnest solicitude as opposed both to indifference and neglect.
The Corinthians had strangely allowed a grievous sin, committed by a church-member, to pass unnoticed, as a matter
of no importance.   The first effect or manifestation of their
godly sorrow was an earnest solicitude on the subject, and a
desire to have the evil corrected; the very opposite of their
former indifference.   It is so in all cases of repentance.   Sins

which had been regarded as of little account, are apprehended in their true character; and deep feeling takes the place of unconcern. *Yea, what clearing of yourselves.* The particle ἀλλά is here and through the verse rendered *yea.* It is used, as in 1, 9, to indicate a gradation—*still more.* 'Not only solicitude, but moreover *clearing of yourselves,*' (ἀπολογίαν.) Their sorrow led them earnestly to apologize for the sin which they had committed. Not to extenuate their guilt, but to acknowledge it and to seek forgiveness. The apology for sin to which repentance leads, includes acknowledgment and deprecation. This apology was addressed to the apostle. They endeavoured to regain his good opinion. Moreover, *indignation,* either at the offence or at themselves that such an offence should have been allowed. They felt angry at themselves for their past misconduct. This is one of the most marked experiences of every sincere penitent. The unreasonableness, the meanness, the wickedness of his conduct rouse his indignation; he desires to seek vengeance on himself. Bengel says the word ἀγανάκτησις is chosen with special propriety, as it denotes a pain of which a man has the cause in himself. *What fear.* Whether fearful apprehension of God's displeasure, or fear of the apostle, depends on the context. The idea is expressed indefinitely. Their repentance was attended by fear of punishment. Doubtless the two sentiments were mingled in the minds of the Corinthians. They had a fear of the wrath of God, and at the same time a fear of the apostle's coming among them displeased and armed with the spiritual power which belonged to his office. The context is in favour of making the latter the prominent idea. *What vehement desire,* either for the correction of the evil complained of, or for the apostle's presence and approbation. In the latter case this clause is a modification of the preceding. It was not so much fear of the apostle as an earnest and affectionate desire towards and for him, that their godly sorrow had produced. As in v. 7 Titus had repeated to the apostle the earnest desire (ἐπιπόθησιν, the same word as here) of the Corinthians for him, it is probable that the same is here meant. *What zeal.* In v. 7 the zeal spoken of is limited or explained by the words (ὑπὲρ ἐμοῦ) *for me.* Without that addition they may be so understood here; zeal or zealous interest in behalf of the apostle manifested by their taking sides with him. The connection, however, with what follows favours the assumption that here the zeal meant is that of which the offender was the object. Zeal for his reformation or punishment *What revenge*, (ἐκδίκησις,) *vindictive justice*. One of the sentiments which godly sorrow had aroused in them was the sense of justice, the moral judgment that sin ought to be punished. This is an instinctive feeling, one belonging to our moral constitution, and therefore a revelation of the nature and will of God. The ground of the punishment of sin is not expediency, nor is it primarily the benefit of the offender, but the satisfaction of justice, or the inherent evil of sin which from its own nature, and apart from the evil consequences of impunity, deserves punishment. Of the six particulars introduced by (ἀλλά) *yea* in this verse, according to Bengel, Meyer and others, "clearing of yourselves" and "indignation" relate to the feelings of the Corinthians towards themselves; "fear" and "vehement desire" to their feelings towards the apostle; and "zeal" and "revenge" to their feelings towards the offender. According to Olshausen, the "apology" relates to their conduct; the "indignation" to their feelings in view of the crime which had been committed; the "fear" to God's displeasure; the "desire" and "zeal" to their feelings towards the apostle, and "revenge" the consequence of all the preceding.

In all things, (ἐν παντί,) in every respect, or, in every point of view. *Ye have proved yourselves*, (συνεστήσατε,) you have set yourselves forth, shown yourselves to be (Gal. 2, 18) *clear*, (ἁγνούς,) *pure*, free from guilt. *In this matter*, or, (without the ἐν, which the older MSS. omit,) *as to the matter*. The Corinthians proved themselves to be free from the sin of approving or in any way countenancing the crime in question. Their sin consisted in not more promptly excluding the offender from their communion. This whole passage, however, is instructive as presenting a clear exhibition of the intimate nature of church fellowship. One member committed an offence. The whole church repents. The godly sorrow which the apostle describes was the sorrow of the church. The effects which that sorrow wrought were common to the church as such. That believers are one body in Christ Jesus, and " every one members one of another," so that "if one member suffers all the members suffer with it," is matter of actual experience.

12. Wherefore, though I wrote unto you, (I did it) not for his cause that had done the wrong, nor for his

cause that suffered wrong, but that our care for you in the sight of God might appear unto you.

Wherefore. That is, because my letter has produced such results. The effects produced by his letter was the end he had in view in writing it. *Though I wrote to you,* i. e. although I interfered with your affairs. His motive in writing he states first negatively and then positively. It was neither for the sake of him who did wrong, nor for him who suffered wrong. His primary object was neither to have the offender punished, nor to secure justice being done to the injured party, viz., the father whose wife the son had married. This is the common and natural interpretation. As, however, nothing is elsewhere said of the father, and as the form of expression in 1 Cor. 5, 1, (γυναῖκα ἔχειν, to marry,) seems to imply that the father of the offender was dead, since otherwise, it is said, there could have been no marriage in the case, various other explanations of this passage have been proposed. Some say that he " who suffered wrong " was the apostle himself; others, as Bengel, say it was the Corinthians, the singular being taken for the plural. Others, as Neander, Billroth, &c., say that ἀδικηθέντος is neuter, *the wrong deed;* so that the meaning is, ' Neither for the offender nor for the offence.' But these explanations are all unnatural and unnecessary. The ordinary interpretation is the only one which the words suggest, and what is said in 1 Cor. 5 is perfectly consistent with the assumption that the father of the offender was still alive. The positive statement of his object in writing is *that our care for you in the sight of God might appear unto you.* The first question concerning this clause relates to the text. Instead of ἡμῶν (*our*), Lachmann, Meyer and others read ὑμῶν (*your*). This latter reading is followed by Calvin and Luther as well as by many of the modern commentators. As the external authorities are nearly equally divided, the decision rests mainly on internal evidence. In favour of the common text is first, the consideration that the manifestation of his love or care for them is elsewhere said to have been his motive in writing his former letter, 2, 4 ; and, secondly, the words πρὸς ὑμᾶς are more easily explained. ' Our care for you might appear unto you,' is plain. But if ὑμῶν is read these words give difficulty. They must be rendered (*apud vos*) " with you." ' Your care for us might be manifest with (i. e. among) you.' That is, that the zeal which you have for us might be brought out so as to be known by yourselves. This, however, would be more naturally expressed by ἐν ὑμῖν or ἐν ἑαυτοῖς, *among yourselves*. Besides, the words "before God," as involving an appeal to the divine omniscience, are more in place if he is speaking of his own zeal, than if speaking of theirs. The immediate context, it must be admitted, is in favour of this latter reading. The apostle had been describing the effects of his letter, dwelling with great satisfaction on the feelings towards himself which that letter had called forth. It was natural for him therefore to say that his object in writing was to bring out this manifestation, and thus reveal themselves to themselves as well as to him. With this also agrees what he says in 4, 9, "To this end also did I write, that I might know the proof of you, whether ye be obedient in all things." Still on the whole the common text gives the better sense. In either case the words πρὸς ὑμᾶς depend on φανερωθῆναι, "might be manifest *towards* (or among) you." So also do the words ἐνώπιον τοῦ θεοῦ, "that our care for you might be manifested *before God*," i. e. in his sight, as what he could approve of. In our version these words are connected with *our care*. "Our care for you in the sight of God." The same sense is expressed by the Vulgate; "ad manifestandam sollicitudinem nostram, quæ habemus pro vobis coram Deo." According to the Greek the natural construction is, "To manifest in the sight of God our care for you."

13. Therefore we were comforted in your comfort : yea, and exceedingly the more joyed we for the joy of Titus, because his spirit was refreshed by you all.

Therefore, i. e. because his letter had led them to repentance. *We were comforted in your comfort*, (ἐπὶ τῇ παρακλήσει ὑμῶν,) on account of your consolation. This, however, does not suit the state of the case. Paul was comforted by their repentance, not by their consolation. To meet this difficulty some make ὑμῶν the genitive of the source; so that the sense would be, 'We were comforted with the consolation derived from you.' The great majority of modern editors read ἡμῶν instead of ὑμῶν, and put a stop after παρακεκλήμεθα. This gives a far better sense. 'Therefore we have been comforted : and besides (ἐπί) our consolation, we have rejoiced exceedingly in the joy of Titus.' Paul had not only the consolation derived from their repentance, but in addition to that, he was delighted to find Titus so full of joy. Compare v. 7. The Vulgate has the same reading and pointing. Ideo consolati sumus. In consolatione autem nostra abundantius magis gavisi sumus super gaudio Titi. *Because his spirit was refreshed by you all.* This is the reason of his joy. Titus rejoiced because his spirit was *refreshed*, (ἀναπέπαυται,) derived rest, according to the comprehensive scriptural sense of the word " rest."

14. For if I have boasted any thing to him of you, I am not ashamed ; but as we spake all things to you in truth, even so our boasting, which (I made) before Titus, is found a truth.

This is the reason why Paul was so rejoiced that Titus was satisfied with what he saw in Corinth. Paul had boasted to him of the Corinthians. He had predicted that he would find them obedient, and ready to correct the evils adverted to in his former letter. Had these predictions proved false, he would have been mortified,—ashamed, as he says ; but as they were more than fulfilled, he naturally rejoiced. *But as we spake all things to you in truth.* No doubt in allusion to the charge of want of adherence to the truth made against him by the false teachers, to which he refers above, 1, 17. 18. As he spoke the truth to the Corinthians, so he spoke the truth of them. We spake *in truth*, (ἐν ἀληθείᾳ,) *truly.* *So our boasting before Titus* (ἡ ἐπὶ Τίτου) *is found a truth*, (ἀλήθεια ἐγενήθη,) *has become truth.* Though it is done incidentally, yet the revelation to the Corinthians that Paul had spoken of them in terms of commendation must have convinced them of his love. This was one of the objects, as appears from the whole epistle, he had much at heart.

15. And his inward affection is more abundant toward you, whilst he remembereth the obedience of you all, how with fear and trembling ye received him.

A continuation of the sentence begun in the former verse. Paul informs the Corinthians that Titus's love for them was greater now than when he was with them. The recollection of their good conduct warmed his heart towards them. *His inward affection*, literally, his bowels, which in the Scriptures is a figurative expression for love, compassion, or any other tender affection. *Whilst he remembereth*, literally, *remembering*, i. e. because he remembers. *Your obedience*, viz., towards him, as appears from what follows. *How with fear and trembling ye received him.* "Fear and trembling" is a common scriptural expression for reverence, or solicitous anxiety lest we should fail in doing all that is required of us. 1 Cor. 2, 3 Eph. 6, 5.

16. I rejoice, therefore, that I have confidence in you in all (things).

This is the conclusion of the whole matter. The first seven chapters of the epistle are intimately connected. They all relate to the state of the congregation at Corinth and to Paul's relation to the people there. The eighth and ninth chapters form a distinct division of the epistle. Here, therefore, we have the conclusion of the whole preceding discussion. The result of the long conflict of feeling in reference to the Corinthians as a church, was the full restoration of confidence. I rejoice that I have confidence in you in all things, (ἐν παντί, *in every thing*). *I have confidence in you,* (θαρρῶ ἐν ὑμῖν,) I have good courage, am full of hope and confidence. 5, 6. Heb. 13, 6. As θαρρέω is not elsewhere constructed with ἐν, Meyer says the meaning is, 'I am of good courage, *through* you.' If this objection to the common explanation be considered of weight, ἐν had better be rendered *before*. 'I stand full of confidence before you, i. e. in your presence.' 1 Cor. 14, 11. The sense, however, expressed by the common interpretation is better.

CHAPTER VIII.

The extraordinary liberality of the Macedonians, vs. 1–6. Exhortation to the Corinthians to follow the example of their Macedonian brethren, vs. 7–16. Commendation of Titus for his zeal in promoting the collection of contributions for the poor, and of the other brethren who were to accompany him to Corinth, vs, 17–24.

Exhortation to liberality to the poor.

To this subject the apostle devotes this and the following chapter. He begins by setting before the Corinthians the liberality of the churches in Macedonia. They, in the midst of great affliction and of extreme poverty, had exceeded their ability in the contributions which they had made for the saints, vs. 1–3. And this not by constraint or in obedience to earnest entreaties on the part of the apostle; but on the contrary, it was they who besought him to receive and take charge of their alms, v. 4. Liberality to the poor was only a part of what they did; they devoted themselves to the Lord, v. 5. The conduct of the Macedonians led the apostle to exhort Titus, as he had already begun the work, to carry it on to completion in Corinth, v. 6.

He begs them, therefore, to add this to all their other graces, v. 7. This was a matter of advice, not of command. He was induced to give this exhortation because others had evinced so much zeal in this matter, and because he desired them to prove the sincerity of their love. What was all they could do for others, compared to what Christ had done for them, vs. 8. 9. The exercise of liberality was a good to them, provided their feelings found expression in corresponding acts, vs. 10. 11. The disposition, not the amount of their contributions, was the main thing, v. 12. What the apostle wished was that there might be some approximation to equality among Christians, that the abundance of one may supply the wants of another, vs. 13–15.

He thanks God who had inspired Titus with so much zeal on this subject, vs. 16. 17. With him he had sent a brother who had not only the approbation of the churches, but had been chosen for the very purpose of taking charge of the contributions in connection with the apostle, vs. 18. 19. Paul was determined to avoid all occasion of reproach, and therefore he associated others with himself in the charge of the money in-

trusted to him, vs. 20. 21. With those already mentioned he
sent another brother of approved character and great zeal, v.
22. Therefore if any one inquired who Titus was, they might
answer, He was Paul's companion and fellow-labourer; or who
those brethren were, they might say, They were the messengers of the churches, and the glory of Christ. Let the church
therefore prove their love and justify his boasting of them,
vs. 23. 24.

1. Moreover, brethren, we do you to wit of the
grace of God bestowed on the churches of Macedonia.

Moreover (δέ) marks the transition to a new subject. *We
do you to wit*, (γνωρίζομεν,) 'we cause you to know.' The
word *to wit*, (Anglo-Saxon, *Witan;* German, *Wissen*,) to
know, and the cognate words, *Wis* and *Wot*, are nearly obso-
lete, although they occur frequently in our version. The
grace of God, the divine favour. The liberality of the Corinthians was due to the operation of the grace of God. The
sacred writers constantly recognize the fact that the freest
and most spontaneous acts of men, their inward states and
the outward manifestations of those states, when good, are
due to the secret influence of the Spirit of God, which
eludes our consciousness. The believer is most truly self-de-
termined, when determined by the grace of God. *Bestowed
on*, (δεδομένην ἐν,) "given in," i. e. given so that it is in. See
1, 22. "Given the earnest of the Spirit in our hearts." In v.
16 of this chapter, διδόντι ἐν is rendered "*put into.*" *The
churches of Macedonia*. Under the Romans Macedonia included the whole of the northern provinces of Greece. The
churches of that region founded by the apostle were those of
Philippi, Thessalonica, and Berœa. Of the extraordinary
liberality of those churches the epistles of Paul furnish numerous intimations. 11, 9. Phil. 2, 25. 4, 15. 18.

2. How that, in a great trial of affliction, the abundance of their joy, and their deep poverty, abounded
unto the riches of their liberality.

A somewhat condensed sentence, meaning, as some say,
that in the midst of their afflictions their joy, and in the midst
of their poverty, their liberality abounded. But this brings
into view two graces, joy in affliction, and liberality in poverty,

whereas the context calls for only one. The meaning rather is, that notwithstanding their afflictions, their joy and their poverty abounded to their liberality. This the grammatical structure of the passage requires. *How that* (ὅτι); the connection is with the verb in the preceding verse, 'I cause you to know that, &c.' *In a great trial of affliction*, i. e. in afflictions which were a great trial (δοκιμή), i. e. a test of their sincerity and devotion. These afflictions were either those which they shared in common with their fellow-citizens, arising out of their social condition, or they were peculiar to them as Christians, arising from persecution. In writing to the Thessalonians, Paul reminds them that they had received the word in much affliction. 1, 6. 2, 14. Comp. Acts 16, 20. 17, 5. *The abundance of their joy ;* i. e. the joy arising from the pardon of their sins and the favour of God, which in 1 Thess. 1, 6, he calls the joy of the Holy Ghost, was abundant. That is, it rose above their sorrows, and produced in them the effect of which he afterwards speaks. *And their deep poverty*, (ἡ κατὰ βάθους πτωχεία,) their abject poverty, or poverty down to the depth. *Abounded unto*, i. e. manifested itself as abundant in relation to. The same verb (ἐπερίσσευσεν) belongs to both the preceding nouns, "joy" and "poverty," but in a somewhat different sense. Their joy abounded unto their liberality, because it produced it. The effect proved the joy to be abundant. Their poverty abounded unto their liberality, because it was seen to be great in relation to it. Their liberality made their poverty, by contrast, appear the greater. *Unto the riches*, (πλοῦτος,) a favourite word with Paul, which he often uses in the sense of abundance. Rom. 2, 4, "Riches of his goodness," for abundant goodness. Eph. 1, 7, "Riches of his grace," for his abundant grace ; 1, 18, "Riches of his glory," for abundant glory, &c. *Of their liberality*, ἁπλότης, which is properly the opposite of duplicity, or double-mindedness, and, therefore, singleness of heart, simplicity, sincerity. Eph. 6, 5. Col. 3, 22. The Scriptures, however, often use a generic term for a specific one, as glory for wisdom, or mercy, or power, which are different forms of the divine glory. So here the general term for right-mindedness is put for liberality, which is a specific form or manifestation of the generic virtue. Comp. 9, 11. Rom. 12, 8. In reference to the poverty of the Macedonian churches, Mr. Stanley, in his Commentary on this Epistle, appropriately quotes a passage from Dr. Arnold's Roman Commonwealth, in which he says, "The

condition of Greece in the time of Augustus was one of deso-
lation and distress. It had suffered severely by being the
seat of the successive civil wars between Cæsar and Pompey,
between the Triumvirs and Brutus and Cassius, and lastly,
between Augustus and Antonius. Besides, the country had
never recovered from the long series of miseries which had
succeeded and accompanied its conquest by the Romans; and
between those times and the civil contest between Pompey
and Cæsar, it had been again exposed to all the evils of war
when Sylla was disputing the possession of it with the general
of Mithridates. . . . The provinces of Macedonia and Achaia,
when they petitioned for a diminution of their burdens, in the
reign of Tiberius, were considered so deserving of compassion
that they were transferred for a time from the jurisdiction of
the Senate to that of the Emperor, (as involving less heavy
taxation.)"

3–5. For to (their) power, I bear record, yea, and
beyond (their) power, (they were) willing of themselves;
praying us with much entreaty, that we would receive
the gift, and (take upon us) the fellowship of the ministering to the saints. And (this they did,) not as we
hoped, but first gave their own selves to the Lord, and
unto us by the will of God.

These verses must be taken together on account of the
grammatical construction. Wherever the reader of the English version sees the frequent use of words in Italics, he may
conclude there is some difficulty or obscurity in the original,
which the translators endeavour to explain by additions to the
text. In these verses there are no less than five such interpo-
lations; three of which materially affect the sense, viz., the
words, *they were, take upon us,* and, *this they did.* The first
point is to determine the text. The words δέξασθαι ἡμᾶς are
omitted in the great majority of the MSS. versions and
Fathers, and seem very much like an explanatory gloss, or an
interpolation analogous to the explanations in Italics so common in our version. They are, therefore, rejected by Griesbach, and by almost all editors since his time. Their insertion
alters the sense materially. If these words are read, Paul
represents the Macedonian Christians as begging him to re-

ceive their contributions and to take upon him the distribution of them. If they are omitted, the sense is, they begged to be permitted to contribute. Granting, however, that these words should be omitted, the construction of the passage is doubtful. Stanley says it is "a sentence which has been entirely shattered in passing through the apostle's mind." He proposes to reduce it to order in the same way that Bengel does, who, however, thinks that, so far from the sentence being shattered, every thing is smooth and easy. He says the word ἔδωκαν sustains the structure of the whole passage; αὐθαίρετοι and δεόμενοι are its nominatives; χάριν, κοινωνίαν and ἑαυτούς are its objects. The sense then is, 'Of their own accord, beyond their ability and with many prayers they gave not their gifts only as a contribution to the saints, but themselves to the Lord and to us.' Any one, however, who looks at the Greek sees that it is very unnatural to make χάριν depend on ἔδωκαν; it belongs to δεόμενοι. The construction, therefore, adopted by Fritzsche, Billroth, Meyer and others is, at least as to that point, to be preferred. Meyer says that to ἔδωκαν there are four limiting or qualifying clauses attached. *They gave*, 1. Beyond their power; 2. Of their own motion; 3. Praying to be allowed to give; and 4. Not as we expected, but themselves. De Wette and many others relieve the harshness of this construction so far as the last clause is concerned by making the sentence end with the fourth verse, and supplying ἔδωκαν in v. 3. "They gave beyond their power, of their own accord, begging to be allowed to take part in the contribution to the saints. And beyond our expectation they gave themselves to the Lord."

As to the connection, ὅτι is evidently equivalent to γάρ, as these verses are the proof of what is said in v. 2. The liberality of the Macedonian churches was great, *for to their power*, (κατὰ δύναμιν,) according to their ability, I bear testimony, and *beyond their power* (ὑπέρ in the common text, in the critical editions παρὰ δύναμιν). Here the word ἔδωκαν is implied. 'They gave beyond their ability,' αὐθαίρετοι, *self-moved*, i. e. spontaneously, without any suggestion or excitement from me.' From 9, 2, it appears that Paul had boasted to the Macedonians that Achaia (the Corinthians) was ready a year ago, and that this had excited their zeal. These two representations are perfectly consistent. In detailing the success of the gospel in Corinth the apostle would naturally refer to the liberality of the disciples. It was the simple mention

of this fact which led the Macedonians, without any exhorta
tion from the apostle, but of their own accord, to make the
contribution of which he here speaks. Our translators by the
insertion of the words *they were* alter the sense of this verse.
They make the apostle say, 'They were willing beyond their
power.' Whereas what he says is, 'They gave spontaneously
beyond their power.' The word ἔδωκαν, *they gave*, though
not expressed until the end of the passage, is clearly implied
from the beginning.

Praying us with much entreaty. The thing for which the
Macedonians so earnestly prayed was, according to the received text and our version, that the apostle would receive
their alms and take upon him the distribution of them. But
by common consent the words δέξασθαι ἡμᾶς (*that we would
receive*) should be omitted, and there is nothing in the Greek
to answer to the interpolated words *take upon us*. The
words are, δεόμενοι ἡμῶν τὴν χάριν καὶ τὴν κοινωνίαν, *begging of
us the favour and fellowship*, (or participation,) i. e. the favour
of a participation. The latter word explains the former; the
favour they asked was that of taking part in *the ministry to
the saints*. The word διακονία, *ministry, service*, is often used
in the sense of *aid* or *relief*. 9, 1. 13. Acts 6, 1. 11, 29. Here,
according to some, the sentence ends. The more common
interpretation supposes καὶ οὐ καθὼς ἠλπίσαμεν to be a new
modification of the principal idea, "and not as we expected,"
i. e. a moderate contribution, *but they first gave their own
selves to the Lord and to us*. This does not mean that they
gave themselves before they gave their alms; but they gave
themselves first to the Lord, then to us; πρῶτον belongs to
κυρίῳ and not to ἔδωκαν. *First* does not mean first in time,
but in importance and order. Compare Acts 15, 28. Exodus 14, 31. The offering was immediately and directly
to Christ, and subordinately to the apostle. By giving
themselves to the Lord the apostle means that not con-
tent with giving their money they had given themselves;
made an entire dedication of all they had and all they were
to their divine Master. This was far beyond his expectations. To understand this expression as indicating that
devotion to Christ was the motive which determined their
liberality is inconsistent with the context. Their inward devotion to Christ was not a thing to take the apostle by sur-
prise; that was involved in their profession of the gospel.
What surpassed his expectations was, that their liberality led

to the gift not of their money only but of themselves. Some say that this means that they offered themselves to go to Corinth or elsewhere to collect money for the poor. But the sense is fuller and simpler as above explained. *By the will of God.* That is, the will of God was the cause of their giving themselves to the Lord, &c. It is (διὰ θελήματος, not κατὰ θέλημα) *by*, not *according to*, the will of God.

6. Insomuch that we desired Titus, that as he had begun, so he would also finish in you the same grace also.

Insomuch (εἰς τὸ παρακαλ.) so that we were induced to exhort Titus. Paul, 1 Cor. 16, 1, had urged the Corinthians to make collections for the poor saints. Titus visited Corinth after that letter was written and made a beginning in this work. When Paul came to Macedonia and found how liberally the churches there had contributed, he urged Titus to return to Corinth and complete what he had so successfully begun. The exhortation therefore addressed to Titus, of which the apostle here speaks, was not the exhortation given him before the visit from which he had just returned, but that which he gave him in reference to a renewed visit yet to be made. Instead therefore of the rendering, *I desired Titus*, it would would be plainer to translate, *I have desired him.* That (ἵνα, not *in order that*, according to the usual force of the particle, but *that*, as expressing the contents of the request), *as he had begun*, (προενήρξατο, a word which occurs nowhere but in this chapter,) *had begun before.* This may mean, 'had already begun,' i. e. begun before the time of Paul's writing; or, had begun before the Macedonians made their collections. The latter is the more probable meaning, since, as appears from v. 10, the Corinthians had commenced this work before the Macedonian churches had moved in the business. *So he would also finish*, i. e. either in the sense of bringing a given work to an end, Heb. 9, 6, or of perfecting an inward grace, 7, 1. *In you*, εἰς ὑμᾶς, in relation to, or, for you. Matt. 10, 10. *This grace also ;* χάριν may here mean either *good work*, or, *grace*, in the ordinary sense of the word. The connection with the following verse is in favour of understanding it in the latter sense. It was a disposition of the mind that Titus was exhorted to bring into full exercise among the Corinthi-

ans. The grace spoken of was something which belongs to
the same category with faith, knowledge, and love.

7. Therefore, as ye abound in every (thing, in)
faith, and utterance, and knowledge, and (in) all diligence, and (in) your love to us, (see) that ye abound in
this grace also.

From this verse onward to v. 16 the apostle urges on the
Corinthians the duty of liberality.   1. Because it was necessary to the completeness and harmony of their Christian character; 2. Because it would be a proof of their sincerity; 3. Because Christ had become poor for their sake; 4. Because it
would redound to their own advantage, inasmuch as consistency required that having manifested the disposition, they
should carry it out in action; and 5. Because what was
required of them was perfectly reasonable.   They were asked
to give only according to their means; and what they were
called upon to do for others, others under like circumstances
would be required to do for them.   *Therefore* is not a proper
translation of ἀλλά (*but*).   The word is often used to mark a
transition to a new subject, and specially where what follows
is an exhortation or command.   Mark 16, 7. Acts 9, 6. 10, 20.
As ye abound, i. e. have in abundance, or, have more than
others, i. e. excel.   *In every thing*, (ἐν παντί,) limited of course
by the context, and explained by what follows, 'every gift
and grace.'   The same testimony is borne in favour of the
Corinthians, 1 Cor. 1, 5. 7.   That the apostle sometimes
speaks so favourably, and sometimes so unfavourably of the
church in Corinth, is to be accounted for by the fact that
some of the people were very good, probably the majority,
and some, especially among the teachers, very much the reverse.   *In faith*.   To abound in faith is to have a strong,
constant, operative faith, sustaining and controlling the whole
inward and outward life.   *In utterance and knowledge*, (λόγῳ
καὶ γνώσει,) the same combination as in 1 Cor. 1, 5.   Here and
there our translators have rendered λόγος *utterance ;* in both
cases it may mean *doctrine*, as it does in so many passages,
especially in such cases as "word of truth," "word of salvation," "word of righteousness," "word of Christ."   The
meaning, therefore, is either that they were enriched with the
gifts of utterance and knowledge, or doctrine and knowledge.

Λόγος is the Christian truth as preached, γνῶσις that truth as apprehended or understood. *In diligence,* (σπουδή,) *earnestness,* a general term for the energy or vigour of their spiritual life, of which their love was one manifestation. In *your love to us.* The expression in Greek is peculiar, τῇ ἐξ ὑμῶν ἐν ἡμῖν ἀγάπῃ, *the love which is of you in us,* i. e. your love (to us) which we cherish in our hearts. That is, which we so highly estimate. Or, simply, *amore a vobis profecto et in me collato.* *That ye may abound.* The ἵνα περισσ. is most naturally explained by supplying some word as in our version, *See* that ye abound. Compare Gal. 2, 10. *In this grace also,* i. e. the grace of liberality. Others here as in the preceding verse make χάρις mean *good work.* But this is not so consistent with the context. Faith, knowledge, and love are not good works so much as divine gifts, and so also is liberality.

8. I speak not by commandment, but by occasion of the forwardness of others, and to prove the sincerity of your love.

The apostle, agreeably to his usual manner, states first negatively, and then affirmatively, his object in what he had said. It was not of the nature of a command. It was not obedience, but spontaneous liberality he desired. The latter may be excited by the exhibition of appropriate motives, but it cannot be yielded to authority. Almsgiving in obedience to a command, or to satisfy conscience, is not an act of liberality. What is not spontaneous is not liberal. Paul, therefore, would not coerce them by a command. His object was to put the genuineness of their love to the test. The nature of the test was suggested by the zeal of the Macedonians. So it was by the occasion of the forwardness of others he was led to put their love to that trial. The real test of the genuineness of any inward affection is not so much the character of the feeling as it reveals itself in our consciousness, as the course of action to which it leads. Many persons, if they judged themselves by their feelings, would regard themselves as truly compassionate; but a judgment founded on their acts would lead to the opposite conclusion. So many suppose they really love God because they are conscious of feelings which they dignify with that name; yet they do not obey him. It is thereby by the fruits of feeling we must judge of its genuineness both in ourselves and others.

9. For ye know the grace of our Lord Jesus Christ, that though he was rich, yet for your sakes he became poor, that ye through his poverty might be rich.

This verse is a parenthesis, the sentence begun in v. 8 being continued in v. 10. Still the connection between this and the preceding verse is intimate and immediate. There are two things indicated and intended in this verse. That self-sacrifice is the proper test of love. And second, that the example of Christ, and the obligation under which we lie to him, should lead us to do good to others. The apostle evidently combines these two thoughts. 'I desire,' he says, 'to put your love to the test of self-sacrifice, *for* ye know that Christ's love was thus manifested;' and, 'You may well be expected to sacrifice yourselves for others, since Christ gave himself for you.' It is not only the example of Christ which is held up for our imitation; but gratitude to Christ for the infinite blessings we receive from him is presented as the motive to liberality. *For ye know.* The fact referred to including the highest mystery of the gospel, viz., the incarnation of the Son of God, or, the manifestation of God in the flesh, and the love therein manifested, is assumed to be known and acknowledged by all who called themselves Christians. Ye know, says Paul, as all Christians must know, *the grace*, i. e. the unmerited, spontaneous love of *our Lord Jesus Christ.* A combination of the most endearing and exalted appellations. *Our Lord*, i. e. the supreme and absolute Lord whom we acknowledge to be our rightful sovereign and possessor, and who is *ours*, belongs to us, in so far as the care, protection, and support of his almighty power are by his love pledged to us. *Jesus Christ.* He who is our Lord is our Saviour and the Christ, God's anointed, invested by Him with supreme dominion. What belongs of right to the Logos in virtue of his divinity, is constantly represented as given to the Theanthropos. See Heb. 1, 2. *That though*, &c. This clause is explanatory of the former. 'Ye know the grace of our Lord Jesus,' that is, 'Ye know that though he was rich, &c.' The grace consisted in, or was manifested by his becoming poor for our sakes. *Being rich*, πλούσιος ὤν, that is, either, as in our version, *Though he was rich*, in the possession of the glory which he had with the Father before the world was, John 17, 5; or, *Being rich* in the actual and constant possession of all divine prerogatives. In the latter case, the idea is that our blessed Lord while here on earth, although he had within himself the fulness of the Godhead and the right and power of possession over all things, yet was poor. He did not avail himself of his right and power to make himself rich, but voluntarily submitted to all the privations of poverty. The former interpretation is commonly and properly preferred. The reference in ἐπτώχευσε, *he became poor*, is not to what our Lord did while he was on earth, but to what he did when he came into the world. The passage is parallel to Phil. 2, 6. "Being in the form of God, and equal to God, he emptied (ἐκένωσε) himself." That is, he so far laid aside the glory of his divine majesty, that he was to all appearance a man, and even a servant, so that men refused to recognise him as God, but despised, persecuted, and at last crucified him, as a man. He who was rich in the plenitude of all divine attributes and prerogatives thus became poor, δἰ ὑμᾶς, *on your account*, out of love to you.   The end to be accomplished by this humiliation of the Son of God, was that, *you through his poverty might be rich.*   Believers are made rich in the possession of that glory which Christ laid aside, or concealed.   They are made partakers of the divine nature, 2 Pet. 1, 4.   That is, of the divine holiness, exaltation and blessedness.   This is divine not only because of its source as coming from God, but because of its nature.   So that our Lord says, "The glory which thou gavest me, I have given them," John 17, 22.   Hence believers are said to be glorified with Christ and to reign with him. Rom. 8, 17.   The price of this exaltation and everlasting blessedness of his people was his own poverty.   It is by his poverty that we are made rich.   Unless he had submitted to all the humiliation of his incarnation and death, we should forever have remained poor, destitute of all holiness, happiness and glory.   It should be observed that moral duties, such as almsgiving, are in the New Testament enforced not so much on moral grounds as on grounds peculiarly Christian.   No man can enter into the meaning of this verse or feel its power, without being thereby made willing to sacrifice himself for others.   And the apostle teaches here, what St. John also teaches, 1 John 3, 17, that it is vain for any man to profess or to imagine that he loves Christ, if he does not love the brethren and is not liberal in relieving their wants.

10. And herein I give (my) advice: for this is ex-

pedient for you, who have begun before, not only to do, but also to be forward a year ago.

The connection is with v. 8. 'I do not command, I, in this matter, viz., in making collections for the poor, give my mind;' γνώμην, in the sense of opinion. Comp. 1 Cor. 7, 6. *For this is expedient for you.* This admits of two interpretations. 'I advise you to make the collection, for this giving to the poor is profitable to you. It not only promotes your own moral growth, but it is demanded by consistency. Having begun this work it would be an injury to yourselves to leave it unfinished.' This is the common, and on the whole the preferable explanation. It satisfies all the demands of the context; and it makes ἐν τούτῳ and τοῦτο refer to the same thing. 'In this matter (of giving) I express my opinion, for this (giving) is profitable to you.' Meyer, Billroth and many others make τοῦτο refer to the immediately preceding words. 'I give my advice, for advising is better than commanding in your case, seeing ye were willing a year ago.' This, however, is not demanded by the context, and lowers the sense. The former interpretation brings out a higher truth than the second. It is for our own good to do good. *Who,* οἵτινες, (being such as those who.) 'It is expedient for you, *because ye began before not only to do* (τὸ ποιῆσαι), *but to be forward* (τὸ θέλειν) *a year ago.* As the will precedes the deed, many commentators assume an inversion in these words, and reverse their order. 'Ye began not only to will, but to do.' This is arbitrary and unnecessary. Others, as do our translators, take the word θέλειν in an emphatic sense, to be zealous in doing. Luke 20, 46. John 8, 44. 'Ye began not only to do, but to do with zeal.' This, however, does not agree with the following verse, where θέλειν is used in its ordinary sense. Others again understand ποιῆσαι of the beginning of the work, and the θέλειν of the purpose to do more. But this requires much to be supplied which is not in the text. Besides it does not agree with the qualifying clause 'a year ago.' According to this explanation the θέλειν does not express what had occurred a year ago, but to the state of mind now assumed to exist and subsequent to the doing begun the year before. De Wette, Winer, and Meyer give a much more natural interpretation. The word προενήρξασθε, as in v. 6, refers to the Macedonian churches. 'You anticipated the Macedonians not only in the work but in the purpose.' That is, before they had begun to make a collection for the poor saints, you had begun; and before they thought of it, you had determined to do it. 'Having thus been beforehand with them it would be to your disadvantage to leave your work half done, seeing that the mere mention of your purpose, 9, 2, roused them to such self-denying liberality.' *A year ago,* (ἀπὸ πέρυσι.) This does not imply that a whole year had intervened, but is analogous to our popular expression *last year.* If Paul, according to the Jewish reckoning, began the year in October, he could properly speak, when writing in November, of an event which happened in the spring, as having occurred last year. An interval of little more than six months, according to this view, from spring to fall, intervened between the date of the first and second epistles of Paul to the Corinthians.

11. Now therefore perform the doing (of it): that as (there was) a readiness to will, so (there may be) a performance also out of that which ye have.

Now therefore, i. e. as there has been the purpose and the commencement, let there be also the completion of the work. Literally, *complete ye also the doing. That,* (ὅπως, in order that,) *as the readiness to will, so also the completion.* Consistency required them to carry out their good intentions openly expressed. *Out of that which ye have,* ἐκ τοῦ ἔχειν, according to (your) property. The preposition ἐκ is not here to be rendered *out of,* but it expresses the rule or standard. Compare John 3, 34. The apostle was not desirous to urge them either beyond their inclination, or beyond their ability. What they gave, he wished them to give freely, and with due regard to their resources.

12. For if there be first a willing mind, (it is) accepted according to that a man hath, (and) not according to that he hath not.

The connection is evidently with the last words of v. 11. They were to give according to their property, *for* the standard of judgment with God is the disposition, not the amount given. The same doctrine is taught by our Lord, Mark 12, 42. *If there be first,* literally, *if there be present;* πρόκειται does not mean *prius adest,* but simply *adest. A willing*

mind, ἡ προθυμία, *the readiness,* or, *disposition. It is;* that
is, the προθυμία (the disposition) *is accepted,* εὐπρόσδεκτος, *acceptable.* It is often used in reference to offerings made to
God. Rom. 15, 16. 1 Pet. 2, 5. Some of the ancient MSS.
introduce the indefinite pronoun τὶς, as the subject of the
verbs ἔχῃ and ἔχει, so our translators insert *man,* 'according
to that *a man* hath, and not according to that *he* hath not.'
The grammatical subject, however, of all the verbs in the
verse is προθυμία, which Paul, according to his custom, per-
sonifies, and therefore says, It is acceptable *according to that
it may have,* (ἐὰν ἔχῃ,) be it more or less; *not according to
that it hath not.* This does not mean that the disposition is
not acceptable when it exceeds the ability to give, or leads to
extravagant gifts. This may be true, but it is not the idea
here intended. The meaning is simply that the disposition is
what God regards, and that disposition will be judged of according to the resources at its command. A small gift may
manifest in one case much greater willingness to give, than a
much larger gift in another.

13. For (I mean) not that other men be eased, and
you burdened.

The reason why he did not wish them to exceed their
ability in giving, is here stated negatively. The positive
statement follows in the next verse. The apostle did not
wish to throw an unequal burden upon the Corinthians. He
did not desire that others should be released from all obligation to give, and they oppressed by it. Not to others ἄνεσις
(relief), and to you θλῖψις (oppression), is his concise expression. According to this view, by ἄλλοις, *others,* we are to
understand other churches or Christians; and by ἄνεσις, relief
from the obligation to give. But this is consistent neither
with what precedes nor with what follows. The equality
which he aims at, is not the equality of the churches in giving,
but that which arises from the deficiency of one class being
made up by the abundance of another. By *others,* therefore,
we must understand the poor, and in this case, the poor saints
at Jerusalem, and by ἄνεσις *release* from the pressure of
poverty, and by θλῖψις the burden of indigence. The meaning therefore is, that Paul did not desire that the Corinthians
should go beyond their ability in giving, for he had no wish
that others should be enriched, and they impoverished. It is

not obligatory on the rich to make themselves poor in order that the poor may be rich. That is not the rule.

14. But by an equality, (that) now at this time your abundance (may be a supply) for their want, that their abundance also may be (a supply) for your want: that there may be equality.

The word ἰσότης means here neither reciprocity nor equity, but equality, as the illustration in v. 15 shows. The ἐκ, as in v. 11, (ἐκ τοῦ ἔχειν,) expresses the rule or standard in giving. That rule is equality; we must give so as to produce, or that there may be, equality. This is not agrarianism, nor community of goods. The New Testament teaches on this subject, 1. That all giving is voluntary. A man's property is his own. It is in his own power to retain or to give away; and if he gives, it is his prerogative to decide whether it shall be much or little. Acts 5, 4. This is the doctrine taught in this whole connection. Giving must be voluntary. It is the fruit of love. It is of course obligatory as a moral duty, and the indisposition to give is proof of the absence of the love of God. 1 John 3, 17. Still it is one of those duties the performance of which others cannot enforce as a right belonging to them. It must remain at our own discretion. 2. That the end to be accomplished by giving is relieving the necessities of the poor. The equality, therefore, aimed at, or intended, is not an equality as to the amount of property, but equal relief from the burden of want. This is taught in the remainder of this verse. 'At the present time,' says the apostle, 'let your abundance be to (γένηται εἰς, extend to, be imparted to, Gal. 3, 14,) their want, in order that their abundance may be to your want, that there may be equality;' that is, an equal relief from want or destitution. 3. A third scriptural principle on this subject is, that while all men are brethren, and the poor as poor, whether Christians or not, are the proper objects of charity, yet there is a special obligation resting on the members of Christ to relieve the wants of their fellow-believers. We are to do good to all men, says the apostle, specially to those who are of the household of faith. Gal. 6, 10. All the directions in this and the following chapter have reference to the duty of Christians to their fellow-believers. There are two reasons for this. The one is the common relation of be-

lievers to Christ as members of his body, so that what is done
to them is done to him; and their consequent intimate relation
to each other as being one body in Christ Jesus. The other
is, the assurance that the good done to them is pure good.
There is no apprehension that the alms bestowed will encour-
age idleness or vice. 3. A fourth rule is designed to prevent
any abuse of the brotherhood of Christians. The poor have
no right to depend on the benefactions of the rich because
they are brethren. This same apostle says, "This we commanded you, that if any man would not work, neither should
he eat," 2 Thess. 3, 10. Thus do the Scriptures avoid, on the
one hand, the injustice and destructive evils of agrarian com-
munism, by recognising the right of property and making all
almsgiving optional; and on the other, the heartless disregard
of the poor by inculcating the universal brotherhood of believers, and the consequent duty of each to contribute of his
abundance to relieve the necessities of the poor. At the same
time they inculcate on the poor the duty of self-support to the
extent of their ability. They are commanded "with quietness
to work, and to eat their own bread." Could these principles
be carried out there would be among Christians neither idleness nor want.

15. As it is written, He that (had gathered) much
had nothing over; and he that (had gathered) little
had no lack.

The moral lesson taught in Exodus 16, 18, is that which
the apostle had just inculcated. There it is recorded that the
people, by the command of God, gathered of the manna an
omer for each person. Those who gathered more retained
only the allotted portion; and those who gathered less had
their portion increased to the given standard. There was as
to the matter of necessary food an equality. If any one at-
tempted to hoard his portion, it spoiled upon his hands. The
lesson therefore taught in Exodus and by Paul is, that, among
the people of God, the superabundance of one should be employed in relieving the necessities of others; and that any attempt to countervail this law will result in shame and loss.
Property is like manna, it will not bear hoarding.

16. But thanks (be) to God, which put the same
earnest care into the heart of Titus for you.

From this verse to the end of the chapter the apostle commends to the confidence of the Corinthians Titus and the two brethren who were to accompany him on his return to Corinth. The object of Titus's first visit was to ascertain the state of the church, and specially the effect of Paul's former epistle. The object of this mission was to bring to an end the collection for the poor which the Corinthians had so long under consideration. Titus had as much zeal in this matter as Paul, and therefore the apostle thanks God *which put into the heart of Titus ;* τῷ διδόντι ἐν, 'Thanks to God giving in, i. e. giving to be in, the heart of Titus.' *The same earnest care for you ;* τὴν αὐτὴν σπουδήν, the same zeal, i. e. the same zeal which I have for you. Titus felt the same interest in the spiritual welfare of the Corinthians, and the same solicitude that they should act consistently, that Paul had so warmly expressed in the foregoing verses. Often, as the occasion offers, it is still well to notice how uniformly the Scriptures take for granted two great fundamental truths which human philosophy finds it hard to comprehend or to admit. The one is that God can and does control the inward acts and feelings of men without interfering either with their liberty or responsibility. The zeal of Titus was the spontaneous effusion of his own heart and was an index and element of his character. Yet God put that zeal into his heart. This is not a figure of speech. It was a simple and serious truth, a ground of solemn thanksgiving to God. The other great truth is that the believer is dependent on God for the continuance and exercise of spiritual life. The Holy Spirit does not regenerate the soul by implanting in it a new principle of life, and then leave that principle to struggle in its own strength for existence and growth. On the contrary, the new birth is the beginning of a constant indwelling of God in the soul, so that both the continuance and exercise of this new life are due to his presence. Yet so congenial and congruous is this divine influence that the life of God in us is in the highest sense our own life.

17. For indeed he accepted the exhortation; but being more forward, of his own accord he went unto you.

This is the proof of the zeal of Titus. Some commentators assume that μέν and δέ are here used instead of οὐ μόνον—ἀλλά, 'Not only did he listen to our exhortation, but fulfilled it with greater zeal as he went forth willingly.' But Meyer gives a better explanation. 'He accepted indeed our exhortation, i. e. he modestly submitted himself to my direction, but being too zealous (σπουδαιότερος) to need an exhortation, he went of his own accord.' He did not require to be urged to go, although in this, as in other matters, he was willing to do as I wished. *He went unto you.* Titus was no doubt the bearer of this epistle, and was with the apostle when it was written. He had not yet gone forth. In epistolary style the writer may use the tense suited to his own position, or to that of his readers. Paul here, and in the following verses, uses the past tense, because when his epistle came to hand the events referred to would be past.

18. And we have sent with him the brother, whose praise (is) in the gospel throughout all the churches.

We have sent. The time is from the stand-point of the reader, as before. *We send with him the brother.* As the name is not given, and as no data are furnished by which to determine who the brother here mentioned was, it is useless to conjecture. It was some one subordinate to Titus sent with him as a companion, some one well known throughout the churches, and who had especially the confidence of the Macedonian Christians, v. 19. But these conditions meet in so many of the persons mentioned in the Acts or Paul's epistles that they lead to no certain conclusion. Whether, therefore, it was Luke, Mark, Trophimus, or some one else, must be left undecided. The question is hardly worth the trouble which commentators have devoted to it. This brother's praise is said to have been *in the gospel.* He was distinguished by his efforts in that sphere; that is, by his zeal and labour in promoting the gospel. *Through all the churches.* If this be taken with the limitation of all the churches of Macedonia, it still is evidence that the brother referred to was specially entitled to the confidence of the Corinthians.

19. And not (that) only, but who was also chosen of the churches to travel with us with this grace, which is administered by us to the glory of the same Lord, and (declaration of) your ready mind.

This brother was entitled to confidence, and might safely be intrusted with the contributions of the Corinthians, not only on the ground of his general reputation, but also because he had been elected for the very purpose of taking charge, together with Paul, of the money collected for the saints. *Chosen*, χειροτονηθείς, literally, chosen by the stretching out the hand, therefore popularly. The word, however, is constantly used for selection or appointment without reference to the mode. Thus Josephus speaks of the king as having been ὑπὸ τοῦ θεοῦ κεχειροτονημένος. Ant. vi. 4. 2. See Wetstein. *Of the churches*, probably by the churches of Macedonia. *To travel with us*, συνέκδημος ἡμῶν, i. e. elected our travelling companion. Acts 19, 29. *With this grace.* The word χάρις means either the disposition, or that which is its expression or manifestation, i. e. either kindness or a kindness. Any free gift is therefore a grace. Here the grace intended is the alms collected for the poor. *Which is ministered by us*, i. e. of which we are the administrators. Paul had undertaken to administer the benefactions of the Gentile Christians among the brethren at Jerusalem, and the brother referred to had been chosen to travel with him and assist him in this service or ministry. *To the glory of the same Lord*, i. e. of our common Lord. The natural construction of this clause is with the immediately preceding words. 'This gift is administered by us to the glory of the Lord.' The only objection to this is that it requires the preposition πρός to be taken as expressing different relations in the same sentence. 'Administered πρὸς δόξαν . . . . καὶ προθυμίαν ὑμῶν (or, ἡμῶν), i. e. to promote the glory of the Lord and to prove your readiness.' Meyer and others therefore refer the clause to χειροτονηθείς; 'chosen that by his co-operation Christ may be honoured and my (ἡμῶν) readiness to labour in the gospel, unincumbered by such cares, may have free scope.' But this is unnatural, and supposes too much to be supplied to make out the sense. If the common text, which reads ὑμῶν, be retained, the sense is plain as expressed in our version. 'The ministration of this gift is for the manifestation of the glory of Christ and of your readiness or alacrity (in giving).' The oldest manuscripts as well as the ancient versions, however, read ἡμῶν, which almost all the modern editors adopt. The sense then is, that the gift served to promote the glory of Christ and to prove the apostle's willingness to serve the poor.

20. Avoiding this, that no man should blame us in this abundance which is administered by us.

The participle στελλόμενοι depends on the verb συνεπέμψαμεν of the verse 18. 'We sent the brother with Titus, avoiding this;' that is, in order to avoid. It was not, however, merely the appointment of a brother to accompany Titus, but also the designation of that brother to take part in the distribution of the alms of the churches that Paul had determined upon in order to prevent misrepresentation. The reference is therefore to the whole preceding sentence. The word στέλλειν, literally, to place, means also to set in order, to prepare, a sense which some adopt here. 'Preparing for, taking care with regard to, this.' The word also means to withdraw, to contract, and hence to avoid, which best suits this place as well as 2 Thess. 3, 6, where the word also occurs. *Lest any one should blame us.* He was determined not to give any one the opportunity to call his integrity into question. *In this abundance which is administered by us;* i. e. in the disposition of the large sums of money committed to his charge. The word ἁδρότης means ripeness, fulness, and then abundance; the nature of which is of course determined by the context.

21. Providing for honest things, not only in the sight of the Lord, but also in the sight of men.

This gives the reason for the precaution just mentioned. It was not enough for the apostle to do right, he recognised the importance of appearing right. It is a foolish pride which leads to a disregard of public opinion. We are bound to act in such a way that not only God, who sees the heart and knows all things, may approve our conduct, but also so that men may be constrained to recognise our integrity. It is a general principle regulating his whole life which the apostle here announces. Προνοούμενος, *providing for in one's own behalf.* The apostle says, He took care beforehand that men as well as God should see that he was honest. Compare Rom. 12, 17, and Prov. 3, 4, in the LXX.

22. And we have sent with them our brother, whom we have oftentimes proved diligent in many

things, but now much more diligent, upon the great confidence which (I have) in you.

Who this second brother was whom Paul sent to accompany Titus and his fellow-traveller, there is no means of determining. The apostle had proved him to be σπουδαῖον, earnest or diligent, ἐν πολλοῖς πολλάκις, in many things many times. *But now,* i. e. on this occasion, *much more diligent* or *earnest.* His zeal and alacrity was greatly excited *by the confidence which he has in regard to you.* He was so assured of success that he entered on his mission with the greatest earnestness. This interpretation, which most commentators adopt, and which in our English Bibles is suggested in the margin, is more natural than that preferred by Calvin, Beza and others. They connect the word πεποιθήσει with συνεπέμψαμεν, 'We sent the brother with them; . . . on account of the confidence we have in you.' This, however, was not the reason for the mission; nor does it suit the context to say, 'we sent him with confidence.' The position of the words is in favour of the explanation first mentioned.

23. Whether (any do inquire) of Titus, (he is) my partner and fellow-helper concerning you : or our brethren (be inquired of, they are) the messengers of the churches, (and) the glory of Christ.

This is a recapitulation, or summary commendation. The language in the original is very concise. *Whether concerning Titus,* i. e. whether I speak of Titus; or, Whether any do inquire concerning Titus; or, without supplying any thing, 'As to Titus.' *He is my partner,* κοινωνός, my associate, one who has a part with me in a common ministry. *And,* specially, *as concerns you my fellow-laborer* (συνεργός). *Whether our brethren,* (they are) *the messengers* (ἀπόστολοι) *of the churches.* The word apostle is here obviously used in its literal, and not in its official sense. These men were surely not apostles in the sense in which Paul was. In like manner, in Phil. 2, 25, Epaphroditus is called the apostle of the Philippians, because he was their messenger sent to minister to Paul at Rome. Both the brethren, therefore, above mentioned, and not only the one of whom it is said specially that he was chosen by the churches, were delegated by the people. They are further said to be *the glory of Christ.* As Christ alone, says Calvin, is the glory of believers, so he is glorified by them. They reflect his glory. They by their holiness lead men to see the excellence of Christ whose image they bear.

24. Wherefore shew ye to them, and before the churches, the proof of your love, and of our boasting on your behalf.

In conclusion the apostle exhorts the Corinthians to prove to these messengers so worthy of their confidence their love, and the truth of the favourable testimony which he had borne to their liberality. *Show the proof* (τὴν ἔνδειξιν . . ἐνδείξασθε) *of your love.* This may mean, 'your love to me;' or, 'your Christian love;' or, as is most natural, 'your love to them.' Give them evidence of your love, i. e. receive them with affectionate confidence; and let them see that my boasting of you was true. *Before the churches;* that is, so that the churches, by whom these brethren were sent, may see the proof of your love. Instead of the received text, which has the imperative ἐνδείξασθε, Lachmann, Tischendorf, Meyer and others, after the older MSS., read ἐνδεικνύμενοι. 'Exhibiting the evidence of your love, &c., (do it) in the presence of the churches.' This whole chapter proves how intimately the early Christians were bound together, not only from the intercourse here shown to exist between the several churches, but from the influence which they exerted over each other, from their brotherly love and sympathy, and from the responsibility which each is assumed to owe to the judgment of the others.

CHAPTER IX.

Continuation of the discourse in the preceding chapter on making collections for the saints.

ALTHOUGH aware of their readiness, the apostle sent the brethren to bring the collection for the poor to an end, lest when the Macedonians who were to accompany him to Cor inth arrived, they should find them unprepared, not so much to their disgrace, as to his mortification, vs. 1–4. He sent the brethren, therefore, that every thing they intended to do might be done in time, and be done cheerfully, v. 5. It was not only liberality, but cheerfulness in giving that the Lord required, vs. 6. 7. God who commanded them to give could and would supply their wants, and increase their graces. They would be the richer and the better for what they gave, vs. 8–10. What he had at heart was not so much that the temporal sufferings of the poor should be relieved, as that God might be glorified by the gratitude and mutual love of believers, and by the exhibition of their Christian graces, vs. 10–14. What are our gifts to the poor compared to the gift of Christ to us? v. 15.

1. For as touching the ministering to the saints, it is superfluous for me to write to you.

This is not a new paragraph, much less, as some have conjectured, a separate writing. It is intimately connected with the preceding. In the last verse of chapter 8, he exhorted them to receive the brethren with confidence, *for indeed* it is superfluous to write about the collection. He exhorted them to show their love to the brethren who were to visit them, for they needed no exhortation to liberality. This is another of those exhibitions of urbanity and rhetorical skill with which the epistles of Paul abounds. The δέ answering to the μέν of this verse is by some said to be found in verse 3. 'It is not necessary *indeed* to write, *but* I send, &c.' Or, if the connection between vs. 2 and 3 forbid this, the μέν may be taken as standing alone, as in 1 Cor. 5, 3. 11, 18. So De Wette. Concerning the *ministering* (περὶ τῆς διακονίας.) The word is often used not only for the ministry of the word, but also for the service rendered in the collection and distribution of alms. Acts 6, 1. 12, 25. Rom. 15, 31. *To the saints.* All believers are called ἅγιοι in the sense of *sacred*, i. e. separated from the world and consecrated to God, and as inwardly renewed and purified by the Holy Spirit. 8, 4. Acts 9, 13. Rom. 1, 7. 8, 27. The saints referred to were of course the poor believers in Jerusalem for whose benefit Paul instituted this collection in the several churches which he had founded. 1 Cor. 16, 1–3. *It is superfluous for me* (περισσόν μοι ἐστί) *to write* (τὸ γράφειν, the infinitive has the article because it is the subject of the

sentence) *unto you.* Paul had written and was about to write
still further on the subject; so that this is to be understood as
only a polite intimation that his writing, so far as they were
concerned, was not necessary. They did not need urging.

2. For I know the forwardness of your mind, for
which I boast of you to them of Macedonia, that Achaia
was ready a year ago; and your zeal hath provoked
very many.

The reason why it was superfluous to write to them was
that they were disposed to act spontaneously. The apostle
says he knew their *forwardness of mind,* (προθυμίαν,) their
readiness or disposition to give. *For which I boast* (ἣν καυ-
χῶμαι, see 11, 30 for the same construction) *of you* (ὑπὲρ ὑμῶν,
for you, to your advantage). Their readiness to give was a
matter of which Paul at that time boasted to the Macedonians
among whom he then was. This does not imply that the
apostle regarded their liberal disposition an honour to himself,
as though it owed its existence to his agency. We are said
to boast of the good qualities of a friend when we proclaim
them to his honour and not our own. *That Achaia was
ready a year ago.* This was Paul's boast, All the Christians
in Achaia belonged to the church in Corinth, although they
did not all reside in that city. See 1, 1. *Was ready,* i. e. to
take part in a collection for the saints. He does not mean
that the collection had already been completed, so that nothing
remained to be done. The context does not justify the dis-
paraging supposition that Paul, to excite the emulation of the
Macedonian Christians, had overstated the fact as to the Corinthians, representing them as having already a year ago made
their collection. *The readiness* to which he here refers is the
readiness of purpose. They were fully prepared to take part
in the work. Others say the apostle had told the Macedonians that the Corinthians had made their collection and were
ready to hand over the money. Those who have sufficient
respect for themselves not to speak disrespectfully of the
apostle, say that he truly believed this to be the fact, and was
now solicitous that the Corinthians should not falsify his assertion by being unprepared. Others, however, as Rückert, (and
in a measure De Wette,) represent the apostle as dishonestly
telling to the Macedonians that the Corinthians had made

their collection, and now to save his credit, he begged the latter to finish the work before he and his Macedonian friends arrived. The whole body of Paul's epistles is a refutation of this interpretation. No man who is capable of receiving the true impress of his exalted character can suppose him guilty of false statement or duplicity. What he told the Macedonians was simply that the Corinthians *were prepared.* What preparation is meant is plain from the context. It consisted in their προθυμία, their alacrity of mind to take part in the work. *A year ago,* 8, 10. *And your zeal,* i. e. your προθυμία, *alacrity,* in this business. The words are ὁ ἐξ ὑμῶν ζῆλος, where the ἐκ may be considered redundant, as our translators have assumed it to be; or, it may be omitted from the text, as by Lachmann; or, the meaning is, the zeal which emanated from you. This last is to be preferred. *Hath provoked.* The word ἐρεθίζειν means to excite, whether the feeling called into exercise be good or bad. In Col. 3, 21, fathers are cautioned not to provoke their children. Here the meaning is that the zeal of the Corinthians had excited the zeal of others. *Very many,* τοὺς πλείονας, the majority, the greater number. Acts 19, 32. It was not every individual of the Macedonian Christians, but the majority of them, whom the zeal of the Corinthians had excited.

3. Yet have I sent the brethren, lest our boasting of you should be in vain in this behalf; that, as I said, ye may be ready.

If the connection is with v. 1, the δέ here answers to the μέν there. 'There is no need to write, *but* I send, &c.' The reference, however, may be to v. 2. 'I boasted of your preparation, *but* lest my boasting be falsified, I send, &c.' *The brethren,* viz., Titus and his two companions, who were about to proceed to Corinth to attend to this matter. Lest our boasting of you *be in vain,* κενωθῇ, be proved unfounded, 1 Cor. 9, 15, i. e. shown to be an empty boast. *In this behalf.* Paul did not fear that the good account which he had given of the Corinthians in other matters should be contradicted by the facts, but only in this one affair of the collection for the poor. *That, as I said, ye may be ready.* This clause is parallel with the preceding. 'I sent the brethren that my boasting be not found vain, i. e. I sent them that ye may be ready.'

It appears from 8, 10 that the Corinthians had avowed the purpose to make a collection for the poor at Jerusalem, and had actually begun the work a year ago. Paul had mentioned this fact to the Macedonians, telling them that the Corinthians were ready to do their part in this business. He now sends Titus and the brethren that the work may at once be completed, and his boasting of them prove to be true. It is plain that he could not have told the Macedonians that the collection at Corinth had already been made, because he not only knew that such was not the fact, but he in this very passage refers to the work as yet to be accomplished. He could hardly say, 'I told the Macedonians you had made your collection a year ago and had the money all ready to hand over,' at the very moment he was urging them to collect it. The simple fact is that he had said the Corinthians were ready to do their part in this business, and he begged them to do at once what they intended to do, lest his boasting of their readiness (προθυμία) should prove to have been unfounded. There is nothing in this inconsistent with perfect truthfulness and open-hearted fairness.

4. Lest haply if they of Macedonia come with me, and find you unprepared, we (that we say not, ye) should be ashamed in this same confident boasting.

Paul was attended from city to city by travelling companions, who conducted him on his way and ministered to him. 1 Cor. 16, 6. Rom. 15, 24. Acts 17, 14. 15. &c. As he was now in Macedonia it was in accordance with the usual custom that Macedonians should attend him to Corinth. *If they come with me*, ἐὰν ἔλθωσιν, *shall have come*, i. e. 'Lest when they come *and find you unprepared*, i. e. unprepared to do what a year ago you professed your readiness to do, *we (that we say not, you) should be ashamed*. The failure would indeed be a cause of shame to the Corinthians, but he delicately substitutes himself. He appeals to their better feelings when he calls upon them to save him from mortification, instead of exhorting them to save themselves from disgrace. *In this same confident boasting*. The words τῆς καυχήσεως are omitted by almost all the recent editors from Griesbach down. They are not found in the MSS. B, C, D, F, G, or the ancient versions. They probably were added by a transcriber from

11, 17. These words being omitted, the text stands, ἐν τῇ ὑποστάσει ταύτῃ, *in this confidence,* i. e. ashamed in relation to this confidence. Comp. Heb. 3, 14. 11, 1. Others take the word in the sense of *negotium,* "in this thing," which is not only unnecessary, but contrary to usage.

5. Therefore I thought it necessary to exhort the brethren, that they would go before unto you, and make up beforehand your bounty, whereof ye had notice before, that the same might be ready, as (a matter of) bounty, and not as (of) covetousness.

Therefore, i. e. in order to avoid the mortification of his boasting being proved vain. *I thought it necessary to exhort the brethren,* (Titus and his companions,) *that they would go before ;* (παρακαλέσαι—ἵνα, as in 8, 6, and often elsewhere, ἵνα is used after verbs signifying to ask, exhort, &c., in the sense of ὅτι.) *Would go before,* i. e. before Paul and his Macedonian companions. *And make up beforehand,* προκαταρτίσωσι, a word not found in the Greek writers, and occurring in the New Testament only in this passage. The simple verb means, to put fully in order, to complete. This the brethren were to do in reference to the collection, before Paul's arrival. *Your bounty,* τὴν εὐλογίαν ὑμῶν, *your blessing.* The word is used in the sense both of benediction and benefaction. The latter is clearly its meaning here, as perhaps also in Rom. 15, 29 ; see also Eph. 1, 3, and in the LXX. Gen. 33, 11. Judges 1, 15. 1 Sam. 25, 27, &c. So in English, *a blessing* is either a prayer for good, or the good itself. *Whereof ye had notice before.* Here the reading is doubtful. The common text has προκατηγγελμένην, *announced beforehand.* Not, however, as our translation has it, announced *to you,* but to others. The benefaction before spoken of, i. e. of which so much has been said. Almost all the critical editions read προεπηγγελμένην, *promised beforehand,* 'your promised benefaction.' And this gives a better sense, as the apostle was urging them to do what they had promised. *That the same might be ready as* a matter of *bounty ;* οὕτως ὡς εὐλογίαν, *so as a blessing,* i. e. as something worthy of the name. This may mean, 'worthy of the name because the fruit of love ;' or, because given freely ; or, because rich, abundant. This last is to be preferred because of the antithesis between εὐλογία and πλεονεξία, because of the explanation in v. 6, and because cheerfulness in giving is afterwards enforced. *And not as* of *covetousness;* literally, not as covetousness, i. e. not such a gift as betrays the avarice of the giver.

6. But this (I say), He which soweth sparingly, shall reap also sparingly; and he which soweth bountifully, shall reap also bountifully.

The words τοῦτο δέ, *but this*, are commonly and most naturally explained by supplying some such words as *I say*, or, *consider*. Others take them as the accusative absolute; 'as to this, however.' Meyer unnaturally makes τοῦτο the object of σπείρων, 'He who sows this sparingly, &c.' That is, in other cases it may be different, but in this spiritual sowing, in this seed of good deeds, the rule always holds good. Our version gives a simple and suitable sense. The only question of doubt in the verse is the meaning of the words ἐπ᾽ εὐλογίαις, which our translators have rendered adverbially, *bountifully.* 'He that sows bountifully, shall reap also bountifully.' This undoubtedly is the meaning as determined by the antithesis, 'He that sows φειδομένως *sparingly*, and he that sows ἐπ᾽ εὐλογίαις *bountifully*.' But the question is how to get that sense out of the words, which literally mean *with blessings.* 'He that sows *with blessings*, shall reap *with blessings*.' The force of the preposition ἐπί with the dative in this place may be explained after the analogy of such passages as Rom. 4, 18. 1 Cor. 9, 10; ἐπ᾽ ἐλπίδι, *with hope*, as expressing the condition under which any thing is done; or after the analogy of such places as Rom. 5, 14, ἐπὶ τῷ ὁμοιώματι, *after the similitude*, as expressing the rule according to which it is done. In either case the preposition and noun may express an adverbial qualification. In this case therefore, ἐπ᾽ εὐλογίαις, *ad normam beneficiorum*, as Wahl translates it, may, as the context requires, mean kindly, freely, or bountifully. Here, as just stated, the antithesis with φειδομένως requires the last, viz., bountifully. The sentiment here expressed is the same as in Prov. 11, 24, "There is that scattereth and yet increaseth; and there is that withholdeth more than is meet, but it tendeth to poverty." It is comprehended also in the wider truth taught in Gal. 6, 7. Our Lord teaches the same doctrine, Luke 6, 38, "Give and it shall be given unto you, &c." Matt. 10, 41, and often elsewhere. It is edifying to notice the difference between the divine wisdom and the wisdom of men. As the proper motive to acts of benevolence is a desire for the happiness of others and a regard to the will of God, human wisdom says it is wrong to appeal to any selfish motive. The wisdom of God, while teaching the entire abnegation of self, and requiring a man even to hate his own life when in conflict with the glory of God, tells all who thus deny themselves that they thereby most effectually promote their own interests. He that loses his life shall save it. He that does not seek his own, shall best secure his own. He that humbleth himself shall be exalted. There can, however, be no hypocrisy in this matter. It is not the man who pretends to deny himself, to humble himself, or to seek the good of others rather than his own, while he acts from a regard to self, who is to be thus rewarded. It is only those who sincerely postpone themselves to others, who shall be preferred before them. We may thence learn that it is right to present to men the divinely ordained consequences of their actions as motives to control their conduct. It is right to tell men that obedience to God, devotion to his glory and the good of others, will effectually promote their own welfare.

7. Every man according as he purposeth in his heart, (so let him give;) not grudgingly, or of necessity: for God loveth a cheerful giver.

Though he wished them to give bountifully, he desired them to do it freely. Let each one give *as he purposes in his heart*, i. e. as he cordially, or with the consent of the heart, determines. This stands opposed to what follows, and, therefore, is explained by it. *Not grudgingly*, ἐκ λύπης, not out of sorrow; i. e. let not the gift proceed out of a reluctant state of mind, grieving after what is given as so much lost. *Or of necessity*, i. e. constrained by circumstances to give, when you prefer not to do it. Many gifts are thus given sorrowfully, where the giver is induced to give by a regard to public opinion, or by stress of conscience. This reluctance spoils the gift. It loses all its fragrance when the incense of a free and joyful spirit is wanting. *For God loveth a cheerful giver;* ἱλαρὸν δότην, *a joyful giver*, one to whom giving is a delight, who does it with hilarity. The passage is quoted from Prov. 22, 9, where the Hebrew means, "A good eye shall be blessed." The LXX. renders the words *quoad sensum*, ἄνδρα ἱλαρὸν καὶ δότην εὐλογεῖ ὁ θεός; a version which Paul adopts for substance. God blesses, loves, delights in, the joyous giver. Let not, therefore, those who give reluctantly, or from stress of circumstances, or to secure merit, imagine that mere giving is acceptable to God. Unless we feel it is an honour and a joy to give, God does not accept the offering.

8. And God (is) able to make all grace abound toward you; that ye, always having all sufficiency in all (things), may abound to every good work.

From this verse to the 11th, the apostle assures them that the liberal and cheerful giver will always have something to give. *God is able.* The sacred writers often appeal to the power of God as a ground of confidence to his people. Rom. 16, 25. Eph. 3, 20. Jude 24. This is done especially when we are called upon to believe something which is contrary to the natural course of things. Giving is, to the natural eye, the way to lessen our store, not to increase it. The Bible says it is the way to increase it. To believe this it is only necessary to believe in the power, providence, and promise of God. God is able to make the paradox, "he that scattereth, increaseth," prove true. *God is able to make all grace abound;* χάριν, favour, gift, whether temporal or spiritual, or both, depends on the context. Here the reference is clearly to earthly good; that kind of good or favour is intended which enables those who receive it to give abundantly. The idea, therefore, obviously is, 'God is able to increase your wealth.' *That ye, having all sufficiency in all things.* The expression here is striking, ἐν παντὶ πάντοτε πᾶσαν, *in all things, always, all.* God is able so to enrich you that you shall have in every respect, at all times, all kinds of sufficiency. The word is αὐτάρκειαν, which everywhere else means *contentment.* This sense Grotius, Meyer and others retain here. 'That having full contentment,' i. e. being fully satisfied and not craving more, you may, &c. This, however, is not so well suited to the context, and especially to the qualifying words, ἐν παντί. It is 'a competency in every thing' of which the apostle speaks. *That ye may abound,* περισσεύητε, *may have abundance.* Phil. 4, 18. The word is used transitively in the first clause of the verse and intransitively in the last. 'God is able to cause your riches to abound, that ye may have abundance *to every good work ;'* εἰς πᾶν ἔργον ἀγαθόν, in reference to, so as to be able to perform every good work. The logical connection is not with the intermediate participial clause, 'that having sufficiency, ye may have abundance,' but with the first clause, 'God is able to cause your resources to abound, that ye may have abundance.' The participial clause expresses simply what, notwithstanding their liberality, would be the result. Having (i. e. still having) a competency for yourselves, ye will have abundance for every good work. There is another interpretation of this passage which the English version naturally suggests. 'That ye may abound in every good work.' But this the Greek will not admit; because it is εἰς πᾶν, κ.τ.λ., and not ἐν παντί, κ.τ.λ. See 1 Cor. 15, 58. Besides, the other interpretation is better suited to the context.

9. As it is written, He hath dispersed abroad ; he hath given to the poor : his righteousness remaineth forever.

The connection is with the last clause of the preceding verse. Paul had said that he who gives shall have abundance to give. This is precisely what is said in Psalm 112. Of the man who fears God it is there said, "Wealth and riches shall be in his house." "He showeth favour, and lendeth." "He hath dispersed, he hath given to the poor; his righteousness endureth forever." The main idea the apostle designs to present as having the sanction of the word of God is, that he who is liberal, who disperses, scatters abroad his gifts with free-handed generosity, as a man scatters seed, shall always have abundance. And this the Psalmist expressly asserts. It may be said that this is not in accordance with experience. We do not always see liberality attended by riches. This is a difficulty not peculiar to this case. The Bible is full of declarations concerning the blessedness of the righteous, and of the providential favours which attend their lot. This Psalm says, "Wealth and riches," or, as the LXX. and Vulgate have it, "Glory and riches shall be in their house;" and our Lord says, that those who forsake all for him shall in this life receive an hundred-fold, houses, lands, &c. Mark 10, 30. These passages were not designed to be taken literally or applied universally. They teach three things. 1st. The tendency of things. It is the tendency of righteousness to produce bless-

edness, as it is the tendency of evil to produce misery. 2d.
The general course of divine providence. God in his providence does as a general rule prosper the diligent and bless
the righteous. Honesty is the best policy, is a maxim even
of worldly wisdom. 3d. Even in this life righteousness produces a hundred-fold more good than unrighteousness does.
A righteous man is a hundred-fold more happy than a wicked
man, other things being equal. A good man is a hundred-fold
more happy in sickness, in poverty, in bereavement, than a
wicked man in the same circumstances. It is, therefore, according to Scripture, a general law, that he that scattereth,
increaseth; he that gives shall have wherewith to give.

His righteousness (i. e. the righteousness of the man who
gives to the poor) *endureth forever*. The word δικαιοσύνη,
righteousness, in Scripture, is often used in a comprehensive
sense, including all moral excellence; and often in a restricted
sense for rectitude or justice. When used in the comprehensive sense, it depends on the context what particular form of
goodness is intended. To return a poor man's pledge is an
act of δικαιοσύνη, Deut. 24, 13; so is giving alms, Matt. 6, 1
(where the true reading is δικαιοσύνην, and not ἐλεημοσύνην).
In like manner the "glory of God" may mean the sum of his
divine perfections, or his wisdom, power, or mercy, as special
forms of his glory, as the context requires. In this passage it
is plain that righteousness means general excellence or virtue,
as manifested in beneficence. And when it is said that his
beneficence shall continue forever, the implication is that he
shall always have wherewith to be beneficent. And this is
here the main idea. He shall always be prosperous; or, as it
is expressed at the close of v. 8, he shall have abundance for
every good work. *Forever* is equivalent to *always*, as εἰς τὸν
αἰῶνα is often used for indefinite duration. Whether the
duration be absolutely without limit, or whether the limit be
unknown or undetermined, depends in each case on the nature
of the thing spoken of, and on the analogy of Scripture.

10. Now, he that ministereth seed to the sower,
both minister bread for (your) food, and multiply your
seed sown, and increase the fruits of your righteousness.

Now; δέ is continuative. God is able to give you abundance, *and* he will do it. This verse is a declaration, and not a wish. Our translation, which makes it a prayer, is founded on the Elzevir, or common text, which reads χορηγῆσαι, πληθύναι, αὐξῆσαι in the optative, instead of the futures χορηγήσει, πληθυνεῖ, αὐξήσει, which are supported by a great preponderance of authorities, and are adopted by Griesbach, Lachmann, Tischendorf, and by the great majority of editors. The sense expressed by the future forms is also better suited to the context. Paul's desire was to produce the conviction in the minds of the Corinthians, which he himself so strongly felt, that no man is the poorer for being liberal. The ground of this conviction was twofold; the explicit promise of God, and his character and general mode of dealing with men. *He that ministereth seed to the sower ;* ὁ ἐπιχορηγῶν, he whose prerogative and wont it is to supply seed to the sower. Such being the character and, so to speak, the office of God, Paul was sure he would supply the necessities of his giving people. The words καὶ ἄρτον εἰς βρῶσιν our translators, after Calvin and others, connect with the following clause, and render καί *both.* "Shall both minister bread for food, and multiply, &c." The obviously natural construction is with the preceding clause, 'He that ministereth seed to the sower, and bread for eating.' (The word is βρῶσις, *eating*, and not βρῶμα, *food.*) This connection is also in accordance with the passage in Is. 55, 10, which was evidently in the apostle's mind, and where the words are, "Seed to the sower, and bread to the eater." This bountiful God *will give and increase your seed.* Your seed means your resources, your wealth, that which you can scatter abroad in acts of beneficence, as a sower scatters seed. He who furnishes the husbandman seed for his harvest, will abundantly supply you with seed for your harvest. *And increase the fruits of your righteousness.* This is parallel with the preceding clause, and means the same thing. 'The fruits of your righteousness,' are not the rewards of your righteousness, either here or hereafter. But 'your works of righteousness,' i. e. of beneficence ; the word δικαιοσύνη having the same sense here as in the preceding clause. As in v. 9, the words "his righteousness remaineth forever" mean that the righteous shall always have the means of being beneficent; so here to increase "the fruits of your righteousness," means, 'will increase your means of doing good.' This sense the context demands, and the words, in their scriptural sense, readily admit. The other interpretation, however, according to which "the fruits of your righteousness" mean the reward of your righteousness, amounts substantially to the same thing; for the reward of beneficence is, according to the context, the increase of the means wherewith to be beneficent.

11. Being enriched in every thing to all bountifulness, which causeth through us thanksgiving to God.

In our version vs. 9 and 10 are regarded as a parenthesis, and this verse is connected with v. 8. "That ye may have abundance for every good work—being enriched, &c." But this is unnecessary and forbidden by the regular connection of vs. 9 and 10 with v. 8. Others supply the substantive verb "ye shall be enriched." Almost all the modern commentators assume the irregular construction of the participle of which so many examples occur both in the New Testament and in the classics. See Eph. 4, 2. 3, 17. Col. 2, 2. 3, 16. Acts 15, 22, &c. The connection is therefore with what immediately precedes. 'God will increase the fruits of your righteousness, (i. e. your resources,) being enriched, i. e. so that you shall be enriched, &c.' The reference is not to inward or spiritual riches, but, as the whole context demands, to worldly riches. 'If you are liberal, God will give you abundance, so that you shall be rich *to all bountifulness,* εἰς πᾶσαν ἁπλότητα. The preposition (εἰς) expresses the design or end for which they shall be enriched. *Bountifulness* or liberality; the word is ἁπλότης, which means sincerity, rightmindedness. Another example of a general term used in a specific sense. See 8, 2. Rom. 15, 12. *Which causes through us,* i. e. by our ministry. Paul had been instrumental in exciting the liberality of the Corinthians and in effecting the contribution for the poor in Jerusalem, and therefore he could say that the *thanksgiving to God* which was thus called forth was *through him.* The good effect of the liberality of Christians was not limited to the relief of the temporal necessities of their brethren; it had the higher effect of promoting gratitude to God. On this idea the apostle enlarges in the following verses.

12. For the administration of this service not only supplieth the want of the saints, but is abundant also by many thanksgivings unto God.

Your liberality produces gratitude, *for* (ὅτι), because, *the*

administration of this service, ἡ διακονία τῆς λειτουργίας ταύτης.
This may mean, 'The administration by me of this service of
yours, i. e. this benefaction of yours, which is a·service rendered to God and his people.' It is a λειτουργία; properly a
public service, but always in the New Testament (except perhaps Phil. 2, 30) a religious service such as was rendered by
the priests in the temple, Luke 1, 23. Heb. 8, 6. 9, 21; or by
the Christian ministry, Phil. 2, 17. Comp. Rom. 1, 9. Or, it
may mean, 'The service which you render by this benefaction.'
The διακονία, ministry, or service, consisted in the λειτουργία,
the contribution. This suits better with v. 13, where διακονία
is used for what the Corinthians did, not for what Paul did.
Not only supplieth. The Greek is somewhat peculiar; ἐστὶ
προσαναπληροῦσα, it is not only fully compensatory . . . but it is
(περισσεύουσα) *overflowing;* the participles being used as adjectives expressing the quality of the thing spoken of. *The
want of the saints.* Their necessities are not only supplied,
but your service overflows, or is abundantly productive of
good; *by means of many thanksgivings to God;* τῷ θεῷ depending on εὐχαριστιῶν as in verse 11.

13. While by the experiment of this ministration
they glorify God for your professed subjection unto the
gospel of Christ, and for (your) liberal distribution unto
them, and unto all (men).

There is the same irregularity of grammatical construction
in this verse as in v. 11; the participle δοξάζοντες here referring
to πολλῶν, as there πλουτιζόμενοι to ὑμῶν. The sense is, 'Many
thank God, *glorifying* him (διὰ τῆς δοκιμῆς τῆς διακονίας ταύτης)
on the occasion of the evidence offered by this service.' The
preposition διά here expresses the occasional, not the instrumental, or rational cause. It is neither *through,* nor, *on account of,* but simply *by,* i. e. occasioned by. The simplest
explanation of δοκιμή, in this passage, is proof, or evidence;
and the genitive, διακονίας, is the genitive of apposition. The
service was the proof. The thing proved by the service rendered by the Corinthians to their poor brethren, is what is
mentioned in the sequel, viz., their obedience and their fellowship with the saints. Meyer makes δοκιμή mean *indoles spec-
tata,* the nature, or internal character. "From the nature of
this service," whereby it proved itself to be genuine, or what

the Christian spirit demanded. Calvin's explanation is, Speci-
men idoneum probandæ Corinthiorum caritati, quod erga fra-
tres procul remotos tam liberales erant; which amounts very
much to what is implied in the first interpretation mentioned.
They glorify God *for your professed subjection*. The words
are, ἐπὶ τῇ ὑποταγῇ τῆς ὁμολογίας ὑμῶν; on account of obedience
to your confession. Ὁμολογία is always in the New Testament
used for the profession, or confession, of Christianity. 1 Tim.
6, 12. Heb. 3, 1. 4, 14. 10, 23. Beza, whom our translators
follow, gives the genitive the force of the participle, *professed
obedience*, i. e. obedience which you profess. Others make it
the genitive of the source, "the obedience which flows from
your confession;" others again make it the genitive of the
object, "obedience to your confession." This gives the best
sense, and agrees best with the analogous expression, "obedience of Christ," 10, 5. *To the gospel of Christ*, εἰς εὐαγ.
These words, it is said, cannot properly be constructed either
with ὑποταγῇ or with ὁμολογίας, because neither ὑποτάσσω nor
ὁμολογέω is followed by εἰς. On this account Meyer connects
the clause in question with δοξάζοντες, 'they praise God—in
reference to the gospel.' But this is forced, and does not
agree with the following clause; as there, εἰς πάντας, if connected with δοξάζοντες, gives no definite sense. De Wette
connects εἰς εὐαγ. with what precedes, 'Your confession—as it
concerns the gospel.' *And for your liberal distribution unto
them, and unto all*. This is the second ground of praise to
God. The words are ἁπλότητι τῆς κοινωνίας, *the sincerity of
your fellowship*. These general terms may, if the context required, be taken in the specific sense, "liberality of your contribution," as is done by our translators; or they may be
understood in their wider and more natural sense. The
ground on which the saints at Jerusalem would praise God
was the manifestation of the Christian fellowship which the
Corinthians cherished not only for them, but for all believers.
It was the consciousness of the communion of saints—the assurance that believers, however separated, or however distinguished as Jews and Gentiles, bond or free, are one body in
Christ, that called forth their praise to God. And, therefore,
the apostle says it was the (κοινωνία) fellowship of the Corinthians not only towards them, (the saints in Jerusalem,) but
towards *all* believers, that was the ground of their praise.
See Phil. 1, 5, for an example of κοινωνία followed by εἰς, as it
is in this verse.

14. And by their prayer for you, which long after you, for the exceeding grace of God in you.

This verse admits of a threefold construction. It may be connected with v. 12, δεήσει being parallel with διὰ πολλῶν εὐχ. 'Your liberality is abundant, or overflowing, (περισσεύουσα,) through many thanksgivings—and by their prayer for you.' That is, our liberality is productive of abundant good, not only by calling forth thanksgiving to God, but also by leading the objects of your kindness to pray for you. This is a full compensation. The prayers and blessings of the poor are their benefactions to the rich, descending on them as the dew on Hermon. Or the connection may be with δοξάζοντες in v. 13. 'They glorify God for your obedience, ... and by their prayer.' But in this case, the natural meaning would be, (δεήσει being co-ordinate with ὑποταγῇ), 'They glorify God for your subjection—and for their prayer.' This does not give a good sense. Believers do not glorify God *for* their prayers. Others, as Meyer, take αὐτῶν ἐπιποθούντων together as the genitive absolute, and καί, not as *and*, but *also*. 'You (Corinthians) manifest your fellowship for them—they also with prayer for you earnestly longing for you.' This gives a pertinent sense. The first mentioned explanation is, however, generally preferred. *For the exceeding grace of God in you.* That is, *on account of*, (διὰ τὴν χάριν,) the surpassing grace, or favour of God manifested towards or upon you (ἐφ' ὑμῖν); in that he had rendered them so liberal, and so filled them with a Christian spirit.

15. Thanks (be) unto God for his unspeakable gift.

According to Calvin, and perhaps the majority of commentators, the gift to which Paul refers, is that spoken of in the context, viz., the grace bestowed on the Corinthians, or the good effect anticipated from their liberality. Confident that the Corinthians would be liberal, and that their liberality would excite the gratitude of their suffering brethren, and cement the union between the Jewish and Gentile converts, the apostle breaks forth in this expression of thanksgiving to God, for bringing about so happy a consummation. But the language is too strong for this. God's unspeakable gift is his Son. This, according to the analogy of Scripture, is that one great, supreme, all-comprehending gift, which is here intended. This is the more natural, because it is Paul's wont, when speaking either of the feeble love, or trivial gifts of believers, one to another, to refer in contrast to the infinite love and unspeakable gift of God in Christ to us. 8, 9. Eph. 5, 1. It is his habit also to introduce ejaculations of adoration or thanksgiving into the midst, or at the close of his teachings or exhortations. Rom. 1, 25. 9, 5. 1 Cor. 15, 17. 1 Tim. 1, 17. The passage, therefore, ought to stand, as we doubt not the vast majority of the readers of the Bible understand it, as an outburst of gratitude to God for the gift of his Son.

CHAPTER X.

Paul deprecates the necessity of asserting his authority and of exercising his power to punish the disobedient, vs. 1–6. He confronts his opposers with the assertion of divinely derived power, vs. 9–11. He shows that he claims authority only over those who were committed to his care, vs. 12–18.

Paul's assertion of his authority and vindication of his apostolic prerogatives.

THE remarkable change in the whole tone and style of this portion of the epistle, from the beginning of the 10th chapter to near the end of the 13th, has attracted the attention of every careful reader. The contrast between this and the preceding portions of the epistle is so great, that some have concluded that they are separate letters, written at different times and under different circumstances. There is no external authority for this conjecture, and it is not only unnecessary, but inconsistent with the facts of the case. The same topics are presented, and there is in 12, 18 reference to the mission of Titus, spoken of in the earlier chapters. It is an adequate explanation of the change in question, that in chs. 1–9, Paul had in his mind, and was really addressing, the faithful and obedient portion of the church, whereas he has here in view the unreasonable and wicked false teachers and their adherents, who not only made light of his authority, but corrupted the gospel, which he was appointed to propagate and defend. He therefore naturally assumes a tone of authority and severity. Satisfied of his divine mission, and conscious of supernatural power, he cautioned them not to rely too much on his forbearance. He was indeed as a man humble, and, if they chose, insignificant; but there was slumbering in his arm an energy which they would do well not to provoke. He had no desire to exercise in Corinth the authority with which Christ had invested him for the purpose of bringing down all opposition. He would give them a fair trial, and wait to see how far they would be obedient, before he punished their disobedience, vs. 1–6. They should not judge by appearance, or set themselves up on the ground of their fancied advantages, because whatever they had, he had in larger measure, vs. 7. 8. He had no intention to frighten them by his epistles —which they said were written in a tone he would not dare to assume when present—for they would find that, when occasion called for it, he could be as bold when present as when he was absent, vs. 9–11. They were subject to his apostolic authority. He usurped nothing in exercising the powers of his office over the churches which he had himself founded. He did not interfere with the jurisdiction of the other apostles, or undertake the special oversight of churches founded by others. Macedonia and Achaia were within the sphere of his operations, and he hoped to preach the gospel far beyond those limits in regions where it had never been heard, vs. 12–16. His confidence was not self-confidence, but confidence in God. His self-commendation amounted to nothing, unless the Lord commended him. Paul constantly felt that in himself he could do nothing, but in the Lord he could do all things, vs. 17. 18.

1. Now I Paul myself beseech you, by the meekness and gentleness of Christ, who in presence (am) base among you, but being absent am bold toward you.

He enters without any preamble or circumlocution on his new subject, and places himself face to face with his unscrupulous opponents. He says, *I Paul myself*. He usually employs the first person plural when speaking of himself. Here, and throughout this context, he makes his individuality promi-

nent, in saying I. This is rendered the more emphatic by the
addition of the word *myself;* αὐτὸς ἐγώ, *I myself,* the man whom
you so despise and calumniate. Comp. Gal. 5, 2. Eph. 3, 1.
Philemon, 19. In this case the expression is so emphatic that
many suppose that Paul here began to write with his own
hand; as though he were so excited, that he seized the pen
from his amanuensis, and says, 'I Paul myself now write to
you.' This, however, is unnecessary, and unsustained by any
thing in the context. *Beseech you by the meekness and gentleness of Christ.* That is, the meekness and gentleness which
belonged to Christ, and which, therefore, his disciples are
bound to imitate. To beseech *by* (διά), is to beseech on account of, or out of regard to. The request is enforced by a
reference to the obligation of Christians to be meek and gentle as was their Lord. Matt. 11, 29. Is. 42, 2. In Rom. 12, 1,
we have a similar expression, "I beseech you by the mercies
of God." See Phil. 2, 1. The words πραότης and ἐπιείκεια differ very much as our words meekness and gentleness do; the
former referring more to the inward virtue, the latter to its
outward expression. As Christians are bound to be meek and
gentle, Paul begged the Corinthians not to force him to be
severe. He describes himself as his opposers described him,
as craven when present, and a braggart when absent. *Who
in presence am base among you.* In presence, κατὰ πρόσωπον,
coram, before, towards the face of any one, here opposed to
ἀπών, *absent.* The word ταπεινός, literally, *low;* then lowly,
humble. It is commonly used in a good sense. Our Lord
says of himself that he was, ταπεινὸς τῇ καρδίᾳ, *lowly in heart,*
and his followers are always described as *the lowly.* But the
word also means *downcast,* as in 7, 6, and thence it sometimes
expresses depression when it is the effect of the want of courage. This is its meaning here. *But being absent am bold
towards you.* Bold, in the sense opposite to base, or craven.
This word also (θαῤῥέω) is commonly used in a good sense,
5, 6. It is only the context which gives it a different shade
of meaning. Paul was regarded by his enemies as in heart a
coward, and his boldness as merely assumed when there was
no danger to confront. No one (except Rückert) now be-
lieves this. True heroism was never more fully exemplified
than in the life of this apostle, who against numbers, wealth
and power, always was true to his convictions; who encountered all manner of dangers and sufferings in the service of
Christ, and whose whole conduct showed that he was ready

not only to be bound, but to die for the name of the Lord Jesus. Acts 21, 13.

2. But I beseech (you), that I may not be bold when I am present with that confidence, wherewith I think to be bold against some, which think of us as if we walked according to the flesh.

The particle (δέ), *but*, serves to resume the exhortation in the first clause of v. 1. There it is (παρακαλῶ ὑμᾶς) *I exhort you*, here it is (δέομαι) *I beseech*. This shows that ὑμᾶς and not θεόν is to be supplied as the object of the verb. The sense is, 'I beseech *you*,' not, 'I pray *God*.' What Paul beseeches of them is, that they would not force him to have recourse to severity. This he expresses by saying, τὸ μὴ παρὼν θαρρῆσαι, *that I may not be bold when present*. The article (τό) serves to render the object of the verb more prominent; and παρών is in the nominative because the subject of both verbs is the same. *To be bold*, i. e. to act with decision and courage; to exhibit the character which the opponents of the apostle said he assumed only when absent. *With the confidence*, i. e. with the conviction of his right to exercise the authority which he claimed, and with the consciousness of power to carry his decisions into effect. *Wherewith I think;* λογίζομαι, which means to reckon, to reason, and then, as here, to purpose. Paul had determined in his own mind that if persuasion failed to bring his opponents to a right state of mind, he would resort to that power with which God had armed him to put down all opposition. The Vulgate gives the word λογίζομαι a passive sense, *qua existimor*, 'which I am thought, or supposed to assume.' So Luther, "die man mir zumisset," *which men ascribe to me*. Bengel and many other commentators adopt the same interpretation. This has the advantage of giving λογίζομαι and the following participle λογιζομένους the same sense. But it is objected to this interpretation that it would require ἀπών to be used. 'The confidence wherewith I am thought *when absent* to assume.' The common interpretation, therefore, is to be preferred. *To be bold.* The word is here not θαρρῆσαι as before, but τολμῆσαι, *to dare;* to act without fear and without regard to consequences. Paul had determined, if forced to it, to set his opponents at defiance and to act with utter disregard of all they could say or do.

The persons against whom he had determined to exercise this severity, were those who *think of us*, he says, *as if we walked according to the flesh.* The word *flesh* sometimes means the body, sometimes it expresses the secondary idea of weakness, sometimes, and most frequently in Paul's epistles, our corrupt nature. Beza gives it here the second of these meanings. He understands Paul as describing his opponents as those who regarded him as weak and cowardly, or, as invested with nothing more than human powers (non alio præsidio freti, quam quod præ nobis ferimus), so that, as Bengel says, "they may despise us with impunity." But this is not only inconsistent with the scriptural use of the word "to walk," which, in its figurative sense, refers to moral deportment, but also with the familiar use of the phrase (κατὰ σάρκα), *after the flesh.* See the next verse, and Rom. 8, 1. 4. 5. 13. The persons referred to were those who regarded the apostle not only as an ordinary man, but as acting under the control of his corrupt nature, governed by selfish or malicious feelings, and relying on himself.

3. For though we walk in the flesh, we do not war after the flesh.

There is here, so to speak, a play on the word *flesh*, which is used in somewhat different senses. Paul did indeed walk in the flesh, he was a man, and a mere man, not only invested with a body, but subject to all the infirmities of human nature; but he did not war after the flesh. What was human and worldly neither determined his conduct, nor was the ground of his confidence. The phrase to be *in the flesh* has various meanings according to the connection in which it is used. In 1 Tim. 3, 16, it is said, "God was manifested in the flesh," i. e. in human nature. In Rom. 8, 8. 9, to be "in the flesh," means to be in an unrenewed state. In Phil. 1, 22. 24, "to live," or, "to abide in the flesh," means to live, or abide, in the body. Here the phrase has substantially the same meaning, but with the accessory idea of weakness and exposure to temptation. 'Though he was a man, and therefore compassed with the infirmities incident to humanity, yet, &c.' "Hic," says Calvin, "*Ambulare in carne* significat in mundo versari: quod alibi dicit, habitare in corpore (supra 5, 6). Erat enim inclusus in corporis sui ergastulo: sed hoc non impediebat quominus Spiritus sancti virtus mirifice se exsereret in ejus infirmitate."

Instead of the general expression " to walk," Paul uses, in the second clause, the more specific term, " to war." *We war not ;* οὐ στρατευόμεθα. Στρατεύω means, to go to war, to make a campaign; στρατεύομαι means, to serve as a soldier, to fight. The war here referred to, is that which the apostle waged against error and every thing opposed to the gospel. This war, he says, he did not conduct (κατὰ σάρκα) *after the flesh ;* that is, governed by the flesh, or relying on it. He was not guided by the principles of ordinary men, who act under the influence of their corrupt nature; neither did he depend for success on any thing the flesh (i. e. human nature) could afford. He was governed by the Spirit and relied upon the Spirit. " What Paul says of himself, is true of all the faithful ministers of Christ. They bear about an incomparable treasure in earthen vessels. Therefore, although they are compassed with infirmities, nevertheless the spiritual power of God is resplendent in them."—CALVIN. The connection of this verse, as indicated by the particle γάρ (*for*), is either with the middle clause of the preceding verse, 'I am determined to be bold towards the opponents of the truth, *for* though I walk in the flesh, I do not war after the flesh;' or, as is often the case in Paul's epistles, the γάρ refers to a thought omitted. 'Some think that I walk after the flesh—*that is not true*—for though I walk in the flesh, I do not war after it.' The latter seems the more natural and forcible.

4. (For the weapons of our warfare (are) not carnal, but mighty through God to the pulling down of strong holds).

This proves that the main idea intended by warring *after the flesh*, is warring with human weapons, relying on human resources. In the war in which Paul was engaged, his confidence was not in himself, not in human reason, not in the power of argument or eloquence, not in the resources of cunning or management, but simply and only in the supernatural power of God. ' We war not after the flesh, for our weapons are not carnal.' That is, such as the flesh, or human nature, furnishes, and which therefore in their own nature are carnal, or human. By *weapons* is, of course, to be understood all the means which the apostle employed in the defence and propagation of the truth. Those means, he says, were *mighty through God*. The words are δυνατὰ τῷ θεῷ, which are variously explained. Some, as Beza, Grotius and others, give the dative the force of the ablative—mighty by God—*afflatu Dei*, as Erasmus expresses it. Others regard the expression as a Hebraic superlative. Others say the meaning is, mighty *for* God, i. e. for his use, weapons which are powerful in his hand. The common explanation is, 'mighty to God,' i. e. such means as even God himself regards as mighty; mighty in his estimation. Of Nineveh it is said it was, πόλις μεγάλη τῷ θεῷ, a city great to God, a version which strictly answers to the Hebrew. Reference is also made to Acts 7, 20, where Moses is said to have been ἀστεῖος τῷ θεῷ, *beautiful to God*, i. e. in his sight; and 2 Peter 3, 14. These weapons were divinely powerful *to the pulling down of strong holds*, πρὸς καθαίρεσιν ὀχυρωμάτων. The last word is most appropriately rendered strong holds, as it is from ὀχυρός (from ἔχω), *haltbar*, what may be held, what is secure from assault. The opposers of the gospel felt that they were so entrenched, so protected by the fortresses which they occupied, that they despised the ministers of Christ and derided their efforts. What these strong-holds were the apostle tells us in what follows. This verse is properly marked as a parenthesis, not only in our version, but in almost all the critical editions of the Greek Testament, because the grammatical construction of v. 5 connects it immediately with v. 3.

5. Casting down imaginations, and every high thing that exalteth itself against the knowledge of God, and bringing into captivity every thought to the obedience of Christ.

As just intimated, the participle καθαιροῦντες (*pulling down*) depends on the verb στρατευόμεθα at the end of v. 3. 'We war—pulling down, &c.' According to this view v. 3 is parenthetical. Rückert, De Wette and others, however, on the ground that v. 4 contains the main idea, which is carried out in v. 8, prefer considering the construction of the passage as irregular, the participle being used here as in 9, 11. 13. They therefore connect this verse with what immediately precedes. 'Our weapons are mighty—in that we pull down, &c.'

What the apostle was thus confident he could cast down were *imaginations* (λογισμούς), *thoughts*, i. e. the opinions, or convictions of those who set themselves and the deductions of their own reason against the truth of God. Compare 1 Cor. 1, 17–31, and Rom. 1, 21–23. *And every high thing* (ὕψωμα), every tower, or fortress; the same as ὀχύρωμα in v. 4. Not persons, but thoughts, are intended by this figure. It is every thing which the pride of human reason exalts against *the knowledge of God;* i. e. that revelation of himself which God has made in the gospel. 1 Cor. 3, 18–20. The conflict to which the apostle here refers is that between truth and error, between the wisdom of God and the wisdom of the world. When the gospel was first proclaimed it found itself in conflict with all the forms of religion and philosophy then prevailing among men. To the wise of this world the gospel appeared as foolishness. It was, however, the wisdom and power of God. The conflict then begun has continued ever since, and is now as deadly as at any former period. Men of science and philosophers are as confident in their conclusions, and as much disposed to exalt themselves, or their opinions against the knowledge of God as ever. There is no doubt as to the issue of this contest. It is a contest between God and man, in which, of course, God must prevail. The instructive lesson which the apostle designs here to inculcate is, that this warfare must not be conducted on the part of the advocates of the gospel, with carnal weapons. They must not rely upon their own resources and attempt to overcome their enemies by argument. They must not become philosophers and turn the gospel into a philosophy. This would be to make it a human conflict on both sides. It would be human reason against human reason, the intellect of one man against the intellect of another man. Paul told the Corinthians in his former epistle, that he did not appear among them as a philosopher, but as a witness; he came not with the words of man's wisdom; he did not rely for success on his powers of argument or of persuasion, but on the demonstration of the Spirit. The faith, which he laboured to secure, was not to be founded on the wisdom of men, but on the power of God; not on arguments addressed to the understanding, but on the testimony of God. That testimony has the same effect which intuition has. It reveals the truth to the mind and conscience as self-evident; and therefore it cannot be resisted. A rationalistic Christian, a philosophizing theologian, therefore, lays aside the divine for the human, the wisdom of God for the wisdom of men, the infinite and infallible for the finite and fallible. The success of the gospel depends on its being presented, not as the word of man, but as the word of God; not as something to be proved, but as something to be believed. It was on this principle Paul acted, and hence he was in no degree intimidated by the number, the authority, the ability, or the learning of his opponents. He was confident that he could cast down all their proud imaginations, because he relied not on himself but on God whose messenger he was.

And bringing into captivity every thought, πᾶν νόημα. This word means either *thought,* or *the mind,* that which thinks. 3, 14. 4, 4. Phil. 4, 7. Hence it may be translated *thought,* as it is in our version; or as in the Vulgate, " omnem intellectum," *every understanding,* and by Luther, " alle Vernunft." Although the modern commentators make an outcry against this latter translation, it really differs little from the former. It does not matter much whether we say that human reason must be subjected, or that all the products of human reason (every thought) must be subjected. It amounts to the same thing. Both forms of statement are equally true. It is the indispensable condition of salvation that our understanding should be brought into captivity, led submissive, as though bound, *into the obedience of Christ,* εἰς τὴν ὑπακοὴν τοῦ Χριστοῦ. Agreeably to the figure in the context, the obedience of Christ is conceived of as a place, or fortress, into which the captive is led. The sense is the same as the dative, τῇ ὑπακοῇ τοῦ Χριστοῦ, would have expressed. We must renounce dependence on our own understanding and submit implicitly, as obedient children, to the teaching of Christ. He who would be wise, must become a fool. 1 Cor. 3, 18.

6. And having in a readiness to revenge all disobedience, when your obedience is fulfilled.

And having in a readiness; ἐν ἑτοίμῳ ἔχοντες, holding ourselves ready, i. e. being ready. He had the ability and the determination to do what he declares he would do. Compare ἑτοίμως ἔχω, 12, 14. The participle ἔχοντες is connected by καί with καθαιροῦντες of the preceding verse. 'We war—casting down all that opposes itself—and ready, &c.' *To avenge all disobedience;* ἐκδικῆσαι, to maintain, or to exact justice, or satisfaction, to punish. *All disobedience,* i. e. every case of disobedience. The gospel, being the word of God, is divinely efficacious, and is certain ultimately to triumph over all opposition. This, however, does not imply that all will obey it. In the apostolic churches, there were those who corrupted the word of God, Judaizing or philosophizing teachers and their followers, who refused to obey the truth. Such persons Paul announced his ability and his determination to punish. They were in the church, for what, he said in his former epistle, have I to do to judge them that are without? 1 Cor. 5, 12. They had voluntarily submitted themselves to his jurisdiction, and he therefore had a legitimate authority over them. What was the nature of the punishment which he threatened, he does not intimate. It may be that he purposed nothing more than excommunication. The fact, however, that the apostles were armed with supernatural power, that they exercised that power for the punishment of offenders, 1 Cor. 5, 5. 1 Tim. 1, 20, and the whole tone of the passage are in favour of the assumption that Paul was determined to use all the means at his command to suppress the insolence, and to destroy the power of the corrupters of the truth in Corinth. He gives what he had said a special application by adding, *when your obedience is fulfilled.* That is, he would not resort to severity until all other means had failed, and until it had become fully manifest who among the Corinthians would submit to God, and who would persist in their disobedience.

7. Do ye look on things after the outward appearance? If any man trust to himself that he is Christ's, let him of himself think this again, that, as he (is) Christ's, even so (are) we Christ's.

Abrupt transitions are characteristic of this epistle. Paul having in the preceding verses so strongly asserted his apostolic authority and supernatural power, turns to those who denied the validity of his claims, and calls upon them to give a reason for skepticism. He was thus led to vindicate his title to the apostolic office and to his special jurisdiction over the church of Corinth. This vindication extends to 12, 18. After which he resumes the subject broached in the preceding verses of this chapter, viz., what he purposed to do when he again visited Corinth.

Do ye look on things after the outward appearance? τὰ κατὰ πρόσωπον βλέπετε. This clause may be taken interrogatively, as by most commentators, or imperatively, or declaratively. If interrogatively, the sense may be, 'Do ye regard, or take into view, only what is external? Do you judge of me from my personal appearance, manner, and speech?' It would seem that a judgment founded on such grounds as these, led the false teachers to regard the apostle with contempt. Or, the meaning is, 'Do you regard only external advantages? Such as being a minister of Christ, being a Hebrew, an Israelite, of the seed of Abraham, &c.' 11, 22. In favour of this view is the use of πρόσωπον in this epistle, 5, 12. 11, 1. See also Matt. 22, 16. Mark 12, 14; the parallel passage in 11, 18 (where κατὰ τὴν σάρκα answers to κατὰ πρόσωπον here); and the context, which goes to show that the things which Paul's opponents regarded, and on which they prided themselves, were their supposed external advantages. Those who take βλέπετε as imperative understand the passage thus: 'Look at what is before your eyes, i. e. at what is evident to all. If you are thus and so, so am I.' Calvin and others take the verb as in the indicative. 'Ye do regard what is external —and therefore despise me.' The first interpretation, for the reasons stated, is to be preferred. *If any man trust to himself.* The use of τίς (any one), in this passage, and of the singular number in vs. 10 and 11, and in 11, 4, has led to the conjecture that there was in Corinth one particular opponent of the apostle to whom in this whole context he refers. But it is evident from the general drift of the epistle that it was a whole class of persons who had arrayed themselves against Paul's authority. *Trust to himself*, πέποιθεν ἑαυτῷ, is persuaded concerning himself, *that he is Christ's.* What that means is somewhat doubtful. It may be taken in the most general sense, 'If any thinks that he is a Christian,' i. e. belongs to Christ as every believer does; or, 'If any man thinks that he is a minister of Christ;' or, 'If any man thinks that he stands in a peculiar relation to Christ.' It is probable from 1 Cor. 1, 10 that there were certain persons in Corinth who said, 'We are of Christ,' as claiming some nearer connection with him than that which belonged to other believers or to other ministers. Whether this claim rested on their having seen Christ in the flesh, or on relationship to his kinsmen, is mere matter of conjecture. Still as the claim existed, it is most likely referred to here. *Let him of himself*, i. e. without its being suggested by others. The fact was so plain that it needed not to be asserted. Let him think *this again*, i. e. let him consider the matter again. The last reflection will convince him that as he is *Christ's, so are we.* There was no relationship which these false teachers could rightfully claim to Christ to which Paul was not equally entitled. They were in no respect his superiors. They had no advantage which did not belong equally to him.

8. For though I should boast somewhat more of our authority, which the Lord hath given us for edification, and not for your destruction, I should not be ashamed.

Paul might have said much more than he had said in what precedes. He was not only all that his opponents claimed to be, but more. He had an authority and power to which they could make no pretensions. He therefore here says that if he had set forth higher claims, he should not be ashamed—facts would not prove those claims to be unfounded. *For though,* ἐάν τε γὰρ καί, *for even in case,* &c. The connection is with the words "we are Christ's." 'We are Christ's, in all the senses in which you can claim to be, *for* we have received more from him.' The greater includes the less. *Somewhat more,* περισσότερόν τι, i. e. somewhat more than was claimed in vs. 3–6, or more than 'being in Christ,' which might be said of others as well as of the apostle. Paul had an *authority* which extended beyond the limits of any claim which he had yet advanced. Ἐξουσία includes the ideas of power and authority, The apostle had authority (i. e. the right to rule) and he had ability, inherent power, to enforce that authority. *Which the Lord hath given* (or rather, *gave*) *to us.* The authority in question was given when he was constituted an apostle, with not only a commission to exercise dominion, but a grace, or inward gift of the Spirit, rendering him infallible as a teacher and investing him with supernatural power. The giver of this authority and power was the Lord, i. e. Christ. Christ, therefore, as the author of supernatural gifts, is a divine person, for to give such gifts is a prerogative of God. The design for which Paul was not endowed, was not his own exaltation, not the accomplishment of any worldly end, not, as he says, "for your destruction," i. e. not that he might be able to put down his personal enemies, but *for edification*, i. e. the building up of the church in holiness and peace. Power in the church comes not from the civil magistrate, nor from the people, but from Christ only. He is, as Calvin says, Solus Dominus et Magister. And this power can be legitimately exercised only for the edification of the church. When exercised for other objects, or for the destruction of the church, then it should be disowned and resisted. Even an apostle, or an angel from heaven, who should preach any other gospel—teach or require any thing contrary to the word of God—would be accursed. And of this contrariety, from the necessity of the case, and from the authority of Scripture, the people, i. e. those who are required to believe and obey, are (at their peril) to be the judges. If they reject a true apostle, their sin is as great as if they gave ear to false teachers. Having the inward teaching of the Spirit, they know of the doctrine whether it be of God.

9. That I may not seem as if I would terrify you by letters.

The connection of this clause (ἵνα μὴ δόκω) is somewhat doubtful. If it belongs immediately to the preceding words, the sense is, 'I should not be ashamed—in order that I should seem,' i. e. God would so order it that I should not appear as an empty boaster. But this is evidently unnatural. The design of God in sustaining the apostle, and giving him a victory over the enemies of the truth, was something higher than preserving him from being regarded as a boaster. A very large number of commentators connect this verse with the 11th, throwing the 10th into a parenthesis. 'That I may not seem to terrify you—let such an one think, &c.' But neither in this way is the connection natural or logical; and v. 11 evidently refers to v. 10, and would not be intelligible if that verse were omitted; verse 11, therefore, is not a parenthesis. A clause with ἵνα, as we have seen before in this epistle, (compare also Gal. 2, 10,) often depends on some word or words omitted but easily supplied from the context. In this case we may supply, '*This I say.*' 'This I say in order that I may not appear, &c.' So Luther ("Das sage ich aber"), Beza, and many others. *As if I would terrify*, ὡς ἂν ἐκφοβεῖν. This is the only instance in the New Testament where ἂν after a conjunction is used with the infinitive. Winer resolves it into ὡς ἂν ἐκφοβοῖμι ὑμᾶς, *tanquam velim vos terrere*, which agrees with our translation. These particles serve to soften the expression, and are equivalent to *as if perhaps*, or, *so to speak*. There is evident allusion to the false representations made by the false teachers, that Paul wrote in the authoritative tone which he assumed merely to frighten his readers, having neither the power nor the purpose to carry his threats into execution. *By letters*, or, *by the letters*, i. e. the letters which he had already written or intended to write.

10. For (his) letters, say they, (are) weighty and powerful; but (his) bodily presence (is) weak, and (his) speech contemptible.

There was reason for his not wishing to appear as assuming a tone of threatening in his letters, *for* this was the very reproach cast upon him. *His letters, they say*, (φησί, here, as often, used impersonally, 'one says,' *sagt man*,) *are weighty* (βαρεῖαι, i. e. impressive) *and powerful*, (ἰσχυραί,) including the ideas of vigour, authority and severity. *But his bodily presence is weak.* This passage, probably more than any other, has given rise to the impression, in accordance with a tradition neither very ancient nor well sustained, that Paul was small in stature, weak and unattractive in his personal appearance. The words here used, however, even supposing that this language of his enemies expressed the truth, do not necessarily imply this. The phrase ἡ παρουσία τοῦ σώματος probably refers not to his personal appearance, but to his deportment. He wrote boldly, but acted feebly. There was not that energy and decision in his acts which one would expect from his language. This was the representation of his enemies; the truth of which, however, the apostle denies. The same remark applies to the next clause, *his speech contemptible.* This does not refer to feebleness of voice, but to the impression made by his oral instructions and addresses. He dared not assume any such authority in speaking to the people that he did in writing to them. The whole history of the apostle, his unceasing labours, his constant journeyings, his innumerable sufferings which he sustained so heroically, prove that he was not physically a man of feeble constitution. And his own declarations, as well as his clearly revealed character, prove that there was no such want of correspondence between his letters and his actions as the false teachers in Corinth, to whom he was probably personally unknown, endeavoured to make the people believe.

11. Let such an one think this, that such as we are in word by letters when we are absent, such (will we be) also in deed when we are present.

Let such an one, i. e. any one, not necessarily implying that there was only one person who had set himself up in opposition to the apostle. *That such as we are in word*, &c. It was admitted that his letters were energetic. He assures them that, when present, his deeds would correspond to his words. His denunciations would not prove idle threats.

12. For we dare not make ourselves of the number, or compare ourselves with some that commend themselves : but they, measuring themselves by themselves, and comparing themselves among themselves, are not wise.

In confirmation of his declaration that his acts would be found to correspond with his words, he adds, 'For I am not like those, who having nothing to recommend them, commend themselves.' *We dare not* (οὐ τολμῶμεν, we cannot bring ourselves to, or, we cannot prevail on ourselves to. Rom. 5, 7. 1 Cor. 6, 1) *make ourselves of the number, or compare ourselves ;* (ἐγκρῖναι ἢ συγκρῖναι, enrol ourselves among, or place ourselves by,) *some who commend themselves.* The reference is obviously to the false teachers, whose only reliance was self-laudation. So far this verse is plain. The latter part of the passage is exceedingly difficult, and has been very variously explained. There are three classes of interpretation, two of which proceed on the assumption of the correctness of the common text, and the third is founded on a different reading. According to the first general view, the αὐτοί refers to the apostle himself. He is assumed to contrast himself, in this verse, with his opponents. The sense, according to some then is, 'They commend themselves, but we, measuring ourselves by ourselves, (i. e. we do not overestimate ourselves, but determine our importance by our performances,) and

comparing ourselves with ourselves, not with these wise men.'
According to this view, συνιοῦσιν, at the end of the verse, is a
participle, and is used ironically in reference to the false teachers. To this interpretation it is objected, 1. That συνιοῦσιν
would require the article in order to express the meaning
given to it; and 2. That it is plainly inconsistent with the
ἡμεῖς δέ of the next verse, which are antithetical to the αὐτοί
of this verse. 'They do so—but we do so.' Others, who
make the latter part of this verse refer to the apostle, refer
συνιοῦσιν also to him. 'We measure ourselves by ourselves,
and compare ourselves with ourselves, we who, as they say,
are unwise.' Then the ἡμεῖς δέ of verse 13th refers to this last
clause. 'They say we are unwise, but we, &c.' This, however, is liable to the same objections, and gives a sense un-
suited to the context. According to the second interpretation, αὐτοί in this verse refers to the false teachers, with whom,
in the next verse, Paul contrasts himself, (ἡμεῖς δέ,) and συνιοῦσιν is the third person plural, as from the verb συνιέω, as in
Matt. 13, 13. 'They measuring themselves by themselves,
and comparing themselves with themselves, are not wise; but
we, &c.' This is the view of the passage adopted by our
translators, after Chrysostom, Calvin, and Luther. It is also
sanctioned by De Wette, Meyer, and Rückert, and many others. These false teachers commended themselves, confined
their views to themselves, despised or disregarded all others,
intruding into other men's labours. Paul, on the contrary,
boasted not of himself; he relied only on God and his grace,
and he kept himself within his own limits, not appropriating
to himself the fruits of the labours of other men. The third
mode of interpreting this passage assumes that the text afforded by the Western, as distinguished from the Eastern manuscripts, is correct. Those authorities omit οὐ συνιοῦσι, ἡμεῖς δέ,
so that αὐτοί (ἡμεῖς) is the nominative to καυχησόμεθα in v. 13,
if that verb be retained. 'They commend themselves; but
we, measuring ourselves by ourselves, and comparing ourselves with ourselves, will not boast as to things beyond our
measure.' Fritsche and Billroth, on the authority of the Co-
dex Clarom., omit also καυχησόμεθα, and connect the participles
μετζοῦντες and συγκρίνοντες with καυχώμενοι of v. 15, thus bringing out substantially the same sense, but rendering the sentence longer and more complicated. The meaning afforded
by this new reading is simple and pertinent. Since, however,
the critical authorities by which it is supported are compara-

tively few and of a secondary class, the great body of editors adhere to the common text. If that text is correct, then the interpretation given in our English version is the most natural and suitable. Calvin applies this whole passage, with his usual vigour, to the monks of his day. Hujus loci expositio non aliunde petenda est quam a monachis: nam quum sint omnes fere indoctissimi asini, et tamen oblongæ vestis et cuculli causa docti censeantur: si quis tenuem modo gustum elegantioris literaturæ habeat, plumas suas instar pavonis fastuose extendit: spargitur de eo mirabilis fama, adoratur inter sodales. At si seposita cuculli larva ventum fuerit ad justum examen, deprehenditur vanitas. Cur hoc? Verum quidem est vetus proverbium: Audax inscitia: sed inde praecipue monachalis insolentissimus ille fastus, quod se metiuntur ex se ipsis: nam quum in eorum claustris nihil sit praeter barbariem, illic nihil mirum, si regnet luscus inter cæcos.

13. But we will not boast of things without (our) measure, but according to the measure of the rule which God hath distributed to us, a measure to reach even unto you.

The words εἰς τὰ ἄμετρα may be taken adverbially, equivalent to ἀμέτρως, *immoderately*, beyond what is proper; or, since in the latter part of the verse μέτρον is used literally, they may be explained as in our version, in reference to things beyond our measure, i. e. beyond the limits of my apostolic labours. This idea is clearly presented in the following verses; but here the contrast with the preceding verse favours the former explanation. The false teachers set no limits to their boasting—self-conceit and not facts determined the character and amount of their assumptions, and therefore their claims were inordinate. Paul expresses his determination to limit his claims to his actual gifts and labours. *According to the measure of the rule*, κατὰ τὸ μέτρον τοῦ κανόνος, i. e. according to the measure determined by the rule, or line, that is, the measure allotted to him. The κανών is the rule, or measuring line, which, so to speak, God used in determining the apostle's gifts and sphere of activity. Paul's boasting, therefore, was not immoderate, but confined to just limits. According to Beza κανών is used metonymically for that which is measured; certum et definitum spatium; the district or diocese measured off to him. But this is not consistent with the ordinary meaning of the word, or with the context. *Which God hath distributed to us ;* οὗ ἐμέρισεν ἡμῖν ὁ Θεὸς μέτρον, for μέτρου ὁ ἐμέρισεν ὁ Θεός, by attraction. This clause is in apposition with κανόνος, and explains what was the rule or line which determined the sphere of his activity. It was not something self-assumed, or self-applied, but something which God had appointed ; *a measure,* he adds, *to reach even unto you.* It is agreeable to Paul's manner to include two or more related ideas in the same form of expression. *To boast according to the measure assigned him,* may mean to regulate his boasting according to his gifts ; or, to boast in reference to what was done within the limits assigned him in preaching the gospel. Both ideas are here united. In opposition to the false teachers, who not only boasted of gifts which they did not possess, but appropriated to themselves the fruits of other men's labours by intruding into churches which they had not founded, Paul says he did neither one nor the other. His boasting was neither immoderate, nor was it founded on what others had done. He invaded no man's sphere of labour. It was his settled purpose to preach the gospel where Christ had not been named, and not to build on another man's foundation. Rom. 15, 20. Acting on this principle he had the right to regard Corinth as legitimately within his field. His assigned limit of labour reached at least that far. He had founded the church in that city ; others had built thereon. 1 Cor. 3, 10. The Corinthians were his work in the Lord. 1 Cor. 9, 1. Over them, therefore, if over no others, he had the authority of an apostle. It is plain, on the one hand, from the New Testament that the apostles had a general agreement among themselves as to their several fields of labour. Paul was to go to the Gentiles ; Peter, James and John to the Jews. Gal. 2, 9. But it is no less plain that they were not confined to any prescribed limits. They had not, as modern bishops or pastors, each his particular diocese or parish. As their authority did not arise from their election or appointment to a particular church or district, but from their plenary knowledge, infallibility, and supernatural power, it was the same everywhere, and in relation to all churches. Hence we find Paul writing to the church in Rome which he had never visited, as well as to others who had never seen his face in the flesh, with the same authority with which he addressed churches which he had himself planted. Peter addressed his epistles to churches within Paul's sphere of labour; and, according to all tradition, St. John presided during the latter years of his life over the churches in Asia Minor, founded by the apostle to the Gentiles. Still it was a matter of courtesy that one apostle should not intrude unnecessarily upon the sphere already occupied by another. Paul, at least, determined that he would not build upon another man's foundation.

14. For we stretch not ourselves beyond (our measure), as though we reached not unto you; for we are come as far as to you also in (preaching) the gospel of Christ.

This verse is generally regarded as a parenthesis, although some commentators make it the beginning of a new sentence. It is logically connected with the last clause of v. 13. 'God assigned us a measure extending to you, *for* not, as not reaching to you, do we unduly stretch ourselves out;' ὑπερεκτείνομεν ἑαυτούς, *do we overstretch ourselves.* The present tense is used, because the reference is to the sphere of the apostle's authority. *For we have come as far as you,* (ἐφθάσαμεν.) 'Our authority extends to you, *for* we have come to you in preaching the gospel.' That is, Corinth was included in the region throughout which he had been the first to preach Christ. The word φθάνω properly means, to come, or be, beforehand; to anticipate; and then, in the aorist, to have come already. See Matt. 12, 28. Phil. 3, 16. 1 Thess. 2, 16. This sense may be retained here. 'We have already come even unto you.' He had already reached them and expected soon to reach beyond them; see v. 16.

15. Not boasting of things without (our) measure, (that is), of other men's labours; but having hope, when your faith is increased, that we shall be enlarged by you, according to our rule abundantly.

If verse 14 is parenthetical, then this verse is connected with the 13th. 'We will boast according to our measure— not boasting immoderately.' *Of other men's labours.* This is explanatory of the εἰς τὰ ἄμετρα. He did not boast of what other men had done. If the connection is with the 14th verse, the participle καυχώμενοι most naturally depends on οὐ ὑπερεκτείνομεν. 'We do not stretch ourselves unduly—not boasting, &c.' The reproach to the false teachers here implied is of course obvious. They had done what Paul refused to do. They came to Corinth after the church had been gathered, assumed an authority to which they were not entitled, and endeavoured to destroy the influence of the apostle to whom the church owed its existence, and the people their hope of salvation. Jam, says Calvin, liberius pungit pseudo-apostolos, qui quum in alienam messem manus intulissent, audebant tamen iis obtrectare, qui sudore ac industria locum illis paraverant.

But having hope, when your faith is increased. This clause the Vulgate renders, 'Habentes spem crescentis fidei vestræ.' This interpretation the words αὐξανομένης τῆς πίστεως (*your faith being increased*) do not admit. Corinth was not the limit which Paul had fixed for his field of labour. He had the purpose, as soon as the state of the Corinthians would allow of his leaving them, to press forward to preach the gospel in regions beyond them. *That we shall be enlarged by you*, ἐν ὑμῖν μεγαλυνθῆναι. Luther, Calvin, Beza, and others, connect ἐν ὑμῖν with the preceding clause—'Your faith being increased among you.' Beza says this is required by the opposite clause, as the advantage was mutual. They were to grow in faith among themselves, he was to enlarge his boundaries. But in this case the words ἐν ὑμῖν are redundant. They belong to the following word, and are to be rendered either *by you*, or, *among you*. This depends on the sense given to μεγαλυνθῆναι. This word is used either literally, as in Matt. 23, 5, "They make broad their phylacteries;" or figuratively, as in Luke 1, 58, "The Lord hath made great his mercy toward her." In every other case where it occurs in the New Testament it means to praise, to declare great. Luke 1, 46, "My soul doth magnify the Lord." So in Acts 5, 13. 10, 46. 19, 17. Phil. 1, 20. This meaning of the word is very commonly retained here. 'I hope to be honoured by you abundantly.' But the object of the apostle's hope was neither to be glorified by them, nor among them. Besides, the following clause ('according to our rule') does not agree with this interpretation. The word, therefore, is to be taken in its more literal sense—'He hoped to be enlarged abundantly (εἰς περισσείαν) according to his rule.' That is, he hoped to preach the gospel far beyond Corinth, agreeably to the line of action marked out for him. The ἐν ὑμῖν may then be rendered, vobis adjuvantibus. They would aid Paul in his future labours. The same idea is brought out by rendering the clause thus, 'To become great among you as to that which is beyond.'

16. To preach the gospel in the (regions) beyond you, (and) not to boast in another man's line of things made ready to our hand.

This infinitive (to preach) is either exegetical, 'We hope to be enlarged, that is, we hope to preach beyond you;' or it is the infinitive of the object, 'We hope to become great among you, in order to preach, &c.' The choice between these explanations depends on the interpretation of the preceding verse. *To preach the gospel in the regions beyond you;* εἰς ὑπερέκεινα (an adverb, *beyond*), *parts beyond*, and with ὑμῶν, *parts beyond you*. Εἰς is not here for ἐν, but means *unto*, as expressing the extent to which. *Not to boast in another man's line;* ἐν ἀλλοτρίῳ κανόνι, within another's line. That is, within the field of labour occupied by another man. *Made ready to our hand.* This is not a literal translation of εἰς τὰ ἕτοιμα. These words belong to καυχήσασθαι, 'Not to boast in reference to things prepared.' The sense is plain; he would not appropriate to himself the fruits of other men's labours.

17. 18. But he that glorieth, let him glory in the Lord. For not he that commendeth himself is approved, but whom the Lord commendeth.

'To glory in the Lord,' is either to regard God as the ground of confidence and source of all good, and to ascribe every thing we have, are, and hope to his grace; or, it is to exult in his approbation. Instead of comforting ourselves with our own high estimate of our attainments and efficiency, or allowing ourselves to be inflated by the applause of men, we should be satisfied with nothing short of the divine approbation. The connection is here in favour of the latter view. 'He that glories should glory in the Lord, i. e. he that rejoices should rejoice in the approbation of God, (not in his own good opinion of himself, nor in the praises of others,) *for* not he who commendeth himself is approved, i. e. is really

worthy of approbation, but he whom the Lord commendeth.'
Paul did not commend himself; his claims were not founded
on the suggestions of self-conceit; neither did he rely on the
commendation of others, his eye was fixed on God. If he
could secure his favour, it was to him a small matter to be
judged by man's judgment. 1 Cor. 4, 3.

CHAPTER XI.

The apostle apologizes for the self-commendation which was forced upon
him, vs. 1–15. He contrasts himself and his labours with the assumptions of the false teachers, vs. 15–33.

Reasons for his self-commendation, vs. 1–15.

HE had just condemned all self-commendation, yet he was
forced to do what had the appearance of self-laudation. The
Corinthians were in danger of being turned away from Christ
by having their confidence in Paul undermined by the mis-
representations of his enemies. It was therefore necessary
for him to present the grounds which he had for claiming authority over them, and for asserting his superiority over his
opponents. Yet so repugnant was this task to his feelings,
that he not only humbly apologizes for thus speaking of himself, but he finds it difficult to do what he felt must be done.
He over and over begins what he calls his boasting, and immediately turns aside to something else. He begs them to
bear with him while he proceeds to praise himself, v. 1, for
his doing so sprang from the purest motive, love for them and
anxiety for their welfare, vs. 2. 3. An anxiety justified by
the readiness with which they bore with those who preached
another gospel, v. 4. He thus spoke because he was on a par
with the chief apostles, and not behind those who among
them claimed to be his superiors, v. 5. They might have
higher pretensions as orators, but in knowledge and in every
thing that really pertained to the apostolic office he was
abundantly manifest among them, v. 6. His refusal to avail
himself of his right to be supported by those to whom he
preached was no offence to them, and no renunciation of his

apostleship, vs. 7–9. He was determined to refuse any pecuniary aid from the Christians in Achaia, not because he did not love them, but because he wished to cut off all occasion to question his sincerity from those who sought such occasion, and because he desired to put the false teachers to the same test of disinterestedness, vs. 10–12. These teachers claimed to be apostles, though they had no more right to the office, than Satan had to be regarded as an angel of light, vs. 13–15

1. Would to God ye could bear with me a little in (my) folly : and indeed bear with me.

The self-commendation of the false teachers was the fruit of conceit and vanity ; with the apostle it was self-vindication. Although so different in character and design, they had one element in common. Both included self-laudation. Both, therefore, are designated by the same word, boasting ; and both, therefore, he calls ἀφροσύνη, a want of sense. *Would to God*, in the Greek simply, ὄφελον, *oh that, I would.* In fact, however, every such exclamation is, in the pious mind, a prayer ; and, therefore, the rendering, 'I would to God,' is neither irreverent nor inaccurate. *Oh that ye could bear with me*, (ἀνείχεσθε, Hellenistic form, instead of ἠνείχεσθε.) The pronoun μοῦ properly belongs to the verb, and not to the following μικρόν τι, as if the sense were, *a little of my folly*. The meaning is, 'Bear with me (μικρόν τι ἀφροσύνης), *as to a little of folly.*' This reading is, on the authority of the majority of MSS., adopted by the later editors. Knapp and others read, μικρὸν τῇ ἀφροσύνῃ, *a little as to folly ;* which amounts to the same thing. *And indeed bear with me.* So Calvin, Beza, and many others, who take ἀνέχεσθε as the imperative. This clause is then a repetition of the first, only more vehemently expressed. The former is a wish, the latter a supplication or demand. But the context does not require this vehemence. A more appropriate sense is afforded by taking the word in the indicative, 'But indeed ye do bear with me ;' i. e. the request is not necessary, I know you are disposed to suffer me to speak as I see fit.

2. For I am jealous over you with godly jealousy : for I have espoused you to one husband, that I may present (you as) a chaste virgin to Christ.

This is the reason either why they should bear with him, or why he was assured that they would do so. That is, the connection is either with the first and principal clause of v. 1, or with the latter clause. It makes but little difference. The sense is better if the connection is with the first clause. 'Bear with my folly—for I am jealous over you.' Ζηλῶ γὰρ ὑμᾶς. The word ζηλόω may mean, I ardently love, or more specifically, I am jealous. The latter, as the figure of marriage is used, is probably the sense in which the apostle uses the word. *With godly jealousy;* ζῆλος θεοῦ may mean a zeal of which God is the object, as in Rom. 10, 2; comp. John 2, 17. In that case Paul intends to say that the feeling which he had for the Corinthians was a pious feeling. It was no selfish or mercenary interest, but such as arose from his desire to promote the honour of God. Or, the meaning is, a zeal of which God is the author; or, a zeal which God approves; or, the zeal which God has. As the people of God are so often represented in the Bible as standing to God in a relation analogous to that of a wife to a husband, so God is represented as being jealous, i. e. moved to deep displeasure when they transfer their love to another object. Is. 54, 5. 62, 5. Ez. 16. Hos. 2. In this view, the apostle means to say, that he shares in the feeling which God is represented as entertaining towards his church. The translation given in the English version includes all the meanings above mentioned; for a godly jealousy (or zeal) is a pious zeal, it is a zeal of which God is both the object and the author, and it is such a zeal as he has. *For I have espoused you to one husband.* It was natural for the apostle to feel this jealousy over them, *for* he stood in a most intimate relation to them. Their union with Christ was his work. 1 Cor. 4, 15. 9, 1. He may compare himself in this verse to a father who gives his daughter to the bridegroom. To this it is objected that Paul became the father of the Corinthians by their conversion; whereas the relation here referred to subsisted before their conversion or espousal to Christ. It is commonly assumed that the allusion is to the office of "the friend of the bridegroom," John 3, 29, (παρανύμφιος,) whose business it was to select the bride, to be responsible for her conduct, and to present her to the bridegroom. In this sense Moses was called παρανύμφιος by the Rabbis, as it was through him the people entered into covenant with God. In either way the sense is the same. Paul's relation was so intimate with the Corinthians as the author of their espousals to Christ, that he could not fail to feel the deepest interest in their fidelity. *I have espoused you.* The verb ἁρμόζω in the active voice is used of the father who betroths his daughter; in the passive of the bride who is betrothed; in the middle voice it is generally used of the man who pledges himself to a woman. The middle form, however, is sometimes used, as in this verse, (ἡρμοσάμην,) in the active sense. *To one husband.* The marriage relation from its nature is exclusive. It can be sustained only to one man. So the relation of the church, or of the believer, to Christ is in like manner exclusive. We can have but one God and Saviour. Love to him of necessity excludes all love of the same kind to every other being. Hence the apostle says he had espoused (betrothed) them to *one* man. This was done in order, in due time, *to present them as a chaste virgin unto Christ.* As in Eph. 5, 27, this presentation of the church to Christ as his bride, is said to take place at his second coming, this passage is commonly understood to refer to that event. Paul's desire was that the Corinthians should remain faithful to their vows, so as to be presented to Christ a glorious church, without spot or wrinkle, on that great day. He dreaded lest they should, in that day, be rejected and contemned as a woman unfaithful to her vows.

3. But I fear, lest by any means, as the serpent beguiled Eve through his subtilty, so your minds should be corrupted from the simplicity that is in Christ.

The apostle adheres to his figure. Though they were betrothed to Christ, he feared that their affections might be seduced from him and fixed on some other object. Men are not jealous until their apprehensions are excited. They must have some reason, either real or imaginary, for suspecting the fidelity of those they love. The ground of the apostle's jealousy was his fear. He feared (μήπως) *lest peradventure.* They had not yet turned aside, but there was great danger that they might yield to the seductions to which they were exposed. There was one standing example and warning both of the inconstancy of the human heart, and of the fearful consequences of forsaking God. Eve was created holy, she stood in paradise in the perfection of her nature, with every conceivable motive

to secure her fidelity. Yet by the subtilty of Satan she fell.
What reason then have we to fear who are exposed to the
machinations of the same great seducer. *As the serpent beguiled Eve;* i. e. Satan in the form of a serpent. *The* serpent,
i. e. the well-known serpent of which Moses speaks. The
New Testament writers thus assume, and thereby sanction,
the historical verity of the Old Testament record. The account of the temptation as recorded in Genesis is regarded by
the inspired writers of the New Testament not as a myth, or
as an allegory, but as a true history. Comp. 1 Tim. 2, 14.
Rev. 12, 9. 15. *Beguiled,* ἐξηπάτησεν, *thoroughly deceived.*
All seduction is by means of deception. Sin is in its nature
deceit. The imagination is filled with false images, and the
foolish heart is darkened. Eve was thus deceived by the subtilty of Satan. She was made to disbelieve what was true, and
to believe what was false. Man's belief, in a very large sphere,
is determined by his feelings. The heart controls the understanding. The good believe the true; the evil believe the
untrue. This is the reason why men are accountable for their
faith, and why the wicked are led captive by Satan into all
manner of error. Eve was deceived by exciting unholy feelings in her heart. Paul's apprehension was lest the Corinthians, surrounded by false teachers, the ministers of Satan,
should in like manner be beguiled. What he feared was that
their *minds should be corrupted.* It was a moral perversion,
or corruption, that he apprehended. *Your minds,* τὰ νοήματα
ὑμῶν. The word νόημα means first *thought;* then that which
thinks, the understanding; and then, the affections or dispositions. Phil. 4, 7. Our translation, "your minds," as including the idea both of thought and feeling, is the most appropriate rendering. *Corrupted from,* is a pregnant expression,
meaning corrupted so as to be turned from. *The simplicity
that is in Christ;* ἀπὸ τῆς ἁπλότητος τῆς εἰς τὸν Χριστόν, 'from
singleness of mind towards Christ.' That is, the undivided
affection and devotion to Christ which is due from a bride to
her spouse. The allusion to the marriage relation is kept up.
Paul had compared the Corinthians to a virgin espoused to
one man, and he feared lest their affections might be seduced
from Christ and transferred to another.

4. For if he that cometh preacheth another Jesus,
whom we have not preached, or (if) ye receive another

spirit, which ye have not received, or another gospel, which ye have not accepted, ye might well bear with (him).

There are two entirely different views of the meaning of this verse, depending on the view taken of the connection. If the association of ideas is with the preceding verse, so that this passage assigns the reason of the fear there expressed, the meaning is, 'I am afraid concerning you, for if a false teacher comes and preaches another gospel, you readily bear with him.' It is a reproof of their credulity and easiness of persuasion to forsake the truth, analogous to that administered to the Galatians. Gal. 4, 6–8. 5, 8. But if this verse is connected with the main subject as presented in v. 1, then the sense is, 'Bear with me, for if a false teacher preaches another gospel you bear with him.' This is to be preferred, not only because the sense is better as more consistent with the context, but also because ἀνέχομαι means to *endure, to put up with*, and supposes that the thing endured is in itself repulsive. In this sense the word is used twice in v. 1, and should be so taken here. 'If a man preaches a new Christ ye would put up with his self-laudation, therefore, you should put up with mine.' The proper force of the verb (ἀνέχομαι) is also against the interpretation given by Chrysostom and followed by many later commentators. 'If any one really preached another gospel (i. e. communicated to you another method of salvation), you would do well to bear with him and receive him gladly.' But all this is foreign to the context. The thing to be endured, was something hard to put up with. It was what the apostle calls folly.

For if he that cometh, ὁ ἐρχόμενος, *the comer*, any one who happens to come. The reference is not to any one well known false teacher, but to a whole class. *Preaches another Jesus ;* not another Saviour, but another person than the son of Mary whom we preached. That is, if he sets forth some other individual as the true deliverer from sin. *Or if ye receive another spirit, which ye have not received.* The gift of the Holy Ghost was secured by the work of Christ. He redeemed us from the curse of the law—in order that we might receive the promise of the Spirit. Gal. 3, 13. 14. The indwelling of the Spirit, therefore, as manifested by his sanctifying and miraculous power, was the great evidence of the truth of the gospel. Hence the apostle, to convince the Galatians of the folly of apostasy to Judaism, says, "This only would I learn of you. Received ye the Spirit by the works of the law, or by the hearing of faith?" Gal. 3, 2; and in Heb. 2, 4, he says, God bore witness to the gospel by the gifts of the Holy Ghost. The apostle here supposes the impossible case that a like confirmation had attended the preaching of the false teachers. 'If,' he says, 'they preach another (ἄλλος) Jesus, and in proof that he is truly a Saviour, ye receive a different (ἕτερος) spirit, i. e. a spirit whose manifestations were of a different kind from those of the Spirit who attests my preaching,' &c. *Or another* (ἕτερος, a different) *gospel, which ye have not accepted.* In the former clause the verb is ἐλάβετε (ye received), in the latter ἐδέξασθε (ye accepted), because, as Bengel says, Non concurrit voluntas hominis in accipiendo Spiritu, ut in recipiendo evangelio. That is, man is passive in receiving the spirit, and active in accepting the gospel. *Ye might well bear with* him. The word is ἀνείχεσθε, in the imperfect. The tense which the context would seem to demand is the present, ἀνέχεσθε, a reading which Lachmann and Rückert, on the authority of the MS. B, have introduced into the text. The other leading verbs of the verse are in the present, 'If one preaches another Jesus, and ye receive another Spirit, and accept another gospel, (in that case,) ye do bear with him.' Instead, however, of saying, 'ye do bear with him,' the apostle is supposed purposely to soften the expression by saying, 'ye might well bear with him;' the particle ἄν being, as often, understood. In this way he avoids the direct charge of tolerating the conceited boasting of the false teachers. Others, as Meyer and Winer, assume an irregularity, or change of construction.

5. For I suppose I was not a whit behind the very chiefest apostles.

The sense here again depends on the connection. If the γάρ refers to v. 4, the reference must be (as so often occurs in Paul's writings) to a thought omitted. 'Ye are wrong in thus bearing with the false teachers, *for* I am equal to the chief apostles.' This, however, is not in harmony with the context. Paul's design is not so much to reprove the Corinthians for tolerating the folly of the false teachers, as to induce them to bear with his. He felt it to be necessary to vindicate himself, and he therefore prays them to bear with him a little in his folly. To this point every thing here refers. They should thus bear with him, 1. Because he was jealous over them with a godly jealousy. 2. Because they would bear with any who really preached another gospel, were that possible. 3. Because he was on a par with the chief apostles. The connection, therefore, is not with v. 4, but with the main subject as presented in v. 1. This also determines the question, Who are meant by the chiefest apostles? If the connection is with v. 4, then the expression is to be understood ironically in reference to the false teachers. 'Ye do wrong to tolerate them, for I am in no respect behind those superlative apostles.' So Beza, Billroth, Olshausen, Meyer, and the majority of the moderns. The reason given for this is, that there is no controversy with the true apostles in this connection, and therefore nothing to call for such an assertion of his equality with them as we find in Gal. 2, 6–11. There is, however, no force in this reason if the connection is with v. 1. 'Bear with me in my boasting, for I am not behind the chiefest apostles.' In this view the reference to the true apostles is pertinent and natural. Paul says, μηδὲν ὑστερηκέναι, that *as to nothing*, in no one respect, had he fallen short, or was he left behind by the chiefest apostles; neither in gifts, nor in labours, nor in success had any one of them been more highly favoured, nor more clearly authenticated as the messenger of Christ. He was therefore fully entitled to all the deference and obedience which were due to the chiefest apostles. The expression τῶν ὑπερλίαν ἀποστόλων, is not in itself bitter or ironical. This is a force which must be given by the connection; it does not lie in the words themselves. It is not equivalent to the ψευδαπόστολοι of v. 13, and therefore there is no more reason why the true apostles should not be called οἱ ὑπερλίαν ἀπόστολοι than οἱ δοκοῦντες εἶναί τι in Gal. 2, 6. The argument, therefore, which the Reformers derived from this passage against the primacy of Peter is perfectly legitimate. Paul was Peter's equal in every respect, and so far from being under his authority, he not only refused to follow his example but reproved him to his face. Gal. 2, 11.

6. But though (I be) rude in speech, yet not in knowledge; but we have been thoroughly made manifest among you in all things.

In Corinth, where Grecian culture was at its height, it had

been urged as an objection to Paul that he did not speak with the wisdom of words. 1 Cor. 1, 17. He was no rhetorician, and did not appear in the character of an orator. This he here, as in the former epistle, concedes. If that were an objection, he had no answer to make other than that his dependence was on the demonstration of the Spirit, and not the persuasive words of man's wisdom. 1 Cor. 2, 4. Εἰ δὲ καί is concessive. 'But if, as is true, I am rude in speech;' ἰδιώτης τῷ λόγῳ, untrained, or unskilful in speech. The word ἰδιώτης means a private person as opposed to those in official station; a commoner as opposed to a patrician; an uneducated, or unskilful man, as opposed to those who were specially trained for any service or work, corporeal or mental. What Paul concedes is not the want of eloquence, of which his writings afford abundant evidence, but of the special training of a Grecian. He spoke Greek as a Jew. It is not improbable that some of his opponents in Corinth, although themselves of Hebrew origin, prided themselves on their skill in the use of the Greek language, and made the apostle's deficiency in that respect a ground of disparagement. *But not in knowledge.* He was no ἰδιώτης τῇ γνώσει. Having been taught the gospel by immediate revelation from Christ, Gal. 2, 12, he had complete possession of that system of truth which it was the object of the apostleship to communicate to men. He therefore everywhere asserts his competency as a teacher instructed of God and entitled to full credence and implicit confidence, 1 Cor. 2, 6–11. Eph. 3, 4. 5. *But we have been thoroughly made manifest among you in all things.* In this clause, after φανερωθέντες, ἐσμέν is to be supplied; ἐν παντί, rendered *thoroughly*, is in every point, or in every respect; ἐν πᾶσιν, *in all things*, so that in every point in all departments he was manifest, i. e. clearly known; εἰς ὑμᾶς, as it concerns you, (not among you, which would require ἐν ὑμῖν). So far from being deficient in knowledge, he stood clearly revealed before them as thoroughly furnished in every respect and in all things as an apostle of Jesus Christ. In nothing did he fall behind the very chief of the apostles. Luther's translation of this clause is, Doch ich bin bei euch allenthalben wohl bekannt. It is in this view a correction of what goes before. 'I am not deficient in knowledge. Yet I am in all respects perfectly known by you; there is no need to tell you what I am.' Beza and Olshausen give the same explanation. This, however, does not agree with what follows in the next verse.

Others again, understand the apostle as here asserting his well established character for purity of purpose and conduct. 'My whole conduct is perfectly open and straightforward for you to see.' There is, however, no impeachment of his conduct referred to in the context, and therefore no call for this general assertion of integrity. It is better to restrict the passage to the point immediately in hand. 'He was not behind the chief apostles; but although rude in speech, he was not deficient in knowledge, and was manifest before them in all things, i. e. in all things pertaining to the apostolic office.' Instead of φανερωθέντες the MSS. B, F, G, 17, read φανερώσαντες, which Lachmann, Rückert and Tischendorf adopt. This alters the whole sense. The meaning most naturally then is, 'I am not deficient in knowledge, but have manifested it in every point in all things.' The majority of critical editors retain the common text, which gives a sense equally well suited to the connection.

7. Have I committed an offence in abasing myself that ye might be exalted, because I have preached to you the gospel of God freely?

Our version omits the particle ἤ (or), which is necessary to indicate the connection. Paul was clearly manifested as an apostle. 'Or,' he asks, 'is it an objection to my apostleship that I have not availed myself of the right of an apostle to be supported by those to whom I preach? Have I sinned in this respect?' Comp. 1 Cor. 9, 4–15. *Have I committed an offence in abasing myself;* ἐμαυτὸν ταπεινῶν, *humbling myself* by renouncing a privilege which was my due. Comp. Phil. 4, 12. It was an act of self-humiliation that Paul, though entitled to be supported by the people, sustained himself in great measure by the labour of his own hands. I humbled myself, he says, *that ye might be exalted,* that is, for your good. It was to promote their spiritual interests that he wrought at the trade of a tent-maker. *Because I preached unto you the gospel of God freely?* This clause, beginning with ὅτι, is exegetical of the preceding. 'Have I sinned humbling myself, i. e. have I sinned because I preached freely?' (δωρεάν, gratuitously). It is clearly intimated in 1 Cor. 9, that Paul's refusing to be supported by the Corinthians was represented by his enemies as arising from the consciousness of the invalidity of his claim to the apostleship. As they had no other objection to him, he asks whether they were disposed to urge that.

8. I robbed other churches, taking wages (of them), to do you service.

To rob is to take with violence what does not belong to us. It is therefore only in a figurative sense the word is here used. What Paul received from other (i. e. the Macedonian) churches, he was fully entitled to, and it was freely given. The only point of comparison or analogy was that he took from them what the Corinthians ought to have contributed. *Taking wages* (λαβὼν ὀψώνιον), or a stipend. *To do you service*, πρὸς τὴν ὑμῶν διακονίαν, *for your ministry*. This expresses the object of his receiving assistance from others. It was that he might minister gratuitously to them.

9. And when I was present with you, and wanted, I was chargeable to no man : for that which was lacking to me the brethren which came from Macedonia supplied : and in all (things) I have kept myself from being burdensome unto you, and (so) will I keep (myself).

It is plain from this verse that when Paul went to Corinth, he took with him a supply of money derived from other churches, which he supplemented by the proceeds of his own labour; and when his stock was exhausted the deficiency was supplied by the brethren from Macedonia. *And when I was present* (παρὼν πρὸς ὑμᾶς), 'being present with you;' (καὶ ὑστερηθείς), 'and being reduced to want;' (οὐ κατενάρκησα οὐδενός), *I was chargeable to no man*, literally, 'I pressed as a dead weight upon no one,' i. e. I was burdensome to no one. The verb here used is derived from νάρκη, *torpor*, hence ναρκάω, *to be torpid*. The compound καταναρκάω, *to be torpid against* any one, (to press heavily upon him,) is found only here and in 12, 13. 14. In confirmation of the assertion that he had been chargeable to no man he adds, *for that which was lacking to me* (τὸ ὑστέρημά μου, *my deficiency*,) *the brethren which came from Macedonia* (rather, 'the brethren having come from Macedonia,') *supplied;* προσανεπλήρωσαν, a double compound verb, to supply in addition. The contribution of the churches were added to what Paul earned by his labour, or, to his diminished stock which he had brought with him to Corinth. The point on which he here dwells is not that he laboured for his own support, but that he received assistance from other churches, while he refused to receive any thing from the Corinthians. His conduct in reference to receiving aid varied with circumstances. From some churches he received it without hesitation; from others he would not receive it at all. He said to the Ephesians, "I coveted no man's silver, or gold, or apparel. Yea, ye yourselves know, that these hands have ministered unto my necessities, and to them that were with me," Acts 20, 34. 35. So also to the Thessalonians he said, "Ye remember, brethren, our labour and travail: for labouring night and day, because we would not be chargeable unto any of you, we preached unto you the gospel of God," 1 Thess. 2, 9. 2 Thess. 3, 8. Among the Corinthians he adopted the same course. Acts 18, 3. 1 Cor. 9, 15–18. Whereas from the Philippians he received repeated contributions, not only while labouring among them, but as he reminds them, "Even in Thessalonica ye sent once and again unto my necessity," Phil. 4, 16; and when a prisoner in Rome they sent by the hands of Epaphroditus an abundant supply, so that he said, "I have all, and abound," Phil. 4, 18. It was therefore from no unwillingness to receive what he knew to be due by the ordinance of Christ, (viz., an adequate support,) 1 Cor. 9, 14, but simply, as he says, to cut off occasion from those who sought occasion. He was unwilling that his enemies should have the opportunity of imputing to him any mercenary motive in preaching the gospel. This was specially necessary in Corinth, and therefore the apostle says, 'In all things (ἐν παντί, in every thing, not only in pecuniary matters, but in every thing else,) I have kept myself from being burdensome unto you, and will keep myself.' He would receive no obligation at their hands. He was determined to assume towards them a position of entire independence. This was doubtless very painful to the faithful in Corinth. They could not but regard it as a proof either of the want of love or of the want of confidence on his part. Still his determination as to this point was settled, and he therefore adds solemnly in the next verse:

10. As the truth of Christ is in me, no man shall stop me of this boasting in the regions of Achaia.

Calvin, Beza, and others, understand this as an oath, or asseveration. Our translators adopted the same view, and therefore supply the word *as*, which is not in the Greek. This interpretation is not required by the text or context. The words are simply, 'The truth (ἀλήθεια, the veracity, truthfulness) of Christ, (i. e. the veracity which pertains to Christ, and which Christ produces,) is in me.' That is, in virtue of the veracity which Christ has produced in me, I declare, *that* (ὅτι, which our translators omit,) *no man shall stop me of this boasting*. Literally, 'This boasting shall not be stopped as to me.' The word is φραγήσεται, which in the New Testament is only used in reference to the mouth. Rom. 3, 19. Heb. 11, 33. 'This boasting as to me shall not have its mouth stopped.' *In all the regions of Achaia;* not in Corinth only, but in all that part of Greece not included in Macedonia. From the Macedonians he was willing to receive aid; from the Christians of Achaia he would not. The reason for this distinction he states negatively and affirmatively in the following verses.

11. 12. Wherefore? because I love you not? God knoweth. But what I do, that I will do, that I may cut off occasion from them which desire occasion; that wherein they glory, they may be found even as we.

That his purpose not to receive aid from the Corinthians did not, as it might seem, arise from want of love to them he solemnly declares. The expression "God knows" in the lips of the apostle, it need not be remarked, implies no irreverence. It is a pious recognition of the omniscience of God, the searcher of all hearts, to whom he appeals as the witness of the strength of his affection for his people. The true reason for his determination to continue to do as he had already done, was, as he says, *That I may cut off occasion from them that desire occasion.* That is, that I may avoid giving those who desire to impeach my motives any pretence for the charge that I preach the gospel for the sake of gain. It is plain from 1 Cor. 9, 15–18, that this was his motive in refusing to receive aid from the Corinthians; and that his special καύχημα, on ground of boasting, was that he preached the gospel gratuitously. He said he would rather die than that any man should take from him that ground of confidence. This of course implies that the purity of his motives had been assailed, and that his object in making "the gospel of Christ without charge" was to stop the mouths of his accusers. *That wherein they glory.* This clause (with ἵνα) depends on the immediately preceding one. He desired to cut off occasion from those seeking it, in order that, if they chose to boast, *they may be found even as we.* That is, he wished to force them to be as disinterested as he was. According to this interpretation, ἐν ᾧ, in the phrase ἐν ᾧ καυχῶνται, does not refer to any special ground of boasting, but to the general disposition. 'Inasmuch as they are so fond of boasting and of setting themselves up as apostles, they may be forced to give over making gain of the gospel.'

Calvin, Grotius, Rückert, and others, assume that the false teachers in Corinth preached gratuitously, and that the reason why the apostle did the same, was that he might not give them occasion to glory over him. In this view the second clause with ἵνα is co-ordinate with the first, and ἐν ᾧ in the last clause refers to their special ground of boasting, and the sense of the whole is, 'I will do as I have done in order that these false teachers shall have no occasion to exalt themselves over me; that is, in order that they be found, when they boast of their disinterestedness, to be no better than I am.' But to this it may be objected, 1. That it is evident from v. 20 of this chapter, and from the whole character of these false teachers as depicted by the apostle, that so far from preaching gratuitously, they robbed the churches. 2. It is clear from what is said in the former epistle that Paul's object was not to prevent his opponents setting themselves forth as his superiors, but to make undeniably manifest the purity of his own motives in preaching the gospel. Others again, admitting that the false teachers received money from the Corinthians, understand the apostle to say, that he refused aid in order that he might take away from the false teachers all occasion for boasting that they were as he was. This, however, was not their boast. They did not claim to be what the apostle was, for they denounced him as an impostor. The first interpretation suits both the words and the context.

13. For such (are) false apostles, deceitful workers, transforming themselves into the apostles of Christ.

The reason assigned in this verse for the determination expressed in the preceding, to cut off occasion from those who sought to degrade the apostle, is, the unworthy character of his opponents. They were so unprincipled and unscrupulous that Paul was determined they should have no advantage over him. The words οἱ τοιοῦτοι ψευδαπόστολοι may be rendered either, Such false apostles *are*, &c., or, Such *are* false apostles. The Vulgate, Luther, Calvin, and the majority of the earlier commentators, give the former interpretation; most of the later writers the latter. The latter is to be preferred because the emphasis is on the word *false apostles ;* and because *such* false apostles would imply that there were other false apostles who were not deceitful workers. *False apostles* are those who falsely claimed to be apostles, as false Christs, Matt. 24, 24, and false prophets, Matt. 11, 15, are those who falsely claimed to be Christ or prophets. An apostle was commissioned by Christ, endowed with the gifts of plenary inspiration and knowledge, and invested with supernatural powers. Those in that age, and those who now claim to be apostles without this commission, these gifts, and these signs of the apostleship, are false apostles. They claim to be what they are not, and usurp an authority which does not belong to them. The fundamental idea of Romanism is the perpetuity of the apostolic office. Bishops are assumed to be apostles, and therefore claim infallibility in teaching, and supreme authority in ruling. If we admit them to be apostles, we must admit the validity of their claims to unquestioning faith and obedience. *Deceitful workers*, i. e. workers who use deceit. They were workers in so far as they were preachers or teachers; but they were not honest; they availed themselves of every means to deceive and pervert the people. To the same persons the apostle refers in Phil. 3, 2, "as evil workers." *Transforming themselves into*, i. e. assuming the character of, *the apostles of Christ*. Though their real object was not to advance the kingdom and glory of Christ, and although they were never commissioned for that work, they gave themselves out as Christ's messengers and servants, and even claimed to have a more intimate relation to him, and to be more devoted to his service than Paul himself.

14. And no marvel; for Satan himself is transformed into an angel of light.

It is not wonderful that false apostles should put themselves forward under the guise of apostles of Christ, and appear and be received as such, for Satan himself, the most evil of all beings, assumes the form of the highest and purest of created intelligences. *An angel of light,* i. e. a bright, pure, happy angel. Light is always the symbol of excellence and blessedness, hence the expressions kingdom of light, children of light, &c. And hence God is said to dwell in light, and the saints are said to have their inheritance in light. It is by no means clear that the apostle refers either to the history of the fall or to Satan's appearing with the sons of God as mentioned in Job 1, 6. It is more probable that the statement rests on the general doctrine of the Bible concerning the great adversary. He is everywhere represented as the deceiver, assuming false guises, and making false representations.

15. Therefore (it is) no great thing if his ministers also be transformed as the ministers of righteousness; whose end shall be according to their works.

If Satan can be thus changed, it is no great thing if his ministers undergo a similar transformation. If a bad angel can assume the appearance of a good angel, a bad man may put on the semblance of a good man. The false teachers are called *ministers of Satan,* that is, they are his servants, 1. In so far as they are instigated and controlled in their labours by him. 2. And in so far that their labours tend to advance his kingdom, i. e. error and evil. All wicked men and all teachers of false doctrine are, in this sense the servants of Satan. He is their master. The false teachers assumed to be *ministers of righteousness.* This may mean, righteous, upright ministers; or, promoters of righteousness in the sense of general excellence. They pretended to be the promoters of all that is good. Or, righteousness may be taken in its peculiar New Testament and Pauline sense, as in 3, 9, where the the phrase " ministry of righteousness " occurs; see also Eph. 6, 15. In these and many other places the word righteousness refers to " the righteousness of God," or, as it is also called "the righteousness of faith." These false teachers professed to be the preachers of that righteousness which is of God and which avails to the justification of sinners in his sight. Satan does not come to us as Satan; neither does sin present itself as sin, but in the guise of virtue; and the teachers of error set themselves forth as the special advocates of truth. *Whose end shall be according to their works.* Satan is none the less Satan when he appears as an angel of light, and evil is evil when called by the name of good. God's judgments are according to the truth. He does not pass sentence on the ($\sigma\chi\hat{\eta}\mu a$) the external fashion which we assume, but on our real character; not on the mask, but on the man. The end, i. e. the recompense of every man, shall be not according to his professions, not according to his own convictions or judgment of his character or conduct, not according to appearances or the estimate of men, but according to his works. If men really promote the kingdom of Christ, they will be regarded and treated as his servants; if they increase the dominion of sin and error, they will be regarded and treated as the ministers of Satan.

16. I say again, Let no man think me a fool; if otherwise, yet as a fool receive me, that I may boast myself a little.

After the foregoing outburst of feeling against the false teachers, the apostle resumes his purpose of self-vindication. He therefore says again what he had in substance said in v. 1. *Let no man think me a fool,* that is, a boaster. Self-laudation is folly; and self-vindication, when it involves the necessity of self-praise, has the appearance of folly. Therefore the apostle was pained and humbled by being obliged to praise himself. He was no boaster, and no one could rightfully so regard him, *but if otherwise* (ϵi $\delta\grave{\epsilon}$ $\mu\acute{\eta}\gamma\epsilon$, the negative is used because although the preceding clause is negative, the idea is, 'I would that no man should regard me as a fool, but if you do not think of me as I would wish, still, &c.') *Receive me,* (i. e. bear with me,) *that I may boast myself a little.* The words are $\kappa\grave{a}\gamma\acute{\omega}$, *I also,* i. e. I as well as others. 'You allow my enemies to boast of what they do, permit me to say a little of what I have done and suffered.'

17. That which I speak, I speak (it) not after the

Lord, but as it were foolishly, in this confidence of
boasting.

That which I speak, ὃ λαλῶ. The apostle uses λαλῶ and
not λέγω, because the reference is not to any definite words
which he had uttered, but general—my talk, or language.
Is not *after the Lord*, i. e. is not such as characterized Christ,
or becomes his disciples. Our Lord was no boaster, and his
Spirit does not lead any one to boast. This is very commonly regarded as a denial of inspiration, or divine guidance in
these utterances. Even Bengel says, " Whatever Paul wrote
without this express exception, was inspired and spoken after
the Lord; " and Meyer says, οὐ λαλῶ κατὰ κύριον, negirt aller-
dings den theopneusten Charakter der Rede. This arises
from a misconception of the nature and design of inspiration.
The simple end of inspiration is to secure infallibility in the
communication of truth. It is not designed to sanctify; it
does not preclude the natural play of the intellect or of the
feelings. When Paul called the High Priest a " whited wall,"
Acts 23, 3, although he apologized for it, he was as much inspired as when he wrote his epistle to the Ephesians. Even
supposing therefore that there was something of human weakness in his boasting, that would not prove that he was not
under the inspiration of God in saying that he boasted, or in
saying that boasting was folly. But this assumption is unnecessary. There was nothing wrong in his self-laudation.
He never appears more truly humble than when these refer-
ences to his labour and sufferings were wrung from him, filling
him with a feeling of self-contempt. Alas! how few of the
holiest of men does it pain and mortify to speak of their own
greatness or success. How often are the writings even of
good men coals on which they sprinkle incense to their own
pride. When Paul said that his boasting was not *after the
Lord*, he said no more than when he called it folly. All that
the expression implies is that self-praise in itself considered, is
not the work of a Christian; it is not a work to which the
Spirit of Christ impels the believer. But, when it is necessary to the vindication of the truth or the honor of religion, it
becomes a duty. *But as it were foolishly*, (ἐν ἀφροσύνῃ, *in
folly*.) That is, speaking boastfully was not religious but
foolish. *In this confidence of boasting*, ἐν ταύτῃ τῇ ὑποστάσει
τῆς καυχήσεως. Ὑπόστασις may mean *matter*, or *confidence*.
' In this particular matter, or case of boasting.' In this sense

it is a limitation of what precedes. He was justified in boasting in this particular matter. It is, however, more consistent with the common use of the word in the New Testament, that here, as in 9, 4, it should be taken in the sense of *confidence*, and ἐν be rendered *with*. 'I speak with this confidence of boasting.'

18. Seeing that many glory after the flesh, I will glory also.

The apostle here assigns the reason of his glorying. His opponents so magnified themselves and their services, and so depreciated him and his labours, that he was forced, in order to maintain his influence as the advocate of a pure gospel, to set forth his claims to the confidence of the people. *Seeing that* (ἐπεί, *since, because*) *many glory*. From this, as well as from other intimations abounding in this epistle, it is evident that the opposition to Paul was headed not by one man, but by a body or class of false teachers, all of whom were Judaizers. They gloried *after the flesh* (κατὰ τὴν σάρκα). This may mean, 'they gloried *as to* the flesh.' Then flesh means what is external and adventitious, such as their Hebrew descent, their circumcision, &c. See v. 22, where these false teachers are represented as boasting of their external advantages. Compare also Gal. 6, 13 and Phil. 3, 4, where the apostle says in reference to the same class of opponents, " If any other man thinketh that he hath whereof he might trust in the flesh, I more." The sense in this case is good and appropriate, but it would require ἐν and not κατά. See 10, 17. 11, 12. 12, 9, &c., &c. Κατὰ σάρκα more properly means *according to the flesh*, i. e. according to corrupt human nature, as opposed to κατὰ κύριον in the preceding verse. These men were influenced in their boasting by unworthy motives. *I will glory also*. Does Paul mean, 'As others glory after the flesh, I also will glory after the flesh'? i. e. as others give way to their selfish feelings, I will do the same. This is the view which many commentators take. They say that κατὰ σάρκα is necessarily implied after κἀγὼ καυχήσομαι, because the apostle had just said that in boasting he did not act κατὰ κύριον, which implies that he did act κατὰ σάρκα; and because in the following verse he makes himself one of ἄφρονες of whose glorying the Corinthians were so tolerant. But the sense thus expressed is neither true nor consistent with the character of the apostle. It is not true that he was influenced in boasting by corrupt feelings; that self-conceit and the desire of applause were in him, as in the false teachers, the motives which governed him in this matter. There is no necessity for supplying κατὰ σάρκα after the last clause. What Paul says is, 'As many boast from unworthy motives, I also will boast.' If they did it from bad motives, he might well do it from good ones.

19. For ye suffer fools gladly, seeing ye (yourselves) are wise.

That is, 'I will indulge in the folly of boasting, for ye are tolerant of fools.' The Corinthians had, to a degree disgraceful to themselves, allowed the boasting Judaizing teachers to gain an ascendency over them, and they could not, therefore, with any consistency object to the self-vindication of Paul. *Seeing ye are wise.* As it is the part of the wise to bear with fools, so the Corinthians in their wisdom might bear with the apostle. Of course this is said ironically and as a reproof. In the same spirit and with the same purpose he had said to them in his former epistle, 4, 8, "We are fools, but ye are wise."

20. For ye suffer, if a man bring you into bondage, if a man devour (you), if a man take (of you), if a man exalt himself, if a man smite you on the face.

They might well bear with Paul since they bore with the tyranny, the rapacity, the insolence, and the violence of the false teachers. The character of these troublers of the church was everywhere the same; see Gal. 1, 7. They were lords over God's heritage, 1 Pet. 5, 3, not only as they endeavoured to reduce the Christians under the bondage of the law, as appears from the epistle to the Galatians, but as they exercised a tyrannical authority over the people. To this the apostle here refers when he says, *If any man bring you into bondage* (καταδουλοῖ), i. e. makes slaves of you. That this is not to be limited to subjection to the Jewish law, is evident from what follows, which is an amplification of the idea here expressed. These men were tyrants, and therefore they devoured, insulted and maltreated the people. *If any man devour (you),* i. e. rapaciously consumes your substance, as our Lord describes the Pharisees as devouring widows' houses, Matt. 23, 14. *If any take* (of you); εἴ τις λαμβάνει; ὑμᾶς is to be supplied as after κατεσθίει in the preceding clause. "*If any take you*," i. e. capture you or ensnare you, as a huntsman his prey. Our version by supplying *of you* alters the sense, and makes this clause express less than the preceding; devouring is a stronger expression for rapacity than 'taking of you.' *If any man exalt himself* (ἐπαίρεται, sc. καθ' ὑμῶν), i. e. if any one proudly and insolently lifts himself up against you. And as the climax, *If any one smite you on the face.* To smite the face or mouth was the highest indignity; as such it was offered to our Lord, Luke 22, 64, and to Paul, Acts 23, 2; see also 1 Kings 22, 24. Matt. 5, 39. Such was the treatment to which the Corinthians submitted from the hands of the false teachers; and such is ever the tendency of unscriptural church-authority. It assumes an absolute dependence of the people on the clergy—an inherent, as well as official superiority of the latter over the former, and therefore false teachers have, as a general rule, been tyrants. The gospel, and of course the evangelical, as opposed to the high-church system of doctrine, is incompatible with all undue authority, because it teaches the essential equality of believers and opens the way to grace and salvation to the people without the intervention of a priest.

21. I speak as concerning reproach, as though we had been weak. Howbeit, whereinsoever any is bold, (I speak foolishly) I am bold also.

I speak as concerning reproach. Κατὰ ἀτιμίαν λέγω means simply *I reproach.* After ἀτιμίαν may be supplied ἐμήν. The sense would then be, 'I say to my own shame, that, &c.;' λέγω being understood as referring to what follows. 'I say to my shame that I was weak.' The Greek is, κατὰ ἀτιμίαν (ἐμὴν) ὡς ὅτι ἡμεῖς ἠσθενήσαμεν; where ὡς ὅτι may, as Winer, § 67, 1, says, be a redundancy for simply ὅτι (5, 19. 2 Thess. 2, 2.) 'I say *that.*' This would be a direct assertion on the part of Paul that he was weak in the sense intended. It is better, with Meyer and others, to give ὡς its proper force, *as, as if.* His being weak was not a fact, but an opinion entertained concerning him. 'I say that (as people think) I was weak.' One class of the Corinthians regarded Paul as weak in bodily presence and contemptible in speech, 10, 10. In reference to this judgment of his opponents he says, 'I acknowledge to my shame that, when present with you (the aorist, ἠσθενήσαμεν, is used), I was weak.' In 1 Cor. 2, 3 he told the Corinthians that he came among them in weakness and fear and much trembling. There was a sense in which he admitted and professed himself to be weak. He had no self-confidence. He did not believe in his own ability to persuade or convert men. He felt the responsibility of his office, and he relied both for knowledge and success entirely on the Spirit of God. His conceited and arrogant opposers were strong in their own estimation; they contemned the mean-spirited apostle, and considered him destitute of all sources of power. The weakness of which Paul here speaks is that which was attributed to him by his enemies. The whole preceding context is ironical, and so is this clause. 'Your teachers are great men, I am nothing compared to them. They are strong, but, I say it to my shame, I am weak. *But*, as opposed to this imputed weakness, I am equal to any of them, I speak in folly.' *Howbeit whereinsoever any is bold* (ἐν ᾧ δ' ἄν τις τολμᾷ), 'But whatever they dare, I dare. Whatever claims they put forth, I can assert the same. If they boast, I can outboast them. If they are Hebrews, so am I, &c.'

The foregoing interpretation of this passage, which assumes that λέγω in the first clause refers to what follows, and that the reproach mentioned had Paul for its object, is given by Storr, Flatt, Meyer, and many others. The great majority of commentators, however, understand λέγω as referring to what precedes and the Corinthians and not Paul to be the object of the reproach. 'I say this to *your* shame.' Compare 1 Cor. 6, 5, πρὸς ἐντροπὴν ὑμῖν λέγω. (In this latter passage, however, it will be remarked that the preposition is πρός and not κατά, as in the passage before us, and that ὑμῖν is in the text, whereas here there is no pronoun used.) The two principal objections to this interpretation are, 1. That if λέγω refers to the preceding verses the sense must be, 'I make this exhibition of the character of your teachers in order to shame you.' This would do very well if what follows carried out that idea; but instead of speaking of the Corinthians, and endeavouring to convince them of their folly in adhering to such men as teachers, he immediately speaks of himself, and shows how he was despised as weak. 2. According to this interpretation there is great difficulty in explaining the following clause. It would not do to say, 'I speak to shame you that I was weak;' or, if ὅτι be made causal, 'I speak to shame you because I was weak,' still the sense is not good. The former interpretation of this difficult passage is therefore to be preferred.

22. Are they Hebrews? so (am) I. Are they Israelites? so (am) I. Are they the seed of Abraham? so (am) I.

In this verse the apostle begins his boasting by showing that in no point did he come behind his opponents. The three designations here used belonged to the chosen people. The Hebrews were Israelites, and the Israelites were the seed of Abraham. The first, as Meyer remarks, is the national designation of the people of God; the second their theocratic appellation; and the third marked them as the heirs of Abraham and expectants of the Messianic kingdom. Or, as Bengel remarks with no less justice, the first refers to their national, and the two others to their religious or spiritual relation. A Hebrew was not a Jew of Palestine as distinguished from the Hellenists, or Jews born out of Palestine and speaking the Greek language. For Paul himself was born in Tarsus, and yet was a Hebrew of the Hebrews, that is, a man of pure Hebrew descent. In Acts 6, 1 the word is used for the Jews of Palestine in distinction from other Jews, but it is obviously not so either here or in Phil. 3, 5.

23. Are they ministers of Christ? (I speak as a fool) I (am) more; in labours more abundant, in stripes above measure, in prisons more frequent, in deaths oft.

In all that related to the privileges of birth, as belonging to the chosen seed, Paul stood on a level with the chief of his opposers; in all that related to Christ and his service he stood far above them. *Are they the ministers of Christ?* Such they were by profession, and such for the moment he admits them to be, although in truth they were the ministers of Satan, as he had said in v. 15. *I more* (ὑπὲρ ἐγώ, where ὑπέρ is used as an adverb). This may mean either, I am more than a (διάκονος) minister of Christ; or, I am a minister or servant of

Christ in a higher measure than they. That is, I am more
devoted, laborious and suffering than they. The latter is the
true explanation as is clear from what follows, and because in
Paul's language and estimation there was no higher title or
service than that of minister of Christ. *I speak as a fool*,
παραφονῶν λαλῶ. This is a strong expression, 'I speak as one
beside himself.' This is said out of the consciousness of ill-
desert and utter insufficiency. Feelmg himself to be in himself both impotent and unworthy, this self-laudation, though
having reference only to his infirmities and to what God had
done in him and by him, was in the highest degree painful
and humiliating to the apostle. It is Paul's judgment of himself, not the judgment which others are presumed to pass
upon him. *In labours more abundant*, ἐν κόποις περισσοτέρως.
There are three ways of explaining this and the following
clauses, 1. In (or, *by*) labours I am more abundantly the servant of Christ. 2. Or, (supplying ἦν or γέγονα,) I have been
more abundant in labours. 3. Or, connecting, as De Wette
and Meyer do, the adverbs with the substantives with the sense
of adjectives, *by more abundant labours*. This latter explanation can better be carried through, and expresses the sense
clearly. *In stripes above measure*, ἐν πληγαῖς ὑπερβαλλόντως,
i. e. *by stripes exceeding measure* (in frequency and severity).
In prisons more frequent, either, as before, 'I have been more
frequently imprisoned,' or, 'By more frequent prisons.' The
sense remains the same. *In deaths oft*, ἐν θανάτοις πολλάκις,
by manifold deaths. Paul, in accordance with common
usage, elsewhere says, "I die daily." He suffered a thousand
deaths, in the sense of being constantly in imminent danger
of death and of enduring its terrors.

24. 25. Of the Jews five times received I forty
(stripes) save one. Thrice was I beaten with rods,
once was I stoned, thrice I suffered shipwreck, a night
and a day I have been in the deep.

These verses are a parenthesis designed to confirm the
preceding assertion that he had laboured and suffered more
in the service of Christ than any of his opponents. In v. 26
the construction is resumed. The apostle had at this period
of his history been scourged eight times; five times by the
Jews and thrice by the Romans. Of this cruel ill-treatment

at the hands of his own countrymen, the Acts of the Apostles contain no record; and of the three occasions on which he was beaten with rods, that mentioned in Acts 16, 22 as having occurred at Philippi is the only one of which we have elsewhere any account. In the law of Moses, Deut. 25, 3, it was forbidden to inflict more than forty stripes on an offender, and it appears that the Jews, in their punctilious observance of the letter of the law, were in the habit of inflicting only thirty-nine so as to be sure not to transgress the prescribed limit. From the distinction which the apostle makes between receiving stripes at the hands of the Jews and being beaten with rods, it is probable that the Jews were at that period accustomed to use a lash. The later Rabbis say that the scourge was made with three thongs, so that each blow inflicted three stripes; and that only thirteen strokes were given to make up the prescribed number of thirty-nine lashes. *Once was I stoned.* Acts 14, 19. On this occasion his enemies supposed he was dead. He must therefore have been rendered for the time insensible. *Thrice I suffered shipwreck.* Of this we have no mention in the Acts. The shipwreck in which Paul was involved on his journey to Rome, was at a much later period. *A night and a day have I been in the deep.* That is, for that length of time he was tossed about by the waves, clinging to a fragment of a wreck. *A night and day* (νυχϑήμερον), i. e. a whole day of twenty-four hours. The Jews commenced the day at sunset.

26. (In) journeyings often, (in) perils of waters, (in) perils of robbers, (in) perils by (mine own) countrymen, (in) perils by the heathen, (in) perils in the city, (in) perils in the wilderness, (in) perils in the sea, (in) perils among false brethren.

Our translators have throughout this passage supplied the preposition *in*. But as ἐν in the preceding verse is used instrumentally, so here we have the instrumental dative, *by journeyings*, *by perils*, &c. It was by voluntarily exposing himself to these dangers, and by the endurance of these sufferings the apostle proved his superior claim to be regarded as a devoted minister of Christ. *Perils of water*, literally, *of rivers;* as distinguished from the dangers of the sea mentioned afterwards. History shows that in the country traversed in

Paul's journeys great danger was often encountered in passing the rivers which crossed his path. *Perils of robbers*, to which all travellers were exposed. Perils from my own countrymen (ἐκ γένους as opposed to ἐξ ἐθνῶν). The Jews were, at least in most cases, the first to stir up opposition and to excite the mob against the apostle. This was the case at Damascus, Acts 9, 23; at Jerusalem, Acts 9, 29; at Antioch in Pisidia, Acts 13, 50; at Iconium, 14, 5; at Lystra, 14, 19; at Thessalonica, Acts 17, 5; at Berea, Acts 17, 13; at Corinth, 18, 12. *From the Gentiles*, as at Philippi and Ephesus. *In the city*, as in Damascus, Jerusalem and Ephesus. *In the desert*. The dangers of the desert are proverbial. Paul traversed Arabia, as well as the mountainous regions of Asia Minor, and was doubtless often exposed in these journeys to the dangers of robbers, as well as those arising from exposure, and hunger and thirst. *Of the sea*, not only in the case of shipwreck before mentioned, but to other and lesser perils. *Perils among false brethren*, referring probably to the treachery of those who falsely professed to be his brethren in Christ, and yet endeavoured to deliver him into the power of his enemies.

27. In weariness and painfulness, in watchings often, in hunger and thirst, in fastings often, in cold and nakedness.

Here the preposition ἐν is again used, but in its instrumental sense *by*. It was *by* these trials and sufferings he proved himself to be what he claimed to be. *By weariness and painfulness*, ἐν κόπῳ καὶ μόχθῳ. These words are thus associated in 1 Thess. 2, 9, and 2 Thess. 3, 8, in both of which places they are rendered "labour and travail." They both express the idea of wearisome toil and the consequent exhaustion and suffering. *By watchings often*, referring to the sleepless nights which he was often compelled by business or suffering to pass. *In hunger and thirst, in fastings often*. The common meaning of the word νηστεία, and its connection with the words "hunger and thirst," implying involuntary abstinence from food, are urged as reasons for understanding it to mean voluntary fasting. But the context is in favour of the common interpretation which makes it refer to involuntary abstinence. Every other particular here mentioned belongs to the class of sufferings; and it would therefore be incongruous to introduce into this enumeration any thing so insignificant and so common as religious fasting. In this the Pharisees were his equals and probably far his superior. They fasted twice in the week. Paul was no ascetic, and certainly did not deny himself food to the extent of making that denial an act of heroism. It is remarkable that we have no record of Paul's ever having fasted at all, unless Acts 13, 3. *By cold and nakedness.* This completes the picture. The greatest of the apostles here appears before us, his back lacerated by frequent scourgings, his body worn by hunger, thirst, and exposure; cold and naked, persecuted by Jews and Gentiles, driven from place to place without any certain dwelling. This passage, more perhaps than any other, makes even the most laborious of the modern ministers of Christ hide their face in shame. What have they ever done or suffered to compare with what this apostle did? It is a consolation to know that Paul is now as pre-eminent in glory, as he was here in suffering.

28. Besides those things that are without, that which cometh upon me daily, the care of all the churches.

This verse is variously interpreted. The first clause, *Besides those things which are without,* is rendered in the same way in the Vulgate. Praeter illa, quae extrinsecus sunt. So also Calvin, Beza, and others. But this is contrary to the usage of the words τὰ παρεκτός, which mean, *the things besides,* i. e. other things; so that the sense of the clause χωρὶς τῶν παρεκτός is, 'Not to mention other things.' The preceding enumeration, copious as it is, was not exhaustive. There were other things of a like nature which the apostle would not stop to mention, but proceeded to another class of trials. That class included his exhausting official duties. *That which cometh on me daily,* viz., *the care of all the churches.* The latter clause is, according to this explanation, assumed to be explanatory of the former. The same view is taken of the relation of the two clauses by Meyer, who renders the passage thus: "My daily attention, the care of all the churches." This latter interpretation assumes that instead of ἐπισύστασις, which is in the common text, the true reading is ἐπίστασις, a reading adopted by Lachmann, Tischendorf, Meyer, Rückert, and others. Both words are used in the sense of concourse, tumult, as of the people, see Acts 24, 12, but the former has also the sense of care, or attention. If the corrected text be adopted, then the interpretation just mentioned is to be preferred. 'Without mentioning other things, (ἡ ἐπίστασίς μου ἡ καθ᾽ ἡμέραν) my daily oversight, the care of all the church.' If the common text, although not so well sustained, be adhered to, the meaning probably is, 'My daily concourse' (*quotidiani hominum impetus*). That is, the crowding upon him every day of people demanding his attention. This is the sense expressed by Luther; "Dass ich täglich werde angelaufen, und trage Sorge für alle Gemeinen." The solicitude which the apostle felt for the churches which he had founded, is apparent from all his epistles; and it may be easily imagined how various and constant must have been the causes and occasions of anxiety and trouble on their account.

29. Who is weak, and I am not weak? who is offended, and I burn not?

That is, he sympathized with his fellow Christians, who were his children in the faith, so that their sorrows and sufferings were his own. This was the consequence not only of the communion of saints, in virtue of which, "if one member suffer, all the members suffer with it; or one member be honoured, all the members rejoice with it," 1 Cor. 12, 26; but also of the peculiar relation which Paul sustained to the churches, which he had himself planted. *Who is weak;* i. e. in faith, or scrupulous through want of knowledge, compare 1 Cor. 9, 22, *and I am not weak?* That is, with whose infirmities of faith and knowledge do I not sympathize? He pitied their infirmities and bore with their prejudices. To the weak, he became as weak. There are men, says Calvin, who either despise the infirmities of their brethren, or trample them under their feet. Such men know little of their own hearts, and have little of the spirit of Paul or of Paul's master. God never quenches the smoking flax. *Who is offended* (σκανδαλίζεται), i. e. caused to stumble, or led into sin; and *I burn not.* That is, *and I am not indignant?* It was not to Paul a matter of indifference when any of the brethren, by the force of evil example, or by the seductions of false teachers, were led to depart from the truth or to act inconsistently with their profession. Such events filled him not only with grief at the fall of the weak, but with indignation at the authors of their fall. Thus his mind was kept in a state of constant agitation by his numerous anxieties and his wide-hearted sympathy.

30. If I must needs glory, I will glory of the things which concern mine infirmities.

Paul's boasting was not like that of the false teachers. They boasted not only of their descent, but of their learning, eloquence, and personal advantages; he boasted only of the things which implied weakness, his sufferings and privations. The future, καυχήσομαι, expresses a general purpose, illustrated in the past, and not having reference merely to what was to come. The persecutions, the poverty, the scourgings, the hunger and nakedness of which Paul had boasted, were not things in which men of the world pride themselves, or which commonly attract human applause.

31. The God and Father of our Lord Jesus Christ, which is blessed for evermore, knoweth that I lie not.

This is a peculiarly solemn asseveration. An oath is the act of calling God to witness the truth of what we say. Here the appeal is not simply to God as God, but to God in his peculiar covenant relation to believers. When the Israelite called on Jehovah as the God of Abraham, Isaac, and Jacob, he recognized him not only as the creator and moral governor of the world, but as the covenant God of his nation. So the Christian when he calls God "The God and Father of our Lord Jesus Christ," recognizes him not only as his Creator, but as the author of redemption through his eternal Son. Jesus Christ is a designation of the Theanthropos, the historical person so named and known, to whom God stood in the relation at once of God and Father. Our Lord had a dependent nature to which God stood in the relation of God, and a divine nature to which He stood in the relation of Father, and therefore to the complex person Jesus Christ God bore the relation of both God and Father.

There is a difference of opinion as to the reference of this passage. Some suppose that the apostle intended by this oath to confirm the truth of the whole preceding exhibition of his labours and sufferings; others, that it is to be confined to the assertion in v. 30, viz., that he would boast only of his infirmi-

ties; others, as Calvin and many others, refer it to what follows, i. e., to the account which he was about to give of his
escape from Damascus. To give this explanation the more
plausibility, Meyer assumes that Paul had intended to introduce an extended narrative of his escape and sufferings, beginning with the incident at Damascus, but was interrupted
and did not carry out his intention. As, however, there is no
intimation of this in the context, it is probable that the reference is to the whole of the preceding narrative. He intended
to satisfy his readers that he had not exaggerated or overstated his sufferings. God knew that all he had said was
true.

32. In Damascus the governor under Aretas the
king kept the city of the Damascenes with a garrison,
desirous to apprehend me.

It is useless to inquire why Paul introduces, as it were, as
an after-thought, this disconnected account of his escape from
Damascus. It is enough that the fact occurred to him when
writing, and that he saw fit to record it. The account here
given agrees with that found in Acts 9, 24. 25, except that
there the attempt to apprehend the apostle is attributed to
the Jews, and here to the governor of the city. There is no
inconsistency between the two. The governor acted no doubt
at the instigation of the Jews. He had no grievance of his
own to redress or avenge. The governor, or *ethnarch*, a term
applied to a vassal prince, or ruler appointed by a sovereign
over a city or province. Governor *under*, literally, *of* Aretas
the king. Aretas was a common name of Arabian kings, as
Pharaoh of the kings of Egypt. A king of that name is mentioned as contemporary with the high-priest Jason, and with the
king Antiochus Epiphanes. The one here referred to was the
father-in-law of Herod Antipas. Herod having repudiated
the daughter of Aretas, the latter declared war against him
and totally defeated his army. Vitellius, proconsul of Syria,
undertook to punish him for this assault on a Roman vassal,
but was arrested on his march by the death of the emperor
Tiberius. It is commonly supposed that it was during this
respite that Aretas, who was king of Petra, gained temporary
possession of Damascus. *Kept the city of the Damascenes,*
not, *besieged the city,* but as it is expressed in Acts, watched

the gates. The words *of the Damascenes* (τὴν Δαμασκηνῶν πόλιν) are omitted in the original edition of 1611 of King James's version, but are now found in all the copies. *With a garrison.* The word is simply ἐφρούρει, *he kept*, or *guarded*. *Desirous to apprehend me.* The governor set a guard at the gates to seize the apostle should he attempt to leave the city.

33. And through a window in a basket was I let down by the wall, and escaped his hands.

Through a window, θυρίς, *a little door*, or *aperture*. This was either an aperture in the wall itself, or, as is more probable, a window of a house built upon the walls of the city. A representation of these overhanging houses as still to be seen on the walls of Damascus, may be found in Conybeare and Howson's life of St. Paul, p. 98 of the 8vo. edition. The same mode of escape was adopted by the spies mentioned in Joshua 2, 15, and by David, 1 Sam. 19, 12.

———◆◆◆———

CHAPTER XII.

The account of a remarkable vision granted to the apostle, vs. 1–6. The other evidences of his apostleship, and his conduct and purposes in the exercise of his office, vs. 7–21.

Paul's revelations and visions.

He would give over boasting, and refer not to what he had done, but to what God had done ; not to scenes in which he was the agent, but to those in which he was merely the subject—to revelations and visions. He had been caught up to the third heavens, and received communications and revelations which he was not permitted to make known. This was to him, and to all who believed his word, a more reliable evidence of the favour of God to him as an apostle than any thing he had yet mentioned, vs. 1–6. With this extraordinary proof of the divine favour there was given him some painful bodily affection, from which he could not be delivered, in order to keep him duly humble, vs. 7–10. This reference to his personal experience was exceedingly painful to him. He had been forced by their unreasonable opposition to speak of himself as he had done; for the external signs of his apostleship should have convinced them that he was the immediate messenger of Christ, vs. 11. 12. They themselves were a standing proof that he was truly an apostle. They were not less richly endowed than other churches founded by other apostles. If inferior at all, it was only that he had refused to be supported by them. This he could not help. He was determined to pursue in the future the course in that matter which he had hitherto adopted; neither by himself nor by others, neither mediately nor immediately, would he receive any thing at their hands, vs. 13–18. All this self-vindication was of little account. It was a small matter what they thought of him. God is the only competent and final judge. His fear was that when he reached Corinth he would be forced to appear as a judge; that not finding them what he desired them to be, he should be obliged to assume the aspect of a reprover, vs. 19–21.

1. It is not expedient for me doubtless to glory. I will come to visions and revelations of the Lord.

The authorities differ much as to the text in this verse. The common text has δή (*indeed, doubtless*) with few MSS. or versions in its support. Many of the oldest MSS. read δεῖ, *it is necessary;* some few δέ, which is adopted by Meyer as the original reading. The difference is only as to the shades of the thought. The idea is that boasting is not expedient; he will pass to something else, or at least to things which implied no agency or superior power on his part. *Is not expedient.* Here again some MSS. read with the common text, οὐ συμφέρει μοι, ἐλεύσομαι γάρ, (*is not expedient for me, for I will come;*) others with Lachmann, Tischendorf, and Rückert, οὐ συμφέρον μὲν, ἐλεύσομαι δέ, (*it is not expedient indeed, but I will come.*) The common text is on the whole to be preferred. Boasting, the apostle says, *is not expedient for me*, either in the sense that it does not become me, is not a seemly or proper thing; or, is not profitable; does not contribute to set my apostleship in a clear light. There is a better way of proving my divine mission than by boasting. The former explanation is better suited to the apostle's mode of representation. He had re-

peatedly spoken of boasting as a kind of folly, something derogatory and painful. He expresses the same feeling here
when he says it is not expedient. *I will come.* Our translators omit the γάρ, *for I will come.* The connection is with a
thought omitted. Boasting is not expedient, (therefore I de-
sist,) *for* I will pass to something else. What follows in the
relation of the revelations made to him, was no self-laudation,
but a recital of God's goodness. *Visions and revelations.*
The latter term is, on the one hand, more general than the
former, as there might be revelations where there were no
visions; and, on the other, the latter is higher than the former, as implying a disclosure of the import of the things seen.
Of the Lord; not visions of which the Lord was the object;
it was not seeing the Lord that he here speaks of, but visions
and revelations of which the Lord is the author. By *Lord* is
obviously to be understood Christ, whose continued existence
and divine power over the thoughts and states of the soul is
hereby recognized.

2. I knew a man in Christ above fourteen years
ago, (whether in the body, I cannot tell; or whether
out of the body, I cannot tell: God knoweth;) such
an one caught up to the third heaven.

He speaks of himself in the third person, " I knew a man."
Why he does this is not clear. He narrates what had happened as though he had been a spectator of the scene, perhaps
because his own activity was so completely in abeyance. *A
man in Christ;* a man who was in Christ; the scriptural
designation of a Christian, because union with Christ makes a
man a Christian. It is the one only indispensable condition
of salvation; so that all who are in Christ are saved, and all
who are out of Christ perish. It is also the plain doctrine of
the Bible that, so far as adults are concerned, this saving
union with Christ is conditioned, not on any thing external,
not on union with this or that external church, but on a personal appropriating act of faith, by which we receive and rest
on Christ alone for salvation. And still further, it is no less
clearly taught that holiness of heart and life is the certain
fruit and therefore the only satisfactory evidence of the genuineness of that faith. *Above fourteen years ago.* The event
referred to in this verse is not the same as that which occurred

at the time of Paul's conversion. That was a vision of Christ to the apostle here on earth, this was a translation of the apostle into heaven; that occurred twenty years before the probable date of this epistle. So that the two agree neither in nature, nor in the time of their occurrence. *Whether in the body or out of the body, I cannot tell.* The point as to which Paul was in doubt, was not the nature of the event, not as to whether it was a mere exaltation of his consciousness and perceptions or a real translation, but simply whether that translation was of the soul separated from the body, or of the body and soul together. Though heaven is a state, it is also a place. According to the scriptural representation, more is necessary to our introduction into heaven than merely opening the eyes to what is now about us and around us. The glorified body of our Lord is somewhere, and not everywhere. *Such an one caught up;* ἁρπαγέντα, *carried away*, the proper term to express a removal from one place to another without the agency of the subject. Paul was entirely passive in the translation of which he here speaks. Comp. Acts 8, 39. 1 Thess. 4, 17, "Caught up to meet the Lord in the air." *To the third heaven.* This means either the highest heavens; or, on the assumption that Paul used the language and intended to conform to the ideas of the Rabbins who taught that there were seven heavens, it means the air, the region of the clouds. He was caught up into the air, and then still further raised to Paradise. The former explanation is to be preferred, 1. Because there is no evidence that the opinions of the Jewish writers, whose works are still extant, were prevalent at the time of the apostle. 2. Because there is no evidence in the New Testament that the sacred writers adopted those opinions. 3. Because if Paul believed and taught that there were seven heavens, that is, if he sanctioned the Rabbinical doctrine on that subject, it would be a part of Christian doctrine, which it is not. It is no part of the faith of the Christian church. 4. Because it is plain that the "third heaven" and "paradise" are synonymous terms; and paradise, as is admitted, at least by those who suppose that Paul here speaks as a Jew, means heaven.

3. 4. And I knew such a man, (whether in the body, or out of the body, I cannot tell: God knoweth;) how that he was caught up into paradise, and heard

unspeakable words, which it is not lawful for a man to utter.

This is a repetition of v. 2, with the exception of the substitution of the word "paradise" for the phrase "the third heaven." *Paradise* is a word of Sanscrit origin, and signifies a park, or garden. It is used in the Septuagint, Gen. 2, 8, in the description of Eden, which was a paradise or garden. The word was early used among the Jews as a designation of heaven, or the abode of the blessed after death, as appears from Luke 23, 43, (compare Ecclesiasticus 40, 17. 28.) In Rev. 2, 7, it occurs in the same sense. *And heard unspeakable words*, ἄρρητα ῥήματα, literally, unspoken words; here obviously the meaning is words not to be spoken, as explained by what follows. *Which it is not lawful for a man to utter.* The communications made to the apostle he was not allowed to make known to others. The veil which conceals the mysteries and glories of heaven God has not permitted to be raised. It is enough that we know that in that world the saints shall be made perfectly holy and perfectly blessed in the full enjoyment of God forever.

5. Of such an one will I glory : yet of myself I will not glory, but in mine infirmities.

Of such a one, ὑπὲρ τοῦ τοιούτου, *for* such a one, i. e. in his behalf; or, ὑπέρ being taken in the sense of περί, *about*, or concerning. This latter gives the better sense. 'Concerning such a person I will glory.' This is equivalent to saying, 'Such an event is a just ground of glorying.' But τοιούτου is not to be taken as neuter, (of such a thing,) as is plain from the antithetical ἐμαυτοῦ. 'Of such a one, but not of myself.' The translation which he had experienced was a proper ground of boasting, because it was a gratuitous favour. It implied no superiority on the part of the subject of this act of divine goodness, and therefore might be gloried in without assuming any special merit to himself. *Of myself I will not glory ;* that is, he would not boast of his personal qualities as entitling him to admiration. *But* (εἰ μή, except) *in my infirmities.* That is, 'I will boast concerning myself only of those things which prove or imply my own weakness.'

6. For though I would desire to glory, I shall not

be a fool; for I will say the truth: but (now) I forbear, lest any man should think of me above that which he seeth me (to be), or (that) he heareth of me.

The connection as indicated by (γάρ) *for*, is not immediately with what is expressed in the preceding verse, but with a thought obviously implied. Paul had said he would not glory concerning himself. The reason for this determination was not the want of grounds of boasting. 'I could do it, *for* if I chose to boast, *I should not be a fool;* i. e. an empty boaster—for I would speak the truth.' *But I forbear* (φείδομαι δέ sc. τοῦ καυχᾶσθαι). Abundant as were the materials for boasting at the apostle's command, justly as he could refer to the extraordinary gifts with which he was endowed, and the extraordinary success which had attended his labours, he did not dwell on these things. The reason which he assigns for this forbearance is that others might not be led to think of him too highly. He did not wish to be judged of by what he said of himself or of his experiences. He preferred that men should judge of him by what they saw or heard.

7. And lest I should be exalted above measure through the abundance of the revelations, there was given to me a thorn in the flesh, the messenger of Satan to buffet me, lest I should be exalted above measure.

As Paul determined not to give occasion to others to think too highly of him, he here tells us that God provided against his being unduly elated even in his own mind. It is a familiar matter of experience that men are as much exalted in their own estimation by the distinguishing favour of their superiors, as by the possession of personal advantages. Therefore the apostle, although he would not boast of himself, was still in danger of being unduly elated by the extraordinary manifestations of the divine favour. The order of the words is inverted. "And by the excess of revelations lest I should be exalted above measure;" ὑπεραίρωμαι, be lifted up above what is meet or right. The expression *excess*, or exceeding abundance, *of revelations* seems to refer not exclusively to the event above mentioned, but to other similar communications made to him at other times. That was not the only occasion on which God had unveiled to the apostle the treasures of divine knowledge. *There was given to me,* i. e. by God.   It was God who sent the trial here referred to, and from God the apostle sought deliverance.   *A thorn in the flesh,* σκόλοψ τῇ σαρκί.   The word σκόλοψ properly means a sharpened stake, a palisade, then any piece of sharpened wood, and specifically a thorn.   This last is the meaning best suited to this passage, and is the one commonly adopted.   Others say the meaning is, "a goad for the flesh," borrowing a figure from oxen, metaphora a bobus sumpta, as Calvin says; others again understand σκολόψ to refer to a stake on which offenders were impaled, or the cross on which they were suspended.   A stake, or cross, for the flesh, would be a figurative expression for bodily torture.   *Flesh* may be taken literally for the body, or figuratively for the corrupt nature.   Calvin and many others take the latter view.   But there is no reason for departing from the literal meaning, which should in all cases be preferred, other things being equal.   The dative σαρκί may be rendered either, *for* the flesh, or *pertaining to* the flesh, i. e. in the flesh.   This last is to be preferred, as it suits the context and is sustained by the parallel passage, Gal. 4, 14, τὸν πειρασμόν μου τὸν ἐν τῇ σαρκί μου.   If this is the true interpretation of the word σάρξ, it goes far to determine the nature of the thorn of which the apostle here speaks.   It cannot be the evil suggestions, or fiery darts of Satan, as Luther, Calvin, and others, understand it; nor some prominent adversary, as many of the ancients suppose; it was doubtless some painful bodily affection.   *A messenger of Satan.*   In the Bible the idea is often presented that bodily diseases are at times produced by the direct agency of Satan, so that they may be regarded as his messengers, something sent by him.   The word Σαταν is used here probably as an indeclinable noun, as in the Septuagint in one or two places, but in the New Testament it is always, except in this instance, declined, nom. Σατανᾶς, gen. Σατανᾶ.   On this account many are disposed to take the word here as in the nominative, and translate the phrase *angel Satan,* i. e. an angel (or messenger) who is Satan.   But inasmuch as Σαταν is at times indeclinable, and as Satan is never in the New Testament called an angel, the great majority of commentators give the same exposition as that given in the English version.   *To buffet me,* ἵνα με κολαφίζῃ, *in order that he* (i. e. the angel or messenger) *may buffet me.*   The use of the present tense seems to imply that "the thorn in the flesh" was a permanent affection under which the apostle continued to suffer. *Lest I should be exalted above measure.* This last clause expresses the design of God in permitting the apostle to be thus afflicted. He carried about with him a continued evidence of his weakness. However much he was exalted, although raised to the third heaven, he could not extract this rankling thorn. And the experience of God's people shows that bodily pain has a special office to perform in the work of sanctification. In the unrenewed its tendency is to exasperate; when self-inflicted its tendency is to debase and fill the soul with grovelling ideas of God and religion, and with low self-conceit. But when inflicted by God on his own children, it more than any thing teaches them their weakness and dependence, and calls upon them to submit when submission is most difficult. Though he slay me, I will trust in him, is the expression of the highest form of faith.

8. 9. For this thing I besought the Lord thrice, that it might depart from me. And he said unto me, My grace is sufficient for thee: for my strength is made perfect in weakness. Most gladly therefore will I rather glory in my infirmities, that the power of Christ may rest upon me.

For this thing, ὑπὲρ τούτου, *in reference to this;* ὑπέρ is here used in the sense of περί. Τούτου may be neuter, *for this thing,* i. e. this affliction; or masculine referring to ἄγγελος, "about this angel or messenger of Satan," &c. This is generally preferred on account of the following clause, ἵνα ἀποστῇ, *that he might depart from me.* I besought the Lord, says the apostle, *thrice.* So our blessed Lord prayed "the third time saying, Let this cup pass from me." Paul was therefore importunate in his petition for deliverance from this sore trial. He says, I besought *the Lord,* that is, Christ, as is clear not only from the general usage of Scripture, but from what follows in v. 9, where he speaks of the "power of Christ." *And he said unto me,* εἴρηκέ μοι. The perfect is used either for the aorist, or in its proper force connecting the past with the present. The answer was not simply something past, but something which continued in its consoling power. Winer, § 41. "He has said;" the answer was ever sounding in the apostle's ears, and not in his ears only, but in those of all his suffering people from that day to this. Each hears the Lord say, *My grace is sufficient for thee*, ἀρκεῖ σοι ἡ χάρις μου. These words should be engraven on the palm of every believer's hand. *My grace*, either, 'my love,' or metonymically, 'the aid of the Holy Spirit,' which is so often meant by the word *grace*. The connection is in favour of the common meaning of the term. 'My love is enough for thee.' These are the words of Christ. He says, to those who seek deliverance from pain and sorrow, 'It is enough that I love you.' This secures and implies all other good. His favour is life; his loving-kindness is better than life. *For my strength is perfected in weakness.* This is given as the reason why the grace or favour of Christ is all-sufficient. That reason is, that his strength is perfected, i. e. clearly revealed as accomplishing its end, in weakness. 'Weakness, in other words, says our Lord, is the condition of my manifesting my strength. The weaker my people are, the more conspicuous is my strength in sustaining and delivering them.' *Most gladly therefore will I rather glory in my infirmities.* The sense is not, 'I will glory in infirmities rather than in other things,' as though Paul had written μᾶλλον ἐν ταῖς ασθενείαις, but, 'I will rather glory in infirmities than seek deliverance.' If Paul's sufferings were to be the occasion of the manifestation of Christ's glory, he rejoiced in suffering. This he did ἡδίστα, *most sweetly*, with an acquiescence delightful to himself. His sufferings thus became the source of the purest and highest pleasure. Καυχάομαι ἐν ταῖς ἀσθενείαις does not mean *I glory in the midst of infirmities*, but *on account of* them. See 5, 12. 10, 15. Rom. 2, 23, &c., &c. This rejoicing on account of his sufferings, or those things which implied his weakness and dependence, was not a fanatical feeling, it had a rational and sufficient basis, viz., *that the power of Christ may rest upon me.* The word is ἐπισκηνώσῃ, *may pitch its tent upon me;* i. e. dwell in me as in a tent, as the shechinah dwelt of old in the tabernacle. To be made thus the dwelling-place of the power of Christ, where he reveals his glory, was a rational ground of rejoicing in those infirmities which were the condition of his presence and the occasion for the manifestation of his power. Most Christians are satisfied in trying to be resigned under suffering. They think it a great thing if they can bring themselves to submit to be the dwelling-place of Christ's power. To rejoice in their afflictions because thereby Christ is glorified, is more than they aspire to. Paul's experience was far above that standard. The power of Christ is not only thus manifested in the weakness of his people, but in the means which he employs for the accomplishment of his purposes. These are in all cases in themselves utterly inadequate and disproportionate to the results to be obtained. The treasure is in earthly vessels that the excellency of the power may be of God. By the foolishness of preaching he saves those who believe. By twelve illiterate men the church was established and extended over the civilized world. By a few missionaries heathen lands are converted into Christian countries. So in all cases, the power of Christ is perfected in weakness. We have in this passage a clear exhibition of the religious life of the apostle, and the most convincing proof that he lived in communion with Christ as God. To him he looked as to his supreme, omnipresent, all-sufficient Lord for deliverance from "the thorn in the flesh," from the buffetings of the messenger of Satan, under which he had so grievously suffered. To him he prayed. From him he received the answer to his prayer. That answer was the answer of God; it implies divine perfection in him who gave it. To what sufferer would the favour of a creature be sufficient? Who but God can say, "My grace is sufficient for thee?" To Paul it was sufficient. It gave him perfect peace. It not only made him resigned under his afflictions, but enabled him to rejoice in them. That Christ should be glorified was to him an end for which any human being might feel it an honour to suffer. It is therefore most evident that the piety of the apostle, his inward spiritual life, had Christ for its object. It was on him his religious affections terminated; to him the homage of his supreme love, confidence and devotion was rendered. Christianity is not merely the religion which Christ taught; but it is, subjectively considered, the religion of which Christ is the source and the object.

10. Therefore I take pleasure in infirmities, in reproaches, in necessities, in persecutions, in distresses for Christ's sake: for when I am weak, then am I strong.

The difference between glorying in infirmities and taking pleasure in them, is that the former phrase expresses the outward manifestation of the feeling expressed by the latter.

He gloried in infirmities when he boasted of them, that is, referred to them as things which reflected honour on him and were to him a source of joy. As they were thus the occasions of manifesting the power of Christ, Paul was pleased with them and was glad that he was subjected to them. *Infirmities* is a general term, including every thing in our condition, whether moral or physical, which is an evidence or manifestation of weakness. From the context it is plain that the reference is here to sufferings, of which reproaches, necessities, persecutions and distresses were different forms. *For Christ's sake.* These words belong to all the preceding terms. It was in the sufferings, whether reproaches, necessities, persecutions or distresses, endured for Christ's sake, that the apostle took pleasure. Not in suffering in itself considered, not in self-inflicted sufferings, nor in those which were the consequences of his own folly or evil dispositions, but in sufferings endured for Christ's sake, or considered as the condition of the manifestation of his power. *For when I am weak, then am I strong.* When really weak in ourselves, and conscious of that weakness, we are in the state suited to the manifestation of the power of God. When emptied of ourselves we are filled with God. Those who think they can change their own hearts, atone for their own sins, subdue the power of evil in their own souls or in the souls of others, who feel able to sustain themselves under affliction, God leaves to their own resources. But when they feel and acknowledge their weakness he communicates to them divine strength.

11. I am become a fool in glorying; ye have compelled me: for I ought to have been commended of you: for in nothing am I behind the very chiefest apostles, though I be nothing.

I am become a fool, &c. This some understand as ironically said, because the self-vindication contained in what precedes was not an act of folly, although it might be so regarded by Paul's opposers. It is more natural, and more in keeping with the whole context, to understand the words as expressing the apostle's own feelings. Self-laudation is folly. It was derogatory to the apostle's dignity, and painful to his feelings, but he was forced to submit to it. And, therefore, in his case and under the circumstances, although humiliating, it was right. *Ye have compelled me.* It was their conduct which made it necessary for the apostle to commend himself. This is explained in the following clause. *For I ought to have been commended of you.* If they had done their duty in vindicating him from the aspersions of the false teachers, there would have been no necessity for him to vindicate himself. They were bound thus to vindicate him, *for in nothing was he behind the very chiefest apostles.* It is an imperative duty resting on all who have the opportunity to vindicate the righteous. For us to sit silent when aspersions are cast upon good men, or when their character and services are undervalued, is to make ourselves partakers of the guilt of detraction. The Corinthians were thus guilty under aggravating circumstances; because the evidences of Paul's apostleship and of his fidelity were abundant. He came behind in no one respect the very chief of the apostles. Besides this they were not only the witnesses of the signs of his divine mission, but they were the recipients of the blessings of that mission. For them therefore to fail to vindicate his claims and services was an ungrateful and cowardly dereliction of duty. By the chief of the apostles, still more clearly here than in 11, 5, are to be understood the most prominent among the true apostles, as Peter, James, and John, who in Gal. 2, 9 are called pillars. Neither here nor in 11, 5 is it an ironical designation of the false teachers. *Though I be nothing.* The apostle felt that what was the effect of the grace, or free gift of God, was no ground of self-complacency or self-exaltation. 1 Cor. 4, 7. 15, 8–10. There were therefore united in him a deep sense of his own unworthiness and impotence, with the conviction and consciousness of being full of knowledge, grace and power, by the indwelling of the Holy Ghost.

12. Truly the signs of an apostle were wrought among you in all patience, in signs, and wonders, and mighty deeds.

This is the proof that he did not come behind the chief apostles. *Truly ;* μέν, to which no δέ answers. The opposition is plain from the connection. 'The signs *indeed* of an apostle were wrought among you, *but* you did not acknowledge them.' So Rückert, De Wette, and others. *The signs of an apostle* were the insignia of the apostleship; those things which by divine appointment were made the evidence of a mission from God. When these were present an obligation rested on all who witnessed them to acknowledge the authority of those who bore those insignia. When they were absent, it was, on the one hand, an act of sacrilege to claim the apostleship; and, on the other, an act of apostacy from God to admit its possession. To acknowledge the claims of those who said they were apostles and were not, was (and is) to turn from God to the creature, to receive as divine what was in fact human or Satanic. This is evidently Paul's view of the matter, as appears from 11, 13–15, where he speaks of those who were the ministers of Satan and yet claimed to be the apostles of Christ. Comp. Rev. 2, 2. These signs of an apostle, as we learn from Scripture, were of different kinds. Some consisted in the manifestations of the inward gifts of the apostleship (i. e. of those gifts the possession of which constituted a man an apostle); such as plenary knowledge of the gospel derived by immediate revelation from Jesus Christ, Gal. 1, 12. 1 Cor. 15, 3; inspiration, or that influence of the Holy Spirit which rendered its possessor infallible in the communication of the truth, 1 Cor. 2, 10–13. 12, 8, in connection with 12, 29 and 14, 37. Others of these signs consisted in the external manifestations of God's favour sanctioning the claim to the apostleship, Gal. 2, 8. To this class belongs fidelity in teaching the truth, or conformity to the authenticated standard of faith, Gal. 1, 8. 9. Unless a man was thus kept faithful to the gospel, no matter what other evidence of being an apostle he might be able to adduce, he was to be regarded as accursed. Gal. 1, 8. To this class also belong, success in preaching the gospel, 1 Cor. 9, 2. 2 Cor. 3, 2. 3; the power of communicating the Holy Ghost by the imposition of hands, Acts 8, 18. 19, 6; the power of working miracles, as appears from the passage under consideration, from Rom. 15, 18. 19, and many other passages, as Heb. 2, 4. Mark 14, 20. Acts 5, 12. 14, 3; and a holy walk and conversation, 2 Cor. 6, 4. Without these signs no man can be recognized and obeyed as an apostle without apostacy from God; without turning from the true apostles to those who are the ministers of Satan. *In all patience,* or constancy. This does not mean that the patient endurance of severe trials was one of the signs of his apostleship, but that those signs were wrought out under adverse circumstances requiring the exercise of the greatest constancy. *In signs, and wonders, and mighty deeds.* These are different designations for the same thing. Miracles are called *signs* in reference to their design, which is to confirm the divine mission of those who perform them; *wonders* because of the effect which they produced; and *mighty deeds* (δυνάμεις) because they are manifestations of divine power.

13. For what is it wherein ye were inferior to other churches, except (it be) that I myself was not burdensome to you? forgive me this wrong.

For. The connection indicated by this particle is with the assertion in v. 12. 'I am not inferior to the chief apostles, for you are not behind other churches.' The fact that the churches founded by Paul were as numerous, as well furnished with gifts and graces, as those founded by the other apostles, was a proof that he was their equal. In other words, as it is said Gal. 2, 8, "He that wrought effectually in Peter to the apostleship of the circumcision, the same was mighty in me towards the gentiles." Comp. 1 Cor. 1, 5–7. *Were ye inferior to other churches*, literally, less, or weaker than. The verb ἡττάομαι (from ἥττων, *less*) has a comparative sense, and therefore is followed by ὑπέρ, *beyond;* 'weak beyond other churches.' The only distinction to the disadvantage of the Corinthians was, that the apostle had refused to accept aid from them. This is not to be regarded as a sarcasm, or as a reproach. It was said in a tone of tenderness, as is plain from what follows. *Forgive me this wrong*. It was, apparently, a reflection on the Corinthians; it seemed to imply a want of confidence in their liberality or love, that Paul refused to receive from them what he willingly received from other churches. In the preceding chapter he endeavoured to convince them that his doing so was no proof of his want of affection to them, or of his want of confidence in their love to him. His conduct in this matter had other and sufficient reasons, reasons which constrained him to persist in this course of conduct, however painful to him and to them.

14. Behold, the third time I am ready to come to you; and I will not be burdensome to you: for I seek not yours, but you. For the children ought not to lay up for the parents, but the parents for the children.

The Acts of the Apostles mention but one visit of Paul to Corinth prior to the date of this epistle. From this passage, as well as from 2, 1 and 13, 1. 2, it is plain that he had already been twice in that city. The words, therefore, *the third time*, in this verse, belong to the word *come*, and not to *I am ready*. The sense is not, 'I am the third time ready,' but, 'I am ready to come the third time.' His purpose was to act on this third visit on the same principle which had controlled his conduct on the two preceding occasions. *I will not be burdensome to you*, I will receive nothing from you. For this he gives two reasons, both not only consistent with his love for them, but proofs of his love. *For I seek not yours, but you.* This is the first reason. He had no mercenary or selfish ends to accomplish. It was not their money, but their souls he desired to win. *For the children ought not to lay up for the parents, but the parents for the children.* This was the second reason. He stood to them in the relation of a parent. In the course of nature, it was the parent's office to provide for the children, and not the children for the parent. You must allow me, says Paul, a parent's privilege. Thus gracefully and tenderly does the apostle reconcile a seemingly ungracious act with the kind feelings which he cherished in himself and desired to excite in them.

15. And I will very gladly spend and be spent for you; though the more abundantly I love you, the less I be loved.

As I am your father, I will gladly act as such, spend and be spent for you; even though I forfeit your love by acting in a way which love forces me to act. This is the strongest expression of disinterested affection. Paul was willing not only to give his property but himself, his life and strength, for them (literally, *for your souls*, ὑπὲρ τῶν ψυχῶν ὑμῶν), not only without a recompense, but at the cost of their love.

16. But be it so, I did not burden you: nevertheless, being crafty, I caught you with guile.

Be it so ; that is, admitted that I did not personally burden you, yet (you may say) I craftily did it through others. This was designed to meet the ungenerous objection which the false teachers might be disposed to make. They might insinuate that although he refused to receive any thing himself, he quartered his friends upon them, or spoiled them through others. *I caught you with guile*, δόλῳ ὑμᾶς ἔλαβον, i. e. I despoiled you by artifice, as an animal is taken by being deceived. This shows the character of the opponents of the apostle in Corinth. That he should think it necessary to guard against insinuations so ungenerous and so unfounded, is proof of his wisdom in refusing to give such antagonists the least occasion to question the purity of his motives.

17. 18. **Did I make a gain of you by any of them whom I sent unto you? I desired Titus, and with (him) I sent a brother. Did Titus make a gain of you? walked we not in the same spirit? (walked we) not in the same steps?**

The best refutation of the insinuation that Paul did in an underhand way by others what he refused to do openly and in his own person, was an appeal to facts. The Corinthians knew the charge to be unfounded. They knew that no one of those whom Paul had sent to Corinth received any compensation at their hands. This was specially true in the case of Titus, his immediate representative. All his messengers followed the example, and doubtless the injunctions of Paul, in bearing their own expenses. The mission of Titus to Corinth here referred to, is not that mentioned in chap. 8, which was not yet accomplished, but that mentioned in chap. 7, designed to ascertain the effect produced by Paul's previous letter. *In the same spirit;* either the same inward disposition of mind, or *with* the same Holy Spirit, i. e. imbued and guided by the same divine agent, who controls the conduct of the people of God. *In the same steps.* Paul and his messengers walked in the same footsteps. That is, they all followed Christ, whose steps mark the way in which his followers are to tread.

19. **Again, think ye that we excuse ourselves unto you? we speak before God in Christ: but (we do) all things, dearly beloved, for your edifying.**

There were two false impressions which the apostle here

designs to correct. First, that he felt himself accountable to the Corinthians, or that they were the judges at whose bar he was defending himself. Second, that his object was in any respect personal or selfish. He spoke before God, not before them; for their edification, not for his own reputation.

Again think ye. Do you again think, as you have thought before. Instead of πάλιν, *again*, the MSS. D, E, J, K read πάλαι, *formerly, long*. This reading is adopted by the majority of modern editors. The sense then is, 'Ye are long of the opinion,' or, 'Ye have long thought.' Comp. εἰ πάλαι ἐπέθανεν, *whether he had been long dead*, in Mark 15, 44. The common reading has so much MSS. authority in its favour, and it gives so good a sense, that it is generally by the older editors and commentators retained. With πάλιν the passage is best read interrogatively. Do ye again think? as they had before done. See 3, 1. 5, 12. They were too much disposed to think that the apostle, like the false teachers, was anxious to commend himself to their favour, and to appeal to them as his judges. He on more occasions than one gives them to understand that he was not under their authority, his office was not received from their hands, and he was not accountable to them for the manner in which he exercised it. See 1 Cor. 4, 3. *Excuse ourselves unto you; ὑμῖν, before you as judges. Excuse, ἀπολογέομαι, to talk oneself off, to plead*, or *answer for oneself.* This was not the position which the apostle occupied. He was not an offender, real or supposed, arraigned at their bar. On the contrary, as he says, *we speak before God;* i. e. as responsible to him, and as in his presence; *in Christ*, i. e. as it becomes one conscious of his union with the Lord Jesus. In all his self-vindication he considers himself as a Christian speaking in the presence of God, to whom alone he was, as a divinely commissioned messenger, answerable for what he said. *All things, dearly beloved, for your edification.* This is the second point. His apology, or self-vindication, had their good, not his reputation or advantage, for its object.

20. For I fear, lest, when I come, I shall not find you such as I would, and (that) I shall be found unto you such as ye would not: lest (there be) debates, envyings, wraths, strifes, backbitings, whisperings, swellings, tumults.

He aimed at their edification, *for* he feared their state was not what he could desire. He feared lest they would not be acceptable to him, nor he to them. What he feared was that the evils to which frequent reference had already been made, should be found still to exist. Those evils were, ἔρεις, *contentions*, such as existed between the different factions into which the church was divided, some saying we are of Paul, others, we are of Cephas, &c., see 1 Cor. 1, 11 ; *envyings*, ζῆλοι, those feelings of jealousy and alienation which generally attend contentions ; θυμοί, *outbreaks of anger ;* ἐριθεῖαι, *cabals.* The word is from ἔριθος, *a hireling,* and is often used of a factious spirit of party ; καταλαλιαὶ and ψιθυρισμοί, backbiting and whisperings, i. e. open detractions and secret calumnies ; φυσιώσεις, *swellings,* i. e. manifestations of pride and insolence ; ἀκαταστασίαι, *tumults,* i. e. those disorders which necessarily follow the state of things above described. This is a formidable list of evils, and it seems hard to reconcile what is here said with the glowing description of the repentance and obedience of the church found in the preceding part of this epistle, especially in chapter 7. To account for this discrepancy some suppose, as before mentioned, that the latter part of this epistle, from ch. 10 to the end, formed a distinct letter written at a different time and under different circumstances from those under which the former part was written. Others, admitting that the two portions are one and the same epistle sent at the same time, still assume that a considerable interval of time elapsed between the writing of the former and latter parts of the letter ; and that during that interval intelligence had reached the apostle that the evils prevailing in the church had not been so thoroughly corrected as he had hoped. The common and sufficient explanation of the difficulty is, that part of the congregation, probably the majority, were penitent and obedient, while another part were just the opposite. When the apostle had the one class in view he used the language of commendation ; when the other, the language of censure. Examples of this kind are abundant in his epistles. The first part of his first epistle to the Corinthians is full of the strongest expressions of praise, but in what follows severe reproof fills most of its pages.

21. (And) lest, when I come again, my God will humble me among you, and (that) I shall bewail many

which have sinned already, and have not repented of the uncleanness, and fornication, and lasciviousness, which they have committed.

The same apprehension expressed under a different form. The word *again* may belong to *coming*, "me coming again;" or with *will humble*, "God will humble me again." This implies that during his second unrecorded visit, Paul was humbled by what he saw in Corinth, and grieved, as he says, 2, 1, in having to use severity in suppressing prevalent disorders. He feared lest his third should prove like that painful second visit. The more obvious and natural connection, however, of πάλιν is with ἐλθόντα, as in our version. 'Lest God will humble me when I come again.' Nothing filled the apostles with greater delight than to see the churches of their care steadfast in faith and in obedience to the truth; and nothing so pained and humbled them as the departure of their disciples from the paths of truth and holiness. Humble me *among you;* πρὸς ὑμᾶς, *in relation to you.*

And that I shall bewail, πενθήσω. The word πενθέω is here used transitively; to mourn any one, to grieve for him. Many suppose that the sorrow here intended was that which arises from the necessity of punishing; so that the idea really intended is, 'I fear I shall have to discipline (or excommunicate) some, &c.' But this, to say the least, is not necessary. All that the words or context requires is, that Paul dreaded having to mourn over many impenitent members of the church. *Many which have sinned already and have not repented,* πολλοὺς τῶν προημαρτηκότων καὶ μὴ μετανοησάντων, *many of those who having sinned shall not have repented.* The προ in προημαρτηκότων is probably not to be pressed, so as to make the word refer to those who had sinned *before* some specific time,—as their profession of Christianity, or Paul's previous visit. The force of the preposition is sufficiently expressed by the word *heretofore.* 'Those who have heretofore sinned.' What Paul feared, was, that when he got to Corinth he should find that many of those who had sinned, had not joined in the repentance for which he commended the congregation as a whole. *Of the uncleanness, &c., which they committed.* According to Meyer, ἐπὶ τῇ ἀκαθαρσίᾳ, κ.τ.λ., are to be connected with πενθήσω, 'I shall lament many on account of the uncleanness, &c.' The position of the words is evidently in favour of the common construction. 'Who have not repented con-

cerning the uncleanness they have committed.' The classes
of sins most prevalent in Corinth were those referred to in v.
20, arising out of the collisions of the different classes or parties in the church; and those here mentioned, arising out of
the corruptions of the age and of the community. To make
a holy church out of heathen, and in the midst of heathenism,
was impossible to any but an almighty arm. And we know
that in the work of sanctification of the individual or of a
community, even Omnipotence works gradually. The early
Christians were babes in Christ, much like the converts from
among the heathen in modern times.

CHAPTER XIII.

Threatening of punishment to impenitent offenders; exhortation to self-examination and amendment; conclusion of the epistle.

Paul's warnings and exhortations.

HAVING previously admonished and warned, he now distinctly
announces his purpose to exercise his apostolic power in the
punishment of offenders, vs. 1. 2. As they sought evidence
of his apostleship, he would show that although weak in himself, he was invested with supernatural power by Christ. As
Christ appeared as weak in dying, but was none the less imbued with divine power, as was proved by his resurrection
from the dead; so the apostle in one sense was weak, in another full of power, vs. 3. 4. Instead of exposing themselves
to this exercise of judicial authority, he exhorts them to try
themselves, since Christ lived in them unless they were reprobates, v. 5. He trusted that they would acknowledge him as
an apostle, as he sought their good, vs. 6. 7. His power was
given, and could be exercised, only for the truth. He rejoiced in his own weakness and in the prosperity of the Corinthians. The object in thus warning them was to avoid the
necessity of exercising the power of judgment with which
Christ had invested him, vs. 8–10. Concluding exhortation
and benediction, vs. 11–13.

1. This is the third (time) I am coming to you: In the mouth of two or three witnesses shall every word be established.

From this it is evident that Paul had already been twice in Corinth. He was about to make his third visit. Those who do not admit that he went to Corinth during the interval between the writing the first and second epistle, say that all that is proved by this verse, is that "once he had been there; a second time he had intended to come; now the third time he was actually coming." Others, still more unnaturally, say he refers to his presence by letter, as Beza explains it: Binas suas epistolas pro tolidem profectionibus recenset. There is no necessity for departing from the obvious meaning of the words. The Acts of the Apostles do not contain a full record of all the journeys, labours and sufferings of the apostle. He may have visited Corinth repeatedly without its coming within the design of that book to mention the fact. *In the mouth of two or three witnesses, &c.* It was expressly enjoined in the Old Testament that no one should be condemned unless on the testimony of two or three witnesses. Num. 35, 30. Deut. 17, 6. 19, 15. In this latter passage, the very words used by the apostle are to be found: "One man shall not rise up against any man for any iniquity, or for any sin, in any sin that he sinneth; at the mouth of two witnesses, or at the mouth of three witnesses, shall the matter be established." This principle of justice was transferred by our Lord to the New Dispensation. In his directions for dealing with offenders he says, "Take with thee one or two more, that in the mouth of two or three witnesses every word shall be established," Matt. 18, 16; see also John 8, 17. Heb. 10, 28. In 1 Tim. 5, 19 the apostle applies the rule specially to the case of elders: "Against an elder receive not an accusation, but before two or three witnesses." In the judgment of God, therefore, it is better that many offenders should go unpunished through lack of testimony, than that the security of reputation and life should be endangered by allowing a single witness to establish a charge against any man. This principle, although thus plainly and repeatedly sanctioned both in the Old and New Testaments, is not held sacred in civil courts. Even in criminal cases the testimony of one witness is often considered sufficient to establish the guilt of an accused person, no matter how pure his previous reputation may have

been. Paul here announces his determination to adhere, in
the administration of discipline, strictly to the rule relating to
testimony laid down in the Scriptures. There are two explanations, however, given of this passage. Some suppose that
Paul merely alludes to the prescription in the Law, and says
that his three visits answers the spirit of the divine injunction
by being equivalent to the testimony of three witnesses. Tres
mei adventus trium testimoniorum loco erunt, says Calvin.
This interpretation is adopted by a great many commentators,
ancient and modern. But the formality with which the principle is announced, the importance of the principle itself, and
his own recognition of it elsewhere, show that he intended to
adhere to it in Corinth. Three visits are not the testimony
of three witnesses. *Every word*, πᾶν ῥῆμα, *every accusation*,
a sense which, agreeably to the usage of the corresponding
Hebrew word, the Greek word ῥῆμα has here in virtue of the
context, as in Matt. 5, 11. 18, 16. 27, 14. *Shall be established*, i. e. legally and conclusively proved.

2. I told you before, and foretell you, as if I were
present, the second time; and being absent now I
write to them which heretofore have sinned, and to all
other, that, if I come again, I will not spare.

The meaning of this verse is doubtful. The words *second
time* (τὸ δεύτερον,) may be connected with *being present* (ὡς
παρών,) or with *I foretell* (προλέγω). If the former, the sense
may be, "I foretold (i. e. when in Corinth), and I foretell, as
though present the second time, although yet absent, to those
who heretofore have sinned, &c." If the latter connection be
preferred, the sense is, "I foretold you, and foretell you the
second time, as if present, although now absent, &c." This
is not consistent with the natural order of the words. Assuming Paul to have been already twice in Corinth, the simplest
explanation of this verse is that given by Calvin, Meyer,
Rückert, and others, "I have said before, and say before, as
when present the second time, so now when absent, to those
who have sinned, I will not spare." Paul gives now when
absent the same warning that he gave during his second visit.
The words προεῖπον and προλέγω are combined here as in Gal.
5, 21 and 1 Thess. 3, 4. "I said before, and I forewarn."
Those who heretofore have sinned; προημαρτηκόσι, to those

who sinned before, not before Paul's second visit, but those who heretofore have sinned, i. e. those who already stand in the category of known sinners, and *to all other*, i. e. to those who were not thus known, who had not as yet offended. *If I come again* (εἰς τὸ πάλιν), *I will not spare*. Paul had forborne long enough, and he was now determined to try the effect of discipline on those whom his arguments and exhortations failed to render obedient. From this, as well as from other passages of Paul's epistles, two things are abundantly manifest. First, the right of excommunication in the church. It is only in established churches controlled by the state, or thoroughly imbued with Erastian principles, that this right is seriously questioned, or its exercise precluded. In his former epistle, chap. 5, the apostle had enjoined on the Corinthians the duty of casting out of their communion those who openly violated the law of Christ. The second thing here rendered manifest, is, that the apostle as an individual possessed the right of excommunication. The apostolic churches were not independent democratic communities, vested with supreme authority over their own members. Paul could cast out of their communion whom he would. He was indeed clothed with supernatural power which enabled him to deliver offenders "unto Satan for the destruction of the flesh," 1 Cor. 5, 5, but this was not all. This presupposed the power of excommunication. It was the ability miraculously to punish with corporeal evils those whom he cut off from the church. This right to discipline, as it is not to be merged into the supernatural gift just referred to; so it is not to be referred to the inspiration and consequent infallibility of the apostles. The apostles were infallible as teachers, but not as men or as disciplinarians. They received unrenewed men into the church, as in the case of Simon Magus. They did not pretend to read the heart, much less to be omniscient. Paul proposed to arrive at the knowledge of offences by judicial examination. He avowed his purpose to condemn no one on his own judgment or knowledge, but only on the testimony of two or three witnesses. This right to exercise discipline which Paul claimed was not founded on his miraculous gifts, but on his ministerial office.

3. Since ye seek a proof of Christ speaking in me, which to you-ward is not weak, but is mighty in you.

This is part of the sentence begun in v. 2. 'I will not spare since ye seek a proof of Christ speaking in me.' Olshausen says the sense of the context is, 'Since they wished to put the apostle to the test and see whether Christ was in him, they had better try themselves and see whether Christ was in them. If Christ was in them, they would recognize the power of God in the apostle's weakness.' This supposes v. 4 to be a parenthesis, and connects ἐπεὶ δοκιμὴν ζητεῖτε of v. 3, with ἑαυτοὺς δοκιμάζετε of v. 5. But this is arbitrary and unnatural, as it is unnecessary, there being no indication of want of continuity in the connection. *A proof of Christ*, may mean, 'a proof which Christ gives,' or, 'a proof that Christ speaks in me.' De Wette and Meyer prefer the former, on account of the following, 'who is not weak,' which agrees better with the assumption that Χριστοῦ is the genitive of the subject. 'Since ye seek a proof or manifestation of Christ who speaks in me, who is not weak.' Calvin's idea is that it was not Paul, but Christ, that the Corinthians were questioning. "It is Christ who speaks in me; when therefore you question my doctrine, it is not me, but him whom you offend." He refers to Num. 16, 11, where murmuring against Moses and Aaron is represented as murmuring against God. Compare also Isaiah 7, 13. The common interpretation, however, is more in keeping with the drift of the whole context. What the false teachers and their adherents denied, was Paul's apostleship; what they demanded was proof that Christ spoke in him, or that he was a messenger of Christ. Since the evidence which he had already given in word and deed had not satisfied them, he was about to give them a proof which they would find it difficult to resist. *Who is not weak as concerns you, but is mighty among you.* The messenger and organ of Christ was not to be rejected or offended with impunity, since Christ was not weak, but powerful. His power had been proved among them not only in the conversion of multitudes, but by signs and wonders, and by divers manifestations of omnipotence.

4. For though he was crucified through weakness, yet he liveth by the power of God. For we also are weak in him, but we shall live with him by the power of God toward you.

Christ is divinely powerful, for though he died as a man, he lives as God. He had a feeble human nature, but also an omnipotent divine nature. So we his apostles, though in one aspect weak, in another are strong. We are associated with Christ both in his weakness and in his power; in his death and in his life. *For though.* The text is doubtful. The common edition has καὶ γὰρ εἰ, *for even if,* which the Vulgate renders *etsi* and the English version *although,* taking καὶ εἰ (*even if*) as equivalent to εἰ καί, *if even.* Many MSS. and editors omit the εἰ. The sense then is, 'For he was even crucified through weakness.' The common text gives a clear meaning, 'For *even if* he were crucified through weakness.' The case is hypothetically presented. *Through weakness,* ἐκ ἀσθενείας. His weakness was the cause or necessary condition and evidence of his death; not of course as implying that his death was not voluntary, for our Lord said he laid down his life of himself; but the assumption of a weak human nature liable to death, was of course necessary, in order that the eternal Son of God should be capable of death. Comp. Phil. 2, 9. Heb. 2, 14, 15. His death, therefore, was the evidence of weakness, in the sense of having a weak, or mortal nature. *Yet he liveth by the power of God.* The same person who died, now lives. That complex person, having a perfect human and a true divine nature hypostatically united, rose from the dead, and lives forever, and therefore can manifest the divine power which the apostle attributed to him. The resurrection of Christ is sometimes referred to God, as in Rom. 6, 4. Eph. 1, 20. Phil. 2, 9; sometimes to himself, as in Matt. 26, 61. Mark 14, 58. John 2, 19. 10, 18. This is done on the same principle that the works of creation and providence are referred sometimes to the Father and sometimes to the Son. That principle is the unity of the divine nature, or the identity of the persons of the Trinity as to essence. They are the same in substance, and therefore the works *ad extra* of the one are the works of the others also. It is not, however, the fact that the resurrection of Christ was effected by the power of God, but the fact that he is now alive and clothed with divine power, that the apostle urges as pertinent to his object. *For we also,* &c. The connection of this clause may be with the immediately preceding one, 'Christ liveth by the power of God, *for* we live.' The life which the apostle possessed and manifested being derived from Christ, was proof that Christ still lived. Or the connection is with the close of the

preceding verse. 'Christ is powerful among you, 1. Because
though he died as a man, he lives; and 2. Because though we
are weak, we are strong in him.' In either way the sense is
substantially the same. In what sense does the apostle here
speak of himself as weak? It is not a moral weakness, for it
is conditioned by his communion with Christ; *we are weak
in him*. It is not subjection to those sufferings which were a
proof of weakness and are therefore called *infirmities;* because the context does not call for any reference to the apostle's sufferings. Nor does it mean a weakness in the estimation of others, i. e. that he was despised. It is obviously
antithetical to the strength or power of which he was a
partaker; and as the power which he threatened to exercise
and demonstrate was the power to punish, so the weakness
of which he speaks was the absence of the manifestation of
that power. He in Christ, that is, in virtue of his fellowship
with Christ, was when in Corinth weak and forbearing, as
though he had no power to vindicate his authority; just as
Christ was weak in the hands of his enemies when they led
him away to be crucified. But as Christ's weakness was
voluntary, as there rested latent in the suffering Lamb of God
the resources of almighty power; so in the meek, forbearing
apostle was the plenitude of supernatural power which he derived from his ascended master. *We shall live with him.*
"Vitam," says Calvin, "opponit infirmitati: ideoque hoc
nomine florentem et plenum dignitatis statum intelligit." As
the life of Christ subsequent to his resurrection was a state in
which he assumed the exercise and manifestation of the power
inherent in him as the Son of God, so the life of which Paul
here speaks, was the state in which he manifested the apostolic
power with which he was invested. There is no reference to
the future or eternal life of which Paul, as a believer, was hereafter to partake. He is vindicating the propriety of his de-
nunciation of chastisement to the disobedient in Corinth.
Though he had been among them as weak and forbearing,
yet he would manifest that he was alive in the sense of having
power to enforce his commands. *By the power of God.*
Paul's power was a manifestation of the power of God. It
was derived from God. It was not his own either in its
source or in its exercise. He could do nothing, as he afterwards says, against the truth. *Toward you;* i. e. *we shall
live toward you.* We shall exercise our authority, or manifest
our apostolic life and power in relation to you.

5. Examine yourselves, whether ye be in the faith; prove your own selves. Know ye not your own selves, how that Jesus Christ is in you, except ye be reprobates?

There are two links of association between this verse and what precedes. They had been trying the apostle, seeking proof of Christ speaking in him. He tells them they had better examine themselves and see whether Christ was in them. Hence the antithesis between ἑαυτοὺς (yourselves) placed before the verb for the sake of emphasis, and δοκιμὴν ζητεῖτε (ye seek a proof, &c.) of v. 3. 'Ye would prove me—prove yourselves.' Another idea, however, and perhaps a more important one is this, 'Ye seek a proof of Christ speaking in me, seek it in yourselves. Know ye not that Christ is in you (unless you be reprobates), and if he is in you, if you are really members of his body, ye will know that he is in me.' The passage in this view is analogous to those in which the apostle appeals to the people as seals of his ministry, 1 Cor. 9, 1, and as his letters of commendation, 3, 2. *To examine* and *to prove* mean the same thing. Both express the idea of trying or putting to the test to ascertain the nature or character of the person or thing tried. *Whether ye be in the faith*, that is, whether you really have faith, or are Christians only in name. This exhortation to self-examination supposes, on the one hand, that faith is self-manifesting, that it reveals itself in the consciousness and by its fruits; and, on the other hand, that it may exist and be genuine and yet not be known as true faith by the believer himself. Only what is doubtful needs to be determined by examination. The fact, therefore, that we are commanded to examine ourselves to see whether we are in the faith, proves that a true believer may doubt of his good estate. In other words, it proves that assurance is not essential to faith. Calvin, in his antagonism to the Romish doctrine that assurance is unattainable in this life, and that all claims to it are unscriptural and fanatical, draws the directly opposite conclusion from this passage. Hic locus, he says, valet ad probandam fidei certitudinem, quam nobis Sorbonici sophistæ labefactarunt, imo penitus exterminarunt ex hominum animis: temeritatis damnant, quotquot persuasi sunt se esse Christi membra, et illum habere in se manentem; nam morali quam vocant, conjectura, hoc est, sola opinione contentos esse

nos jubent, ut conscientiæ perpetuo suspensæ hæreant ac
perplexæ. Quid autem hic Paulus? reprobos esse testatur
quicunque dubitant an possideant Christum, et sint ex illius
corpore. Quare sit nobis hæc sola recta fides, quæ facit ut
tuto, neque dubia opinione, sed stabili constantique certitudi-
ne, in gratia Dei acquiescamus. Elsewhere, however, Calvin
teaches a different doctrine, in so far as he admits that true
believers are often disturbed by serious doubts and inward
conflicts. See his Institutes, Lib. iii. cap. ii. 17, and Lib. iv.
cap. xiv. 7. 8.

Know ye not your own selves how that Christ is in you.
This version overlooks the connecting particle ἤ (*or*), the force
of which indeed it is not easy to see. It may be that the
apostle designed in these words to shame or to rouse them.
'Examine yourselves, *or* are you so besotted or ignorant as
not to know that Christ is in you; that some thing is to be
discovered by self-examination, unless ye are no Christians at
all.' It may, however, be a direct appeal to the consciousness
of his readers. 'Do you not recognize in yourselves, that is,
are ye not conscious, that Christ is in you.' The construction
in this clause is analogous to that in 1 Cor. 14, 37 and 16, 15.
'Know yourselves that, &c.,' equivalent to 'know that.'
Winer 63, 3. The expression *Christ is in you*, does not mean
'Christ is among you as a people.' It refers to an indwelling
of Christ in the individual believer, as is plain from such passages as Gal. 2, 20, "Christ liveth in me," and Gal. 4, 19.
Rom. 8, 10. Christ dwells in his people by his Spirit. The
presence of the Spirit is the presence of Christ. This is not a
mere figurative expression, as when we say we have a friend
in our heart—but a real truth. The Spirit of Christ, the Holy
Ghost, is in the people of God collectively and individually,
the ever-present source of a new kind of life, so that if any
man have not the Spirit of Christ he is none of his. Rom. 8, 9.
Unless ye be reprobates. The word *reprobate*, in its theologi-
cal sense, means one who is judicially abandoned to everlasting perdition. Such is obviously not its sense here, otherwise
all those not now converted would perish forever. The word
is to be taken in its ordinary meaning, *disapproved, unworthy
of approbation.* Any person or thing which cannot stand the
test is ἀδόκιμος. Those therefore in whom Christ does not
dwell cannot stand the test, and are proved to be Christians,
if at all, only in name.

6. But I trust that ye shall know that we are not reprobates.

In v. 3 Paul had said that the Corinthians sought δοκιμήν (evidence) that Christ was in him as an apostle. He exhorted them to seek evidence that he was in them as believers. If they should prove to be (ἀδόκιμος) without evidence, he was satisfied that they would find that he was not ἀδόκιμος. The δοκιμή (or evidence) of Christ speaking in him which he proposed or threatened to give, was the exercise of the apostolic power which resulted from the indwelling of Christ, and therefore proved his presence. He was loath, however, to give that evidence; he would rather be (ἀδόκιμος) without that evidence; and he therefore adds,

7. Now I pray to God that ye do no evil; not that we should appear approved, but that ye should do that which is honest, though we be as reprobates.

Now I pray God that ye do no evil; that is, I pray that ye may not give occasion for me to give the evidence of Christ speaking in me, which I have threatened to give, in case of your continued disobedience. So far from desiring an opportunity of exhibiting my supernatural power, I earnestly desire that there may be no occasion for its exercise. The interpretation which Grotius, and after him Flatt, Billroth, and others give of this clause, 'I pray God that I may do you no evil,' is possible so far as the words are concerned, as ποιῆσαι ὑμᾶς κακόν may mean either, *to do you evil,* or, *that you do evil.* But to do evil is not to punish. And had Paul intended to say, 'I pray God that I may not punish you,' he certainly would have chosen some more suitable expression. Besides, ποιῆσαι κακόν is the opposite of ποιῆτε τὸ καλόν (*ye may do right*) in this same verse. *Not that we should appear approved,* &c. This and the following clause give the reason of the prayer just uttered. The negative statement of that reason comes first. He did not desire their good estate for the selfish reason that he might appear, i. e. stand forth apparent, as δόκιμος (approved), as one concerning whom there could be no doubt that Christ dwelt in him. There were different kinds of evidence of the validity of Paul's claims as a believer and as an apostle; his holy life and multiform labours; signs and wonders; the apostolic power with which he was

clothed; his success in preaching, or the number and character of his converts. The good state of the Corinthian church
was therefore an evidence that he was approved, i. e. could
stand the test. This, however, as he says, was not the reason
why he prayed that they might do no evil. That reason, as
stated positively, was, *that ye should do that which is honest.*
That is, it was their good, and not his own recognition, that
he had at heart. *Do what is honest,* τὸ καλὸν ποιῆτε, that ye
may do the good, the beautiful, what is at once right and
pleasing. *Though we be as reprobates,* ἀδόκιμοι, *without approbation.* Paul was earnestly desirous that the Corinthians
should do what was right, although the consequence was that
he should have no opportunity of giving that δοκιμήν (evidence) of Christ speaking in him which he had threatened to
give, and thus, in that respect, be ἀδόκιμος, *without evidence.*
There is such a play on words in this whole connection that
the sense of the passage is much plainer in the Greek than it
is in the English version. This view of the passage is simple
and suited to the connection, and is commonly adopted.
Calvin and others interpret it more generally and without
specific reference to the connection. "Concerning myself,"
he makes the apostle say, "I am not solicitous; I only fear
lest ye should offend God. I am ready to appear as reprobate, if you are free of offence. Reprobate, I mean, in the
judgment of men, who often reject those who are worthy of
special honour." This is the general sense, but the peculiar
colouring of the passage is thus lost.

8. For we can do nothing against the truth, but
for the truth.

This verse is connected with the last clause of the preceding. 'We shall, in one sense, be ἀδόκιμοι (without evidence)
if you do what is right, *for* we can do nothing against the
truth, but are powerful only for the truth.' That is, 'We can
exercise the apostolic and supernatural power which is the
evidence of Christ speaking in us, only in behalf of the truth.'
By *the truth* is not to be understood moral excellence, or rectitude—a sense indeed which the word ἀλήθεια often has when
antithetical to unrighteousness; nor does it mean judicial rectitude specifically, i. e. that standard to which a judge should
be conformed, or, as Bengel explains it, "the exact authority
to be exercised over the Corinthians;" but it means truth in

its religious, scriptural sense; that revelation which God has made in his word as the rule of our faith and practice. This passage is of special interest as fixing the limits of all ecclesiastical power, whether ordinary or miraculous. The decision of the apostle, if against the truth, availed nothing in the sight of God; the supernatural power with which he was invested forsook his arm, if raised against God's own people. The promise of our Lord, that what the church binds on earth shall be bound in heaven, is limited by the condition that her decisions be in accordance with the truth. The doctrine of the extreme Romish party that acts of discipline are effectual in cutting off from the true church and the communion of God, even *clave errante*, i. e. when the church errs in her knowledge of the facts, is utterly inconsistent with Paul's doctrine. He claimed no such power.

9. For we are glad, when we are weak, and ye are strong : and this also we wish, (even) your perfection.

If connected with the preceding clause the sense of this verse is, ' We can act only for the truth, *for* we have no desire to exercise our power to punish; we are glad when we are weak.' The meaning is better if this verse is regarded as coordinate with verse 8, and subordinate to v. 7. ' We desire that you should do right, though we appear as ἀδόκιμοι (without evidence), for we are glad when we are weak.' That is, we are glad when we have no occasion to exercise or manifest our power to punish. This is evidently the sense in which the word *weak* is to be here taken. It does not mean weak in the estimation of men, that is, despised as unworthy of respect. *And ye are strong*, i. e. such as cannot be overcome. They were strong when they were good. Their goodness was a sure protection from the disciplinary power of the apostle. *This also we wish*, viz. *your perfection*. That is, we are not only glad when you are strong, but we pray for your complete establishment. *Perfection*, κατάρτισις, from καταρτίζω, in the sense *to put in complete order*. Paul prayed that they might be perfectly restored from the state of confusion, contention, and evil into which they had fallen.

10. Therefore I write these things being absent,

lest being present I should use sharpness, according to the power which the Lord hath given me to edification, and not to destruction.

Therefore, i. e. because I desire your good, and because I prefer to appear ἀδόκιμος, *without proof,* so far as the proof of my apostleship consists in the exercise of my power to punish. This is the reason why the apostle wrote these exhortations and warnings, *lest being present I should use sharpness,* i. e. be obliged to exercise severity in dealing with offenders. The expression is ἀποτόμως χρήσωμαι, where ὑμῖν must be supplied, 'lest I should use *you* sharply.' *According to the power.* The word is ἐξουσίαν, which includes the ideas of ability and authority or right. Paul was invested both with the authority to punish offenders and with the power to carry his judgments into effect. *Which the Lord hath given me.* His authority was not self-assumed, and his power was not derived from himself. They were the gifts of the Lord, the only source of either in the church. *The Lord* is of course Christ, whose divine power and omnipresence are taken for granted. Paul everywhere as much assumes that the Lord Jesus is invested with divine attributes and entitled to divine worship, as God himself. Nothing can be more foreign to the whole spirit of the New Testament than the idea, that Christ, having finished his work on earth as a teacher and witness, has passed away so as to be no longer present with his people. The whole Scriptures, on the contrary, assume that he is everywhere present in knowledge and power, the source of all grace, strength and consolation, the object of the religious affections, and of the acts of religious worship. *For edification, and not for destruction.* This not only expresses the design with which Paul was invested and endowed with apostolic power, but it teaches that the power itself could be exercised only for good. Christ would not sanction an unjust decision, or clothe the arm of man with supernatural power to inflict unmerited punishment. The apostles could not strike a saint with blindness nor deliver a child of God unto Satan. The church and its ministers are in the same predicament still. They are powerful only for good. Their mistaken decisions or unrighteous judgments are of no avail. They affect the standing of the true believer in the sight of God no more than the judgments of the Jewish synagogues when they cast out the early disciples as evil. Truth and holiness are a sure defence against all ecclesiastical power. No one can harm us, if we be followers of that which is good. 1 Peter 3, 13.

11. Finally, brethren, farewell. Be perfect, be of good comfort, be of one mind, live in peace; and the God of love and peace shall be with you.

The severe rebukes contained in the preceding chapters, are softened down by the parental and apostolic tone assumed in these concluding verses. He addresses them as brethren, members of the family of God and of the body of Christ. *Farewell*, χαίρετε; literally, *rejoice*, or, *joy to you*. It is used often in salutations, as Hail! On account of what follows it is better to take it as an exhortation to spiritual joy. *Rejoice*, i. e. in the Lord. In Phil. 3, 1 and 4, 4 we have the same exhortation, χαίρετε ἐν κυρίῳ. Joy in redemption, rejoicing in our union and communion with the Lord is one of our highest duties. Blessings so infinite as these should not be received with indifference. Joy is the atmosphere of heaven, and the more we have of it on earth, the more heavenly shall we be in character and temper. *Be perfect*, καρτίζεσθε, *reform yourselves;* correct the evils which prevail within and among you. *Be of good comfort*, παρακαλεῖσθε, which may be rendered, *exhort one another*. This latter interpretation is perhaps preferable, because more distinct from the preceding command. The exhortation to rejoice includes that to be of good comfort. *Be of one mind*, τὸ αὐτὸ φρονεῖτε, be united in faith in feeling, and in object. Cognate with this is the exhortation, *Live in peace*. One of the greatest evils prevailing in Corinth, as we learn from 1 Cor. 1, 10–12, was the contentions of the various parties into which the church was divided. *And the God of love and peace*, i. e. God is the author of love and of peace, *shall be with you*. The existence of love and peace is the condition of the presence of the God of peace. He withdraws the manifestations of his presence from the soul disturbed by angry passions, and from a community torn by dissensions. We have here the familiar Christian paradox. God's presence produces love and peace, and we must have love and peace in order to have his presence. God gives what he commands. God gives, but we must cherish his gifts. His agency does not supersede ours, but mingles with it and becomes one with it in our consciousness. We work

14

out our own salvation, while God works in us. Our duty is
to yield ourselves to the operation of God, and to exert our
faculties as though the effect desired were in our own power,
and leave to his almighty, mystic co-operation its own gracious office. The man with the withered hand, did something when he stretched it forth, although the power to move
was divinely given. It is vain for us to pray for the presence
of the God of love and peace, unless we strive to free our
hearts from all evil passions. *Shall be with you ;* shall manifest his presence, his glory and his love. This gives perfect
peace, and fills the soul with joy unspeakable and full of glory.
It is the restoration of the original and normal relation between God and the soul, and secures at once its purification
and blessedness. He who has the presence of God can feel
no want.

12. Greet one another with a holy kiss.

The kiss was the expression of fellowship and affection.
It was and is in the East the common mode of salutation
among friends. A *holy* kiss, is a kiss which expresses Christian communion and love. It was the usage in Christian as-
semblies for the men to kiss the minister and each other,
especially at the celebration of the Lord's supper. It did not
go out of use in the Western churches until about the thir-
teenth century, and is still observed among some eastern
sects. It is not a command of perpetual obligation, as the
spirit of the command is that Christians should express their
mutual love in the way sanctioned by the age and community
in which they live.

13. All the saints salute you.

The saints, in scriptural usage, are not those who are
complete in glory, but believers, separated from the world,
consecrated to God, and inwardly purified. This term, therefore, expresses the character and the relations, not of a class
among God's people, but of the disciples of Christ as such.
They are all, if sincere, separated from the world, distinguished from men of the world as to their objects of desire
and pursuit, and as to the rules by which they are governed;
they are consecrated to the service and worship of God, as a
holy people; and they are cleansed from the guilt and con-

trolling power of sin. They are therefore bound to live in accordance with this character. *All* the saints, i. e. all those in the place in which Paul then was. The communion of saints includes all believers who feel themselves to be one body in Christ. *Salute you*, that is, wish you salvation, which includes all good.

14. The grace of the Lord Jesus Christ, and the love of God, and the communion of the Holy Ghost, (be) with you all. Amen.

This comprehensive benediction closes the epistle. It includes all the benefits of redemption. First, *the grace*, or *favour*, of the Lord Jesus Christ. This is the theanthropical designation of our blessed Saviour. It includes or indicates his divine nature, he is our Lord; his human nature, he is Jesus; his office, he is the Christ, the Messiah, the long-promised Redeemer. It is the favour, the unmerited love and all that springs from it, of this divine person clothed in our nature, and who as the theanthropos is invested with the office of Messiah, the headship over his own people and all power in heaven and earth, that the apostle invokes for all his believing readers. Every one feels that this is precisely what he, as a guilty, polluted, helpless sinner, needs. If this glorious, mysteriously constituted, exalted Saviour, Son of God and Son of man, makes us the objects of his favour, then is our present security and ultimate salvation rendered certain. *The love of God.* In one view the love of God is the source of redemption. God manifested his love in giving his Son for us, Rom. 5, 8. But in another view the love of God to us is due to the grace and work of Christ. That is, the manifestation of that love in the pardon, sanctification and salvation of men, was conditional on the work of Christ. We are reconciled to God by the death of his Son. His death as a satisfaction for our sins was necessary in order to our being actually introduced into the fellowship of God and made partakers of his love. Therefore the apostle puts the grace of Christ before the love of God, as, in the sense mentioned, the necessary condition of its manifestation. *And the communion* (κοινωνία, the participation) *of the Holy Ghost.* The primary object of the death of Christ was the communication of the Holy Spirit. He redeemed us from the curse of the law that we might receive the promise of the Spirit, Gal. 3, 13. 14.   It is the gift of the Holy Ghost secured in the covenant of redemption by the death of Christ that applies to us the benefits of his mediation. As the gift of the Spirit is secured to all the people of God, they are κοινωνοί, joint partakers, of the Holy Ghost, and thereby made one body.   This is the ground of the communion of saints in which the church universal professes her faith.

The distinct personality and the divinity of the Son, the Father, and the Holy Spirit, to each of whom prayer is addressed, is here taken for granted.   And therefore this passage is a clear recognition of the doctrine of the Trinity, which is the fundamental doctrine of Christianity.   For a Christian is one who seeks and enjoys the grace of the Lord Jesus, the love of God, and the communion of the Holy Ghost.

THE END.